THE OTTOMAN

AND

THE SPANISH EMPIRES,

IN THE

SIXTEENTH AND SEVENTEENTH CENTURIES.

BY

LEOPOLD RANKE.

TRANSLATED FROM THE LAST EDITION OF THE GERMAN, BY

WALTER K. KELLY, ESQ. B.A.

OF TRINITY COLLEGE, DUBLIN.

LONDON: WHITTAKER AND CO., AVE MARIA LANE.

MDCCCXLIII.

Library of Congress Cataloging in Publication Data

Ranke, Leopold von, 1795-1886.
  The Ottoman and the Spanish empires, in the sixteenth
and seventeenth centuries.

  Reprint of the 1843 ed. published by Whittaker,
London.
    1. Spain—History—House of Austria, 1516-1700.
  2. Turkey—History—1453-1683. I. Title.
  DP171.R3613   1975   946'.04   78-153628
  ISBN 0-404-09266-7

Reprinted from an original copy in the collections
of the Historical Society of Pennsylvania

From the edition of 1843, London
First AMS edition published in 1975
Manufactured in the United States of America

AMS PRESS INC.
NEW YORK, N. Y. 10003

ADVERTISEMENT.

THE History of the Popes, &c., which has already appeared in this series, constitutes in the original German the last three of four volumes, entitled, collectively, "Sovereigns and Nations of Southern Europe in the Sixteenth and Seventeenth Centuries." The first of these volumes comprises the two historical treatises which are now for the first time presented to the English reader. These will be found to be in every respect worthy of the industrious, conscientious, and judicious author of the first-named history. Whilst they possess a high intrinsic interest as substantive works, they must obviously be regarded also as in some degree necessary complements to the history of the Papacy. The relations between that power and the Most Catholic King in particular were so numerous and important in the sixteenth and seventeenth centuries, that the political history of the latter becomes in fact an integrant and prominent part of that of the popes.

To accommodate purchasers, a double title, general and specific, is given; so that both divisions of the general subject may be bound together under a common title, or either may be had separately in the form of a distinct work.

CONTENTS.

THE OTTOMAN EMPIRE.

INTRODUCTION.

THE SPANISH EMPIRE.

INTRODUCTION.

AUTHOR'S PREFACE.

THERE was a time when the power, and, in a great measure, the civilization of Europe, seemed to have their chief seat in the South ; a time when the Ottoman empire and the Spanish monarchy had grown up, face to face, to an overtopping greatness, dangerous to neighbouring and remote nations, and when no literature in the world could compare with that of Italy.

Another followed, in which the Spanish monarchy, far from asserting its force over friends or foes, was rent and sub-divided by foreign politics, in which Italy, as well as Spain, was pervaded by a civilization of no native growth ; and in which the Ottomans ceased to be feared, and began themselves to fear. These changes, we know, constitute, in no small degree, the distinctive features that mark, respectively, two periods in modern history.

What then produced these changes ? How did they arise ? Was it through the loss of decisive battles, or the invasion of foreign nations, or the stroke of inevitable disasters ? They were mainly the result of internal developments ; and these are what the present work proposes to investigate. As it contemplates the period filled by the vigour and seeming bloom of the two nations in question, from 1540 to 1620, or thereabouts, it traces in the germ what succeeding times brought forth.

It will, I think, be admitted, that even the more authentic and pains-taking works on the history of late ages, engrossed, as they are, with the events of political or religious strife, which occurred from day to-day, afford us but little information respecting the gradual revolution in the inward organization and economy of nations. Had I relied on these works only, I should never have accomplished my own, imperfect as it is ; nay, I should never have undertaken it. But fortunately I found other aids, which afforded a more complete body of information ; aids, frequently, of extraordinary value, and yet still unknown, which it is a main object of this work to bring within the circle of general knowledge. I purpose going through them upon another occasion, singly and in detail ; still I think it necessary to give a general description of them in this place.

If, after the numerous labours of able men, posterity still feels how short-coming are the historical works belonging to the period in question, this feeling must have been much more strongly experienced by contemporaries ; above all, by those who were called on to take an active part in public affairs. These men soon turned from printed works, in which comprehensiveness of range and fluency of expression were the chief things aimed at, to manuscript documents of more veracity. We have essays recommending the formation and study of collections of this kind ; we have such collections themselves in our possession. Among their contents the Venetian Relationi hold by far the most conspicuous place.

Placed repeatedly in the midst between two parties, having relations not only of politics, but still more of trade and commerce with half the world, not strong enough to rest wholly on her own strength, and yet not so weak as to be obliged inactively to wait what should be done by others, Venice had occasion enough to turn her eyes in every direction, and to form connexions in every quarter. She frequently sent her most experienced and able citizens to foreign courts. Not content with the despatches on current affairs regularly sent home every fourteen days, she further required of her ambassadors, when they returned, after an absence of two or three years, that they should give a circumstantial account of the court and the country they had been visiting. This was delivered in the council of the Pregadi, before men who had grown old in the service of the state, and who had, perhaps, themselves discharged the self-same embassies, or might soon be called on to do so. The reporter laboured to pourtray the person and character of the sovereign to whom he had been accredited, his court and his ministers, the state of his finances, his military force, his whole administration, the temper and feeling of his subjects, and, lastly, his relations with other states in general, and with Venice in particular. He then laid at the feet of his Signoria the present made him by the foreign potentate. Sometimes these reports were very minute, and occupied several evenings in the delivery : we can see how the reporter breaks off, when arrived at the end of some division of his subject, to take breath. Sometimes, at least in earlier times, they were delivered from memory : they are all interspersed with direct addresses to the Doge and the assembly : their style and matter every where shows the freshness of personal observation ; every man strove to do his utmost ; he had an audience worthy of a statesman. The Venetians are not unfrequent in their praises of this institution. " In this way we learn, respecting foreign states, what it is alike serviceable to know in peace, and when discord has broken out ; we can draw also from their measures lessons for our own administration ; and the inexperienced are thus forearmed and prepared for public

B

business. Whilst a scholar knows only the past, and a reconnoitrer can only communicate what is present, an ambassador, deriving credit from the importance of his country, and from his own, will easily make himself familiar with both, and be enabled to furnish satisfactory information." Others, on the contrary, not unfrequently found fault with the republic for this anatomy, as they called it, of foreign courts and states. They thought the Venetian ambassadors over-eager in prying into likings and dislikings, favour and disfavour, resources and designs of sovereigns, and far too liberal when the question was, how to discover secrets. Men who have taken an active part in business, and who have been personally privy to details, always possess a knowledge of existing things, and of the immediate past, of decisive positions and of ruling interests, which is hidden from the crowd, and which dies with themselves. The ambassadors of Venice gathered up no small stock of such knowledge in almost all the courts of Europe, for the behoof of their Signory. Their reports were inserted in the archives of the state.

How rich must these archives have been ! A law, passed as early as 1268, enjoins the ambassadors to note down and communicate whatever they could observe, that might be interesting to the government. The word " Relatione" came into use after 1465. Giovanni Casa, speaking of a report made by Gaspar Contarini, in 1526, says, that it was delivered after the usage of their predecessors. The republic continued this practice to the last days of her existence, and there is still extant a report of the Venetian embassy touching the commencement of the French revolution, which is full of striking and impartial revelations. But these performances obtained most note at the period the regular embassies came in vogue, and when Venice was strong and respectable in the eyes of other powers, namely, in the sixteenth century : between 1530 and 1620, we find them sometimes made use of, frequently alluded to, and continually copied and communicated. They constituted the chief part of the politico-historical collections we have spoken of.

But these contained many other important pieces besides. Similar reports were likewise called for, at times, by the Pope, the King of Spain, and the Dukes of Ferrara and Florence. Ex-ambassadors drew up instructions, full of detailed information for their successors. High functionaries and governors of provinces were inducted into their offices by their predecessors, or by others possessed of the necessary knowledge. There was a multitude of letters in circulation. All things of this kind were stored up in the above-mentioned collections, to afford materials for a conception of the then existing world. For us that world is long gone by : we can easily see how a consecutive series of such reports would necessarily become for us direct history, and that, too, such a one as we are now looking for ; one that deals not so much with individual occurrences as with the general aspect and condition of things, and with the development of inherent principles. But doubly valuable must these collections have been for contemporaries themselves : only the question presents itself, how could they have come into existence ? If, as we are assured, it was no very difficult matter to get hold of those same MSS., provided one spared neither money nor trouble, still, it may be asked, how did so singular a traffic in private state papers arise, and how did it become general ?

We have some information on this point too. In the year 1557, Paul IV. bestowed the cardinal's hat on Vitellozzo, of the house of Vitelli, a house that, for a considerable while, had been mixed up in all Italian movements. Vitellozzo himself had long in his hands all the papers of the Caraffeschi, who thought to revolutionize all Italy. He collected from Italian, French, and Spanish archives, invaluable memorials for the history of modern Rome. The popes esteemed him the best versed, of all men, in their affairs ; he was called the Interpreter of the Curia ; he always proved himself full of talent, apt, and docile. This cardinal was held to be the founder of the study of political MSS. " I will not omit to mention," says the author of an essay entitled, Memoranda for the Roman See, " that the endeavour to gain information from MSS, was principally introduced by Cardinal Vitellozzo, of glorious memory. If he was not the first to set up the practice, at least he gave it new animation. His excellency was exceedingly eager on this point; he took the utmost pains to get together written pieces from various places, and spent a great deal of money for them. To such an extent did he push his exertions, that his archives were surpassingly rich, and commanded universal wonder." The practice came very speedily into vogue. Cardinals and papal nephews established archives of their own, for similar collections ; and we find instances of such-a-one being recommended to another as a man who had a quiet, noiseless way of going to work, and bringing together many fine things. Pallavicini found such collections in the possession of Cardinal Spada, in the Borghese Palace, and he employed them in the composition of his History of the Council of Trent. Cardinal Francesco Barberini deposited another, in a long series of volumes, in the library that still bears his family name. Another was kept in the library Della Vallicella, founded at the same period by San Filippo Neri. Collections similarly composed are to be found in the Vatican, and in the mansions of the Chigi and Altieri families. But why attempt to enumerate them ? Rome was full of them ; Rome (says one reporter), where every thing is known, and nothing kept silent ; Rome (says another), a registry of all state transactions. It will not be supposed that every collector went back to the first fountain-heads. One copy produced twenty others ; and Vitellozzo's collection will probably have been the mother of the rest. A lively movement was continually kept up in this range of pursuit by the addition of new pieces. How should it have been difficult for a reigning nephew, the ambassador of a powerful sovereign, or an influential cardinal, to get possession of state papers, which, after all, did not always contain the very secrets of current negotiations, but were merely drawn up for the advice and guidance of the rulers ? At any rate, the Venetian Relationi, to which the state historiographers unambiguously allude, and collections of which in foreign libraries Foscarini mentions without suspicion, bear the full stamp of genuine authenticity. Collectors seem to have assisted each other by mutual exchanges. When we consider the ample stock that is extant of these writings, the wide range, and the abundance of their contents, it almost seems as though, even after the art of printing was in practice, there existed for the knowledge of modern history a literature apart, but only in manuscript ; a literature declared secret, and yet so diffused that works newly circulated excited public attention, and called forth replies ; a literature almost wholly unused, as regarded general knowledge, and yet rich, in manifold, instructive, well-written works.

These collections did not remain confined to Rome. The archduke Cosmo of Tuscany appointed a man expressly to bring together and obtain copies of everything that had appeared there for a long while. In Venice, Agostino Nani had a stock of similar manuscripts. The library of Paris has so ample a store of Venetian Relazioni, that it seems almost in a condition to supply the place of the Venetian archives. They have also found their way to Germany.

The royal library of Berlin contains a collection like those formerly made in Rome, and comprised in forty-eight vols. folio, of which forty-six are entitled Informationi Politiche. It is made up of writings of the same kind, reports, particularly of Venetian ambassadors, instructions, and memoranda for high functionaries entering on office, narratives of conclaves, letters, speeches, reflections, and notices. Each volume contains no small number of these, but not arranged in any order. The heads under which they might be ranged, such as the times and the places to which they relate, the languages in which they are composed (for though far the majority are written in Italian, some are in Spanish and some in Latin), have not been made the basis of any classification ; no other order of succession is observed than that in which the copies came to hand ; the same work recurs two or three times. The bulk however of what we find in this collection belongs to a definite and not very extensive circle. Some of the documents relate to the fourteenth and fifteenth centuries ; but these are not many, and are already known : perhaps only two amongst them may be deserving of reconsideration. It is not till we come to the sixteenth century that we find ourselves presented with a more varied store year by year. Instructions, reports, and letters fall most thickly between 1550 and 1580. After this, single points of time of pre-eminent importance for the general politics of Europe, 1593, 1606, 1610, 1618, present us with extraordinary abundance of materials. As we proceed, we find them continually decrease in frequency. The last manuscript is of the year 1650. Most of them are fairly written, revised by a corrector, and pleasanter to read than many a printed work. They are of very various worth : it is unnecessary to state that there are many excellent pieces among them.

Twenty years ago Johann Müller had thoughts of publishing extracts and notices of the Berlin collection. He devoted himself with great animation to its study, particularly in September 1807, and an essay is extant in which he describes the general impression made on him by the first volume. But he left Berlin in the October of the same year. It was no more permitted him to carry out this design than others of greater magnitude with which his noble soul was filled.

The ducal library, too, at Gotha contains volumes of kindred matter. There are three large ones, and one smaller, in folio : they are the more important for us, as their contents are confined to Venetian Relationi. When Frederick-William, a sovereign who participated vividly in the general movements of his times, kept his court as administrator of electoral Saxony between 1502 and 1601 on the Hartenfels at Torgau, George Köppen presented him with at least two out of those three volumes, which are marked as his property. Possibly he collected them when travelling in Italy.

I can never sufficiently extol the kindness with which I was allowed the use of these manuscripts. Along with a volume of just the same kind which fell into my own possession, I had before me fifty-three folio volumes full of the greatest variety of papers, comprising perhaps upwards of a thousand larger and smaller treatises, from which I was at liberty to select whatever seemed particularly suitable to my purposes. For these it was my good fortune to find them copious in materials.

In truth, these manuscripts relate to almost all Europe. The pope sends his nuncios now to Switzerland, now to Poland, and here we have their reports. The connexions of Venice stretch afar : we possess reports on Persia and Moscow, above all on England : they meet us however but sparingly, and one by one. It strikes me as singular, that neither in our own, nor as it seems in other collections, is there to be found a single report on Portugal by a Venetian ambassador *. As Rome and Venice constitute the centres of the politics here disclosed, so the manuscripts chiefly throw light on that southern Europe about the Mediterranean, with which those powers were most directly connected. Repeatedly do we accompany the bailo of the Venetians along the well known coasts to the capital of that Ottoman empire which was for them so formidable a neighbour, to the divan of the vizier, and to the audience hall of the sultan. Not unfrequently we accompany the ambassadors of the republic to the court of Spanish kings, whether they stood in the midst of an agitated world, in Flanders or in England, or kept their state in the quiet of Madrid. Piedmont, Tuscany, Urbino, and sometimes even Naples, are visited by special envoys ; but these are most constantly to be encountered in the Vatican and the Belvedere at Rome, in confidential discourse with the pope, in close relation with the pope's nephews and with many a cardinal, always engaged in the most weighty affairs, which keep their attention alive to every turn of things in that changeful court. Here we can take our place. Here we have native works instructing us as to a host of individual circumstances. The nuncios return to Rome after defending the rights of papal camera in Naples or in Spain, or consulting perhaps with the Catholic king on enterprises of great moment. Here Venice in her turn is made the subject of report, and so closes this circle.

Were it but continuous and unbroken ! But in the midst of wealth we are sensible of our poverty.

---

* (Note to the second edition.) There have since indeed been found a couple of Relationi on Portugal, besides many others, with the aid of which the present work might have been considerably enlarged. But having engaged in studies that carry me far from this range of subject, I must make up my mind to leave the work unchanged in essentials. I beg the reader too to regard it for the future as a work of the year 1827. In the new edition, which I publish only to meet the demands of the public, I have merely sought to improve the style here and there.

As a whole there is much ; but when we look to particulars, great wants are apparent. Printed works, no doubt, by learned men, afford us welcome aid and manifold information : but still we remain in the dark on many points ; many questions arise and are not solved. We feel like a traveller who has roamed over even the less known heights and valleys of a country, and who then not only investigates individual points with more minuteness, but believes himself too to have acquired novel and true views of the whole, yet still feels the wants under which he labours even more sensibly it may be than the acquisitions he has made, and has now no more earnest wish than to return and make his inspection complete. Meanwhile he is allowed to communicate even his imperfect observations. The like permission I ask for myself and my attempts.

Let the reader then accompany me, in the times of which our manuscripts chiefly treat, to those southern nations and states which then maintained a pre-eminent position in Europe.

The diversity of the European nations was far more striking in the sixteenth and seventeenth centuries than at present ; it was fully discernible in their systems of warfare. If the nations of Germanic and Roman origin every where furnished their territories with fortresses, and cultivated the use of artillery for the attack or defence of such strongholds ; if they took the field with no very numerous forces, and placed their chief reliance on their infantry ; the other nations on the contrary encountered each other on horseback in open and unfortified plains, and if a castle was any where to be seen, it served only to guard the treasures of the sovereign. Poland possessed so numerous a cavalry that it has been expressly computed that Germany, France, and Spain together would have been incapable of bringing a similar one into the field. The grand prince of Moscow could lead 150,000 mounted men to war ; the Szekler in Hungary alone were estimated at 60,000, the forces of the woiwodes of Transylvania, Moldavia, and Wallachia, at 50,000 horsemen ; to these were to be added the Tatar nations, whose lives were passed on horseback. It will at once be perceived that this difference must have inferred a thorough diversity upon all other points.

The supremacy among the second of these two classes of nations belonged to the Ottomans ; Hungary bore their yoke ; the principalities obeyed them ; and the Tatars yielded them military service. They belonged indeed essentially to the latter, but they had the advantage over them of the institution of their Porte. Among the first class the Spaniards were predominant. Not only were they rulers over a good portion of Italy, but Charles V. carried them also into Germany ; they maintained themselves in at least half the Netherlands ; Philip II. was once king of England ; another time he had his armies at once in Provence and Bretagne, in Picardy and Burgundy, and his garrison in Paris. To match with him, the Italians asserted not physical force indeed, but the only supremacy left them, that of talent and address. This was evinced, not merely on occasions such as when cardinal Pole, during his administration in England, consulted with none but the Italians who had accompanied him thither, or when the two Medicean queens filled France with their own countrymen, though this too had its significance ; but above all through their literature, the first of modern times which combined a deliberate cultivation and perfecting of form with scientific comprehension. To this were added accomplishments in various arts. We find that the only engineer in Poland, about the year 1560, was a Venetian ; that Tedali, a Florentine, offered to make the Dniester navigable for the dwellers on its banks, and that the grand prince of Moscow had the castle in his capital built by an Italian. We shall see that their commerce still embraced half the world.

Whilst these three nations made themselves formidable or conspicuous among the rest, they encountered each other directly in the Mediterranean ; they filled all its coasts and waters with life and motion, and formed there a peculiar circle of their own.

The Spaniards and the Italians were very closely knit together by the ties of church and state. By the former, because after the general departure from its communion, the dwellers alone beyond the Pyrenees and the Alps remained wholly faithful to the Roman see. By the latter, because Naples and Milan were Spanish. Often was Madrid the abode of young Italian princes, of the Roveri, the Medici, the Farnese, and Rome the residence of young Spaniards desirous of cultivating their minds. The Castilian poets adopted the forms of the Tuscan masters ; all the martial fame of the Italians was won in Spanish campaigns.

The Ottomans set themselves in violent contrast to both. The Spaniards they encountered victoriously on the African, the Italians on the Greek coasts. They threatened Oran ; they attacked Malta with their whole force; they conquered Cyprus, and swarming round all the coasts they carried danger even into the haunts of peace. They were opposed therefore not alone by the old maritime powers of the two peninsulas ; in Tuscany and Piedmont new knightly orders were founded for this strife ; the pope himself yearly despatched his galleys in May from Civita Vecchia to cruise against them ; the whole force of the two nations took part in this contest. Those fair coasts and many named seas that beheld in their antique grandeur the rise, the rivalry, and the extinction of the Shemitic, and the Greco-Roman sea dominions, that saw the mastery won successively by Arabs and by German Christians, were witnesses to a third struggle, when Ottomans came forth instead of Arabs, when Spaniards and Italians (for no other people stood by them in this cause, and the French were often leagued with the foe) had need to put forth all their strength to uphold the Christian name on the Mediterranean. Hereby was formed for the most immediate and vivid exertion of all the powers of these nations, a circle in which they are most at home, and which is often the horizon involuntarily bounding the thoughts and the fancy of their authors. The strife gave their genius free and vigorous play. It contributed to work out in them that singular mixture their minds then exhibited ; a mixture of pride and cunning, of illusion and eagerness to discover the mystery of things, of romantic chivalry and insidious policy, of faith in the stars, and implicit devotion to religion.

Let us now enter into this circle, among these nations.

THE OTTOMAN EMPIRE.

INTRODUCTION.

HUMBLE indeed is the description the Ottomans give of their own origin. They relate that Othman, the founder of their empire and name, himself followed the plough with his servants, and that when he wished to break off from work at noon he used to stick up a banner as a signal to call them home. These servants and none besides were his first followers in war, and they were marshalled beneath the same signal. But even he, they add, had in his day a forecasting of his house's future greatness, and in a dream he beheld a tree grow up out of his navel that overshadowed the whole earth *.

The new power that arose in Asia Minor having now established itself on its northern coasts, it chanced one day, as the story continues, that Soliman, the grandson of Othman, rode along the shores of the Hellespont, passing on through the ruins of ancient cities, and fell into a silent reverie. "What is my khan thinking of?" said one of his escort. "I am thinking," was the reply, "about our crossing over to Europe †." These followers of Soliman were the first who did cross over to Europe : they were successful; and Soliman's brother, Amurath I., was he who conquered Adrianople.

Thenceforth the Ottoman power spread on the further side of the Hellespont, east and west from Brusa, and from Adrianople on this side northwards and southwards. Bajazeth I., the great-grandson of Othman, was master here of Weddin and Wallachia, yonder of Caramania and Cæsarea.

Europe and Asia, both threatened by Bajazeth, rose up to resist him. Europe however fell prostrate at Nicopolis; and though Asia, for which Timur stood forth as champion, was victorious, still it did not destroy the dominion of Bajazeth. It was but fifty years after this defeat that Mahomet II. took Constantinople, the imperial city whose sway had once extended far over both quarters. The victor was not content with seeing the cities on the coasts of the Black Sea and the Adriatic own his supremacy; to bring the sea itself under subjection he built a fleet; he began to conquer the islands of the Ægean one after the other; and his troops showed themselves in Apulia.

There seemed to be no bounds to the career of victory. Though Bajazeth II. did not equal his predecessors in valour, still his cavalry swept Friuli, his infantry captured fortresses in the Morea, and his fleets rode victorious in the Ionian Sea. But he was far outstripped by his son Selim and his grandson Soliman. Selim overcame the Mamelukes of Cairo, who had often been victorious over Bajazeth; and he caused the Chutbe or prayer to be pronounced in his noble name in the mosques of Syria and Egypt *. Soliman effected far more than he. One battle made him master of Hungary, and thenceforth he trod in that kingdom as in his own house. In the far east he portioned out the territory of Bagdad into sandshakates according to the banners of his troops. That Chaireddin Barbarossa, who boasted that his turban stuck on a pole scared the Christians and sent them flying for miles into the country, served him and made his name dreaded over the whole Mediterranean. With amazement and awe men reckoned up thirty kingdoms, and nearly 8000 miles of coast, that owned his sway. He styled himself emperor of emperors, prince of princes, distributer of the crowns of the world, God's shadow over both quarters of the globe, ruler of the Black and of the White Sea, of Asia and of Europe †.

Foundations of the Ottoman Power.

If we inquire what were the bases on which rested the essential strength and energy of this empire, and therewith the success of its efforts, our attention will be arrested by three things, viz. the feudal system, the institution of slavery, and the position of the supreme head.

Every country overrun by the Ottomans was immediately after its conquest parcelled out according to banners and scymitars into a multitude of fiefs. The design was, the protection of the country once well provided for within and without, to keep its original conquerors ever ready for new achievements. The great advantage of this system will be obvious, when it is considered that every possessor of the moderate income of 3000 aspers (sixty to a dollar) was required to hold a man and horse in

---

* Leunclavii Historiæ Musulmanæ Turcorum de monumentis ipsorum exscriptæ, iii. 113.

† Leunclavii Annales Osmanidarum, p. 10.

* See Selim's diploma of investiture in Hammer's Staatsverfassung und Staatsverwaltung des osmanischen Reichs, Bd. i. § 195.

† Soliman's letter to Francis I. Garnier, Histoire de France, xxv. p. 407.

constant readiness for war, and another mounted soldier was to be furnished for every additional 5000 aspers; that in this way Europe could supply 80,000, Natolia 50,000 sipahi (the name of this cavalry); that to raise this force nothing more was requisite than an order to the two beglerbegs of the empire, from whom it found its way to the commanders of the banners, the sandshakbegs, and through them to the commanders of the squadrons, the alaibegs, and so on to every possessor of a fief, large or small, of a siamet or a timar, whereupon the muster and the march followed forthwith[*]. Now comes the question how was the feudal system kept free from that principle of inheritance which has always prevailed in our feudal institutions? These fiefs conferred no title of nobility, neither were they properly entailed on sons. Soliman ordered that if a sandshakbeg with an income of 700,000 aspers left behind him a son a minor, the latter should receive nothing but a timar of 5000 aspers, with the express obligation of maintaining a mounted soldier out of the proceeds. There exist multitudes of similar ordinances appointing to the son of a sipahi a larger timar if his father died in the field, a smaller if he died at home, but in all cases but a small one[†]. "Therefore," says Barbaro, "there is among them neither nobility nor wealth; the children of men of rank, whose private treasures are taken possession of by other grandees, enjoy no personal distinction[‡]." Still there did exist even here a principle of inheritance, but an inheritance not so much of individuals as of all together, not of the son from the father but of generation from generation. It was a fundamental law that no one should obtain a timar but the son of a timarli[§]. Every one was obliged to begin his career from the lowest grade. Putting all this together we behold in the timarli a great community, tracing its origin essentially to the first companions of Othman, but afterwards numerously recruited by the events of war and by voluntary submission; a community void in itself of distinction of ranks, save such as is conferred by bravery, fortune, and the sultan's favour, which has imposed the sultan's yoke on the empire, and is ready to do the same by all the other realms of the world, and if possible to parcel them out in like manner among its own members.

This correlation must have unfolded itself by a natural process of development, out of that originally subsisting between the lord and his warlike servants, which, if I err not, much more resembled the personal subjection of the Mamelukes to the emirs, than the free allegiance owned by the bands of the west towards their condottieri[||]. But a much more peculiar institution, for which I know not whether a parallel ever existed before or since, was the education of stolen children for soldiers or statesmen in the service of the sultan.

Every five years it was the practice to make a seizure of the children of the Christians in the empire. Small bands of soldiers, each under a captain furnished with a firman, marched from place to place. On their arrival the protogeros assembled the inhabitants with their sons. The captain was empowered to carry off all between the age of seven and that of manhood, who were distinguished for beauty or strength, or who possessed any peculiar talent or accomplishment. He brought them like a tithe, as it were, to the court of the grand signor. Others were carried thither from the campaigns, as the portion of the booty by law reserved to the sultan. No pacha returned from an expedition without bringing the sultan a present also on his own part of young slaves. Thus were there gathered together at the Porte children of various nations, the majority of them natives of the country, but besides them Poles likewise, Bohemians and Russians, Italians and Germans[*]. They were divided into two classes. One of these was sent, especially in earlier times, to Natolia, where they served among the peasants, and were trained up as Moslem; or they were kept in the serai, where they were employed in carrying water, in working in the gardens, in the barges, or in the buildings, being always under the inspection of an overseer, who kept them to their tasks with the stick. But the others, those who appeared to give evidence of superior qualities (many an honest German was persuaded that it was only by the help of evil spirits the fact was so happily discriminated), passed into one of the four serais, that of Adrianople or of Galata, or the old or the new serai of Stambul. Here they were lightly dressed in linen or in cloth of Salonichi; they wore caps of Brusa stuff; every morning they were visited by teachers, each paid eight aspers daily, who remained till evening instructing the children in reading the law and in writing[†].

At the appointed age they were all circumcised. Those who were engaged in severer tasks became janissaries in process of time; those who were brought up in the serai were made either sipahi, (not feudatory but paid,) who served at the Porte, or higher state functionaries.

Both classes were kept under strict discipline. Soranzo's Relatione informs us how the first named class especially was exercised by day in every kind of self-denial as to food, drink, and comfortable

---

[*] Relatione di Constantinopoli del C¹ Sg^r Bernardo Navagero, MS. "Li sanzacchi sono obligati tener prima un allaibeg, che è un luogotenente del suo sanzacco, poi timarioti overo spahi, li quali sott' il governo d'allaibeg sono con lui insieme sottoposti all' obedienza del sanzacco." Later writers, Marsigli for instance, mention alaibegs only on the frontiers.

[†] Canunname of Soliman to the beglerbeg Mustafa, Hammer, i. 349. Order of the same to Lutfi Pacha, ib. i. 364.

[‡] Relatione del C¹ Marcantonio Barbaro MS. "Li descendenti loro vanno totalmente declinando et restano affatto privi d'ogni minimo grado."

[§] Canunname of Aini, Hammer, i. 372.

[||] Schlözer's 7th section in the Origg. Osman, p. 150, with the motto "C'est tout comme chez nous," only points out the resemblance between Othman and a Sforza, which however is but a general one, but not their difference, which to me seems much stronger.

[*] All Relationi, printed and unprinted, are full of the "scelta di piccoli giovanetti figliuoli di Christiani," as Barbaro expresses himself. Of the booty in war Morosini says, (Constantinopoli del 1584, MS.) "Vengono presentati quotidianamente al Gran Signore da suoi generali, cosi da terra come da mare, quando tornano dalla guerra."

[†] Morosini: "Sono posti nel serraglio proprio del Gran Signore, nel serraglio di Galata, in quello del hipodromo ed in quello d'Adrianopoli: nelli quali 4 serragli continuamente si trovano il numero di 5 o 6 mila giovanini, quali non escono mai da detto serraglio, ma sotto una grandissima disciplina vengono ammaestrati et accostumati di buonissima creanza." The rest is from Navagero.

clothing, in laborious hand labours, in shooting with the bow and the arquebus; how they passed the night in a long lighted hall, watched by an overseer who walked up and down continually and allowed them no rest *. Were they then enrolled among the janissaries ; did they enter those conventlike barracks in which the various odas observed such strict community in their economy that their military ranks derived their names from mess and soup, they continued to practise obedience, not only the young in silence and subjection to their elders †, but all of them under such strict rules that none durst pass the night beyond the walls, and that whoever suffered punishment was bound to kiss the hand of the muffled individual who inflicted it upon him.

In no less strict discipline lived the young people in the serai, every ten of them under the inspection of an inexorable eunuch, and employed in similar exercises to the others, to which however were added literary and somewhat knightly tasks. Every three years the grand signor allowed their departure from the serai. Those who preferred remaining rose in the immediate service of their lord, according to their age, from chamber to chamber, with a constant increase of pay, till they reached perchance to one of the four great offices of the innermost chamber, whence the way lay open to the dignity of beglerbeg, of capitan deiri, i. e. admiral, or even of vizier. Those, on the other hand, who availed themselves of the permission were received, each in accordance with his previous rank, into the first four regiments of paid sipahi serving at the Porte, which were more trusted by the sultan than his other body guards ‡. Merrily did they scamper out through the gates, decked in their new finery and swinging the purse of gold they had received as a present from the grand signor.

A German philosopher once proposed a system of education for children, which was to be carried on apart from the parents in a special community, and in such a way that a new will should take the place of the old one. Here we have such an education. Here is total separation, strict community, the formation as it were of a new principle of life. The youths thus brought up forgot their childhood, their parents, their homes, knew no native land but the serai, no lord and father but the grand signor, no will but his, no hope but of his favour; they knew no life but one passed in rigid discipline and unconditional obedience, no occupation but war in his service, no personal purpose unless it were plunder in this life, and in death the paradise thrown open to him who fought for Islam. What the philosopher proposed in idea for the purpose of

training up youth in morality, religion, and communion, was here put in practical execution centuries before his day, to the development of a spirit at once slavish and warlike.

This institution perfectly fulfilled its intentions. Busbek, an Austrian ambassador at the court of Soliman, whose report is among the most celebrated and the best authenticated, cannot help overflowing with admiration as he describes the rigorous discipline of these janissaries, now seeming like monks, now like half statues, their extremely modest garb, the heron plume on their head-dress perhaps excepted, their frugal habits of life, and the way in which they season their carrots and turnips with hunger *. Under their discipline brave and dignified men were produced, to the amazement of all beholders, out of lads who had run away from an inn, a kitchen, or a convent school in some Christian country. They would suffer no one among them who had been brought up in the ease and softness of a parental dwelling. It cannot be denied that in decisive engagements they alone preserved the empire. The battle of Varna, one foundation of all the Ottoman greatness, would have been lost but for them †. At Cossowa the Rumelian and the Natolian force had already taken to flight before the evil Jancu, as they called Johann Hunniades; but these janissaries won the victory ‡. They boasted that they had never fled in battle §. The fact is admitted by Lazarus Schwendi, long a German commander-in-chief against them ‖. They are designated in all reports as the nerve and the core of the Ottoman forces. It is a highly remarkable fact, that this invincible infantry was formed in the east just at the time (since 1367) that in our side of Europe the Swiss, foot soldiers likewise, devised and practised their equally invincible order of battle. Only the former consisted solely of slaves, the latter of the freest men of the mountains.

The same discipline imposed on the janissaries was equally observed with the sipahi and the servants of the serai, who were to rise thence to higher dignities. Inwardly to resist this discipline, and to return, should occasion offer, to Christendom, was an effort that demanded the soul of a Scanderbeg. Hardly will another example be found of one of these youths returning to the parents from whose arms he had been torn and to his old home. And how should they? There was no hereditary aristocracy to interpose their claims, and dispute with them the rewards of their valour or their talents ¶: on the contrary they were themselves destined to fill all the highest dignities of the empire, all the sandshakates; the aga of the janissaries was taken from their body; not only the whole government of the country, but the command too of its armies was in their hands ; every one saw before him a field of exertion, a career in life, with which before his eyes he might forget that he was a slave. Nay

* Soranzo, Viaggio MS. " Gli Azamogliani (Adshem Oglan) hanno un gran luogo, simile a un convitorio de frati: dove ciascuno la sera distende il suo stramazette et coperta; e vi si corica, havendo prima li guardiani accese per il lungo delle sala lampade."

† Soranzo: " Sono obligati i Giannizzeri nuovi a servire i più vecchi et anteriori nello spendere, apparecchiare et altri servitii."

‡ Morosini: " Quelli della stanza del tesoro escono spahi della prima compagnia con 20—22 aspri di paga; quelli della stanza grande e piccola del proprio serraglio, dove sta S. M., escono medesimamente spahi della prima e seconda compagnia con 18—20 aspri; quelli delli altri tre serragli escono della 3 e 4 legione con aspri 10—14 di paga." Respecting these sipahi see also Libri iii delle Cose de' Turchi. Aldine press F. 15.

* Augerii Gislenii Busbequii legationis Turcicæ Epistolæ iv. Frankf. 1595, p. 200, 15, 78. Ejusdem de re militari contra Turcas instituenda Consilium, p. 352.

† Callimachus, Experiens de clade Varnensi, in Oporinus, p. 311.

‡ Leunclavii Historiæ Musulmanæ d. i. T. m. e., p. 519.

§ Paulus Jovius, Ordo militiæ Turcicæ, p. 221.

‖ Lazari Suendii, Quomodo Turcis sit resistendum consilium, in Couring's collection. Helmst. 1664, p. 383.

¶ This is particularly dwelt on by Ubertus Folieta de causis magnitudinis imperii Turcici, Leips. 1595, p. 6.

on the very contrary the condition of these men seemed possessed of high charms in the estimation of those Christians who longed for adventures and brilliant promotion. Many voluntarily left their native land to seek their fortunes among these slaves. On their part they kept their own body rigorously aloof from foreign admixture, not suffering any born Turk, nor even the son of a grand vizier, though the father had risen from their own ranks, to become a sandshak*. Their sons entered the fifth and sixth corps of the paid soldiers, or into the number of the feudatory sipahi, or timarli, among whom the empire was portioned out, and continually augmented and reinvigorated that body.

Such was this institution of slaves. " It is in the highest degree remarkable," exclaims Barbaro, that " the wealth, the administration, the force, in short the whole body politic of the Ottoman empire reposes upon, and is intrusted to men born in the Christian faith, converted into slaves, and reared up Mahometans." On this institution depends the character and the form of government of the Turks.

If we have now made it clear that the power of this empire, so far as those constitute the true power whose activity is apparent, consisted of two corporations, the timarli and that twofold body of slaves, the larger moiety of which constituted the élite of the army on horseback and on foot, and the smaller had the administration and the executive in its hands, it is no less obvious that war was absolutely necessary to the empire on account of both these corporations ; on account of the timarli, because their numbers grew continually by additions from among the slaves, and so there was a constant need of acquiring new timars ; and on account of the janissaries and the paid sipahi that they might practise what they had learned, and not be spoiled by sitting down inactively at the serai †.

It is in war that we behold the physiology of this warlike state in all its genuine character. The timarli are seen marshalled beneath the banners of their respective corps ; they carry bows and quivers, iron maces and daggers, scymitars and lances ; they know how to use these various weapons at the right moment with the utmost dexterity ; they are trained with rare skill to pursue and to retire, now to hang back in alert suspense, now to dash forward and scour the country. Their horses too claim attention ; they come chiefly from Syria, where they have been reared with the utmost care, and fondled almost like children. Judges indeed remarked that they were somewhat ticklish to the stirrup, apt to swerve aside, and hard mouthed ; this however was rather the fault of the riders, who used tight bits and short stirrups‡ ; otherwise the animals proved

tractable, serviceable, as well on mountainous and stony ground as on the plain, indefatigable, and always full of spirit. The most accomplished riders were furnished from many a district. It was surprising to see them hurl their maces before them, gallop after them, and catch them again ere they fell *. Turning slightly round, with the horse at full speed, they would discharge their arrows backwards with unerring aim. Next to these the Porte sent forth its paid sipahis and its janissaries. The former, in addition to their scymitars, were armed with those lances, by the small flags on which they were distinguished ; some also were furnished with bows. A few were equipped with coats of mail and morions, but rather for show than for service ; their round shields and their turbans seemed to them defence enough. The janissaries lastly marched in long flowing garments, armed with scymitar and arquebus, in their girdles the handjar and the small hatchet ; dense in their array, their plumes like a forest.

It was as though the camp was the true home of this people. Not only was it kept in admirable order, so that not an oath or an altercation was to be heard, no drunken man, no gambling was to be seen in it ; nor anything to be found in it that could offend either sight or smell †. It was also to be remarked that the life the soldier led at home was but meagre and sorry compared with the magnificence of the camp. For every ten janissaries the sultan maintained a horse to carry their baggage ; every five and twenty had a tent that served them in common ; in these they observed the regulations of their barracks, and the elder were waited on by the younger. No sipahi was so mean that he did not possess a tent of his own. How gallant and glittering was their array as they rode in their silken surcoats, their particoloured richly wrought shield on their left arms, their right hands grasping the costly mounted sword, feathers of all hues waving in their turbans. But surpassingly splendid was the appearance of their leaders. Jewels hung round their horses' ears ; saddles and housings were studded with others ; chains of gold hung from their bridles. The tents shone with Turkish and Persian decorations ; here the booty was laid up ; a numerous retinue of eunuchs and slaves was in attendance.

Religion and morals were in harmony with this martial tendency that pervaded the whole being of the nation. It has frequently been remarked how much Islamism promoted arms, how strongly the belief it inculcated in an inevitable destiny tended to inspire with courage in the fight. Besides this,

* Barbaro: " Nè possono patire che nè un figliuolo de' primi visir sia fatto sangiacco."

† Valieri, Relatione di Constantinopoli, MS. " Si va discorrendo, che essendo stato quel imperio per suo instinto quasi continuamente lontano della pace non possi in alcun tempo star lungamente quieto, ma ad una guerra fa succeder l'altra, e per desiderio de nuovi acquisti e per la necessità che stimano d'havere d'impiegar la militia, la quale facilmente può causare seditioni, tumulti et novità. Li corpi grossi con mosso si mantengono e si fanno più robusti e con l'otio si impiono di malo humore. . . . . Li fiumi, che corrono, conservano l'acqua sana."

‡ See the Relatione of Floriani, MS., particularly p. 217.—

" Portano i morsi stretti, le selle picciole, le staffe large et corte." [The broad stirrup pointed on the inner side, serves the Turkish rider for a spur.—TRANSLATOR.]

* These accomplishments are best described in the Relatione of 1637, though it remarks that they had then grown rare : " tanto che ridotti si trovano in rarità.—Ferendo in oltre cosi bene con l'arco che mentre corre velocemente il destriero, di saetta armano l'arco,—et rivoltandosi a dietro con l'arco seguitado dall' occhio scoccano lo strale, e colpiscono dove disegnano ferire."

† See, for somewhat earlier times indeed, Cuspinianus de militari instituto etc. Turcorum in Cæsaribus, p. 579, and for the times before us Busbequius. Floriani : " Dalla grandezza e dalla commodità che ha il Turco in campagna, si vede chiaramente ch'egli è nella sua propria residenza, e che nelle terre egli è più tosto forestiero che cittadino."

it was the opinion in the sixteenth century, that the numerous ablutions which prevented the uncleanliness to which so many diseases owe their origin in camps, and even the prohibition of wine, were laudable and well considered measures. For in the first it cost inordinate trouble to procure wine and to convey it to the camp ; and when it was there, how many disorders did it give rise to in western armies *. It was even thought that the daily habits of the Turks might be traced to the necessities of the camp. In Morosini's opinion the Turks sat on a plain carpet stretched on the ground, and ate on the ground, and slept where they had eaten, that they might find nothing strange which the life of the camp and the tent rendered indispensable †. Be this as it may, the Ottomans assuredly regarded themselves above all as warriors. In the edicts of Constantinople, by way of distinguishing them from the Christians, the latter are called citizens, while the former are styled soldiers, askery ‡.

Now, taking into consideration all these facts, first, that all were slaves (and most so those who stood highest), trained unceasingly to unconditional obedience ; that there was not a man among them possessed of any independent rights, of family property, jurisdiction, or retainers ; that every career depended on the beck of the sultan, from whom his slave expected either magnificent rewards, or degradation and death ; and lastly, that the whole system was thoroughly military in its organization, that the state was warlike and its business war ;— taking all this into account, it is very clear that the sultan was the soul of this singularly constituted body, the origin of its very movement, and above all, that he too, if he would reign, must needs be of a warlike spirit. Bajazeth II. proved this by experience in his old age. When he could no longer take the field, disorder followed upon disorder, and he was at last compelled to give way to his martial son. Soliman, on the other hand, was altogether the ruler suited to that warlike state. Whilst his lofty stature, his manly features, and his large black eyes beneath his broad forehead, plainly bespoke the soldier §, he displayed all the vivacity, all the open-handedness and the justice that make a ruler beloved and feared. He would hardly ever have desisted from campaigns of conquest. It is very possible, indeed, that we shall never be able thoroughly to fathom his designs ; but thus much we know, that the Multeka‖, a law-book he caused to be compiled, most pressingly inculcates war against the unbelievers as an universal duty : they were to be called on to embrace Islam or pay the capitation tax, and if they refused both alternatives, they were to be pursued with arrows, and all implements of war, and with fire, their trees should be cut down, their crops laid waste. The fanatical book which is

known unto us under the name of Trumpet Peal of the Holy War, a book which omits no exhortation, no promise, no command by which believers could be excited to the frenzy of a religious war, that bids the mussulman cling till death to the horse's forelock, and live in the shadow of the lances, till all men own the creed of Mahomet, was translated into Turkish towards the close of his reign *, probably for the immediate use of the youth of the serai.

Digression respecting the modern Greeks in the Sixteenth Century.

But whilst the Ottomans were disturbing and threatening the world, how lived they in whose country they had reared their empire ?

Whilst the whole southern range of Asia, a native seat of civilization, no longer beheld aught but tyrannous rulers and peoples condemned in masses to hard servitude, the Ottoman transplanted this desolation to Europe. A state of things of this nature usually has two great epochs. As long as the dominant power is intrinsically strong, the conquered passively endure ; flight itself is courage ; the boldest retreat to inaccessible mountains. But as those grow weak, these rise up to isolated deeds of violence, to the wild retaliation of robbery and murder. So the Mahrattas rose against the Moguls, the Lores and Kurds against the Sofis, and the Wechabites, the children of the desert, against these same Ottomans.

The Greeks in Soliman's time were in the stage of obedience. They had no part in war, politics, or public life, save as renegades or serfs. Their charaz †, the wretched produce of their toil, wherewith they purchased the right of existing, filled the treasury of the Ottoman. There is nothing a nation more needs than an abundance of noble men who devote themselves to the common weal ! The Ottoman regularly carried off the flower of the Greek youth to the serai. On this institution he founded at once his own strength and subjection. He fed upon their marrow.

Many superior Greeks, to please their lords, accommodated themselves to this enervation. No few descendants of the noble families of Constantinople, which had in earlier days themselves been native oppressors, farmed the revenues of the sultan. Palaiologoi and Kantakuzenoi were remarked in the capital, Mamaloi and Notaradai in Peloponnesus, Batazidai, Chrysoloroi, and Azanaioi in the ports of the Black Sea. Such as combined with these employments those commercial pursuits in which we find the Greeks engaged now in Moscow and now in Antwerp, could speedily arrive at great wealth. Michael Kantakuzenos was able in the year 1571 to make a present of fifteen galleys to the sultan : when he rode on his mule through the streets, six servants ran before him, and seventeen followed him. These rich Greeks adopted oriental manners under the Ottomans, as they assumed those of Italy under the Venetians. They wore the turban, they imitated the domestic ar-

---

* These remarks are made by Floriani.

† " Quelli popoli, come quelli che hanno sempre fatto professione delle cose della guerra, hanno sempre usato il modo del viver nelle case loro che è conforme a quello che è necessario in campo."

‡ Muradgea d'Ohsson, from the decrees of Muhammed II Tableau de l'empire Othoman, ii. 268.

§ Navagero 237. " Ha il fronte largo e un poco prominente, gli occhi grossi e neri, il naso acquilino e un poco grandetto a proportione delle altre fattezze, e ha il collo un poco lungo."

‖ Extract from book xiii. of the Multeka in Hammer i. 163.

---

* Preface by Johann Müller to Hammer's translation of this book, p. 7.

† Navagero, Relatione : " Il carazzo è il tributo che pagano tutti li Christiani che habitano il paese, le persone un ducato per testa, le pecore aspro uno et mezzo per testa."— It was otherwise at a later period. For the manner in which the charaz was exacted from poor herdsmen in 1676, see Spon et Wheler, Voyage de Grèce, ii. 41.

rangements of their conquerors ; they delighted in gorgeous finery. Their women wrapped their hair in golden nets, and decked their foreheads with diadems of pearls ; heavy jewelled drops hung from their ears ; their bosoms were covered more with golden chains than with drapery *. It was as though every man was in haste to enjoy an uncertain prosperity, as though he felt the hand of the tyrannous ruler suspended over him. Michael Kantakuzenos was in vain so submissive, nay, so liberal handed, to the sultan : the latter at last sent his capidji bashi, had him hanged before the door of the stately house he had built himself at Achilo, and his treasures carried to the serai †.

The poorer people dragged on their days in want and servitude. A great part of the country was waste, depopulated, and ruined. What could thrive in the land where every sandshak strove to extort double the income assigned him, where rapacious contractors often filled his place ‡, and where every Osmanli bore himself as unlimited lord and master ? The people of the islands were decidedly better off. We find Lemnos and Lesbos very well cultivated in the year 1548. We see the people tilling their fields, planting their vines, attending to their springs and watercourses, and cultivating their gardens. Here they remained true to themselves.

The people still manifested the noble qualities of their native stock. The sweet tone of Homeric words still lived in Chios : they still counted in those days fourteen villages of the Laconians in Peloponnesus, where a Greek almost identical with the ancient was spoken : the Athenians were still remarked for their surprising memory and their melodious voices : even in the household utensils the artistic forms of ancient sculpture have always been perceptible. So likewise in their social life there were preserved some elements of their former civilization. The symposia of the men were everywhere found adapted as of old to a lofty strain of conversation ; where arms were allowed, they had those armed dances which were kept up for whole days by men girt with the sword, and arrayed with bow and quiver §. The active and spontaneous ingenuity of the Greek character in labour and recreation, with sword and shield, above all at sea and on shipboard, was proverbial ‖.

* The most important authorities on this head are the writings, letters, and notices collected with care and love by Martin Crusius, who styles himself φιλέλλην, and who was the first that was justly entitled to the name. They are contained in his Turcogræcia, Basle, 1584, fol. pp. 91. 211. 225. 485.

† The rich lord Michalis, whose death is described in the oldest of the Greek songs lately published by Fauriel, which he found written in the characters of the sixteenth century. (Τραγουδία 'Ρωμαϊκά. Ausg. von Müller, 1. 94) is doubtless none other than our Michael Kantakuzenos. This event excited the strongest sympathy. There exists an essay on the subject, "Per qual causa e come è stato impiccato Michael Cantacuseno a dì 3 Marzo a Achilo davanti la porta di casa sua." Turcogr. 274. It is a pity it has not been preserved entire. The 'Ιστορία πολιτικὴ Κωνσταντινουπόλεως (ib. p. 43) concludes with a reference to it.

‡ Navagero and Barbaro's Relationi.

§ These and many other traits are noticed by Bellon in his Observations de plusieurs singularités en Grèce, i. ch. 4. ch. 25, and elsewhere. See also Turcogr. 489. 209. 216. 430.

‖ A rhyming proverb, still older than that oldest poem

There was no room however for the free expansion of the mind, where the energies were directed only towards the most immediate necessities, and the whole state and being was debased. The language became overladen with Bulgarian, Turkish, and Italian words : it fell into a hundred degenerations of barbaric forms. No instruction was to be thought of, for there existed no instructor. So soon as men do not acknowledge nor seek to acknowledge the laws of the creation, its operations begin to stultify the soul and bewilder it with illusions : these Greeks were wholly possessed by a fantastic view of nature and her works. There remained only one element in which their mental life could give itself expression : they retained that utterance of nature, song. The Athenians were pre-eminently rich in lays in the sixteenth century *. We can imagine of what kind they were, when we find lovers sitting together and vying which shall outdo the other in repeating them. They were undoubtedly that well-known kind of song that accompanies with its monotonous and almost sad strains the joys and the sorrows of a simple life. Its subjects were joy, the sweets of love, and family endearments ; sorrow, death, and separation ; and then that loneliness that charges the moon with its greetings, that makes the birds its messengers, wanders with the clouds, has the stars and the sea for its confidants, and animates the lifeless world with a fancied sympathy.

Thus does the people, once in the enjoyment of a life in which the human race beholds its pride and centuries their paragon, return to the condition of nature, after having lived for long ages constrained within narrow forms, if not dishonourably, yet without renown. It pictures to itself its old forefathers as giants. An ancient grave stone is, by its account, the manger of Alexander's horse.

But the return is not complete. How could they, if totally dismembered, maintain their nationality in the face of the victorious foe ? On the contrary, religion and priesthood exercised over them their wonted sway.

Through these it was that the Greeks were rigorously severed from the Ottomans. Historical works written in the sixteenth century call the sultan " the accursed " even in the midst of his victories, and his people " the strangers." Justice administered by the Ottomans was a thing sedulously avoided ; legal proceedings were presided over by the elders, by the good men of the various localities, and by the priests ; whoever withdrew from their authority was put under a ban sometimes with his whole house. The Greek woman who married a Turk was excommunicated †. They paid their charaz to the Turks, they endured what could not be remedied ; but in other respects they kept aloof from their oppressors ; the state to which they chose to belong was different from theirs ; it was the hierarchy.

This hierarchy was built on the established subordination of all priests to the patriarch of Constantinople. Even the patriarchs of Jerusalem, Antioch, and Alexandria, owned him for their head. His high priesthood was acknowledged over

mentioned above, is given by Crusius from the lips of a Greek, Turcogr. 211.

* Zygomalas to Crusius: μέλεσι διαφόροις θέλγουσι τοὺς ἀκούοντας ὡς σειρήνων μέλη.

† Turcogræcia, 25. 220.

the whole eastern world, from the cataracts of the Nile almost to the Baltic, from Armenia to the Ionian islands. He sent his exarchs every year into the provinces to receive the dues of the patriarchate from the metropolitans. Every five years he set out in person to visit his dioceses, to allay disputes, and to give them his blessing *.

While his authority was thus wide in its range, it was no less minute in its application to the most individual details of life. There was nothing in which he was not appealed to. A lady who had married in Chios, and who was now, upon the death of her husband, ill-treated by laymen and priests, applies to him for succour. A certain person has had the water cut off from his garden: he lays the matter before the patriarch. A daughter by a second marriage has engrossed the whole inheritance; the daughter by the first marriage claims her share, and applies to the patriarch who is the father of the fatherless †. Mirzena, a noble lady of Wallachia, entreats the patriarch to select husbands for her daughters from among the Greeks of higher rank ‡.

Must not this subjection, especially in matters of litigation, have been irksome to many? What may it have been that bent their necks to the patriarch? Such is human nature, that whole nations may pass under the sway of an error, and that error may subserve their best interests ; the germs by which life is propagated may find shelter under such a covering. The whole force of the patriarchs consisted in excommunication. And what was there in this so coercive and formidable? The conviction was entertained that the body of a man cursed by the patriarch did not perish in the earth. So long as the devil had hold of the soul, so long the bonds of the flesh could not be loosed, till the patriarch recalled the curse. The illusion was insisted on, even to the sultan, and confirmed by dreadful examples. There is no doubt that it was predominant in the sixteenth century, and that it was the terrific cause that forced the refractory to obedience §.

But others obeyed cheerfully. With joy they gazed on the holy cross erected on the patriarchion, and visible afar from land and sea. The patriarchion itself, near a church of the Virgin on an eminence in Constantinople, an enclosed court with a few trees containing the residence of the patriarch, was in their eyes a holy spot ‖. None passed its gates without laying the hand on the breast, bowing, and making the sign of the cross as he proceeded on his way. It was believed for certain that yonder church of the Virgin shone like the sun even in the darkness. They even went the length of directly coupling these things with the Deity. " When we behold the priests and deacons advance in the sticharies and ovaries, surround

* Gerlachii Literæ, ad Crusium, Turcogr. p. 502, and Crusii Annotatt. p. 197.

† The letters on these subjects are all given in the third book of the Turcogræcia.

‡ See the above mentioned Italian narrative, respecting Michael Kantakuzenos.

§ Ἱστορία πολιτικὴ Κωνσταντινουπόλεως, p. 27. Ἱστορία πατριαρχικὴ, p. 133. Another example in the Ἱστορία πατρ. p. 151. Heineccius, De absolutione mortuorum tympanicorum in Ecclesia Græca.

‖ A little sketch of this, but after the removal of the cross, is given in the Turcogr. p. 190.

the throne and bend their heads in prayer, they are like the angels of God as they place themselves round the heavenly throne to offer up their ' Holy is God !' Nay, with God himself on his heavenly throne may be likened the patriarch, who represents on his earthly throne a person of the Trinity, namely, Christ. The sanctuary of the beatified, an earthly paradise, has God made and no human hand * !"

The thoughts in which a man completes his daily routine of life demand a mental terminus; they seek to connect themselves with whatever is supremely high. Strange as the result was in this case, yet to the power of the priests founded thereon is to be ascribed the salvation of the Greek nationality. Under this protection the Greeks cherished and cultivated that hatred to the Turks, and that peculiar character, of which they now reap the advantage.

On the decay of the Ottoman Power.

Thus we behold two hostile and irreconcilable communities in one state : yet they are closely linked together ; the rulers draw vital force, and ever fresh renovation from the vanquished. We revert to the former.

Weighing once more the facts we have observed in their case, we perceive that the instinct of despotism here contrived for itself three organs; first, immediate slaves, who, commencing with personal service, executed the will of their lord in peace or war; men promoted for their talents, brought up in the ways of the Ottomans, of tried obedience, old in their master's favour, and partakers in the splendour of his sway ; next, that twofold bodyguard, mounted and on foot, that was wont to guard the sultan when he reposed, and to accompany his victorious career when he took the field; these as well as the former were slaves of the serai, but their slavery involved a kind of precedence over others : lastly, those feudatories that held the conquered empire partitioned out among them, and who hoped to conquer and share among them the rest of the world, though without ever acquiring any possession independent of the sultan's nod. We perceive that this so constituted organization had need of two things : it needed for its animation a man filled himself with a vivid spirit and free and mighty impulses; and to give it movement and activity it required continual campaigns and progressive conquests; in a word, war and a warlike chief.

All this seemed to subsist under Soliman in almost complete perfection. When it was considered how an inviolable usage imposed some brilliant enterprise or another on every new sultan, how even the religious ambition of being the builder of new mosques, was connected with the conquests of new countries, for through these they were to be endowed; and how no enduring resist-

* At the end of the Ἱστορία πατριαρχική. Turcogr. lib. iii. p. 184. Καθὼς ἡ θεότης κάθηται ἐπὶ θρόνου εἰς τὸν οὐρανὸν, οὕτως καὶ αὐτὸς ὁ δεσπότης ὁ φέρων τὴν εἰκόνα τοῦ ἑνὸς τῆς ἁγίας τριάδος Χριστοῦ τοῦ Θεοῦ ἡμῶν κάθηται ἐπὶ τοῦ θείου θρόνου τοῦ ἐπιγείου. Ἔναι (ἔστι) δὲ καὶ λέγεται αὐτὸς ὁ ναὸς τῆς παμμακαρίστου ἐπίγειος οὐρανὸς, νέα Σιὼν τὴν ὁποίαν ἔκτισεν ὁ Κύριος, καὶ οὐκ ἄνθρωπος. This is founded on older opinions, such as put forth by Simeon Thessalonicensis, περὶ τοῦ ναοῦ.

ance was to be expected either in the east from the manifestly weak empire of the Persians, nor in the west from Christendom, which had fallen into discord about the truth of its faith ; under such circumstances even intelligent men might well fear that the course of these victories would carry the Turks to universal monarchy.

Whilst men thought thus, whilst they were filled with dismay and uttered gloomy forebodings as they compared the might and the valour of the Ottomans with those of the western nations, whilst it was shown in treatises that the Turks were invincible, and why they were so[*], just then alterations took place among the latter which produced an essential revolution in the condition of their empire.

The empire needed warlike sovereigns; it began to experience a dearth of them : it needed the unswerving discipline of its military institutions, and its slave education ; this became corrupted : it needed continual conquests; they began to fail. Our purpose is to show how all this took place.

The Sultans.

The contrast has long been remarked in the west, that subsisted between all the sultans before Soliman and all those after him. Nor has it escaped the notice of the orientals. It is alleged that the grand vizier Mustafa Kiuperly frequently complained, that all the sultans since Soliman were without exception fools or tyrants ; that there was no help for the empire if it did not get rid of that most perverted stock [†].

Now as Selim II. may be regarded as the first founder of this new line, as he shall have had a great influence over it, whether by his example or by the qualities inherited from him by nature, it is a very remarkable fact that he did not obtain the throne by right, but in preference to a better brother by his mother's craft and his father's cruel and violent deed.

Soliman had an elder son, the son of his youth, Mustafa, who was just like himself, and of whom the people thought that they were indebted for him to a special favour of Heaven, so noble, brave, and high-hearted they thought him; of whom his father deemed that he reflected the virtues of his ancestors, and who was wont to say of himself, he hoped yet to do honour to the house of Othman [‡].

How came it then that Soliman bore such ill will to the inheritor of those qualities by which he had achieved his own greatness ?

If it must be admitted on close consideration that the institution of a harem is intimately associated with a military despotism, and that an exclusive passion for one woman is incompatible with it, because it attaches to home and gives occasion to many uncongenial influences, there was reason for serious apprehension in the very fact that Soliman

devoted himself wholly to his slave Roxolana; but it was truly alarming that he broke through the established order of the harem, deposed the mother of the heir apparent, to whom the foremost rank belonged of right, and raised Roxolana to the condition of a wife.

I find a letter of Codignac, a French ambassador at the Porte[*], who relates the following origin of this event:—Roxolana wished to found a mosque for the weal of her soul, but the mufti told her that the pious works of a slave turned only to the advantage of her lord ; upon this special ground Soliman declared her free. This was immediately followed by the second step. The free woman would no longer comply with those desires of Soliman which the bondswoman had obeyed, for the fetwa of the mufti declared that this could not be without sin. Passion on the one side and obstinacy on the other at last brought it about that Soliman made her his wife. A treaty of marriage was ratified, and Roxolana was secured an income of 5000 sultanins [†].

This being done, the next and most perilous thing was, that Roxolana desired to procure the succession for one of her own sons instead of Mustafa. This was no secret to any one. It was supposed that she had no other motive for connecting herself with the grand vizier Rusthen by bestowing one of her daughters on him in marriage [‡]. When it was seen that Rusthen sought every where to establish sandshaks and agas of his own selection, and to make himself friends by gifts out of his great wealth § (it was said that he possessed fifteen millions, and could roof his house with gold), that he promoted his brother to be capudani derja, captain of the sea, all this was looked on as pointing one way, namely, that in case of Soliman's death, the capudan derja should keep Mustafa, who had seated himself in Amasia, away from Europe ‖. Soliman's personal intentions were regarded with decidedly less alarm. If Mustafa's mother, who was with him, and whom he esteemed very highly, daily warned him to beware of poison, it was on the part of her fortunate rival she feared it, and as it is said not without reason. The Turks believed that the struggle would first break out after the father's death, and that the result would very possibly turn out fatally for the empire.

But in this they were mistaken. The very qualities that seemed destined to exalt Mustafa to be the head of the empire, those which made him dear to the people, were perilous to him with his

---

* A Monsignor di Lodeva, Amb. in Venetia, 3 Ott. 1553. Lettere di Principi, iii. 141.

† Ubert Folieta gives a precisely similar account in his De causis magnitudinis imperii Turcici, vol. iii.

‡ Navagero. "Li disegni della madre, così cara al Signore, et quelli del magnifico Rusten, che ha tant' autorità, non tendono ad altro fine che a questo, di fare in caso che morisse il patre herede del imperio Sultan Selim, figliuolo di lei et cognato di lui."

§ Commentarii delle cause delle guerre mosse in Cipro MS. Informatt. xvii. 73. "Si è veduto un di questi (gran-visiri) chiamato Rusten venire a tante richezze che lasciò morendo 15 millioni d'oro."

‖ Navagero : "Capitano di mare è suo fratello, il quale farà che continui in quest' officio per questo respetto, o levandolo metterà persona confidentissima : che a prohibire il Sultan Mustafa dalla successione dello stato, non è via più secura d'impedirli il passo che con un armata."

---

* E. g. "Discorso sopra l'imperio del Turco, il quale ancorche sia tirannico e violento, è per essere durabile contra l'opinione d'Aristotele et invincibile per ragioni naturali," MS. Busbek and Folieta argue to the same effect.

† Marsigli, Stato militare del imperio Ottomano, 1, 6, p. 28.

‡ Navagero, Relazione ; classical on this point. "La fama che ha di liberale et giusto fa che ogn'uno lo brama;" p. 246, a. "Solimano ha detto che Mustafa li par sia degno descendente della virtù de suoi passati;" p. 247, b. "Mustafa per essere più delli altri magnanimo et generoso ... suole dire che egli è nato ancor per far honore alla casa Ottomana."

father. If every one wished him the inheritance of the throne, if the janissaries gave open proof how earnest was the good will they bore him, if not a slave of his father's passed through the range of his government without being captivated by his kindness or his bounty, the people remarked how good it was of Mustafa, that with such general good wishes in his behalf he never showed any resentment at his father's bestowing far greater marks of favour on his brothers than on him * ; but the father remarked nothing but those connexions which seemed to him of a suspicious character. The name of Mustafa seemed to throw him into agitation. It did the son little service that he sometimes sent presents of handsome horses to the Porte ; that when he was aware of his father's unfavourable feelings he never turned his foot, never turned his face, as he said himself, in the direction of his father's court, that he might not provoke his anger. Finally, when an alliance was talked of which Mustafa proposed forming with Persia, when Rusthen complained of the devotion of the janissaries to the person of the former in a campaign in the east, Soliman set out thither in anger and summoned his son before him. The latter might undoubtedly have escaped by flight, he might probably have been able to resist ; but his mollah told him that eternal blessedness was better than dominion over the whole earth ; and, guiltless as he was, he could hardly bring himself to fear the worst. He obeyed the summons, having first divested himself even of his dagger. The worst did befal. The mutes fell upon him ; Soliman looked out from behind a thick curtain, and with threatening eyes urged them on : they strangled Mustafa †.

The padichah had still two sons left, both by Roxolana, Selim, the elder, on whom the right of succession now devolved, and Bajazeth, the younger, more like his father, more affable and more beloved, but destined by the inveterate usage of the Turks to certain death. After many a quarrel, and many an attempt at insurrection on the part of the younger, open war at length broke out between the two brothers during their father's life. Mustafa, a pacha of whom we shall have frequent occasion to make mention, boasted that it was he decided the contest. He said, that Selim having actually fled the fight, he hastened after him, and went so far as to seize his horse by the bridle ; whereupon Bajazeth, seeing his brother return and the fight renewed, was seized with despair and determined to fly to Persia ‡. He fled, but he did not succeed in escaping. The shah

allowed Soliman's executioner to seek him even there, and to strangle him. So hard was the struggle necessary to enable Selim to ascend the throne of Othman. It is not unlikely that his younger, it is in the highest degree probable that his elder brother would have inherited those warlike and manly qualities by which that house had become so great : but Selim, who preferred the society of eunuchs and of women, and the habits of the serai to the camp, who wore away his days in sensual enjoyments, in drunkenness and indolence, had no such gifts. Whoever beheld him and saw his face inflamed with Cyprus wine, and his short figure rendered corpulent by slothful indulgence, expected in him neither the warrior nor the leader of warriors. In fact nature and habit unfitted him to be the supreme head, that is the life and the soul, of that warlike state *.

With him begins the series of those inactive sultans, in whose dubious character we may trace one main cause of the decay of the Ottoman fortunes. Many were the circumstances that contributed to their ruin.

The ancient sultans took their sons with them to the field, or sent them out upon enterprises of their own without any jealousy. Othman was still living when his son Orchan accomplished the most important thing effected in his day, the conquest of Prusa. Again, the most important event under Orchan, the expedition to Europe, was accomplished under the command of his son Soliman. Succeeding sultans departed from this practice. They kept their sons aloof from themselves and from war, in a remote government under the inspection of a pacha †. At last it was thought better to shut up the heir apparent as a prisoner till the moment he was to ascend the throne ‡.

But when that moment was come, when he was become sultan, what was then his business ? Marsigli narrates how the privilege of the janissaries, of being compelled to take the field only when the sultan did so likewise, was taken from them by Soliman. It is a question whom Soliman most injured by this measure, the janissaries or his own race. Since the janissaries, the élite of the forces, were indispensable, the sultans would have continued under the necessity of marching with them in every war ; they would not have sat down the livelong year in the harem, which was now become the most pernicious of all their institutions, and wasted there all the energies of life in effeminate pleasures.

Some nobler qualities may be discovered in no few even of the latter sultans. The education and the habits of the serai, of which I have already spoken, but above all their unlimited despotic

* Navagero. "Una cosa è maravigliosa in lui, che si trova havere mai non tentato di fare novità alcuna contra il patre, et stando li fratelli, figliuoli dell' altra matre, vicini a Constantinopoli et uno anco nel serraglio, esso però tanto lontano sta quieto.

† See the extract from Busbequii Legationis Turcicæ Epistola i. p. 50, which is the source of most of the narratives of this transaction, and that from the Lettera di Michiele Codignac a Monsignor di Lodeva, Lettere di Principi, iii. 145, which, though less noticed, is more circumstantial and accurate.

‡ Floriani, Descrittione dell' imperio Turch. MS. 230. "Non restò egli (il Bassa Mustafa) di ricordar modestamente al Signore (una cosa) che giova Beglierbei di Maras et ch'egli (Selim) era gia posto in fuga da Bajazet suo fratello, lo prese per le redine del cavallo andandogli prontamente in ajuto."

* Barbaro, 294. "Delle quali laudabile conditioni (di Solimano) non viene gia detto nè anco dalli proprii Musulmani che d'alcuna Selim sia stato herede, benche di tanti regni sia stato possessor. Questo principe è di statura più tosto piccola che altrimente, pieno di carne, con faccia rossa e più tosto spaventosa, d'età di 55 anni, a quali è commun judicio che pochi n'habbi ad aggiungere per la vita che tiene." Relatione di Constantinopoli et Gran Turco, MS. 531. "Quando li figliuoli del Grand Turco sono di età di 13 anni, si circoncidono et fra 13 giorni li convien partire et si mandano per governo in qualche luogo di Natolia e in vita del Gran Turco sempre sono tenuti fuora della città."

‡ Muradgea d'Ohsson, Tableau général de l'empire Ottoman ; Paris, 1787, fol. i. 294.

power, by virtue of which they were not bound to regard, unless they pleased, any fetwa of their mufti, a power so exalted, that their excesses were declared to be the result of divine inspirations, enticed them to give way to their more ignoble qualities, and to suffer these gradually to become their second nature *. Such absolute power is not made for man. The people are not so petty and so mean as to be able to endure it. Neither will a ruler ever be found great enough to exercise it without being himself thereby utterly perverted.

What fair hopes did Amurath III., the son of Selim, afford ? In striking contrast with his father, he appeared temperate, manly, given to study, and not averse to arms. He displayed, too, a very praiseworthy beginning of his reign. What I read of him in our Relationi strikes me as especially admirable in a Turkish sultan. Every one is acquainted with that horrid custom, in compliance with which the sultans made it their first business after the death of their father to have their brothers murdered †. It did not exist in primitive times ; the brothers of Othman fought in his battles;. but it gradually became established and inviolable. Now Amurath, says the Relatione, being tender-hearted, and unable to endure the sight of blood, would neither seat himself on the throne of the sultans, nor have his accession proclaimed, till he had first secured from death his nine brothers who lived with him in the serai ‡. He talked on this matter with his muallim, with the mufti, and other learned men. But so imperative seemed the necessity of this practice, that he could make no impression upon any of them ; on the contrary, he was himself constrained to give way, after holding out for eighteen hours. He then summoned the chief of the mutes, showed him his father's corpse, and gave him nine handkerchiefs to strangle his nine brothers. He gave them him, but with tears.

There was in him a certain tincture of humanity, a trace of poetical studies, and a sort of resolution. Once, when he had the history of his ancestors read to him, he asked the by-standers which of the wars carried on by his predecessors they thought the most difficult ? They answered, " Without doubt the Persian." " That," he rejoined, " will I undertake § ;" and he did so. German ambassadors described him as clever, sober, and just, a master in the art of rewarding and punishing ||.

Such he was in the first beginning of his reign. But not all men faithfully retain the character evinced by them in their youth. The process of

development goes on even in manhood, and not always from harshness to mildness, from turbulence to sedateness. Some there are who, from modest, staid, and quiet youths, become passionate, boisterous, and insufferable men.

Amurath's character unfolded itself far otherwise than had been expected. In the first place, he gave himself up to inactive retirement. Personally he shunned war, and even avoided the chase *, and passed his day in silence and melancholy, shut up in the seclusion of the palace with mutes, dwarfs, and eunuchs. He now suffered two insatiable passions to obtain the mastery over him ; the one was the passion for women, which he indulged to the destruction of all his energies, and to the violent aggravation of his predisposition to epilepsy ; the other was the passion for gold. The story had run of Selim, how he had the sequins that flowed in to him from many a realm cast into a huge ball, and rolled by the mutes into the cistern in which was contained his private treasure, the chasineh †. In Amurath was observed an almost involuntary fondness of coined metal. It sounds almost like a tale of mythology, when we read that he had made for him a quadrangular marble pit like a well, into which he every year cast nearly two and a half millions of gold, all in sequins and sultanins. He would strip the gold ornaments from old works of art, coin them into money, bearing the characters of his name, and throw them into the pit. Over the entrance to it, which was fastened up with the utmost care, stood the bed in which he slept ‡. Be this as it may, certain it is that the tribute of repeated presents was a sure means for securing the continuance of his favour, and that appointments very soon became venal. It may be asserted, that he, the head of this empire, let himself be suborned as it were. So strongly was he influenced by his unfortunate craving for pelf.

When the creature had gone through his daily routine, that is to say when he had given that audience during which the presents brought by ambassadors or petitioners were carried before the windows so that he could have sight of them,—an audience in which he did nothing but give ear to the ambassadors, who were led before him with almost running speed and then led off as rapidly §,

* Muradgea d'Ohsson, Tableau Général de l'emp. Ott. Code religieux, i. 95.

† Relatione di Const. e di Gran Turco. " Per obligo di lege di stato Ottomano fa il successore strangulare tutti li fratelli maschi che si trovano nel serraglio, e se qualchune si truova fuori, lo manda incontinente a far morire sino bisognando con farli guerra."

‡ Ib. " Sultan Murat essendo pietoso di non poter vedere far sangue, stette 18 hore, che non volse sedere in seggio imperiale nè publicare la sua venutà nella città, desiderando e trattando prima di liberare li 9 fratelli maschi carnali. . . . Piangendo mandò li muti." Leunclavius and Thuanus (lib. lix.) allude obscurely to this.

§ Morosini, Rel. MS. 372. " Essendoli risposto, che indubitamente la più difficile era questa che potevano far li Signori Ottomani con Persiani : replicò Sua Maestà, La ho in animo di far io."

|| Gerlachius ad Hailandum, 1 Aug. 1576, in Crusii Turcogr. 499.

* Soranzo, Relationi o diario di viaggio MS. " Lontano dei negotii—non essendo punto bellicoso nè amatore d'essercitii militari,—ritenendosi insino dalle caccie, particolar piacere de suoi precessori."

† Relatione di Const. e G. T. " Selim cominciò ad usare di fondere tutto l'oro che veniva dall' entrate de regni et farne una palla grande, quale faceva mettere rozzolando per terra dalli muti in quella cisterna accio non rivelassero niente."

‡ Relatione di 1594. " Nella propria camera ha fatto una buca quadra molto profonda, in guiza d'un pozzo, cinta di finissimi marmi et la via impiendo tutta d'oro." The Rel. di Const. e G. T. agrees with this. " Sono le bocche serrate con tre coperchi di ferro conchiave et sopra vi sono murate da tre palmi, che non appare ci sia cosa alcuna."

§ Soranzo of his own audience : " Ciascheduno era messo in mezzo de capigi bassi cioè mastri di camera, et pigliato strettamente per le mani e maniche era condotto a piedi del signore, dove inginocchiatosi gli veniva porto da uno di loro due una manica della sua veste a baciare, il che fatto era reconduto indietro con la faccia sempre volta verso il Signore : et intanto che si faceva questa ceremonia, passava il presente portato da i capigi, cioè da portieri, dinanzi a una finestra della camera del signore accio lo potesse vedere."

stare at them with his large, lacklustre, melancholy eyes, and perhaps nod his head to them; when he had done this he went back to his garden, where in deep sequestered spots his women played before him, danced and sang, or his dwarfs made sport for him, or his mutes, awkward and mounted on as awkward horses, engaged with him in ludicrous combats, in which he struck now at the rider now at the horse, or where certain Jews performed lascivious comedies before him [*].

Was this a fit head for a state founded on war, and having its existence in war?

Neither were his successors so. Our Relationi are silent as to Mehemet; but we know independently of them that this weak monarch was less a ruler than he was ruled. Ahmed was nobly endowed by nature. He ascended the throne in his fourteenth year; it was not till near the end of his reign that he was a man. He then showed himself clement, active, full of noble designs. He less regretted the loss of ships taken by the Christians when they were his own than when they were the property of poor Moslem. He chose rather to declare a man insane who had thrown a stone at him, than to punish him [†]. He revived and maintained an incorruptible justice, and personally sifted all grievances to the bottom; highly was he reverenced for this by the people, who reaped the immediate benefit of these qualities. But he had far greater things still in view. Daily to be seen on horseback, in the chase, busy with the bow and quiver, his thoughts were bent on war. When he read the deeds of Soliman it seemed his longing not only to equal these but to surpass them [‡].

But nothing of the kind befel. Since the empire, just then weakened by wars and insurrections, probably wanted in fact the strength for great enterprizes; since the sovereign was thus perhaps withheld from actual deeds, and compelled to entertain himself with mere intentions, the result was that his mind, which could not put forth its whole force in great enterprises, was easily disgusted and satiated with pettier occupations. Unlimited power reacted singularly on Ahmed. He was neither used to encounter nor inclined to endure contradiction from others; but he constantly contradicted himself. His thoughts seemed often in direct variance with each other; he repented of his acts in the moment even of their performance; he recalled his orders in the very beginning of their execution. Even his daily life was filled with a violent spirit of unrest; there was no place, no occupation, no enjoyment in which he did not soon find dissatisfaction [§].

* Relatione di 1594.

† Valieri, Relatione di Constantinopoli: "Si dimostra assai amatore della loro legge et della giustitia et del bene de suoi sudditi, il che lo fa amare del popolo tutto, et quando può havere notitia d'uno aggravio, se ne risente grandemente e ne fa la provisione. Et negli accidenti delle gallere prese da Fiorentini et Spagnuoli s'andara consolando con dire che la perdita non fosse di Mussulamani, ma toccasse al suo solo interesse. Non inchina al sangue, anzi più tosto in alcune occurrenze si è dimostrato di natura mite."

‡ "Spiriti grandi nutrisce con la memoria di sultan Soliman, che va frequentemente leggendo con pensiero non pure d'imitarlo ma di superarlo."

§ Ibid. "La mal cupidità troppo cercando perde et dopo molta fatica subitamente getta quello che avidamente ha capito, et dal abondanza delle delizie nasce la satietà et dalla satietà la nausea. La leggierezza quasi turbine volge intorno tutte le cose."

Thus all his endeavours were destined to run to waste, and his schemes to vanish in air.

Among all his successors there was absolutely but one possessed of genuine innate vigour; this was Amurath IV. But we shall see how his character turned out, and how little he was a sovereign capable of ruling a people.

In short, from the period of Soliman's unfortunate marriage with Roxolana, the organization of the Ottoman polemarchy began to lack the head in which its life was centred. The sultans continued to be emirs like their ancestors, with a warlike confederacy of slaves. What must needs have been the result, so soon as the spirit of the confederacy became alienated from the emir? If the despotism had need of the slaves, the slaves had need of the despot.

Viziers.

But can it have been that no remedy was to be found in the constitution against an evil, the inevitable occurrence of which, at least occasionally, might have been so easily foreseen?

There exists among the Ottomans an institution fitted to prevent the effects of incapacity in the sultan, the institution of the Veziri-aasam, that is of the grand vizier. This officer they are accustomed to style an unlimited deputy, an essential feature in the world's order, nay a lord of the empire [*]. A great portion of the public weal depends on him, since he holds the administration, and when the sultan is incapable the whole executive power, in his hands. The grand difficulty is only to find a man, who, taking upon him his master's duties, possesses likewise all the virtues which the latter wants.

Now it must be admitted that under Selim II. this power was committed to the hands of the fittest man that could be found, a Bosnian named Mehemet. He was brought from the house of his uncle, a priest of Saba, as a young slave into the serai; and there he had climbed thus high in dignity. As Selim seldom saw or spoke to any one but him; as the sultan was used to leave the whole routine of business to him, so that all propositions from foreign ambassadors, all reports from the interior of the kingdom, were submitted to him alone, and all measures in consequence were determined by him; as he had the appointment to all posts, and the disposal of all honours and dignities, as the whole body of civil and criminal jurisdiction rested with him, we may admit the truth of Barbaro's remark that he was the only ear in the empire to hear, and the only head to determine. The weal and the woe, the substance and the life of every subject were in the hands of this slave of Saba. It was matter of amazement how he contrived to fulfil all his various avocations [†]. Not only did he hold his public divan on the four appointed days from an early hour till noon, giving audience upon

* Hammer, Staatsverfassung der Osmanen, i. 451; ii. 84.

† Barbaro, 296: "Chi potrà dunque con ragione comprendere che basti il tempo a tante e così diverse attioni et come vi possa esser tanta intelligenza che a così importante governo supplisca? nè però è mai impedita audienza a qualsivoglia ancora che minima persona ad ogni sua commoda satisfattione." Not a trace of this whole passage is to be found in the copy of this Relatione in the Tesoro Politico, i. p. 87.

so many diverse questions that the dragoman of Venice, for example, thought it necessary to be constantly present that he might be ready with his answer on the spot, should any unexpected complaint be sent in from the frontiers; but he also gave audience in his own house both on the other days, and on these after the close of the divan. Every man, though he were the lowest, might address him; the hall was always full; yet not a sound was heard but that of the man who was stating his case, or of the secretary reading a petition. The decision was given on the spot, irrevocably, and for the most part to the satisfaction of the parties concerned. Presents of slaves and horses, of costly textures, silks, and, above all, gold flowed abundantly into his house. There was a running fountain of gold therein, says Barbaro[*]. Rivers of gold and silver streamed into it, says Floriani. Nor was he a man to hoard up these good things. Three thousand men ate daily at his table. In no few places in Europe and Asia were seen mosques, baths, and aqueducts, bridges and dams erected by him. He was particularly fond of founding caravanserais, in which travellers were entertained gratis for three days together with bread, rice, and meat, and also with fodder for their horses.

Mehemet was not puffed up by this fortune, this power and greatness. He is one of the noblest of his nation whose memory has come down to us. He was always found kind and pacific, sober and religious, without vindictiveness, and without rapacity. Even at the age of sixty-five his aspect was that of a hale and vigorous man, handsome in person, tall and of stately presence[†].

Two things perhaps conduced to the moderation of his character. If it is one of the most difficult problems for regular constitutions to counteract the arbitrary will of the higher functionaries of state, a problem for the sake of which recourse is mainly had to them, it is on the other hand a most remarkable fact, that the problem is in a certain degree solved by despotism itself; not however by law but by caprice, by the caprice of the despot's self. Mehemet saw his fortune and his life at the mercy of any small error, any trifling fault, that might produce a bad impression on the sultan. Add to this, that at this time there were besides the grand vizier others too at the Porte, the so called viziers of the cupola; who, though their business seemed to be chiefly to obey and execute orders, yet they sometimes, though unfrequently, had access to the sultan, as for instance, when the latter rode to the mosque, or when he held a divan on horseback, or when it was afforded them by a confederacy in the serai. Among these were two vehement opponents of Mehemet, Piali, who was also a son-in-law of Selim, and that Mustafa who decided the battle against Bajazeth, and who believed himself to possess no small claims on his master's gratitude. Sometimes they succeeded in carrying some point against him. When Selim thought of distinguishing his reign by some exploit, they were for an attack on Cyprus; Mehemet was for a bolder enterprise. The sultan's nature inclined to the easier undertaking, and its speedy success in the hands of his rivals was near bringing Mehemet into jeopardy. His intense inward emotion was visible in his face when he spoke of their persecutions[*]. He now took double heed to his ways. It were impossible to describe the deliberation, the forethought, with which he engaged personally in the smallest things. That he might not provoke envy he forbore from adorning Constantinople with his architectural works.

He erected there nothing but a small mosque; yet this was the monument of his misfortune. It will be remembered that he was the son-in-law of the sultan. He buried his twelve children in that mosque.

He was successful in maintaining his position at the summit of power under three sovereigns. The last two, Selim and Amurath, were indebted to him for their quiet accession to the throne. For Selim's sake he kept the death of Soliman before Sighet concealed. When Selim died he made a secret of his death likewise. He privately summoned young Amurath from Asia. Mehemet welcomed him in the garden, where he arrived by night sooner than expected, and under the tree where he had sat himself down[†], and led him into the imperial apartments. How completely seemed the whole power of the empire to be then in his hands. He made the sultan sit still, they say, sent for the young man's mother, and asked her, was that her son, Sultan Amurath? when she replied in the affirmative he raised his hands to heaven, thanked God, and offered up the first prayer for the weal of the new sultan.

Now, if the arbitrary power of the sultans was not unprofitable for the viziership, so long as the former remained within certain bounds, it could not fail to be fatal so soon as it was guided rather by distrust than by prudence, and so soon as it came to be exercised too often.

---

[*] Barbaro, 287: "Hora no quali crede la S. V. siano quelle (le richezze) di Mehemet Bassa: poiche oltre l'infiniti donativi minori ne sono molti ancora di 20, 30 et anco di più di 52 miglia scudi l'uno; ma qui non debbo io allargarmi, lasciando che da se medesime le S. V. lo considerino, sapendo che non si fa mentione di grado o d'altra cosa di gratia o di giustitia in quell' amplissimo imperio che egli non ne sia riconosciuto abondantemente, aggiongendovi di più che ogn' uno per essere stabilito et accresciuto di honore et d'utilità lo tributa quasi del continuo, onde si può quasi dire che sempre nella casa sua corre un fonte d'oro." Of this passage too, nine leaves before the former one, there is no trace in the printed copy.

[†] Barbaro: "Nelle fatiche mai manca, responde gratamente, non s'insuperbisce per la suprema dignità che tiene, nè mancò per essere genero di Signore.—Ha la moglie giovane assai bella, et con tutto che sia egli più di 65 anni, si fa però più giovane: et ogni anno fa un figliuolo, ma tutte gli muorono." Besides Barbaro we have also made use of Floriani (223—229, MS.), a classical authority as to Mehemet.

[*] Relatione del Barbaro delli negotii trattati di lui, MS. 380. "Il Bassa in estremo si dolse di quello ch'era successo, et venendo alle lagrime si rammaricava quanto fosse da suoi emuli perseguitato, si come anco molte volte ha fatto meco con molta afflittione dell' animo suo."

[†] Morosini, Constantinopoli del 1584, MS. 353. "Trovata una galeotta gionse a mezza notte in Constantinopoli, et accostandosi al giardino del suo serraglio, non trovato il Buttigi Basso il quale havea ordine d'aprirli la porta che entra in serraglio; smontato della galeotta si ripose a sedire nel giardino fuori della mura sott' un albero, nel qual luogho di poi ha fatto fare una bellissima fontana." The rest is told at full length. A similar account is given in Sagredo, Memorie Istoriche de Monarchi Ottomanni, p. 617.

Mehemet's well-earned reputation caused Amurath III. some jealousy, and he favoured the subordinate viziers of the cupola in opposition to him [*]. But before this was productive of any mischief to Mehemet, he was murdered by an incensed timarli, whom he had deprived of his timar, perhaps with justice, and who made his way into the vizier's house in the disguise of a beggar. Thus fell a man with whom, as Floriani says, the virtue of the Turks descended to the grave.

At least vigour and dignity were missed in the viziers who succeeded him. Viziers of characters mutually the most opposite followed each other in rapid succession. From the hands of Achmet, first an opponent and now the successor of Mehemet, a good old man on the whole, who, above all, would not endure a thought of corruption [†], the administration was transmitted to that Mustafa who had fought against Bajazeth and against Cyprus. Though seventy years old, and of fearfully repulsive aspect, with thick brows overhanging his eyes, and shadowing his swarthy features ; though infamous for his cruel deeds, especially in Cyprus, Mustafa yet knew how to conceal that impetuous and violent temper, of which he had so often given proof, under polished manners, flattering speeches, and a gracious manner of reception.

For a while he exercised only the functions without the titles and dignities of his office : it is said that he laid violent hands on himself in disgust at his not receiving the seals [‡]. Among the viziers of the second rank was an Albanian from the neighbourhood of Scutari, named Sinan, who alone of seven brothers had remained in the serai till he reached one of the four highest dignities, that of a chokahdar (who supports the hem of the sultan's mantle) whence a prospect opened to him of appointments to important offices. Upon this he took advantage of Mehemet's quarrel with Mustafa, to ingratiate himself with the former, and of Amurath's incipient aversion to Mehemet to make good his footing with the sultan [§]. The men of the west noticed in him a striking resemblance to cardinal Granvella. This is no compliment to the cardinal. Sinan paraded his shameless want of principle openly and without reserve [‖], and laughed when he thought he had appalled any one by his bravadoes. It was a fact, that he had been at an earlier date successful in some warlike exploits in Arabia and on the coasts of Africa. Upon his now marching against the Persians he boasted that he would fetch away the shah from Casbin and bring him to Constantinople ; and when he came back, not only without the shah, but even without having

ing achieved anything worth mentioning, he never theless bragged that he had conquered a country for fifty sandshaks. But upon his venturing to hint, as the war in Persia was proceeding unfavourably, that it needed a shah to combat a shah, —he fell into disgrace.

Totally different again in character was his successor Sciaus, a Croat, polished, agreeable, affable, courteous, and a man of address. On the day when having set out to accompany his sister to her husband [*], he was waylaid by the Turks, taken prisoner along with his brother and two sisters, and carried into slavery ; he had surely little hopes of such high rank and fortune as awaited him. But what an unenviable fortune it was after all. Amurath did not bear with him long.

Amurath even abandoned the consecrated custom of his predecessors, of taking their state functionaries and viziers only from among their slaves. The only leader who acquired renown in the Persian war was Othman Pacha. Though his father had been a beglerbeg, and his mother the daughter of a beglerbeg, and he was perhaps of the best blood in the empire next to the imperial family ; the sultan nevertheless fixed his choice on him. Othman, however, paid but too soon with his life for his gallant enterprises in Persia.

Upon this Amurath departed still more widely from the practice of his forefathers. He turned again to the deposed vizier, but only for a short while [†]. Sinan, Sciaus, and a third named Ferhat, were seen to relieve each other as it were by turns, and there was witnessed the establishment of a ceremony for the deposition of a vizier. A messenger from the sultan suddenly made his appearance in the apartments assigned the vizier, and having first demanded of him the seal he carried in his bosom, he made him a sign that he must begone, after which he finally clapped the door to behind him. It was opened again for the new comer, who however had soon to share the same fate. Whether it was rather distrust or caprice that induced the sultan to make such continual changes, at any rate it was believed that his conduct in this respect had much to do with his greediness for gold. Sinan sometimes gave 100,000 sequins, sometimes 200,000 to re-establish himself in his vacillating favour. The capudan Cicala made no secret of it that he must set out on a cruise for booty, to enable him to present the sultan with 200,000 sequins, otherwise he had reason to fear his dismissal ; and in fact his rivals had already been summoned to the court [‡].

Things continued under the succeeding sultans as under Amurath. Under Achmed, too, we see viziers of the most opposite character following

---

[*] Soranzo, Diario MS. 465. " Venuto al imperio Sultan Amurath, cominciò Mehemet declinare della solita gratia et favore, cercando il Signore ogni occasione di levargli il credito et autorità acquistatasi in vita del patre."

[†] Floriani : " Haveva (Achmet) più tosto nobil natura che testa di negotii."

[‡] Soranzo : " Mustafa se ne mori per disperatione, o come altri vogliono, s'attossicò, come ingratamente remunerato di tante imprese da lui condotte a felice fine."

[§] The details of these matters are to be found exclusively in Soranzo.

[‖] Floriani : " E' Sinan ambitioso inconstante contumelioso enfiato imprudente impudente superbo e nella pratica senza nessuna sorte di maniera civile. E ancho chiamato da Turchi multo aventuroso." Soranzo agrees in this unfavourable estimate of his character.

[*] So I understand Soranzo, 467 : " Pervenuto in mano de Turchi con modo si può dire tragico, perchè accompagnando insieme con un suo fratello due sorelle a marito (this however admits of another interpretation) diede in una imboscata de Turchi.......E il più trattabile et cortese."

[†] Relatione di 1594: " Con diversi pretesti il più delle volte leggieri gli fa, come dicono loro, Manzoli (le nom de Mazoul répond à déplacé, déstitué, Ohsson II. 272), cioè gli depone ; se ben dopoche gli ha fatto vivere un pezzo senza dignità et governo et ben mortificati, torna poi con il mezzo de danari e de presenti a ricevergli in gratia."

[‡] Ibid. "Il Signore prontamente accettò il consiglio di Ferrat Bassa, che lo persuase a chiamar a Constantinopoli Giafer, famoso capitano di mare, per accrescere maggiormente al Cicala la gelosia."

C

each other *. Now it is a Mehemet, a pacific, quiet, only not sufficiently resolute man, who however duly hears every one, and endeavours to comprehend the arguments laid before him. Now it is a Nasuf, an irritable and violent Albanian, who gives ear to others with reluctance, is always prone to the most violent courses, and with whom the Venetian bailo complains that he has fallen into a sea of difficulties.

The consequence of this new practice was, that whilst the head of the government was constantly changed, the manner and course of the administration, and the principles and usages of the higher functionaries were unsettled and subjected to no fewer changes. Above all, it ensued that the viziers, too dependent on the caprice of the sultan, were incapable of making good the latter's faults.

If then the sultan himself happened not to be the man who could guide the state, if his vizier moreover was hindered from acquiring that independence and that stability, without which no administration is possible, on whom then devolved the conduct of public affairs, from whom did the internal movements of the state receive their impulse?

What constantly befals Oriental despotisms occurred in this case likewise; here, too, caprice called up some one who was able to master it. A new system of government grew up, situated in the hands of the favourites within the palace, such as the sultan's mother, or his wives, or his eunuchs.

We have seen the influence exercised by Roxolana: under Amurath too the women had much sway, and Sinan maintained himself chiefly through the protection of a countrywoman of his own, an Albanian, in the harem †. But even under this sultan the weightiest affairs were in other hands than the vizier's. While all other offices were fluctuating, Capu Agassi, aga of the gate of bliss, as they phrase it, head of the household and chief of the white eunuchs, maintained his credit unabated ‡. He contrived to flatter his master's tastes, sometimes with ornaments for the female slaves of the harem, which he procured from Venice, and for which he sent at times impracticable orders §; sometimes with an agreeable present, were it only a golden vessel filled with fragrant oil. He once contrived to have a sumptuous gal-

lery erected in the serai without its being observed by Amurath: when it was finished he took him thither. It was placed in one of the most beautiful spots in that garden so remarkable for its fair situation, with a prospect over both seas. He threw it open before the eyes of the astonished sultan, and presented it to him. In this way he perfectly secured his good will. He had a thousand opportunities of turning this to account. As he alone laid petitions before the sultan, as he was the sole bearer of news to him, it was easy for him to exert an influence over his master's opinions. He often set persons at liberty who had been imprisoned by a pacha; frequently he contrived to have orders issued contradictory to others that had just preceded them, so that the pachas were thrown into confusion, and knew not what to do *.

This manner of government became gradually inveterate. One at least of his wives had so much influence over Ahmed, that he never refused her a request; she was complete mistress of his inclinations. But still greater was the influence of the kislar aga, that is the chief of the black eunuchs, the superintendent more peculiarly of the harem. He had always the ear of the sultan, he could direct his will as he pleased: how many a project of the vizier Nasuf did he singly defeat! In outward appearance too, in manners, in the number of his servants, he was almost on an equality with his master †. It was necessary to keep well with both the favourites: to effect this was a prime endeavour with foreign ambassadors. The lady was to be won with little civilities, with rare perfumes and costly waters ‡. With the kislar it was necessary to go more earnestly to work. Large fowl, says Valieri, require good feeding: people who have gold in abundance are not to be had at a cheap rate §.

In this way there arose, within the walls of the harem, an interest opposed to the vizier, and by which he was himself ruled, and placed and displaced; not a general interest of the empire, nor a personal one of the sultan's, but an interest of women and of eunuchs, who now assumed the lead of this warlike state ‖.

The harem possessed yet another influence. As the sultans began to give not only their sisters and their daughters, but also their slaves in marriage to the great, it followed that these women carried the manners of the serai into private houses ¶. What a wide departure was now made from the

---

* Valiere speaking of the time of Ahmed: "Lo stato del primo visir et d'ogn' altro ministro di quel governo è lubrico assai, restando la sua grandezza appesa a debolissimo et picciolissimo filo. Avviene che o per piccolo disgusto che prende il re o pure per incontro d'altri accidenti et alle volte per brama di novità viene deposto dal governo et abbandonato e negletto, et se vivo, resta poco men che sepolto nella miseria."

† Of the female superior too of the harem, the Kadun Kietchuda, the Rel. di 1594 says; "Venetiani se vagliono molto del favore di questa donna presso il Signore, sendo hor mai chiari che ella ottiene cio che vuole et il più delle volte lo fa mutar pensiero."

‡ Ibid. "Di natione Venetiano, nato bassamente, ma di bellissimo ingegno, è perfido Turco il quale si è tirato tanto innanzi nella gratia del Signore, che in la sola sua persona ha unito due carichi principali della camera, cioè il titolo et carico proprio del capi aga et anco di visir bassa."

§ Ibid. "Ne risente Venetia perche hora il Bailo hora mercanti Venetiani hanno da lui carichi et disegni di cose quasi impossibili, come ultimamente volse un raso cremisino che fosse simplice raro e nondimeno che havesse il fondo del rovescio d'oro, et altre cose molto difficile et di gran spesa."

---

* Ibid passim. That this was generally known appears from the Ragionamento del re Filippo al suo figlio, MS. which ascribes to Amurath a "seguir contrario al deliberato."

† Valieri: "Lascio in dubio veramente qual sia il re."

‡ Ibid. "Mi sono ingegnato d'insinuarmi con la regina: con alcune gentilezze, che li riuscivano care, sopra ogni altra cosa, d'odori et d'altre acque di suo gusto, l'ho resa inclinata alla casa: onde ben spesso faceva offerirmi l'opera sua."

§ Ibid. "Ma ogni spesa con questi è benissimo impiegata"

‖ On this turn of the viziership see also Businello, Historical notices of the Ottoman monarchy, section xi.

¶ Relat. di 1594. "Manda alcune delle sue schiave—pregato anco della Cagianandona, fuori, maritandole a suoi schiavi più favoriti. E di qui ha presa forza la corruttela de costumi turcheschi.......Non più sedono in terra ma in sedie di velluto e d'oro d'infinita spesa; nè si contentano d'una sola e semplice vivanda, come si usava a tempo di Solimano, ma sono introdutti li cuochi eccellentissimi, li pasticci, le torte, li mangiari composti."

old simplicity of the camp from which the nation had set out. They began to cover their seats with cloth of gold ; they slept in summer on the finest silk, and in winter wrapped in costly furs. A pair of shoes belonging to a Turkish lady of rank seemed worth more than the whole dress of an European princess. In lieu of the simple fare of Soliman's time they outdid all the delicacies of Italy.

Now if this had an injurious influence from the mere fact that even the humbler classes gradually became used to live in this way, it was a still worse result that the great were compelled by their expenses, and prompted by the sultan's example, to do or suffer every thing for gold. If ever the rearing up of slaves to high places in the sultan's household had been attended with a good effect, this was now utterly destroyed. Justice was venal; every office had its price. But as every thing was liable to be lost again at any moment, the consequence was everywhere tyranny, extortion, desolation, and despair. Constantinople indeed increased; but it was because men thought themselves somewhat more secure there than under the grasp of the pachas and their feudatories, or because more was to be earned by a town trade than by agriculture. The empire declined whilst its capital increased [*].

Military Forces.

If the conclusion must be admitted, that the corruption of the sultans and that of the system of government which have hitherto formed the subject of our inquiries, were related to each other as cause and effect, and were both to be traced to one origin; there were other alterations which arose independently of the former, and only co-operated with them to one result.

Important changes took place in the warlike organization itself as well as in its head; and, first, in that institution which was the core and the sinews of all the others, the institution of the janissaries.

It is very well known how important the janissaries were in the beginning ; it is no less known what they came to be at last; both facts are strikingly obvious. It is less clear, but certainly not less deserving to be known, how this decay took place.

When we put together the scattered notices in our Relationi, we discern some stages of this transition.

In the first place let us recollect that the janissaries were originally prohibited from marrying, and even to a late period they adhered to the custom of not suffering any woman near their barracks. On no account, says Spandugino, were they to take wives[†]. Despotism, like the hierarchy, required people wholly devoted to itself, separated by no care for wife or child, by no domestic hearth, from the only interests they should know, the interests of their lord. But now marriage was allowed the janissaries, and that undoubtedly as early as in Soliman's reign; at first indeed only to such of them as were less fit for actual service, or who were

stationed on the frontiers, but gradually to all without exception [*]. This change alone must have produced no little mutation in the habits and way of thinking of the soldiery.

But another change immediately came forth from the first, and directly threatened the very vitality of the institution. The question was, what was to be done with the children of the janissaries ? The fathers demanded that their sons should be received into their body. We learn from the Relatione of Giovanfrancesco Morosini, and as far as my investigation has gone, from it alone, that they obtained this favour on the accession of Selim II. to the throne. It is very well known that the grand vizier Mehemet thought it expedient to keep secret the death of Soliman before Sighet. It was not till the army had begun its march homewards after the conquest of that place, and had already reached Belgrade, not till Selim, who had set out from Asia upon the first secret intelligence sent him by Mehemet, had arrived at the same point, that the death of the late sultan and the accession of the new were proclaimed at one and the same moment[†]. It now happened, as Morosini relates, that Mehemet, who was never very lavish of the imperial treasure, did not bestow upon the janissaries the present usual on the accession of a sultan, particularly as they had dispersed on the march home. Incensed at this they betook themselves to their quarters, with muttered threats that they would let it be seen in Constantinople who and what they were. They arrived before the sultan; they escorted him into the capital; but when the line of march was arrived before their odalar, their quarters, they halted, stepped forth, and declared that they would not suffer the sultan to enter the serai unless he satisfied their demands. Now their demands were not only to the effect that they should be granted the accustomed gratuities, and that their pay should be raised, but what is of most importance to our present consideration, that their sons, for whom the state had already condescended to make provision, should be admitted into the janissary corps as soon as they were grown up[‡]. In vain the viziers dismounted from their horses to still the mutiny with fair words; in vain the aga of the janissaries went among them, with his head enveloped in the handkerchief used for strangling, and implored them not to put this insult on the sultan; the

---

[*] Soranzo, 1581 : "Si maritano come più lor piace; *il che gia non li era* permesso se non ad alcuno posto nelie frontiere overo consumato delle guerre, ma tutto con licenza et gratia dell' Aga." That this was the case under Soliman, is stated in Libri tre delle cose de Turchi, Venice 1539, p. 18.

[†] Here likewise Morosini is exclusively our informant. "Alla qual gionta (the vizier's) ritrovandosi Sultan Selim accampato fuori della città; ricevè il corpo, al quale subito fatto secondo il costume turchesco la sua oratione, ipsofacto lo consegnò ad Acmad Bassa Visir che lo dovesse condurre in Constantinopoli et sepelirlo nel giardino della sua moschea; appresso postosi Sultan Selim a sedere realmente, li fu bacciato la mano."

[‡] Morosini : "Le dimande di Giannizzeri erano queste, che essendo stati dati loro solamente 2000 aspri di presente per uno et tagliati in parte il modo del accrescimento del loro soldo, fossegli accresciuto il presente sino alla somma di 3000 aspri, come avea fatto Sultan Solimano, et che il accrescimento del soldo loro fosse nel medesimo modo,—che i loro figliuoli subito nato dovessero secondo il solito *essere descritti al pane et dopo cresciuti in età dovessero medesimamente essere fatti Giannizzeri.*"

---

[*] Relat. di 1594: "Chi non può fuggire in altro paese, si salva in Constantinopoli. Onde si inganna chi da questo argomenta la grandezza del imperio, poiche imitando il corpo humano si veggono le vene correre per tutte le parti del corpo et non allargarsi ne ramificare vicino al cuore."

[†] Trattato di Theodoro Spandugino de costumi de Turchi, printed in Sansovino's collection, p. 113. "I detti Genizzeri in alcun modo non possono prender moglie."

viziers were forced to give way, the aga to with-draw. They did not suffer the sultan to enter the serai till in his name, and in his presence, the aga had promised all they demanded; they did not throw open the gates till Selim once more made them the same promise with his own lips, and raised his hands above his head in testimony of his vow. They then opened the gates, fell into rank, and saluted their sovereign with a full volley from their arquebuses. The next divan ratified what had been thus granted them.

Now if it was constitutional with this body-guard to be made up of young people, who had lost all knowledge of their parental home, this principle was now decidedly violated, and that not exception-ally, but by distinct enactment. Ere long the sons of the janissaries were seen in the ranks of that corps. It was impossible that they should have undergone the full rigour of discipline that had once been enforced.

It may readily be conceived that this facilitated the passage to a third innovation. When that Persian war in which Amurath embarked, because it seemed the most arduous of all Ottoman enter-prises, proved in reality to be very difficult, con-sumed whole armies and afforded no conquests ; when it made great havoc in the ranks of the ja-nissaries, and it was urgently necessary to recruit these in every way, it was then not enough that their sons should be admitted among them, admis-sion was likewise granted to other native Turks, and to Mussulmen of all nations, men unpractised, undisciplined, and incapable of all discipline *. This was carried to such a pitch as to produce an inter-nal division in the body. How should the veterans, who had borne a part in Soliman's wars, have deemed this promiscuous rabble worthy comrades in arms ? There was often reason to fear that they would come to mutual hostilities.

The door was thus flung open widely to every abuse. The metamorphosis made rapid way. Under Soliman the janissaries took themselves wives ; under Selim II. they had their sons en-rolled among them; under Amurath III. they were forced to admit among them native Turks, of totally different descent, who had not gone through their training; under Ahmed this warlike body was already brought to such a condition, that the pri-vates when stationed through the country or on the frontiers began to ply to trades, to engage in com-merce, and, satisfied with the advantage of their name, to think little of war and arms †.

How badly now did they stand to their arms ! A Frank could not refrain from laughing to see them

shoot. They clutched the stock of their piece tightly in their left hand, while with the right they applied the match; and so childish was their fear of the explosion that they hurriedly turned away their heads *. How far did they now fall short of their old invincible renown ? It passed soon into a proverb, The janissary has surely a good eye and good legs, the former to see if the cavalry waver, and the latter to run away with all speed there-upon.

If the janissaries were no longer capable of de-fending the empire as before, they now turned against the sultan the strength and the arms they had hitherto employed against his foes. Even in former times the rigour of their discipline had not always sufficed to keep them under subjection; that rigour was now relaxed †, but their old refractori-ness remained, along with their old rights and pre-tensions. When all those personal qualities of the several members are lost which may at some time have conferred privileges on any society or body corporate, still the spirit of the body does not depart, but clings to its prerogatives with aug-menting pertinacity. The insolence of these forces was insufferable. They compelled sultan Amurath to deliver up to them deftardars and pachas to be strangled. They slew a pacha of Cyprus, and Amurath sent them another. Fearing that the new man, however complaisant he affected to be, would punish them for what they had done to his predecessor, they promised him obedience at first, and lulled him into security ; then, when they saw their opportunity, they surrounded him and his staff, and killed them all‡. Thus were the slaves become tyrants.

One question now remains, when did the prac-tice cease of pressing Christian boys into the ser-vice of the palace ? It may be supposed that this was gradually abandoned from the time native Turks began to be employed. Marsigli, who made his observations in 1680, assures us, that the cus-tom had long fallen into desuetude §. Valieri, on the other hand, whose Relatione belongs to the year 1618, describes it as in full operation. We must conclude therefore that it was left off between 1630 and 1650. I find no trace of it in the Rela-tione of 1637. This was unquestionably the great-est good fortune that befel the Greeks. How could they have entertained a thought of rising, nay of at all sustaining themselves as a body, had the practice of regularly carrying off the flower of their youth into slavery been persisted in ? It is not till after this usage had ceased, not till the seventeenth century, that we first meet with a

---

* Relatione di 1594: "Gia scelti homini fatti d'ogni natione—non hanno in loro altro che crudeltà, insolenza et disobedienza verso li capi loro." Discorso dello stato del Turco, in the Tesoro politico i, 99. "Sono stati anco as-critti al luogo dei Giannizzeri nati Turchi contra l'ordine invecchiato di quella porta, che non ha mai usata, se non per estraordinario favore, di far Gianizzero nessun altro se non rinegato."

† Valieri: "Resta assai alterata questa militia et nella gente et nella disciplina; perche molti Turchi nativi sono ascritti in luogo d'altri, et la maggiore parte è sparsa nel paese, che fattasi con la nostra voce casalini attendono alla mercantia et ad ogni commercio senza curarsi d'altro, bastan-doli il commodo che apporta il nome de Giannizzeri, che è grande." Perhaps the gradations of the change will some-time or other be more accurately intelligible from more cir-cumstantial accounts.

* Relat. di 1637 : "Un tenero figliuolino si mostrerebbe più ardito."

† Relat. di 1594: "La militia e relassata da quella prima et ottima sua disciplina; perche la falange de Giannazzeri, da cui valore sono sempre dependuti tutti li acquisti di questo imperio, a pena retiene la prima imagine ; non essendo più educati con quella esatta disciplina, passando per quei cimenti che solevano li vecchi. . . Per il che non è maraviglia che siano pieni li avisi di tante scelerità da loro commessi sino in Constantinopoli su gli occhi del signore et sotto il medesimo Sinan Bassa."

‡ Leunclavii Supplementum Annalium Turcicorum, p. 93.

§ Marsigli, dello stato militare, i. c. 6, p. 27. "Ad instanza de timarli, de siameti, de beg et beglerbeg è molto tempo che fu levato quel crudel tributo che queste nationi Chris-tiane doveano dare con un certo numero di figli."

klepht, celebrated in the national songs, Christos Milionis *.

It is self-evident that these great changes, decisively influencing the whole constitutional economy of the empire, must have extended to the other slaves destined to the sultan's service. As early as the times of Selim II. the custom ceased of entrusting the higher offices of state exclusively to the Christian-born slaves brought up in the serai. Barbaro says, the sons of Turks are now admitted to these offices by a pernicious stretch of partiality ; an irregularity disapproved of by many, and which in his opinion was sure to be pernicious to the empire†. And in fact it was not long before a dearth of able men was thought to be evident. Only as the sultan still continued to keep the serai full of slaves, come whencesoever they might, as with the natural leaning of every despot he went on bestowing the highest stations on favourite slaves, the revolution could not be so complete in this case as in the others.

It is easy too to see that the janissaries would necessarily communicate their own corruption to the sipahi at the Porte. The Persian war had a two-fold mischievous effect on the sipahi, since it not only cost them men, but also completely ruined that excellent breed of horses they had hitherto employed, and which had contributed not a little to their renown. Among the sipahi too were admitted native Turks and people of all sorts ‡ ; they too were always prompt to mutiny. In the year 1589 they compelled Sultan Amurath to reinstate Sinan, who had recently been dismissed, in the rank of grand vizier §.

The condition of the timars was not very intimately connected with what we have been considering ; but they too could not escape participation in the general corruption. I find no account, either in print or in manuscript, of the manner in which they underwent change. It is fortunate therefore that there exist two unquestionably genuine reports by Turks, which throw some light on the subject. Aini, a feudal officer under Sultan Ahmed, remarks that in old times it had been almost impossible for any other than the son of a sipahi to obtain a timar ; but subsequently this regulation had fallen into neglect, and even the lowest persons made pretensions to be timarli ‖. The question is how and when did this occur ? If I am not mistaken this may be discovered from a decree of Soliman ¶. He is given to understand, he says in that document, that the sons of the raajas who had obtained fiefs, were excluded from the timars under the pretence that they were foreigners, that they were plundered of their berat, that is their patents, and that contrivances were used to obtain firmans to eject them. He strongly censures this. " How should the inhabitants of my territories and states," he says, " be foreigners with respect to each other ? Sipahi and raajas are alike

my servants, and should dwell quietly beneath the bounteous shadow of my favour." From this it is to be inferred, that the inferior classes had obtained under Soliman, and with his approval, those advantages of which Aini complains. He complains because this innovation undoubtedly gave occasion to a multitude of irregularities. It is not well to alter or meddle too much with institutions on the steady subsistence of which rests the stability of a state. The consequence of these innovations was, that the sandshaks and pachas, indebted for their own promotion to the sultan's inclination to favour his slaves, imitated the example, and seized the opportunity to bestow fiefs on their own slaves, often worthless fellows. Having once succeeded in this they went further. They had already begun to apply the timars more to their own service than to that of the state; they now made them wholly subservient to their own profit, without maintaining the troops required by law. It was soon noticed in the serai how profitable this was to them ; but those who might have stopped the abuse, instead of doing so indulged in it themselves. What had hitherto been done only by the governors of provinces, was now practised by the central authorities. They began to dispose of the timars as gratuities, without regard to their military destination *. Then followed gradually what Aini complains of, that for the space of twenty or thirty years no muster was held, that a sandshak, instead of a hundred sipahi scarcely furnished fifteen, and that frequently not a tenth part of those registered in the books were actually forthcoming †. A chief cause of Nasuf's fall was that he attempted to stem this disorder. He employed for a while twenty scribes daily to aid him in his inquiries and in preparing new books, so that he might insist on the maintenance of the due number of sipahi ‡. But great loads, says Valieri, are not easily moved; he who attempts to divert rivers from their course exposes himself to danger. Nasuf was unable to abolish the abuse; the attempt proved his ruin.

Thus we see the three foremost soldieries of this state fall simultaneously into manifest decay. They show plainly enough in themselves how this happened. Still the corruption of the other institutions had also assuredly an important influence upon them. A state is so intimately interwoven as a whole, that the fatal evil which has seized on one part overspreads the rest. The thing occurs, without our being able to say precisely how it occurs.

Frontiers.

It is certain that under Soliman the Ottoman empire, as it surpassed all others in intrinsic strength, so likewise was it more threatening than any other power to the rest of the world.

---

* Τραγούδια 'Ρωμαικὰ, p. 2.

† " Ben è vero che a questi tempi con corruttela et scandalo si va introducendo con favor figliuoli de Turchi."

‡ Relat. di 1594: " Così hanno perduti non pure quei vigorosi cavalli ma anco le razze; et però sendo fatti li spahi d'ogni sorte d'huomini ... teme tanto più il Signore che questa gente povera et avida desideri mutatione di stato."

§ Sagredo, Memorie de Monarchi Ottomani, 683.

‖ Kanunname of Aini, Hammer, Staatsverf. der Osm. i. 372.

¶ Kanunname to the beglerbeg Mustafa, Hammer i, 3. 50.

* Valieri: " Il numero è impossibile che si sappia ; perche molti timari si sono perduti per la dishabitatione del paese ; molti sono possessi dalle fatture del serraglio, avuti in assegnamento di propria entrada ; et molti viene detto esser tenuti anco dalli medesimi Visiri et Grandi della porta et del serraglio et de suoi ministri che con favore nelle vacanze facilmente se ne impadroniscano."

† Aini's Kanunname, Hammer i, 372.

‡ Valieri: " Volse Nasuf, gia primo Visir, venir indietro di questo negotio et deputò più di 20 scrivani per caverne l'intiero et farne un nuovo catasto, per ritrovare il numero et reintegrarlo. ... Ma la moltitudine interessata non ammette nè vuole regola, ma ben spesso cambio la novità con la testa dell'autore."

It nevertheless appears from our investigations, that under this very same Soliman the internal strength of this empire became afflicted with grave maladies. Under him the influence of women in the harem first gained the ascendancy ; under him those edicts were issued that gave the chief occasion to the change in the disposition of the timars ; under him the janissaries began to have wives ; through him it came to pass that the least worthy of his sons ascended the throne. Nor was this all. If a state has been founded on conquest, if it has hitherto known no pause to its progressive conquests, can any one doubt that the shock to it will be severe when the progress is stayed, and conquest ceases ? Under Soliman, warlike and victorious as he was, the empire yet began to have boundaries. In the east he encountered in Persia a weak people indeed, that intrinsically was by no means able to cope with him, but still a people who venerated their shah as a god, and even made vows to his name in their sicknesses *, that left their territory widely exposed to the foe, but not till they had first laid it waste, so that the assailants could never reach the fugitive defenders, and had enough to do to avoid being themselves assailed on their retreat. Christendom was Soliman's other foe, and it must be owned it was weakened by internal dissensions. Now if the establishment of the Austro-Spanish power was in any point of view a fortunate thing for Christendom, it was so inasmuch as it was fitted by circumstances, and had inherent strength enough, to resist the Turks at once in Africa, Italy, and Hungary. In this way it has earned the gratitude of all Christian nations. It crossed and resisted both the directions taken by the Turkish power in its outspread westward, the continental and the maritime. What tedious sieges were required to capture single small towns in Austrian Hungary ! What vast efforts were made to no purpose before Malta ! Those two nations, that had once set bounds to the broad empire of the Romans, the German, namely, and the Persian, should these be subjugated by the Turks, by whom they were now both assailed ?

Such by all means were the hopes of the Turks and the fears of the rest of the world. If decay was present, it was little more than an alteration in the moral impulses still lurking within, and not to be at once discerned either by friend or foe.

When Selim II. came to the throne, two enterprises presented themselves to him, both in that maritime direction towards the west which Mahomet II. had opened. The one was against Spain †, the prime foe of the Muhamedan name ; an enter-

prise glorious for its boldness even should it fail, but should it prosper, one that promised the grandest results. That kingdom was just then thrown into serious peril by the insurrection of the Moors, whose numbers were computed at 85,000 families. They even sent repeatedly to Constantinople, and most urgently besought the aid of their brethren in faith. The other enterprise was against Venice and Cyprus. The Venetians had been peaceful, compliant, almost submissive, always with presents in their hands for the sultan and his vizier. If the capudan when cruising abstained from piracy in their waters, they were never slack in remembering it to him. They were of all foreigners the most liberal to the dragomans, as the latter remarked in their books *. Cyprus was already half subdued, and as an Egyptian fief yielded a tribute of 8000 ducats. Here there were no oppressed Muhamedans, nor any great glory to be acquired. On the contrary, it would be necessary to break a peace just sworn.

Sultan Selim did not ponder what were the manliest, the grandest enterprises, and the most useful to his fellow believers ; he only considered what might be the easiest, the surest, and the nearest conquest. A landing could hardly be prevented in Cyprus. If it came then to sieges, as it would be sure to do, how should any resistance be made by the capital Nikosia ? the reason for making which town the capital was merely that it lay between mountains that tempered the heat of the climate. The fall of Nikosia would necessarily infer that of the whole island. Some even went the length of supposing that Venice would never engage in earnest war for the defence of Cyprus † ; it had too urgent need of Turkish goods for its commerce, and of Turkish corn for its sustenance. In spite of the repeated and strenuous opposition of Mehemet, and often as the mufti called attention to the distresses of the unfortunate Moors, distresses it was the sultan's indefeasible duty to relieve, still Selim's unwarriorlike ambition decided for the attack on Cyprus ; his army embarked, landed, conquered the capital, and took the island.

And now, strange to say, the easier undertaking proved to be attended with more dangerous consequences than could ever have ensued from the more difficult one.

Had Spain been attacked, Venice would never have resolved on lending that country her strenuous aid ; the neighbourhood of the Turks on all her frontiers would have been too alarming to allow of this ‡. But when Venice was attacked,

---

* Relatione di Mr· Vincenzo delli Alessandri delle cose da lui osservate nello regno di Persia, MS. Berol.: "Si tiene felice quella casa che può havere qualche drappo o scarpe di esso Re, overo dell' acqua dove egli si ha lavato le mani, usandola contra la febbre. Non pur i popoli, ma i figliuoli e Sultani parendoli, di non poter ritrovare epiteti convenienti a tanta grandezza, gli dicono: Tu sei la fede nostra et in te crediamo: così si osserva nelle citta vicine fino a questo termino di riverenza, ma nelle ville e luoghi più lontani molti tengono che egli, oltre l'havere lo spirito della profetia, riusciti li morti et faccia altri simili miracoli."

† Mehemet was in favour of this enterprsie. Relatione dello stato· "Concetto gia fu di Mehemet di assaltare la Spagna per gettare sopra di lei li Mori." . . . . Relatione di Barbaro delli negotii trattati da lui con Turchi per lo spatio di sei anni, MS. "Mehemet proponendo con buone ragioni il soccorrere i Mori in Spagna ribellati dal re catholico,

dimostrando quanto maggior gloria e profitto dovesse apportarli quella impresa."

* Navagero, Relatione : "Ibraimbei (Dragomano) m'ha detto molte volte, haver veduto il libro di Sanusbei, ove erano scritti li doni che li facevano tutti li principi et altri che negotiavano a questa porta, e ritrovato che niun altro li dava tanto nè così spesso come la Signoria di Venetia, al che molte volte ho riposto che così la Signoria vuole trattare li suoi buoni amici."

† Barbaro delli negotii trattati : "Niun altra causa haveva mosso più l'animo del Signore al tentare l'impresa di Cipro che il persuadersi d'ottenere la cession di quel regno senza contrasto d'armi ; sì come i maggiori della Porta si lasciavano chiaramente intendere, mossi sì per la poca estimation che tacevano delle forze di questa republica come anco per il timido modo col quale s'era seco proceduto."

‡ This is hinted at in Avvertimenti di Carlo V. al re il Filippo II. "Che sia il Turco per rompere prima con i

since it was the interest of Philip II. to keep the war, which would otherwise have threatened him at home, in remote waters, the consequence was, a confederation of the two maritime powers. It was joined by the pope ; three fleets stood together to sea to meet the Turks.

The naval like the military force of the Turks was constituted with a view to continuous conquest. The timars in the islands, the holders of which served in the fleet, were similar to those on the mainland. The Turks ruled the Mediterranean in war and piracy ever since that day in the year 1538, when Chaireddin Barbarossa attacked with wonderful daring, and vanquished the far superior fleet of the Christians at Prevesa. They believed that the Christians would never venture again to stand before them in open fight. This superiority endured till the year 1571. The individual must often stand for the whole ; the vicissitudes in human events are often determined by the talent and the will of one distinguished man. The Turks were now confronted by a youth who for daring, energy, fortune, and grand conceptions might well be compared with Chaireddin Barbarossa ; this was Don John of Austria. The Christians were victorious under his command ; the Turks had no equal to oppose to him ; the day of Lepanto broke down the Ottoman supremacy.

But it must not be supposed that the maritime power of the Turks was nothing before Chaireddin's time, and that it was instantaneously reduced again to nothing by Don John. Growth and decay are the slow work of time ; those two remarkable days only mark two great crises.

The Turks lost all their old confidence after the battle of Lepanto *. They were soon conscious of the vices in their naval system. The grand defect was, that they would only condescend to bear arms, leaving all the rest to slaves †. Slaves were compelled to build their ships, and these men, as it was not their own affair, carelessly employed unseasoned wood : the consequence was, that the vessels, however handsomely they might be constructed in other respects, were prone to leak, and that usually out of several hundred galleys, hardly fifty were to be found seaworthy. They employed slaves linked in a chain to navigate their vessels. But as they nevertheless treated their crews as slaves, that is to say not as men, the

majority of them perished. Barbaro saw the fleet return five times, and each time completely unmanned. Under these circumstances, if ever they came to an engagement, the captains had no longer the prospect of making prizes before them, but might foresee the loss of their slaves to the enemy, if they were faithful, or their insurrection if they were not so. There was nothing they more dreaded than coming to close quarters with the Christians in the open sea.

The bad condition of the fleet, the worthlessness of the working crews, and that spiritless temper of the armed men, which first made glaringly obvious all those other defects that had before been covered by courage and good fortune, lastly, the enormous costs of equipment, for a long while made Selim's successors averse to enterprises of magnitude by sea, and necessarily produced a pause in this branch of the Turkish conquests.

But as yet there was no cessation to their continental efforts. The lust of dominion over the world was too deeply rooted in the minds of these sultans. Though himself so unmanly, and under such unmanly guidance, Amurath nevertheless carried on continual wars for conquest, and this freely and spontaneously, to the no small diminution of the treasures he amassed with such eagerness *. He would never grant a peace except upon the most unequal conditions. That love of conquest, which covets only the acquisition of territory, whether it be that it takes delight in the active occupations of war, or that it may be indulged without the necessity of leaving home, is equally insatiable as voluptuous lust or the greed of gold ; it seems to depend upon the self-same principle in the mental constitution as these two passions.

Be this as it may, Amurath embarked in two wars, the Persian and the Hungarian, that eventually exhausted the best energies of the empire. The two presented him with totally distinct difficulties. In Persia he had to do with a country destitute indeed of castles and towns, but likewise without villages or inhabitants for a space of six or seven days' journey †. His troops no doubt marched unresisted through wide tracts of this purposely devastated frontier land; they established themselves beyond it in Shirvan, built vessels in Temicarpi, and navigated the Caspian, and even founded a fortress in Tauris, above the lofty mountain range that divides Iran from Mesopotamia. Yet these were no conquests to afford means of filling treasuries and building mosques. Even the country which the conquerors held with some degree of security was not capable of being divided out into timars. For as the remnants of the inhabitants either fled to the mountains, where they defied control, or into the interior of Iran, where there was no getting at them; there remained no subjects either to maintain the timarli and his

---

Venetiani che con voi, non è verisimile, perche potrebbe stimare che in tal caso haverebbe insieme ancora voi ; ove rompendo primo con voi, può sperare che i Venetiani si sieno almeno stare di mezzo, sì per la loro desistenza gia tant' anni dall' armi, sì ancora per haverli esso fitte l'unghie adosso et quasi il freno in bocca posto per rispetta dell' isola di Candia et di Cipri."

* Barbaro : "E' levata non solo a Turchi quella superba impressione che Christiani non ardirebbono affrontarli, ma in contrario sono al presente gli animi loro talmente oppressi da timore che non ardiscono affrontarsi con gli nostri, confessando essi medesimi che le loro gallere sono in tutte parte inferiori alla bontà delle nostre, così di gente più atta al combattere, come dell' artiglieria et di tutte altre cose pertinenti alla navigatione ; et veramente è così."

† Floriani : "I Turchi non hanno applicato il pensiero a nessun esercitio e massimamente a quello delle cose maritime." Barbaro : "Nelle cose maritime non hanno li Turchi vocabolo della lingua loro, ma tutti sono greci o franchi." [The Turks have not a single naval term proper to their own language, but all borrowed from those of the Greeks or the Franks.]

* Relat. di 1594. "Ha bisognato il paese tenere in freno con forti, che costano ad esso Amurath un tesoro. . . . . Del quale rispetto si valsero assai gli emuli di Mustafa, mostrando che egli con poco giudicio haveva divisato di pigliar la porta della Persia, poichè si è scoperto che questo è un tarlo et una ruina perpetua all' erario del Signore."

† "Le fortezze del Re di Persia sono al presente l'haver fatto desertare i paesi verso i confini del Turco per ogni parte in sei o sette giornate di cammino, et quelli castelli che vi erano li ha fatto ruinare per assicurarsi tanto più." Vincenzo degli Alessandri, Relatione di Persia.

horse, or to pay the capitation tax. Amurath had to make up his mind to build castles, and to pay the garrisons out of his privy purse [*]. Only the longing to possess every country that had ever borne the hoof-prints of Ottoman horses, only the illusive belief that he was destined to be lord of the east and of the west, could ever have induced him to prosecute wars in which his people had to contend more with hunger and the inclemency of the elements than with the sword of the foeman; and in which his generals had to strive no less against the mutiny of their own men than against the resistance of the enemy. Ere long too the dissensions of the Persian princes, which had hitherto been subservient to the success of the Turks, came to an end, and the throne of Persia was ascended by Shah Abbas, a very different man from these descendants of Othman, affable and estimable, energetic, brave in the field, and victorious [†]; a sovereign who, after successful wars in Khorasan, allying himself with those Georgians who boasted that every man of them was a match single handed for five Turks, soon won back the lost frontiers. They used to say in the sixteenth century, that these frontiers were for the Turks what Flanders was for Spain.

But if the sultan had some partial success in Persia, at least in the beginning, this was not the case in Hungary. The dreams of his commanders of carrying the dominion of the Porte into Germany and Italy, or at the least of conquering Bohemia [‡], were crossed by difficulties, different in kind from those encountered in Persia, but no less formidable. These were the military dispositions on the frontiers, important fortresses, and, in the beginning at least, the decisive hostility of Transylvania, and the vacillating temper of Wallachia [§]. This is not the place to go into the history of this war. It is clear that the Ottoman conquests had met with that check, which it was foreseen even in Soliman's time they would one day sustain. The Persians and the Germans remained unvanquished. Thus then the main lines of march pursued by the Ottoman victories being three, one by sea in the Mediterranean, and two by land, in the east and in the north-west, we see that in all three they halted, in the first under Selim, and in the last two under Amurath.

[*] Relatione dello stato etc. di 1594, f. 495. "Li soldati turchi non vogliono accettar timari, poiche non hanno il modo di far lavorare i terreni, con i quali possano notrire i cavalli descritti per nuovi timarioti in augumento dell' esercito. Le gabelle delle paese acquistati non rendon alcun utile. Onde conviene ad Amurath pagare li presidii dal suo Casna."

[†] Giacomo Fava, Lettera scritta in Spahan a dì 20 Luglio, 1599. Tesoro politico ii. 258.

[‡] Relat di 1594 : "Iattavano di voler passare l'Austria et voler andare in Bohemia, nel qual regno havevano molte loro spie per torre in nota li fiumi, le fortezze et il sito del paese, sperando per quella loro alterezza turchesca di acquistar facilmente tutti quei paesi mettendo inanzi al Signore che con questi si farebbe ricchissimo il suo esercito." [They boasted that they would overrun Austria and enter Bohemia, in which kingdom they had numerous spies reconnoitring the rivers, the fortresses, and the posture of the country, hoping, with their Turkish arrogance, that they would easily acquire all those territories, and suggesting to the grand signor how much these would enrich his army.]

[§] Laurentii Soranzi Ottomanus, in Conring's collection, is classical on this head. See also Anonymi Dissertatio de statu imperii Turcici cujusmodi sub Amuratho fuit, in the same collection, particularly p. 325.

Posture of the empire under Amurath IV.

Wholly altered was now the aspect of the Ottoman empire from that presented in former times. That inward energy was lost which had knit together the military monarch and his army and fitted them for continuous conquests. The helm of state was in the hands of favourites within the serai, of women and eunuchs. The sovereign's body guards, that had once given him victory and security, were now destitute of their ancient valour and discipline. Neighbouring nations had no more reason to dread the Osmanlis than any other foes, and might sit down more at ease, relieved from their former incessant mortal combats for freedom or bondage.

But the elements of this state, that before had worked together to such mighty achievements abroad, now turned their force against each other in intestine strife.

It has been repeatedly asserted, that the old notion of the sultan's unlimited authority was erroneous; that he was restricted now by the hierarchy of the ulemas, and now by the power of the soldiery [*]. And in point of fact both these often gave their lord and chief no little trouble.

But if it be considered that the sultan is first iman and khalif, of whom an article of faith declares that he is invested with absolute authority, that every one is subordinate to him, and that none must be recognized as co-ordinate with him [†] ; a second, that he needs neither be just, nor virtuous, nor in other respects free from blame [‡] ; and finally, a third asserts that neither tyranny on his part nor other faults justify his subjects in deposing him [§] : if these things be considered, how were it possible to withstand him without rebellion, that is, without violation at once of his person and of the law ? When Amurath IV. annulled a first principle of Muhammedanism, and allowed the use of wine, did the ulemas, who should have been the guardians of the holy law, resist him ? The mufti, the head of the whole hierarchy, is after all but the deputy of the sultan, who appoints him and can depose him at pleasure [||].

Had the soldiery then the right of resisting, either by themselves or in concert with the ulemas ? Muradgea remarks that every revolution affecting the throne was still invariably regarded as illegitimate, as an offence against the consecrated majesty of the sovereign.

The truth is, that people take in practice the right that is not conceded them by theory. The sovereign shall command without restriction ; the subject shall obey unconditionally : but it frequently happens that the latter feels strong enough to

[*] After Marsigli, particularly Toderini, Literature of the Turks, vol. i. p. 64.

[†] Omer Nesséfy's Catechism, with Sadeddin's Explanations, article 33.

[‡] Omer Nesséfy, article 36.

[§] Ibid. art. 37, ap. Muradgea d'Ohsson, Tableau etc. i. p. 95.

[||] Muradgea : Du Scheik-ul Islam ou Mouphty, Tableau etc. ii p. 259. Relatione di 1637 : " Di poi che il Gransignore ha privato di vita il precessore di questo (Mufti) conoscendo non voler la legge superiore alla sua volontà, deposta ogni autorevole forma di trattare, si serve di sommissione." [Since the grand signor put the predecessor of the present Mufti to death, the latter, seeing that the grand signor would own no law superior to his own will, has laid aside all pretensions to authoritative conduct, and is all submission.]

defy the sovereign's will, and the sovereign feels too weak to enforce his commands. It then comes to a struggle between the commander and the commanded.

After the death of Ahmed I. it seemed as though the janissaries would completely subjugate the throne and seize the power of disposing of it as they pleased. Ahmed had been clement enough to spare his brother Mustafa. The latter was idiotic, so much so that his unconnected words were thought to embody oracles *. Notwithstanding this, the janissaries brought him forth and set him on the throne of the sultans, which till then had never passed but from father to son. It was their pleasure soon afterwards to depose him again, and to enthrone Othman, the son of Ahmed. No one ever felt more burthened by their intolerable fraternity than Othman. But when he showed symptoms of an inclination to withdraw from them (it is said he wished to transfer the seat of empire to Damascus or Cairo) they instantly rallied against him, and brought out his idiot uncle, dragging him up with a rope from the subterranean dungeon in which he lay as it were entombed. He thought they brought him forth to die ; but death was destined for his nephew, the throne for him. It may easily be imagined how he filled it. We are told, though I know not whether we are to understand the story in a proverbial or in a literal sense, that he flung money into the sea, saying that the fishes ought to have something to spend †. He made most serious inroads on the treasures collected by Selim and Amurath. At last the janissaries bethought them, and set him aside for Amurath IV., Ahmed's second son.

But with him they became involved in deadly strife. Amurath on arriving at manhood possessed extraordinary bodily strength and agility. He was one of the best of riders, and sprang with ease from the back of one horse to another's. He flung the djereed with unfailing precision ; he drew the bow with such force that the arrow shot further than the ball from the hunter's gun, and he is said to have sent it through an iron plate four inches thick ‡. In other respects there was little to distinguish him. Whilst his mother (whom the author of our report found in her forty-fifth

year still beautiful and engaging, and besides this good-natured, virtuous, wise, and above all bountiful) continued to maintain the influence she had acquired under Ahmed, whilst the viziers were changed after every less prosperous campaign, and the soldiery fluctuated between mutiny and obedience, he himself passed his time in his athletic exercises, or surrounded with buffoons and musicians he indulged in wine, which he loved to a drunken excess. At last it was a great insurrection of the sipahi and the janissaries that gave his character its final bent. The insurgents murdered all who then possessed his confidence, the grand vizier, the aga of the janissaries, the deftardar, and even a boy, merely because he was liked by the sultan. He resolved to punish them*. Not being able to do this by open force, he had the ringleaders secretly assassinated one after the other, and their corpses were often seen at morning floating upon the sea. In this way he got rid of them assuredly, but the passion for murder was thus awakened within him. Perhaps it is not an erroneous supposition, that after these private executions had given him the first taste for blood, he was confirmed in it by the desire for amassing treasure to which they afforded aliment. What could well have been more profitable to him than the execution of one of his grandees? That of Rezep Pacha alone brought him in a million. This opinion cannot however be affirmed with certainty: the most pernicious passions are those that take most rapid possession of the soul; but true it is, at all events, that he was filled with a raging thirst for blood. This was evident even in the chase. His pleasure was not in the pursuit of the game ; this was driven together by many thousand men, and his whole delight was in slaughtering it when thus collected. It was computed in the year 1637, that he had executed 25,000 men within the last five years, and many of them with his own hand. He was now terrific to behold. His savage black eyes glared threateningly in a countenance half hidden by his dark brown hair and long beard ; but never was its aspect more perilous than when it showed the wrinkles between the eyebrows. His skill with the javelin and the bow was then sure to deal death to some one. He was served with trembling awe. His mutes were no longer to be distinguished from the other slaves of the serai, for all conversed by signs. While the plague was daily carrying off fifteen hundred victims in Constantinople, he had the largest cups brought from Pera, and drank half the night through, while the artillery was discharged by his orders †.

<hr />

* Relatione di 1637 : "Andando da lui per interpretatione di sogni et per altre risposte, come gli antichi facevano con oraculi, a quali mentre spropositatamente responde senza alcuno imaginabile senso, tengono vi si includino gran misterii nel oscurità di quel dire, venerandolo come profetico."

† Ibid. "Nel corso di pochi mesi che per fortuna potè impugnare lo scettro, rese così povera la camera imperiale che Murad suo nepote, quando all' imperio fu assunto, non haveva denaro per fare alle militie il solito donativo : et cio perche Mustafa in grandissima copia a tutti ne prestava, dandone sino alli pesci del mare, dicendo che era bisogno che havessero ancora loro da spendere." See also Majolino Bosaccioni, Vite d'alcune Imperatori Ottomani, in Sansovino's collection, edition of 1654, p. 345.

‡ Ibid. "Gioca di zagaglia con non poca maestria, così fieri colpi menando che alcuna volta lo scherzo tramutato in tragedia ha più della battaglia che del gioco o dello spasso : non potendosi alcuno agguagliare alla robustezza del braccio suo, col quale piega si facilmente la durezza di ogni arco che sbarra la saetta più lontana che fa la palla d'un archibuzzio di caccia ; havendo alcuna volta per esperimentar la sua forza, trapassato con frezza una lastra di ferro grossa quattro et più dita." The accounts in Kantemir (Osman. Geschichte, i. 380) are in a style of eastern hyperbole.

* Ibid. "Comprobando la mia opinione l'essere lui vissuto con assai placida et humana natura sin al 1652, havendo promosso et eccitato alla strage l'arroganza et insolenza delle sue militie, quando con così poco rispetto et timore del Signore loro et disprezze della legge propria volsero che nelle mani gli desse vivi per stratiarli a lor modo il Visir grande, l'aga de Gianizzeri, un suo favorito garzone, per il quale pianse nel darlo dirottamente, et il Gran Tesoriero del Divano o Camerlengo, che vogliamolo dire."—Siri, Mercurio, libro i. p. 173, displays on the whole but moderate acquaintance with the subject.

† Ibid. "Non passan due mesi che ho inteso per lettere da quelle parti, che discorrendo un giorno (Amurath) con un suo favorito della peste che allhora andavo publicando i progressi suoi con ascendere a somma di mille et cinquecento et seicento il giorno, ... disse, che lasciasse che Dio nella stagione d'estate castigasse i cattivi, che poi nel

Violent remedies may be of good effect against deeply rooted evils. But in this man murder was no longer a means, but an indulgence. It is not thus that states are renovated. Nor did it prove so in his case. His excessive rigour undoubtedly tamed the refractory soldiery. Along with the use of coffee and tobacco he forbade them those meetings in which they sat whole days giving themselves up to those half-exciting, half-stupifying indulgences, and plotting together [*]. He compelled the sipahi to change their dress at his pleasure, and he cleared the streets of their noise and turbulence. He turned out the unserviceable members of the janissary corps, and forced the efficient men to take the field in spite of their dispensations. He restored order in the timars that were dispensed from the serai. But with all this he could not bring back courage and victory to his troops. The sipahi missed the bounty of former sultans, and as their pay was not sufficient for them, they often abandoned pay and service together. The janissaries seemed now made to strike terror into the men of the west only by their looks and their shouts, not by their arms. In presence of the enemy they displayed neither training nor courage. Their aga having marched on one occasion from Constantinople with the whole body of the janissaries, he reached Aleppo with only three thousand, the rest having all gone off by the way. The posts in the army which were formerly coveted with eagerness and sought for by bribery and every other means, were now as sedulously shunned. The earliest condition of the Ottoman army was now brought back, and the timarli once more appeared as its choicest portion. But even the best of them, those who were posted on the Hungarian frontiers, and kept in practice by the continual wars, were no great soldiers ; the Christians congratulated themselves, that, luckily for the faithful, God had given the Turks but little ability [†]. Their battle array was compared to the aspect of a bull ; threatening, seemingly perilous, but to be overcome with judgment and address by a far inferior force. No great achievements could be looked for under this condition of the army, in which the less important household troops of the sultan, and those belonging to the pachas, now found opportunity to push themselves forward. Amurath made a campaign for the recovery of

Bagdad, and he actually captured the city ; but if he did, it was only by driving back the fugitive soldiers to the fight with his sword, and killing his vizier with his own hand.

But, after all, strong and self-sustained as Amurath might seem, he was not free from the influence of the serai. He divested his pious mother indeed of her credit and authority, and twice banished her to the old palace. She had nothing in her power unless it were to mitigate the effects of some of his evil deeds by presents, or to redeem unfortunate debtors from prison, that she might thereby obtain the blessings of Heaven for her son. But, on the other hand, he gave himself up without reserve to his favourites. There are a multitude of stories about his fondness for the drunken Mustafa. Our Relatione mentions his silahdar, a Bosnian, who enjoyed his full favour. Amurath gave him a special body guard of 3000 men, who were implicitly at his command, and exalted him so that he would no longer attend the divan, because he was too proud to pay deference to the grand vizier, and he bestowed his daughter upon him. The sultan used to say, that this man was perfectly on a par with himself. Indeed, whoever made a present to the master did not forget the servant; the one would have been in vain without the other.

We know that the sultan loved gold. We are assured that neither prayers nor intercessions, neither law nor justice availed with him so much as gold, for which he displayed a thirst there was no allaying [*]. There was no need of seeking sumptuous stuffs or costly manufactures for him ; the number of purses presented to him was all he looked too. Hence every one strove to appear poorer than he really was. The use of gold and silver utensils was shunned ; men hid their money, and dreaded lest they should provoke the sultan's two passions at once, his rapacity and his thirst for blood. Such was the manner in which Amurath swayed the state. Undoubtedly he filled his exchequer ; undoubtedly he secured his personal safety, and he died in his bed as padishah. But the means of terror that made him secure paralyzed the energies of the empire ; the sword that won him wealth robbed the realm of those men, of those names that awed Christendom [†].

Conclusion.

The Ottoman empire was founded not by a people, not by a ruling stock, nor yet by soldiers freely combined ; but, if we are not wholly mistaken, by a lord and his bondsmen. Like the khalifs, whom we picture to ourselves with the Koran in one hand and the sword in the other, this warlike family, filled with a wild religious delusion, and fired with the lust of conquest, flung themselves on all their neighbours, and thought to sub-

---

verno sariano stati i buoni sovvenuti da lui, et per guardarsi da quel pericolo che lui minacciava la malincolia, volendo scacciare da lui fece portare una gran copia di vini, et con più grandi bicchieri che in tutta Pera si potevano ritrovare diede principio ad un dilettevole giuoco."

[*] Relatione di 1637 : "Li ha levato il modo di più potersi unire a conspirare contro la sua persona con la prohibitione del tabacco, con pena di forca da essere irremissibilmente eseguita et di tutti quelli ridotti dove si beveva il caffè, che è un' acqua nera che fanno d'una specie di zece che vien dal Cairo, molto giovevole al capo et al stomacho et cio perche non habbino occasione come facevano prima, d'ivi fermarsi et l'hore et i giorni intieri a discorrere et far radunanze." All the other particulars are from the same Relatione.

[†] Ibid. "I più pregiati sono i confinanti di Buda nel regno d'Ungheria e i confinanti di Bossina col stato della rep. Veneta; havendogli gli essercitii frequenti nell' armeggiare con discapito loro continuo. Sono arditi alla zuffa poco meno delli nostri, da quali giornalmente vanno apprendendo qualche gesto nell' armi, assuefacendosi all' uso delli terzetti e pestoni d'arcione, senza però progressi considerabili per la poca attitudine che gli vien permessa del cielo a prò dei fideli."

[*] Ibid. "Arse di questa sete dell' oro nel diletto che prese impatronandosi di un milione di zecchini che trovossi nelle facultà di Rezep Bassa suo cognato, quando levò gli la vita : il quale tanto affannossi a bere che fatto idropico più che possiede, più brama."

[†] Ibid. "Come successe a miei giorni ad Abasa Passa, —il quale mentre si persuase di vedere soggiogata la Polonia et forse poi debellata la Christianità con somministrar nella mente regia vasti pensieri et speranze di felicissimi eventi, quando meno pensava, precipitò della gratia, restando estinto con un pezzo di laccio. Et il simile occorse al capitain del mare Zafer Passa."

jugate the world. The name of the lord has properly become that of the whole body.

Now, when the ties between the lord and the bondsmen grew slack, when the inward impulse declined, and the efforts for conquest were checked in mid career, there ensued what might have been expected ; things fell into more natural bearings towards each other. That they should return completely to a natural condition was not possible, since they had set out from a principle at variance with humanity, from despotism. This principle was propagated anew through every subordinate member, and so became inextinguishable.

After the Ottomans ceased to be conquerors they remained encamped in the midst of their old strongholds. There is a proverb, that no grass grows where the foot of an Ottoman horse hath once trodden ; and it seems amply confirmed by the desolation of the fairest countries of the world fallen under their sway. It is true that many of them possess virtues that adorn the man ; they are lauded as free from falsehood, stedfast, beneficent, and hospitable ; but they have never attained to a liberal developement of the intellectual powers ; they have evermore remained barbarians. Their conceptions of what is beautiful in material things scarcely extend beyond the charms of gold and of women ; they evince hardly a trace of a disposition to bring home the natural world to their understandings by a cognizance applied to the reality of things, not to the illusions of fancy ; they live and move among the relics of a nobler existence, and they heed them not. Errors there are that engross and penetrate the whole soul, that render the eye purblind to all that is intellectual and to the brightness of truth, and that cramp life in, within the bounds of a dull self-sufficiency. Such errors are theirs.

Yet their state cannot be denied the possession of a certain inward vitality. It is always conceivable that a sultan should return to the qualities of his predecessors, and brace anew the relaxed sinews of the empire: such a possibility was admitted by Muradgea d'Ohsson in his own day. Or a vizier may overcome the obstacles thrown in his way by the serai and the body-guards, and arouse the people to greater endeavours. This was really the case with the Kiuprilis. The first of these made use of the body-guards to rid himself of the favourites in the serai who stood in his way ; after this he contrived to master the soldiery in their turn, and thenceforth he kept them busy with war after war. The Ottomans were then at least a match for their neighbours. They conquered Candia from the Venetians, and often appeared victoriously on their frontiers.

Thus they have continued to subsist for centuries even in their decay. It has been their good fortune, first, that there has broken out in the east no national movement like those of old to which they owed their own success ; and next, that since the European policy has reached its mature growth, there exists in the west that jealousy with which each of our states is watched by all the rest severally and collectively : this has always in their utmost dangers procured them allies, and brought them safety.

THE SPANISH EMPIRE.

INTRODUCTION.

WE turn from the east to the west, from a Turkish slave-state to a Romano-German monarchy.

The total contrast strikes us instantaneously; the contrast between a state of which the sovereign is lord and unlimited proprietor, and one which, based on individual freedom, confers just so much authority on the sovereign, as is requisite to defend that freedom from foes without and foes within. The oriental monarch is sole autocrat among serfs, and even the ancient Roman imperial authority had merged into that condition : the Germanic sovereign, on the contrary, is the protector of the common freedom, the upholder of personal rights, the safeguard of the country.

If the distinction is even still striking and self-evident, it was yet more so in former times, when there reigned in the east monarchs of distinguished personal qualities, who swayed their states at will in perfect subjection and unity; whilst in the west privileges, and the chartered and indefeasible rights of individuals and of subordinate assemblies, restricted and hindered the power of the sovereign.

The latter was the condition of the Spanish empire. It was far from being a state in our sense of the word, a state of organic unity, pervaded by a single ruling interest. It had not been so put together by conquest that any one province had lost its local rights, or that any leading division could have asserted and maintained its pretensions to command the rest: but it consisted of co-ordinate parts, each of which had its own rights; of a multitude of separate provinces of German, French, Italian, Castilian, Catalonian, and Basque tongues; provinces of dissimilar traditions and customs, unlike laws, discordant character, yet homogeneous rights. If we ask what it was that cemented these various provinces together, and kept them combined, we find that it was no inherent community of interests, but a casual inheritance that had joined them to each other; and that even when war was the immediate efficient cause of their union, it was always a war of inheritance, and they were combined together under the sovereign upon whom they devolved. The principle of inheritance was not however identical throughout them all, and the sovereign stood in a different relation to each several country composing the empire. The long title given themselves by the princes of the house of Habsburg was no mere piece of ostentation, as the French court was pleased to consider it, but their monarchy was in reality quite different in Castile from what it was in Sicily or in Aragon : in Flanders they were nothing but counts, in Guipuscoa their authority was founded on the fact that they were barons and hereditary lords of the country; whilst the American possessions belonged to them as a sort of crown domains. This diversity in the nature of their authority is indicated by their titles.

If we now proceed to contemplate this monarchy and its development in the course of a century, we find two antagonizing forces present themselves to view. Though the sovereign was limited in all points, yet he acquired prominent importance from the fact that the union of the whole body was centered in his person ; but for him it would not have existed. Frequently we see him called upon to direct the energies of the several countries in a common enterprize; he seeks to rule them all upon one general principle. Will the provinces be able under these circumstances to maintain their separate existence, and to abide by their ancient usages? Or will the sovereign force them into more intimate coalition? Will he compel them to perform his will? They confront him in their individuality.

This division constitutes the foremost subject of our inquiry. It is not our purpose to set forth in detail the relations in which the monarchy stood to the rest of Europe; we must take some notice of these, but only as a subordinate consideration. Our intention is rather to set before the reader the struggle within the range of the empire itself, between the supreme authority and the isolated interests of the several provinces. First we shall consider the character and the designs of the rulers, including the kings and their councils; secondly, the resistance they encountered in the several provinces, and the greater or less success with which they combated this; lastly, the state economy they now established, and the conditions in which the provinces were placed.

Our views are not aimed however merely at the general aspect of the combined whole: it is not by such means alone that nature and history engage our sympathy. Man fixes his eye with lively curiosity, first of all, on the individual object. Happy is he to whom it is granted to comprehend it at once in the essence of its being, and in the fulness of its peculiar phenomena.

CHAPTER I.

OF THE KINGS.

Charles V.

IN the pictures which the old legends give us of their heroes, they now and then set before us some who spend a long period of their youth sitting idly at home, but who, when they have once bestirred themselves never rest again, but rush on from enterprise to enterprise, with indefatigable buoyancy of spirit. It is not till the energies are fully aroused that they find the career befitting them.

Charles V.* may be compared with the characters of such a cast. He was but sixteen when he was called to the throne, but he was far from having then arrived at the condition suitable for under-

* Though he was the first of his name of Spain, we continue to give him the designation by which he was known to the rest of Europe.

taking its duties. People were long disposed to apply to him a nickname given his father, because he relied too implicitly on his counsellors. His constant byeword was, "Not yet." A. Croi completely governed him and his whole realm. Even whilst his armies were subjugating Italy, and winning repeated victories over the bravest enemies, he himself sat still in Spain, and was regarded as insensible and indifferent, weak and dependent. Such he was thought to be till 1529, when he appeared in Italy in his thirtieth year*.

How very different did he show himself there from what had been expected! for the first time how totally his own master, and how fully decided! His privy council had been unwilling that he should go to Italy, had warned him against John Andrew Doria, and suggested to him suspicions as to Genoa. It was beheld with astonishment that he nevertheless went to Italy, that he reposed his confidence in that very Doria, and that he persisted in his determination to disembark in Genoa. So it was throughout. No minister was observed to possess any preponderating interest; Charles himself gave no evidence of passion or precipitation, but all his resolutions were mature, all were deliberately weighed; his first word was his last†.

This was the first thing noticed in him; next to that, how personally active, how industrious he was. It required some patience to listen to the long speeches of the Italian ambassadors; he took pains to understand the complicated relations of their sovereigns and powers. The Venetian ambassador was surprised to find him not a little more accessible and free of speech than he had been three years before in Spain‡. He expressly selected a lodging in Bologna, from which he could visit the pope unobserved, that he might do so as frequently as possible, and arrange all disputed points with his holiness.

From that time forth he began to direct his negotiations, and to lead his armies in person ; he began to hasten continually from country to country, wherever the wants of the moment and the posture of affairs required his presence. We find him now at Rome complaining to the cardinals of the implacable hostility of Francis I., now in Paris courting and winning the favour of Estampes§ ; frequently in Germany presiding at the diet for the appeasing of religious discord, and again in the cortes of Castile exerting himself to have the tax of the Servicio voted. These are peaceful occupations: but we often see him at the head of his army. He crosses the Alps into France, and overruns Provence ; he advances to the Marne, and strikes terror into Paris. He then turns away to the east and the south. He checks the victorious career of Soliman on the Raab ; he seeks and

* Micheli, Relatione d'Inghilterra, MS.: "L'imperatore da ognuno o de la maggior parte era tenuto per stupido o per addormentato, et poi si può dire che ad un tratto et inespettatamente si suegliasse et riuscì così vivo, così ardito et così bravo come sa Vostra Signoria." [The emperor was thought by all, or almost all, to be stupid or lethargic, and then he awoke, as it were, all at once, and became so full of life, so ardent, and so brave, as your signory is aware.]

† Storia Florentina di Messer Benedetto Varchi, ix. 228. 233. Sigonius, de vita Andreae Doriae, 243.

‡ Contarini, Relazione di Bologna. Marzo, 1530, MS.

§ Zenocarus a Scauwenburgo: De republica et vita Caroli Maximi. Gandavi, 1560, fol. p. 175.

assails the crescent at Algiers. The army that had served him in Africa follows him to the Elbe, and the war cry of Spain is heard on the heaths of Lochau. Charles is now the busiest sovereign in the world. He frequently sails across the Mediterranean, across the Ocean. Meanwhile his mariners are discoverers in unploughed seas, his soldiers conquerors of untrodden lands. Even at such remote distance he remains their ruler and their lord. His motto, " More, further," is gloriously realized.

Such is his life contemplated as a whole ; full of activity after unusually long repose. It may be remarked that the same phenomena, at first inertness and a passive looking on, by and by action, continually recur in the several circumstances of all his most stirring life.

Although the general cast of his will was thoroughly determined, still his resolutions were taken but slowly, and step by step. His first reply to every proposal was indefinite, and it was necessary to beware of taking his vague expressions for a positive sanction *. He then pondered over the matter, repeatedly turned over the arguments for and against, and put the whole train of reasoning into such perfect connection and sequence, that whoever granted him his first proposition was forced to admit his last. He paid a visit to the pope at Bologna, with a paper in his hand, on which he had accurately noted down all the points they had to discuss †. Granvella was the only one to whom he used to communicate every intelligence, every proposal ; the ambassadors always found that minister instructed as to every particular, even to the very words they had uttered. All measures were determined between him and Charles. These resolutions were taken slowly: Charles frequently delayed the courier for some days beyond the appointed time.

But when things had been brought thus far, there was no power in the world that could bring him to change his mind. It was said he would let the world perish rather than do anything upon compulsion ‡. There never was an instance known of his having been forced into anything by violence or by danger. He once made a frank confession on this point, saying to Contarini, " I am naturally given to abide obstinately by my own opinions." " Sire," replied the other, " to abide by sound opinions is not obstinacy but stedfastness." " Ay, but," said Charles, " I sometimes abide by unsound ones §."

But from resolving to executing the way is still long. Charles felt an involuntary repugnance to taking things in hand, even though he very well knew what was to be done. Tiepolo says of him ||,

that in the year 1538, he dallied so long that his cause was endangered, nay, actually injured in some degree. Pope Julian III. was aware of this; he knew that Charles revenged him no doubt, but that he must first receive some thrusts before he would bestir himself *. The emperor often wanted money too : the entanglements of policy offered him a thousand grounds for hesitation and reflection.

While he was obliged to wait he kept his eye incessantly on his enemies. He watched them so narrowly that ambassadors were astonished to find how well he was acquainted with their governments, how happily he conjectured beforehand what they would do †. At last came the occasion, the favourable or the urgent crisis. Then he was all alert, then he put into execution what he had perhaps pondered over for twenty years.

Such was the policy which his foes regarded as detestable craft, his friends as a paragon of prudence. At any rate it can hardly be regarded as an effect of choice, of deliberate volition. Thus to lie still, to gather information, to await, and not till long after to rise and strike the blow, all this was the very nature of this monarch.

In how many other things did he display the same disposition ! He punished, but not till he had borne a great deal. He rewarded, but not indeed at once. Many had to linger for years unpaid, and then he would provide for them with one of those fiefs or benefices, of which he had so many at his disposal that he could enrich whomsoever he pleased, without any cost to himself. By this means he brought others to endure any hardships that might befal them in his service.

When his servants were putting on his armour he was observed to tremble all over : but once fully caparisoned he was full of courage, so much so that it was thought he was emboldened by the notion that an emperor had never been shot ‡.

Such a man, full of calmness and moderation, affable enough to accommodate himself to various persons, strict enough to keep many at once in subjection, appears to have been well fitted for presiding over a combination of several nations. It is alleged in praise of Charles that he conciliated the good will of the Netherlanders by his condescension, of the Italians by his shrewdness, and of the Spaniards by his dignity. But what had he wherewith to please the Germans ? His nature was incapable of attaining to that truehearted openness, which the German nation assuredly acknowledges, loves, and reveres in its men of distinction and high station. Though he willingly imitated the manner in which the old emperors bore themselves towards princes and lords ; though he took pains to assume German habits, and even wore his beard after the national fashion then in Germany §, still he was always looked on as a foreigner by the Germans. A mounted artilleryman, whom he urged angrily to make more speed, let him feel the whip ; a

---

* Relazione del Cl. Monsignor Marino Cavallo, MS. : " Parla molte volte ambiguo, quando importo: di modo che si gli ambasciatori non sono b_n cauti, può S. Maestà et li consiglieri dire con quella dubietà parole che intendere possono a questo et a quell' altro modo."

† Contarini. " Il papa mi ha detto, che ragionando con lui (Carlo) portava un memoriale notato di sua mano di tutte le cose che haveva a negotiare, per non lasciarne qualch' uno."

‡ Cavallo: " Lascierà più tosto ruinare il mondo che fa cosa violentata."

§ Contarini : " Qualche fiate io son fermo in le cattive."

|| Relazione del convento di Nizza, MS. " Nelli pericoli delle cose sue proprie ritarda qualche volta tanto che patiscono prima qualche incommodo."

---

* Lettera, MS. del Papa a Giovambattista di Monte.

† Cavallo, 240 : " Conosce eccellentissimamente la natura di tutti li principi con chi lui negotia, et in questo spende gran tempo ad instruirsene di avantaggio. Però quasi mai s'inganna de pronostici che fa di questa eccellentissima republica."

‡ Zenocarus a Scauwenburgo.

§ Ibid. p. 168.

landsknecht at Algiers even levelled his weapon at him [*], both these men having taken him for a Spaniard. He fell at variance with the feelings of the nation, particularly after the war of Schmalkalde. His two opponents were called the Magnanimous; but he, Charles of Ghent, as he was called, was said to have laughed slily to think how he had taken the honest elector prisoner, and with what craft he had seized the person of the landgrave in Halle! Whilst the Italians praised his simple habits, marking how he rode into their towns with his brilliant and richly dressed escort, himself wrapped in a plain cloak [+], the Germans found something to set off against this. When he was surprised by a shower of rain outside the walls of Naumburg, he sent into the city for his old bonnet, meanwhile putting the new one he was wearing under his arm. " Poor emperor, thought I to myself," says Sastrow, " warring away tons of gold, and standing bareheaded in the rain for the sake of a velvet cap [‡]." In short, he was never quite at home in Germany. The dissensions of the country consumed all his exertions without affording him renown ; the climate was prejudicial to his health ; he was not well acquainted with the high German tongue ; the majority of the nation misunderstood and disliked him.

It was late when his life began to be self-dependent, and its decline was early. His growth was long retarded, and a variety of aliments were sought to help it forward [§]. His constitutional development was unusually backward, till it was observed in the year 1521 that he was getting a beard and becoming more manly [||]. From that time he enjoyed a long period of healthy adolescence. He began to love field sports. He more than once lost himself so far in the Alpuxarra, and in the Toledan moors, that no one could hear his horn, and he had to trust to some Morisco guide to show him the way home in the evening, lights being already placed in the city windows, and the bells rung to call the people to search after him [¶]. He jousted on horseback sometimes in the lists, sometimes in the open field ; he practised with his gun and his gineta ; nor did he recoil from exercises on foot [**]. The proposal to terminate his quarrel with Francis I. by single combat was on his part, at least, made in perfect seriousness. We have a portrait of him at this period of his life, the mouth closed and somewhat imperious, the eyes large and fiery, the features compressed ; the figure is full length, and he holds a hound by the collar. Gradually, however, yet too soon, the discrepancy began to show itself, which is noticed in most of his portraits between the upper and the lower half of his countenance. The lower half projects, the mouth is open, the

eyelids droop. At the moment when he first entered fully into active life, his healthy vigour was already gone, and it was with a strange feeling of envy he marked the eager appetite with which his private secretary, come fresh from a journey, devoured the roast meat set before him. In his thirty-sixth year, just as he was dressing in Naples, to make himself pleasing forsooth to the ladies, as he owns, he observed the first white hairs on his temples. It was to no purpose he had them removed ; they always came again [*]. In his fortieth year he felt his strength half gone. He missed the old confidence in himself and in his fortune ; and it is remarkable that his memory was more tenacious of facts that had occurred to him before that year than after it, though the latter were so much more recent [†]. From that time he became particularly subject to the gout. He was obliged to travel for the most part in his litter. At times, indeed, he still brought down a stag or a wild hog in the chase ; but usually he was obliged to content himself with going into the woods with his gun and shooting crows and daws. His enjoyment was to remain within doors, where his fool forced a half smile from him as he stood behind his chair at table, and his steward of the household, Monfalconet, amused and delighted him with his happy replies [‡]. But his malady grew upon him apace. The gout, says Cavallo in 1550, flies frequently to his head, and threatens with sudden death. His physicians urgently advised him to leave Germany ; but the increasing entanglement of public affairs kept him fast in those regions. The tendency to gloomy solitude which had long possessed him, now acquired overwhelming strength; it was in point of fact the same that had so long kept his mother in the world a stranger to the world. Charles saw no one he had not expressly summoned to his presence. It often vexed him even to sign his name. The mere opening of a letter gave him a pain in his hand. He used to be for hours on his knees in a chamber hung with black, and lighted with seven tapers. When his mother died, he sometimes fancied he heard her voice calling him to follow her [§].

In this condition he resolved to quit life before he was yet removed by death.

2. *Philip II.*

If an intelligent man pondered over the posture of the world in those days, what must he have expected of the son of such a father ?

It was manifest that only a sovereign of liberal feelings, only one more disposed to gratify the world and to enjoy it than to dispose of it after his own views, and capable of allowing others a spontaneous course of action, would have been in a condition, if not to reconcile the discordant feelings of the nations, at least to soothe them, and prevent the outbreak of

* Sepulveda, de Rebus Gestis Caroli V. lib. xi. p. 19.
† Ripamonte, Historia Mediolanensis ap. Græv. Verri, Storia di Milano, ii. 321, from Burigozzo.
‡ Bartholomäi Sastrowen, Herkommen, Lebenslauf, u.s.w. Bd. ii.
§ Thomas Leodius, de vita Frederici Palatini, iii. 10.
|| Petrus Martyr : Epistolarum Opus, Ep. 734.
¶ Sandoval : Vida y hechos del Emperador Carlos, xv. p. 811.
** Cavallo : "Ha giostrato bene a lizza et a campo aperto. Ha combattuto alla sbarra. Ha giocato a canne et caroselle et *ammazzato il tauro*, et brevemente tutto quello che alla ginnetta et alla brida si può fare."

* Extrait de la Relation du voyage de M[r] l'amiral de Chatillon vers l'Empereur Charles, in Ribier and in the Appendix to Rabutin's Mémoires : Collect. Univers. xxxviii. 483.
† Hormayr : " From papers never before made use of" in the Archiv für Geographie, Historie, &c. Jahrg. 1810, p. 8.
‡ Cavallo : "Il barone Monfalconetto, suo maestro di casa il quale in vero, per l'argutie et prontezze sue e per la libertà che si piglia di dire ogni cosa, è di giocondissima et dilettissima pratica al imperatore."
§ Extrait. Zenocarus, Hormayr. Galuzzi, Storia del Granducato di Toscana, i. 2. 208.

their passions. It was plain that the heir of the Spanish monarchy, destined to the sovereignty over such heterogeneous countries, had need of manners marked by dignified condescension and affability, and of a cheerful temper to win the confidence of every individual. If this was undoubtedly to be wished, it might also perhaps have been expected. It might have been supposed that a sovereign, brought up under a sense of his great destiny, would have elevated his soul to a nobler view of things than such as is usually afforded by the narrowing influences of a meaner station. Reared in the feeling that he was the head of the nobility, should he not have sought to fashion his character to that cheerful, engaging chivalry, that sits so well on the young?

When Philip left Spain for the first time, and presented himself in other countries, the first thing remarked in him was the great external resemblance he bore to his father. There was the same white rather than pale visage, the same fair hair, the same chin and mouth. Neither was tall; Philip was somewhat less in stature, more neatly made, and weaker than his father *. The comparison was soon carried further. The son's features did not seem to indicate the acute penetration that characterized those of the father. It was perceived that Philip, far from vying with the latter in natural affability, was far surpassed by him in that respect. Whilst Charles was used, when escorted home by princes of the empire, to turn round, take off his hat, offer his hand to each and dismiss him with marks of amity, it was remarked with displeasure, that when the same attention was paid to Philip, he never once looked round him, but straight forward, as he ascended the steps to his apartments †. He took no delight in the chase, or in arms; he even declined the invitations of his father, preferring to remain at home, and to converse with his favourites ‡. It was evident that he lacked all those qualities that engage the affections of the people : the Italians and the Flemings were not a little averse to him, the Germans decidedly so.

It seemed, however, on his second departure from Spain in 1554, as though he abjured his former haughty, repulsive bearing, as though he sought to resemble his father in his outward deportment, and had got rid of that foolish fancy of which he was accused, namely, that he the son of an emperor was more than his father, who was but the son of a king. He displayed more condescension and affability, gave audience readily, and returned satisfactory answers §. But in reality there was no change in him. He took heed to himself, because he wished to please the English, over whom he desired to be king. He nevertheless retained that

proud, isolated impassibility which the Spaniards call *sosiego* *. Sympathy and frankness were no virtues of his ; he did not even concern himself to display a bountiful character ; he showed himself averse to all personal participation in war.

From the time he returned to Spain after the peace of 1559, he never quitted the peninsula again. Even there he abstained from travelling from place to place, as his father and the kings before him had done. He fixed his royal residence in the castle of Madrid, and only left it to pursue that dreary road, shadowed by no tree, enlivened by no brook, that led to the Escurial, which he built among small naked hills, in a stony valley, as a residence for monks of the order of San Geronimo, and as a sepulchre for his father; or to go in spring to Aranjuez, where indeed he accompanied the chase to the mountains, and condescended to alcaldes and monteros, but without asking them a word about any thing else than their offices, or suffering them to speak of any thing besides their business. " Every one," says Cabrera, " was duly regarded according to his station †." At times we find him in the woods about Segovia, and once in Lisbon ; but with these exceptions always at home. At first he used to show himself there on popular holydays, afterwards he suffered himself to be seen only once or twice a-year in a gallery leading from his residence to his chapel ; and in his latter years he desisted even from this, and remained constantly shut up in his apartments ‡. The habitual expression of his face and figure was that of imperturbable calmness, a gravity carried to the utmost pitch, and its effect was felt to be exceedingly depressing. Even practised and esteemed orators were put out when they stood before him, and he measured them as usual with his eyes from head to foot. " Compose yourself (Sosegaos)," he would then say to them. He used to smile slightly in replying to any one §.

Philip II. lacked, as we see, the physical activity of his father. He was no friend to those constant journeys, those hurried excursions to all places, wherever the sovereign's presence seemed necessary. He agreed with those who had applauded Ferdinand the Catholic, because he had rather caused his foreign wars to be carried on, than directed them in person, and who called to mind that even the armies of Charles had been more successful under the command of Pescara and Leira than under his own ‖. Philip carried on war, but he remained aloof from it. A stirring life makes the soul more open, freer, and warmer. If there was always a certain rigidity of temper ob-

---

* Micheli, Relatione d'Inghilterra : " E il re Filippo la stessa imagine dell' imperatore suo patre conformissimo di carne et di faccia et di lineamenti, con quella bocca et labro pendente et con tutte l'altre qualità dell' imperatore, ma di minore statura."

† Sastrowen, i. 269.

‡ Cavallo, Rel. " Ha piacere di starsi in camera co' suoi favoriti a raggionare *di cose private*, et se talhora l'imperatore lo manda in visita, si scusa *per godere la solita quiete*."

§ Micheli. " Ha il costume et maniere dell' imperatore imitando per quanto può le vie et attioni sue di dignità et humanità, havendo del tutto lasciata quell' altierezza con la quale uscì la prima volta di Spagna et riuscì così odioso."

---

* Tiepolo, MS. " E' di natura tardissimo, essendo flegmatico di complessione, et è anco per volontà tale per osservar maggior decoro nelle cose sue."

† Cabrera, Felipe el segundo, p. 598.

‡ Thom. Contarini, Rel. della Spagna anno 1593, MS. Informat. Politt. xi. 474: " Soleva per il passato lasciarsi vedere dal popolo una o due volte l'anno per un corridore che dalle sue stanze passa nella sua capella, ma hora sta sempre ritirato."

§ Tiepolo, Relat. della Spagna : " E ajutato d'un poco di suo riso, che fa ordinariamente nel rispondere et rende ad ognuno molto amabile."

‖ Micheli, 76 : " Levata la necessità di andarvi so che può li occorrere di far guerre: egli stima et approva più il proceder del re cattolico suo avo, che le faceva fare tutte per mano dei suoi capitani senza andarvi lui in persona, che'l proceder dell' imperatore suo padre, che ha voluto farle lui : et a questo lo consigliano li Spagnuoli, li suoi intimi."

servable in Philip, it might possibly have been owing to the want of this activity.

On the other hand, Philip inherited from his father a larger share of the latter's energy in the affairs of the cabinet. True he avoided, even here too, all immediate intercourse with others, and we neither find him negotiating in person, nor taking part in the sittings of the council of state. But we shall see how the machinery of his government was so arranged that all the affairs of his wide spread empire tended to his table as to a common centre. Every resolution of his council of any importance was laid before him on a sheet of paper, on the margin of which he noted his own views and emendations*. The petitions and the letters addressed to him, the suggestions of his ministers, and the secret reports, were all laid before him in his closet. His business and his pleasure was to read them, to reflect upon, and to reply to them. Seated there, sometimes assisted by a trusty secretary, but often quite alone, he governed the large portion of the world subject to his sway, and exercised a kind of inspection and control over the rest; there he set in motion the hidden machinery that moved a great portion of the public affairs of the age. His diligence in this occupation was indefatigable. We have letters written by him at midnight : we find him dispatching the unpleasant affairs of Flanders at one of his country seats, whilst his carriage halted on his way to join the queen. If he had to be present at an entertainment, he fixed it for a day on which there was at least no regular post to send off. He did not make his short journeys even to the Escurial without taking his papers with him, and perusing them by the way. As Margaret of Parma and Granvella, though inhabiting the same palace, communed together more by letter than by word of mouth, so he too wrote innumerable notes to his confidential ministers: Antonio Perez had two chests full of such autographs. Thus he was beyond comparison the most fully employed man of business in the world. His attention to his finances was uninterrupted, and we find him at times more accurately informed respecting them than his presidents†. He wished to know every thing that concerned his dominions. He had materials collected for a general statistical account of Spain for his own use, six volumes of which work are still preserved in the Escurial‡. But he wished his information to extend even to particulars. He had correspondents in every diocese, who reported to him how the clergy and the holders of the benefices conducted themselves. He had always a prelate at each of the universities who acquainted him how the members of the colleges were versed in the sciences. Those who were candidates for any place he usually

knew, even before they were presented, as well as though he had been personally acquainted with them : he was aware of their character and their peculiarities; and once, when they were speaking to him in praise of a certain person's learning and ability, he retorted, " You say nothing to me of his amours *." Thus he ruled his dominions in peace ; in turbulent times he redoubled his attention. It excited wonder to see, when the troubles broke out in Flanders, how accurately he was informed about all persons who might have had any leaning to the new opinions, how exactly he knew, not only their meetings, but also the age, appearance, character, and intercourse of each ; and how, instead of receiving information from Margaret on these matters, he was, on the contrary, able to impart it to her †. Now, it was just in the same manner he managed his foreign affairs. He had at all the leading courts, not only public ambassadors who sent him reports, or came to Spain to give him information by word of mouth, but he had also secret emissaries whose letters were addressed directly to himself. A historian might well cherish the wish that he might share with this king the comprehensive and thorough knowledge he possessed of his own times. Philip sat and read all these reports, and concentrated all their contents, and directed them to his own ends. He weighed them for himself. If he thought good he communicated them to one or other of his confidential ministers ; if not, he buried them in perpetual silence ‡. Thus he lived in complete solitude, and yet was personally acquainted, as it were, with the whole world ; secluded from its contemplation, and yet its real governor ; himself in almost motionless repose, and yet the originator of movements that affected all the world. Grown old and grey, weary and dim-sighted over his toils, he still did not give them up. His daughter, the infanta Isabella, who was moulded entirely after his own heart, for whom he had a cordial regard, and to whom he would go even at night, and communicate to her some welcome news, used to sit for three or four hours with him ; and though he did not admit her into all his secrets, still she helped him to read the petitions and memorials of private persons, and to provide for the affairs of the home administration §.

Now what was the aim of such incessant industry throughout his long life ? Was it the welfare of the kingdoms of which he swayed the sceptre ? the prosperity of his subjects ? This might have been supposed in the beginning of his reign, so long as he seemed to abjure his father's schemes, and

---

* " E diligentissimo nel governo dello stato, et vuole che tutte le cose di qualche importantia passino per le sue mani, perche tutte le deliberationi di momento gli sono mandate da i consiglieri, scritte sopra un foglio di carta, lasciandone la metà per margine, nella quale poi S. M. ne scrive il suo parere, aggiungendo, scernendo et corrigendo il tutto a suo piacere. E sopravanzandole tempo lo spende tutto in rivedere et sottoscrivere suppliche etc., nel che s'impiega 3 o 4 hore continue, sì che non tralascia mai per alcuno minimo punto la fatica."

† See a calculation by Philip in a letter to Eraso, Cabrera, 1166.

‡ Rehfues, Spanien nach eigener Ansicht, iv. S. 1348.

* Cabrera, p. 1064, and elsewhere. The Cortes expressed a wish in 1554 that visitadores should be secretly sent to all the pueblos to inquire into the habits of the regidores, the judicial personages, and the knights. Peticion xxviii.

† Strada, who himself possessed more than one hundred letters from Philip to Margaret, De Bello Belg. iv. p. 81.

‡ Contarini. " Usa S. M. una squisitissima secretezza nelle cose sue, ... ma è altro tanto desiderosa di scoprire i disegni et secreti degl' altri principi, nel che impiega ogni cura et diligentia, spendendo una infinita quantità d'oro in spie in tutte le parti del mondo et appresso a tutti i principi, et queste spie spesse volte hanno anco ordine d'indrizzare le lettere a S. M., la quale non communica le cose importanti a persona alcuna et solamente quelle di Fiandra al duca di Parma."

§ Contarini: " Ajutandogli ella a leggere queste tali scritture." Cf. Strada ii. lib. vii. p. 216.

his thirst for glory, and to look only to his own dominions. But he soon began to play a very busy part in the complicated affairs of Europe. Was it then his purpose, as it was perhaps in his power, to heal the wounds of his times? We cannot affirm either the one or the other. Obedience and the catholic faith at home, the catholic faith and subjection in all other countries, this was what he had at heart, this was the aim of all his labours. He was himself devoted, with monkish attachment, to the outward observances of the catholic worship. He kissed the hand of a priest after mass, to show archdukes who visited him what reverence is due to such men. To a lady of rank, who stood upon the steps of the altar, he said, " That is no place either for you or me." How diligently, with what care and expense, did he gather the sacred relics from all countries that had become protestant, that such precious things might not be lost to catholicism and Christendom *. This was surely not from indwelling religion ; yet a sort of indwelling religion, capable of swaying the moral character, had grown up in him, out of the conviction that he was born to uphold the external service of the church, that he was the pillar of the church, that such was his commission from God. If by this means he brought it to pass, that the majority of Spaniards, full of the like feelings, did, as an Italian says, " not merely love, not merely reverence, but absolutely adore him, and deem his commands so sacred, that they could not be violated without offence to God † ;" at the same time, by a singular illusion (if indeed we are justified, in supposing his conduct to have sprung from an illusion of his own, and not to have been deliberately pursued to delude others), he came to regard the progress of his own power and the progress of religion as identified, and to behold the latter in the former. In this he was confirmed by the people of the Netherlands, who revolted simultaneously from him, and from the pope. In truth, the zeal that animated him was none other than that which had actuated Charles the Bold and Maximilian I., the zeal, namely, of exalting the Burgundian and Habsburg house, which had become conjoined with religious purposes since the days of Charles V., only the union of these two motives was much stronger in him : and if he sought to conquer England, and to obtain the crown of France for his nephew and his daughter, it was with the full persuasion that he was acting for the best interests of the world, and for the weal of souls. If, on the one hand, his reserve and his gravity unfitted him for presiding over the nations he ruled with kindness, affability, and as a father ; on the other hand his narrow and fanatical constitution of mind placed it far beyond his power to become the reconciling spirit of his distracted times ; he was, on the contrary, a great promoter and augmenter of the discord.

Two points are further to be remarked, with reference to his administration. The one, as regards his ministers ; the other, as regards the means he employed to obtain his ends.

Whether it was from the compulsory pressure of his multitudinous businesses, or that he was induced thereto by personal confidence, he left his ministers great freedom, and an open range of action. Espinosa was long called the monarch of Spain * ; Alva had his hands free in the Netherlands. We will look more minutely into the changes of his ministers, and their position. He seemed to be dependent on, and ruled by, many of his confidential advisers. Moreover, it was to no purpose any one proffered a complaint against these men : his first answer was, that he relied on his advisers ; and however often their accusers returned to the charge, they were always met with the same reply. People complained, that not only the interests of foreign powers, but those of the king himself, were betrayed and ruined through the private feelings and passions of these ministers †. Now, it is very well worth noting his manner of dealing with them. To their best suggestions he seemed to lend but half an ear, and for a while it was as though they had said nothing ; but at last, he put their ideas into operation, as though they had proceeded from himself. He used to say, that he stayed away from the council of state, in order that the passions of the several members might be free to display themselves the more unreservedly, and that if he had but a faithful reporter of all that passed, he could have no better means of information ‡. But he went still farther than this. He suffered incensed enemies to pursue each other into his very cabinet, and he received the memorials of the one party against the other §. As the close secresy he observed on all things was notorious, no one scrupled to confide to him the most private matters, and things that would never have been imparted to any other. Such communications did not always produce the full effect intended, but some of them did ; and Philip was always filled with suspicion. Never was it easier for any one than for him to withdraw his accustomed confidence, and to stint in his wonted favour. For awhile he would conceal his secret displeasure. Perhaps the minister had important matters still in hand, perhaps his personal co-operation was necessary for the accomplishment of some purpose. So long as the case stood thus, he dealt with him warily as with a foreign power, and frequently, meanwhile, would neither comply with the minister's desires, nor absolutely reject them. But at last, his displeasure broke out all at once. Cabrera remarks of no few, that his disfavour was their death. So much may have been implied by the saying proverbial at his court, that it was not far from his smile to his dagger. The whole spirit of his favourites hung on his good will ; without it they sank into nothingness.

As he changed his ministers, so too he changed the measures they were to carry out, ever keeping

* Micheli ; above all Cabrera.

† Relatione e sommario dell' historie antiche et moderne di Spagna, in the Tesoro politico i. Contarini : " Questa opinione che di lui si ha, rende le sue leggi più sacrosancte et inviolabili."

* Famianus Strada, de Bello Belgico, i. lib. vi. p. 161.

† Tiepolo : " Il ritrovar poi S. M. per ottener più di quello ha fatto il detto consiglio è cosa in tutto superflua : per il che da se non risponde cosa alcuna, ma si rimette a quello è stato risoluto. Il che causa senza dubio danno ai negotii. Spesso avviene che il giuditio di suoi ministri è corrutto o da interesse particolare o da alcuna passione."

‡ Cartas de Antonio Perez.

§ For instances see Cabrera passim. He mentions " papeles que le davan emulos invidiosos y malos por odio y pasion."

D

his ends steadily in view. How numerous, and how various, were the courses he struck out in the affairs of Flanders alone *. It is a mistake, to suppose he knew how to adopt no other devices than those of force. Undoubtedly he acquiesced in Alva's cruel measures, not however from cruelty, but for the sake of the result he expected. When this did not ensue, he selected Requesens for the express reason, that he was a moderate man, and commissioned him to employ milder means †. He sent don John, who was acceptable to the people of the Netherlands, because he appeared to be their countryman ‡, with definite orders to conclude a peace. Failing in this, he again reverted to force. In this he may be compared to his great grandfather, Maximilian, who was continually adopting new means to arrive at his ends : only Maximilian broke off at an early stage of his proceedings, whilst Philip always pushed matters to the very utmost ; Maximilian always seemed highly excited, Philip invariably maintained the most unruffled composure. Never did he give way to any impulse of temper §. There never arrived a despatch from Flanders, however good or bad its news, that could produce the least change in his countenance. On receiving the first intelligence of the victory at Lepanto, the greatest that had been achieved by Christendom for 300 years, he said, " Don John risked a great deal," and not a word more. Upon the greatest mischance that could befal him, the loss of his fleet, on which he had exhausted the resources of Spain, on which he had built the grandest hopes, and which he had deemed invincible, he said, " I sent it out against men, and not against the billows ;" and having said this, he seemed perfectly calm. The only gesticulation he was observed to make, when anything occurred quite contrary to his expectation, or when any word let fall provoked him very much, was that same one which is noticed in the gravest Arabs ; he clutched his beard in his hand.

There are in this dismal life some spots of surpassing gloom. Why was his son Don Carlos disposed to rebel against him ? It is now but too certain that he wished to do so. Assuredly the prince presented a decided contrast to his father ; the latter, particularly at first, all calm and pacific ; the former, on the contrary, fired with an enthusiastic love of arms, ardently attached to the soldiery, and of an impetuosity of character that disdained to conceal ambition, cruelty, or any other passion. He displayed a brilliant munificence, strikingly opposed to the king's frugality ||. The

more restrictions there were imposed on him, the more passionate became his inclinations. He was still very young when the question began to be agitated of entrusting him with some lieutenancy. But this was not done. He had reason to expect a greater degree of independence from his marriage, which was already negotiated and agreed on ; but the father took to himself the son's destined bride. As often as a war broke out he longed to join in it, and he always was forced to remain at home. At last he made it the sole object of his wishes, that the pacification of the Netherlands should be committed to him : Alva was preferred to him. Thus this impetuous spirit, shut out on all sides from active exertion, and driven back upon itself, was thwarted and irritated to madness. Now would Carlos kill Alva, and escape by flight from his father ; now had he no rest day or night, till he cried out that he meditated a deed against a man he hated, for which he besought absolution beforehand, till he was frantic enough to give the theologians of Atocha grounds for surmising that his father was the hated foe whose life he threatened *. Did his father then leave him to pine away and die in prison ? Or is the story really true, that the coffin in which Carlos lay was opened, and his head found severed from his body ? Be it enough to say, that Philip lived on such deplorable terms with his son, that he must either fear every thing at his hand, or doom him to death without pity.

This matter had no doubt some influence on the subsequent discipline practised by this monarch with his children. When he had his heir apparent, Philip, brought up for an unusual length of time, and with injurious severity, among women, it was thought that he bore Don Carlos in mind †. He took care not to give him a grandee for his tutor. He did not even suffer, as it is said, that his son and his faithful daughter, Isabella, should speak with each other unknown to himself.

He lived, however, to see the natural and inevitable result of all this. As his end drew nigh he saw his kingdom exhausted of men, and burdened with debts, his foes and his revolted subjects powerful, alert, and provided with means of attack ; but the successor, who might have remedied those evils, and resisted those enemies, he saw not. His son was wholly incapable. It is said that this conviction once quite overcame him. He bewailed it to his son-in-law, Albert of Austria, and to Isabella, whom he greatly loved : " To his grace in bestowing on him so great a realm, God had not been pleased to add the grace of granting him a successor capable of continuing to rule it. He commended the realm to them both." The old

---

* This was remarked by Cabrera, lib. xi. p. 869. " El rey catolico haviendo usado para reduccion de los Flamencos del rigor, blandura: castigo, perdon : armas, paz : y sin fruto.

† Cabrera mentions the " medio di concerto y blandura que S. Magestad havia mostrado querer provar tras los de las armas y rigor."

‡ Lippomano, Relatione di Napoli.

§ Contarini : " E' gravissimo in tutte sue operationi, si che non esce mai parola della bocca sua nè atto alcuno dalla sua persona che non sia molto bene ponderato et pesato. Modera felicissimamente tutti i suoi affetti."

|| Tiepolo : " E nelle attioni sue così ardente et si può dir precipitoso. Si sdegna facilmente et prorumpe tanto che si può dir crudele. .... E amico della verità et nemico de buffoni. Si diletta di gioie, perche di man sua ne intaglia.

Stima poco ognuno, se ben è grande, parendoli a gran lungo che nessun li possa pareggiare. Suol dire : Chi debbe far elemosine, se non le danno i principi ? E' splendidissimo in tutte le cose et massime nel beneficiar chi lo serve." Soriano (MS.) thus describes Carlos : " E' simile al padre di faccia, è però dissimile de costumi ; perchè è animoso, accorto, crudele, ambitioso, inimicissimo de buffoni, amicissimo de soldati."

* L'histoire de l'huissier, in Llorente, Hist. de l'Inquisition, iii. 151. It has been sufficiently proved in recent times that Carlos perished through his irregularities in prison. (Note to the second edition.)

† Khevenhiller's account of 1621. Annal. Ferdin. ix. 1270.

king said this with tears, he who had shed no tears at the death of his children *.

3. *Philip III.*

The Spaniards have a book relating to Philip III., which ascribes many virtues to that monarch. If I mistake not, human virtues are of two kinds : in the one case their active impulses are directed outwards, and are expansive in their nature ; in the other, these are turned inwards with a self-contracting force : and whilst the virtues of the former class belong more to the stronger minded, and those of the latter to the weaker, it is the due combination of both that constitutes the faultless man. Now just such a combination does the book we speak of ascribe to the king : it describes him as brave, open-handed, and sage, and at the same time clement, pious, and chaste. Why then was Philip II. alarmed at the prospect of being succeeded by a son so well endowed ? Why did he think of setting governors over him ?

Poreño, the author of the book, does not leave us in doubt. For what is the bravery he extols in Philip ? It is that he controls himself, and refuses to take vengeance. In what consists his open-handedness ? He makes donations to churches, founds colleges, and sends money to the Persians, that they might keep the Turks employed, and hinder them from infesting the coasts of Spain. Lastly, wherein does his sagacity display itself ? In the fact that he submits to be instructed, that he shapes his course according to the judgment of others †. And so vanish all his active virtues.

We have seen how Charles V. was so constituted, that his nature could hardly attain to a free exercise of its powers ; but it did arrive at that stage of growth at last ; that monarch was indefatigable in the field and in the council. Again, we saw how one half of this active capacity remained for ever denied to Philip II.; how sedulously that sovereign avoided all energetic movements, all personal contact with others ; but in solitude and in his cabinet he too was unwearied in his labours. Philip III. could brace himself to neither of these courses. He was very far from taking delight in a stirring life in the field or in the fight ; but he also resigned to others the business of the cabinet.

Don Philip III. was of a small, well-shaped person, with a small, round, agreeable, white and red face ; he had the family lips. He had been taught to display a certain air of dignity when he appeared in public ; but naturally he was altogether cheerful and unpretending in his appearance. He had passed his youth in weakness, obedience, and not very profitable occupations. An unhealthy nurse had communicated to him a malady of which he never thoroughly got rid : it was not till his fourteenth year that he cut his

second teeth, so slowly did his constitution unfold. He was certainly not entirely destitute of the talent to comprehend ; nevertheless his tutor, Loaisa, with all his minute and pedantic rigour, did not carry him much further than grammar and a smattering of St. Thomas. Was it the trial befitting a prince's mettle, that they made him support theses and syllogisms in the Escurial ? Above all they instilled into him the strictest obedience to his father, and never was that duty more inviolably observed by a son. The charge has been gravely alleged against Loaisa that he educated the prince with a view to ruling him at a future time *.

At any rate, the prince seemed from the first more fitted and more inclined to receive impulses from others than to impart them. When his father announced to him that he should now take part in the affairs of state, that he should return as a man to the chamber he had left more like a child, he said not a word, kissed his father's hand, and remained the same as ever. Even when Philip showed him the portraits of three young princesses, one of whom he might select for his bride, and repeatedly urged him to make his choice, there was no bringing him to a decision, " for his father's will was his taste." He left it, so to speak, to death to decide for him †. Two of the three princesses died.

After the death of his father, when he himself became king, he resigned all authority from the very first into the hands of the duke of Lerma, as we shall presently see. Other sovereigns have done something of the same kind, but only that they might be free to pursue their pleasures. He knew no pleasures to which he could wish to devote himself. What he seemed to have most taste for was travelling, playing at ball, and throwing dice till a late hour of the night. But his fondness even for these amusements was not very decided. It was plain after all that he only played to pass away the time, not for any gratification such occupations afforded him ‡.

Thus he appears in this world without taking part in it, without acquiring any active character, without suffering himself to be tempted to the indulgence of any passion. He blushes and casts down his eyes if a lady looks upon him with vivacity in the palace. He affirms, and we may really take his word for it, he looks upon a beautiful woman only from thankfulness to God for having made so perfect a creature §.

But no ! there is something in him that does at

* Relatione della vita del re di Spagna et delli privati. " Pate tutta via una certa infirmità et la chiamano usogie (?) Don Francesco de Avila, marchese di Velada, fu quello a cui si raccomandò et comise la custodia di questo principe : e Garzia de Loaisa, che morse arcivescovo di Toledo, fu maestro per insegnarli le scienze et virtù christiane et politiche che bisognano a così gran discepolo. Questi hebbero per scopo, poiche il padre era vecchio, infermo et molto vicino alla morte, di allevare S. M. in maniera che'l potessero reggere et, maneggiare come loro tornava commodo et quasi tiranneggiarlo. Questo scopo hebbe più di ogn' altro il Loaisa."

† Khevenhiller, Annales Ferdinandei, an. 1598.

‡ Relat. della vita, etc. " Dei gusti non si è potuto scoprir più che il correre la posta, far viaggi, giocare a pillotta et a caccia, et in questa materia tirare più che alli uccelli. . . . . Gioca ancora et molto bene a dadi buona parte della notte, et questo più per spassarsi che per dilettarsi del gioco."

§ Poreño, Dichos y hechos de Felipe III. c. iv. p. 299.

* Rel. della vita del re di Spagna, MS. " Gli disse che egli ben sapeva il gran valore et le qualità dell' infanta, che erano tali che in essa et in suo marito haveva poste le sue speranze : già che dio per li suoi peccati, ancorche gli havesse fatto gratie di tanti regni et dominii, non gli haveva per reggerli et governarli dato figliuoli : perchè il principe non era che un ombra di principe, non havendo talento per comandare, di maniera che dubitava che non dovesse essere occasione di molti gran danni alla sua casa."

† Poreño, Dichos y hechos del Rey Don Felipe III. cap. ii. vii. xi.

times incite him to action. There lives within him, interwoven with the very core of his existence, a spirit of rigorous Catholic devotion, whether inherited from his father or implanted in him by education. How often meeting with the procession of the host does he accompany it even beneath the poorest roof! It is with great unwillingness he returns from Valladolid, whither the court had been transferred, to Madrid; but he does so because his confessor tells him it is for God's service. He kneels down before a poor friar to receive his blessing, and thinks his indisposition relieved when he has obtained it. After the death of his wife there needs a heavenly voice to comfort him, speaking in very choice Castilian; yet he does not conceive the least suspicion *.

This turn of thought sometimes impels him to active exertion. It seems to him an important duty to bring all men to acknowledge " the mystery of the immaculate conception of the angel queen, the most holy Mary." For this he consults with his learned men, for this he makes his bishops and archbishops write to Rome, and is ready even to make a pilgrimage thither on foot if necessary ; nor can his children afford him greater delight than by repeating, " Holy Mary conceived without sin."—" So, my children," he answers, " do I also believe †."

But all the results of his religious promptings were not equally inoffensive. We see him making warlike preparations in the year 1609. The veteran Spanish troops are summoned from Spain. The galleys of Naples and Sicily, of Castile, of Portugal and Catalonia, put to sea, and the names of Doria and Santa Cruz, are heard again upon the waters. The king makes a vow to St. James, and to his wife, the Blessed Virgin, to obtain success in the proposed attempt. And for what was all this done? What was the enemy to be encountered ? The campaign was against a people that raised its corn and its sugar for the kingdom, against the poor Moriscoes of Valentia, who had long been baptized and disarmed. The crime imputed to them was certainly not very clear; their grand fault was that they were not yet thoroughly Catholic. And, behold, an image of the Virgin has wept; whole clouds of steaming sweat have oozed from another; the bell of Velilla has struck : now is the king fully determined; he will not hear one word of remonstrance. And now when all has been accomplished, when the streets of Valentia have been strewed with corpses, when so many Moors have perished by sea under the cruel treatment of their robberlike captors, and scarcely a third part of them have been landed in Africa; then goes the queen and lays the foundation-stone of the church she had vowed, and the king undertakes his pilgrimage to St. Jago ; whilst the Spaniards reckon up 3700 battles fought within the last 800 years between them and these Moors, now finally expelled; and they appoint a solemn holyday for an everlasting memorial of this enterprise ‡.

If religious opinions were the sole causes that

could prompt Philip III. to action, so were they also the only source of his uneasiness. Before we can fully understand the how and the wherefore of this matter, we must take more minute note of the administration of his favourites. Here it is enough to state that the thought smote him at last, he had done sinfully in conceding so much power to those favourites; and that no consolatory arguments were strong enough to assure him of that blessedness in another world, for which he had lived a life of such purity, chastity, and devotion to the church; so that he departed in a kind of despair *.

Conclusion.

These are the three sovereigns whose administration we propose considering further. But first it is well worth our noting how like each other, and yet how different they were.

The Spanish line of the house of Habsburg is remarkable for having continued itself by marriages exclusively within its own family.

The wife of Charles V. was his own niece by blood; that wife of Philip II. who bore him his heir, was of the house of Austria, and so likewise was the queen of Philip III. Philip IV. married his own niece, and from the marriage sprang Charles II., the last scion of the house of Habsburg in Spain.

From this may have arisen the fact, that in no other race have the children so much resembled their parents in form and features as in this. There is a curious substantiation of this fact in our Relationi. Leonardo Moro pourtrays king Philip IV. in the very words employed by Soriano to describe Philip II.; whether it was that this was an accidental coincidence, or that Moro saw the description of the grandfather to be quite applicable to the grandson.

Now where education, circumstances, and habits of life are the same, it is not at all unlikely that the physiognomy of the soul should be as hereditary as that of the body, a fact of which we daily see thousands of instances ; maxims and thoughts may pass consciously or unconsciously from father to son ; but is the force, the indwelling energy that alone constitutes the man of action, that gives him his value and his influence on society, is this too hereditary ?

We know the prophetic words spoken of the Merovingian race by the bride of Childerick, on her nuptial night, and how they proved but too true. The race of Pepin long brought forth men and heroes, and Charlemagne was surrounded by valorous sons. The nation had sworn never to depart from them. But from that time forth there was a continual descent, generation after generation, down to weaklings, who remained all their lives in a state of non-age. Three nations were constrained to abjure them in spite of the oath. The Spanish line of the house of Habsburg may be compared with the sons of Pepin and the Merovingians.

We are here verging on the mysteries of life, where it is fed by hidden and sometimes sealed fountains. This only we may venture to assert, that the man is not fashioned by nature alone.

---

* Davila, Vida y hechos de Felipe III., p. 81 et seqq.
† Poreño, cxii. " De su devocion," p. 330.
‡ Geddes, The History of the Expulsion of the Moriscoes out of Spain, in Miscellaneous Tracts, i., particularly p. 106. Our information is taken from Poreño, pp. 282. 291, and Davila, an. 1610, authors not made use of by Geddes.

* Khevenhiller, an. 1621, p. 1250.

CHAPTER II.

Of the Court and the Ministers.

IF we have duly comprehended the character and habits of the monarchs before us, we shall understand as a matter of course what was the position of their ministers. We shall conclude that they could not have possessed any extraordinary importance under Charles V. ; that the personal qualities of Philip II. afforded them scope for free action upon all beneath them, and for a considerable re-action upon himself ; and that lastly, under Philip III. they must have been omnipotent.

But it is not enough to know this. It is perhaps necessary to be acquainted with the intimates, the immediate organs of the monarchs of independent character ; but it is much more important to become acquainted with those on whom much, with those on whom everything, depended. Contemporaries too felt this. The Relationi belonging to the times of Charles V. have reference chiefly to the general form of his court and state ; those pertaining to Philip II. carry us further into the heart of the subject ; and when we come to the times of Philip III. we find the description of the ministries the chief theme of the Relationi. It is just the same with the printed works. The information they give us respecting Charles V. is not very minute ; they are much more so respecting Philip II., but still there is something suppressed; but as to Philip III., they make no concealment. The importance of a thing augments the attention with which it is regarded. We, too, shall both voluntarily and of necessity adhere to the same course of proceeding ; voluntarily, in consideration of the nature of our subject, and of necessity, by reason of the character of our materials.

1. The Court and State of Charles V.

The court of Charles V., it must be owned, was of much importance at the time when he had not yet overcome the obstacles to his own freedom of action inherent in himself. It was a thoroughly Burgundian court, constituted exactly after the fashion of those of Philip the Good and Charles the Bold ; it consisted of gentlemen *. The immediate servants of the prince were persons of princely blood † : they were under the directions of a lord high chamberlain, who slept in the chamber of the prince, by whom a table was daily provided for them. The household was full of inferior persons of gentle blood ‡. Some of these served as armed retainers ; others waited at table, and served bread and wine ; several of them had been brought up

in the household. All these were under a grand steward of the household, a mayor-domo-mayor, or patron of the court as they called him. Such were the provisions for the service of the household. But when the monarch left the palace, the functions of the master of the horse came into play ; for not only was the whole retinue of heralds and trumpeters, of saddlers and tent-keepers, under his control, but his services were particularly required when the monarch set out for a tournament, or armed for battle. On these occasions he dressed the monarch in his armour, and received him on his return ; and he was in his immediate proximity in the busiest moments *. With these three officers was associated the father confessor †. He had the control of the two preachers, the chaplains, and those forty musicians who constituted the most perfect choir in the world, and upheld the fame of the Netherlands as the native place of music. The confessor could moreover boast that the sovereign was under his influence in his most solemn and perhaps his most important moments.

We see what were the four chief personages of the court, and it is not to be denied that at first they had great influence on the administration of the state. This has always been so in Germanic nations. There is sometimes reason to doubt which was the original of the two, power and princely dignity, or service about the royal person. The high offices of the German electors certainly admit of no doubts of the kind ; but in the case of the palatines of the West Goth kings, which was the earlier of the two, their functions in the palace, or their rank in the kingdom ? Was the power of a major domus derived from his position about the Frankish kings, or was that position conferred on one already possessed of power ? Be this as it may, Chievres, lord high chamberlain to Charles V., established an almost unlimited authority over the kingdom, upon the almost constant proximity in which he stood to the sovereign. Maingoal de Lanoi, the same monarch's master of the horse, a man of no remarkable intrinsic ability, but who had won his sovereign's favour ‡, found means thereby to make his own importance acknowledged in the weightiest affairs of Europe. It caused the Spanish grandees no little mortification, on the arrival of Charles in the country, to find the first places occupied by Flemings, and themselves excluded from every station immediately about the king's person. This very circumstance contributed to excite the comunidades to their insurrection.

Now, if the chief personages of the court possessed such decisive influence, the younger members also might look forward to various stations of weight and dignity. No few young men of noble blood, most of them younger sons of great houses, served the court as chaplains, as private priests, and chanted vespers in their surplices. They performed these services, because they were destined for clerical honours, and the disposal of these was

---

* Olivier de la Marche, Mémoires, App. Collect. Univers. tom. ix.

† Cavallo : "Ha S. M. 36 gentilhuomini della camera sua, alli quali non si da più che un scudo il giorno di provisione, et questi per il più sono principi e di parentado di principi." [His majesty has 36 gentlemen of his chamber, who receive each only a scudo a day, and these are for the most part princes and of princely extraction.]

‡ Ibid. "Li gentilhuomini della casa sono intorno a cento, tenuti a servire con armi et cavalli in ogn'un occasione, come allo stato loro ci conviene: delli quali secondo i meriti suoi si eleggono quelli che si chiamano della bocca et sono intorno a 50: oltre al servitio d'armi et cavalli servono al mangiar dell' imperatore."

* Cavallo : "Il grand scudiero, che è cavaliere del ordine del tosone, è tenuto armare di sua mano l'imperatore."

† Ibid. "Vi è l'elemosiniero : .... vi sono cantori, al numero forse di quaranta, la più compita et eccellente capella della christianità, eletti da tutti i paesi bassi, che sono hoggidì il fonte della musica:—sono poi inferiori ministri : —vi sono due predicatori, un Francese, l'altro Spagnuolo : et tutti questi sono sotto il confessore."

‡ Petrus Martyr, ep. 758. Varchi, Stor. Fiorent. ii. p. 10.

in the hands of the court. At the end of from six to ten years, they obtained a bishopric or an abbey*. If a young Croi, on the arrival of Charles in Spain, obtained the first prelacy in the kingdom, the arch-bishopric of Toledo, he was undoubtedly indebted for this to his connexion with the court. Was it likely it should have been otherwise with secular appointments? Was it likely the sovereign should not bethink him, in the first place, of those he had known from their youth upward? The court became a nursery for the state. Obviously it was to be regarded as the centre of the whole system of public life. It is plain how dangerous it were, if a sovereign should become too dependent on its members.

We cannot contemplate this court, or the others of those times, without making one general observation. If we reflect how influential was the education of the nobility, how important in its effects on all the rest of society must have been the change in its notions of what was noble, respectable, and desirable, it will not appear superfluous to inquire, how it was that the knight passed into the cavalier. The qualities that make the knight are valour guided by lofty aims, inviolable fidelity to the suzerain to whom he has pledged his allegiance, and disinterested devotion as regards the fair sex. The cavalier's characteristics are superior personal endowments and accomplishments, which he employs according to the received notions of honour ; as regards his sovereign, unconditional obedience, and the complaisance of a courtier; as regards women, address in winning their favour. The broad-sword is the weapon of the former, the small sword that of the latter. It seems to me that courts, such as was the Burgundian court under Charles V., and such as it further became under his successors, contributed not a little to bring about this change. There were always about forty pages brought up in them. In what were they instructed? In the whole course of modern training for young men of rank. Dancing and vaulting, riding and fighting ; not much science or literature †. Now if the hope of obtaining gracious marks of his favour from the sovereign, prompted to submissive deference towards him ; and if the cavalier's daily occupations forced him to attain peculiar proficiency in the before-mentioned exercises, he soon acquired, moreover, a certain gallantry, particularly when the consort of the sovereign likewise kept her court. That tone of feeling, which has been set before us by Calderon, unfolded itself among the Spaniards, to whose minds the catholicism of their monarchy gave a peculiar kind of elevation.

When Charles began to act for himself, he completely dissolved the connexion of the court with public affairs. Nassau and Büren, who played important parts there in the year 1630, and who stood particularly high in the emperor's favour *, had no share in the administration of the state. After Nassau's death, the post of lord high chamberlain was abolished †, and we do not find that the so called somiglier du corps, who took the duties of the suppressed office upon him, was ever of much importance. Alva was grand steward of the household, but he never had any decided influence under Charles ; and if he did possess some weight ‡, he owed this to other things than his position at court. We hear no more of the power of the grand-master of the horse after Lanoy. The father confessor alone, whose office, as we have seen, constituted an important feature of the court establishment, was of course not to be dispensed with by Charles. There were so many clerical affairs to be discussed, so many that related to the councils, to Turks and Moors, to new Christians and protestants, besides many others, in which he needed the aid of a ghostly counsellor. On all these the father confessor was consulted. It was perceived, however, that he had need to put forward his opinions with all modesty, and to back them by cogent arguments, if he would have them attended to §. It is only over weak natures that confessors have obtained a paramount control. It is no bad proof of the independence with which Charles bore him, that we hear nothing of factions at his court, nothing even of remarkable visitations of disfavour.

Thus gradually vanishes the influence at first exercised by this court ; institutions of state arise, which are independent of the court.

But as the provinces of the Spanish realm had distinct administrations, it became a question of commanding interest, how far Charles would have the power to give these a certain unity. The most peculiar institution we find at his court is a supreme administrative council, selected from the several councils of all the provinces. " His majesty," says Cavallo, who is our sole informant on this subject, " has a council for the government of his states collectively, consisting of several *regents* (the superior members of the colleges are so called), one from Sicily, one from Naples, one from Milan, one from Burgundy, one from the Netherlands, one from Aragon, and one from Castile ; and in addition to these, there are two or three doctors. These councillors deliberate on all important matters that concern the emperor or the empire at large ; each member takes care to make himself acquainted with the concerns of his own province, and reports thereon. The younger Granvella, bishop of Arras, is president of this council ∥." If the utility of

---

* Relat. di Contarini : " Amatissimi da Cesare."

† Ordine della casa : Monsr di Prata is here styled secondo ciamberlano, Monsr di Rye somiglier.

‡ Cavallo : " E vero che per ceremonia più che per altro ha ammesso il duca d'Alva."

§ Ibid. " Questo confessore entra in tutti li consigli dove si trattano cose pertinente alla conscientia, et per questo viene ammesso dove si parla di guerra et anco si parla di giustitia, et particolarmente quando si consultano le denominationi de beneficii, ... d'*usure* et quasi di tutte le cose che faccia l'imperatore. Bisogna che lui con destrezza non manchi di dire l'opinion sua fondatamente et con buona ragione et veda di diria con tanta modestia che sia accettata la verità: altrimenti fa poco frutto et diminuisce l'autorità sua infinitamente."

∥ Cavallo : " Li quali tutti insieme massime nelle cose d'im-

---

* Cavallo. " Sono de secondogeniti de suoi principi, personaggi di gran qualità de suoi stati, li quali, havendo servito sei, dieci o talhor più anni, sono rimunerati con pensioni, abbatie, vescovati, si come pare a S. M."

† Cavallo : " Ha S. M. da 20 in 40 paggi, figliuoli di conti et signori suoi vassalli et anco alcuni d'altra natione, per il vivere de quali S. M. paga un sesto di scudo (they had according to the Ordine della casa a governatore, who provided for them, and received five scudi a month for each): di più li veste ogn'anno, ma non molto sontuosamente : gli tiene maestri che gl'insegnano bellare et di giuoco di spada, cavalcare, volteggiare a cavallo et un poco di lettere."

such a council would be obvious even in a monarchy possessed of an organic unity, how much more must this have been the case in an empire made up of co-ordinate, and almost independent kingdoms. Its members might be looked on as at once organs of the executive, and as representatives of their native states. If, on the one hand, they were bound to uphold the several local interests against that of the general body, on the other hand, they could not be blind to the necessity for combination; they could not obstinately stand out against this ; and the provinces must have found it easier to obey what was enjoined by a council, in which they saw one of their own people sitting as a member *, than what was imposed on them by absolute authority, without appeal. In such a council, too, there was a greater facility for duly balancing the mutual relations of the provinces.

This council, however, was not considered singly sufficient. There was, certainly, need of another, of more strict unity, for the control of the complicated monied affairs of the empire. The emperor had a council of finance, which he consulted on the state of his income and expenditure, the loans he proposed to make, and the interest he was willing to grant †. The respective characteristics of these two councils I imagine to have been, that the one demanded what the other unwillingly granted.

There was over both these, in the latter part of the reign of Charles, a council of state, which, however, was of but little importance. Alva and the father confessor were members of it. Cavallo asserts, that this council had but little to do.

The emperor was fond of taking counsel of a single individual ; Gattinara and the elder Granvella successively enjoyed his confidence. Gattinara was an Italian, from the foot of the Alps, who acquired his experience in the administration of Upper Burgundy. We have letters of his that bespeak a certain boldness even to the sovereign's face, and in contradiction to him, and the most lively sense of honour. " I would live in accordance with the laws of honour," he says, " though no one saw me, though I lived in the heart of a forest." These letters are remarkable for the happy art with which they always hit the very central point of policy‡. We know, however, that their author's influence was not paramount. Though a man of penetration, and firmly rooted in the favour of Charles, still he could not enforce his views on important occasions. It has already been mentioned how close and constant was the community of ideas between Granvella and his master. The emperor sent him every report, and all the negotiations carried on with foreign ambassadors ;

and Granvella used, every evening, to send the emperor a note containing his notions respecting the business for the following day. When an oral consultation was held between the two, the confessor was indeed admitted to it, but he had no part in the decision *. Now, neither do we find it said of Granvella that he led Charles ; it is only said that he agreed with his master.

The execution of those matters which were thus determined between the king and his confidential advisers, was further discussed with the two councils. The chanceries, one of which had charge of matters pertaining to the Germanic empire, another, of those of the Italian states independent of that empire, and third, of those of Spain, made out the orders which were then transmitted to the several provincial administrations.

We see how much the unity of the whole body politic was centred in the person of the emperor. No doubt he encountered multiplied limitations in the constitutions of his dominions, the policy of his neighbours, and the frequently inauspicious turn of affairs ; still we find him, to the very close of his life, always firm and independent of extraneous influence in the exercise of supreme authority.

2. The first Ministry of Philip II.

We have seen that the calm and reserved nature of Charles had pliancy enough to accommodate itself to various nations. We admit that his reign was conspicuous for the personal independence he maintained, and for the equal regard he extended to all his dominions.

Did his son succeed him as well in his system of government as in his rights ?

Again and again in the history of the house of Habsburg, we find it endeavouring to coerce one nation by means of another, and to rule such as were ill-disposed to it by foreign aid. Rudolf I. subjugated the Austrians with the help of Swabians, many a man of whom marched with him on foot, and ere long acquired an income of 10,000 marks, and against whose permanent dominion Austria vainly struggled †. To make himself master of the Netherlands, Maximilian made use of the resources of Austria, of those troops Gaudenz von Ems brought him from the Tyrolese wars, and of German auxiliaries. Again, Philip I. entered Spain with Flemish and German troops ; and it was to Flemings that Charles at first entrusted the government of Spain.

But Charles corrected himself, and in his later years we find Spaniards, Flemings, and Italians treated by him with equal favour.

But a peculiar re-action exhibited itself under Philip II. As the Spaniards acquired the habit of regarding themselves, though not altogether justly, as the victors in the Italian and German wars, and the founders of the monarchy, as their pride arrogated to themselves the first rank among the nations constituting the same, and that so success-

---

portanza consultano et giudicano ogni cosa particolare pertinente all'imperatore o alli stati, et separamente ogn'uno di loro della sua propria provincia s'instruisce et riferisce a gli altri, sollecitando l'espeditione : capo de quali tutti è Monsignor d'Arras : et questi hanno di provisione dall' imperatore da mille scudi sino in 1500 l'anno."

* Respecting the Neapolitan member, see Giannone, Storia di Napoli, xxx. c. 2. The Cortes of Madrid, 1552, Petic. i. say that two members of the council of Castile must always accompany the imperial court.

† Cavallo : " Sono vi poi a parte di tesoriere consultori, che sono ragionati (perhaps ragionatori), e con il consiglio d'alcuni di questi S. M. piglia a cambio."

‡ His letters to Margaret, governess of the Netherlands, in the Lettres de Louys XII. vol. iv.

* Cavallo : ".Si serve l'imperatore del consiglio suolo di Monsignor Granvella. La cosa si risolve tutta fra l'imperatore et Monsignor Granvella. Rare volte, anzi dico rarissime, sono discrepanti fra loro d'opinione o conclusioni,—non solo nelli negotii di stato, ma in qual altra cosa possa occorrere a lui, come d'andare, stare, far venire, licentiare et risolvere tutte le cose."

† Albertus Argentinensis, ap. Urstis, ii. p. 103.

fully, that the two sons of Charles, the legitimate Philip, and the illegitimate Don John, both insisted on being nothing but genuine Spaniards*, so they gradually made pretensions to a predominant share in the general government. Philip admitted their claims. The first deviation from Charles's system was that Philip regarded Castile as the head of the empire. Next, the council composed of natives of the several provinces disappeared. After Philip took up his residence permanently in Spain, and indeed, in consequence of that circumstance, he adopted a system of administration by which the other territories were treated as subordinate provinces of Castile. There had for some time existed distinct councils for judicial affairs, for the inquisition, the knightly orders, and the Indies, and now certain new ones were added to these, namely for Aragon, for Italy, and for the Netherlands; and though the latter were essentially quite different from the former, they seemed so only in incidentals†. All these councils were in immediate contact with the king. True, he never was present at their sittings; but he made it a practice, at least in the earlier part of his reign, to have their resolutions brought forward in a *consulta*‡. It continued, certainly, to be the custom for some native representatives to sit in these committees, but the former sittings and consultations in general assembly fell into disuse.

The care of the general body of the realm lay principally with the privy council. May this have consisted of members selected from the various territories of the Spanish empire?

The manner in which Philip II.'s privy council of state was constituted, is highly deserving of notice. While he was yet *principe* he had a court assigned him, constituted in the Burgundian fashion, and made up almost wholly of Castilians. The duke of Alva was grand steward of the household; Don Antonio de Toledo, of the same family as Alva, was master of the horse; Figueroa, count of Feria, likewise nearly related to Alva, commanded the Spanish body-guards. Among the chamberlains (for the office of lord high chamberlain, abolished by the father, was not continued in the household of the son) we remark especially Don Ruy Gomez de Silva; he was a scion of the Portuguese branch of a family extensively ramified in Spain and Portugal, and he became conspicuous for the decided favour in which he stood with Philip. These were the persons essentially constituting the court of the *principe* §. How great must our surprise be to

see him after he had become king, though he had his father's system of business before him, though he was not so young as to give himself up to whomsoever chance happened to place near him, forming, nevertheless, his privy council out of these same persons, and committing to their guidance the affairs of the whole united empire. Alva, Toledo, Ruy Gomez, and Feria, were all members of this council. Two other Spaniards were associated with them, Manrique de Lara, the queen's mayor-domomayor, and the duke of Francavilla. On the other hand, neither the victories of Emanuel of Savoy, nor the ties of blood between the king and Ottavio Farnese, nor the old services of Ferrante Gonzaga, nor the recent and distinguished services of Egmont, were potent enough to give them a place in the council. Even the younger Granvella, who had been engaged ever since his youth in the policy of the monarchy, was invited to the sittings only on occasions when his presence was indispensably necessary, but on all others he was really excluded from the general deliberations *. It was thought enough to give him a post in the Netherlands, an important one no doubt, but not commensurate with his former position. Whatever consideration was bestowed on the others, seemed only to be with a view to preventing them from giving themselves up to any foreign potentate, and to keeping them in some degree in good humour †.

Such was the first shape assumed by Philip II.'s council of state, and whatever enlargements it received were made in the same spirit. We find admitted into it the presidents of the council proper of Castile, of the council of inquisition, of that of the orders, and of the old council; we do not find in it a president of Aragon; and if a president of Italy sat in it, it was that same Francavilla, who had been a member of it already, before the time of his presidency.

Through these two changes, the suppression of the general administrative council, and the metamorphosis of the privy council into a completely Castilian shape, Castile was decidedly exalted to be the head of the empire; the greatest influence over the remaining territories was afforded to the Spaniards. "The king," says Soriano, "has no regard but for Spaniards; with these he converses, with these he takes counsel, with these he rules‡." What was the effect of this we shall have to consider by and by: the question at present is, what was the shape assumed by the supreme administration, and how far did Philip remain independent or dependent with regard to it? In the beginning of his reign king Philip adopted the following course: after the first hours of morning he gave audience to foreign ambassadors; he then heard mass

* Lippomano on Don John: "in somma vuole essere tenuto Spagnuolo in tutte le cose."

† Sommario dell' ordine che se tiene alla corte di Spagna circa il governo delli stati del re catolico, MS., thus enumerates the eleven councils: "Il consiglio delle Indie—di Castilia, (i. e. the supreme court of judicature of Castile)—d'Aragona—d'inquisitione—di camera (a part of the supreme court before-mentioned)—dell' ordini—di guerra, (i. e. the privy council, with the addition of some persons acquainted with military affairs)—di hazienda—di giustitia—d'Italia—et di stato"

‡ Tiepolo: "Non si trova mai S. M. presente alle deliberationi nei consigli, ma deliberato chiama una delle tre consulte, secondo che il negotio gli aspetta: l'una è di Spagna, l'altra delle Indie et la terza d'Italia, alla qual sempre si ritrova."

§ Sandoval, Vida y hechos del Emperador Carlos V. ii. 756.

* Soriano: "Monsignor d'Aras, se bene è stato adoperato tanto dall' imperatore nelle cose grandi et se bene resti con quel suo grado col re, però non va nel consiglio et non vien chiamato se non s'ha da trattar cosa che habbi difficoltà o che non si possa nascondere."

† Soriano: "Più per bisogno che s'havea di lui (Ferrante Gonzaga) che per volontà che havessero di favorirlo."

‡ Soriano adds: "Contro il costume dell' imperatore fa poco conto d'Italiani et di Fiamenghi et manco di tutt' i Tedeschi. Et se bene intratiene huomini principalissimi d'ogni natione delli suoi regni, però si vede che non vole admettere alcuno nelli consigli secreti." In another place: "I Spagnuoli come figliuoli primogeniti sono più cari et più favoriti. A questi si danno li premj, a questi li honori."

in his chapel; after this he dined publicly; and after dinner he received the petitions, and heard the requests of his subjects. In all matters laid before him, he referred to his counsellors; all statements were reduced to writing by a secretary, and sent to the functionaries to whose department they belonged*. Their decisions were communicated to the king in the consultas he appointed; or, as was afterwards the exclusive practice, they were given in to him on a sheet of paper. The petitioners now received the king's final reply confirmed by his signature.

Now if the king, as Tiepolo assures us was still the case in 1567, made it a regular practice to ratify the decisions of the privy council except in matters concerning Flanders, and those of the other functionaries except in matters of grace†, it is essential that we should know the conditions of these functionaries, and particularly the intrinsic constitution of the privy council, from which issued the most important decisions.

Now it happened that the two leading personages in the privy council, Ruy Gomez de Silva, and the duke of Alva, set themselves in decided mutual opposition.

Ruy Gomez had ingratiated himself with his lord and master by his personal address, and by the talent with which he played the discreet courtier. Modest in questioning, and concise in his replies, not much given to debating, seeking to know no more than his sovereign chose to imply, and keeping every thing secret, not exalting his house beyond a moderate degree of splendour, he perfectly fell in with Philip's ways. It was by an easy and unassuming, a helpful and compliant alacrity in service, that he won his favour; and he was very well aware that he must hold fast by these qualities. He was content to carry his point, even though the means were not altogether agreeable. It was his opinion, that if a man had a better insight into any matter than his sovereign, he should carefully avoid letting the latter ever become aware of this; that it was not so much by direct advice as by covert hints a man should accomplish his ends; that one should be the Mæcenas of his Augustus, and then would he be held meritorious before God and man. Cabrera calls him a lucky pilot in the perilous gulf of the court; but he was unquestionably more than this, he aimed at preserving more than himself‡.

A very different man was Alva, with nothing of these arts and these discreet considerations. His influence he owed to his distinguished merits as a subject of the monarchy, to his hair grown grey in the service of its kings, to his experience, his reputation in war, and his ever determined soul. He desired to maintain or to augment that influence, but by no personal suppleness. If he desired practical power, he wished likewise for its visible semblance. He evinced towards the throne the bitterness of wounded pride that feels it has an unlimited lord above it. It was not said for the first time in the days of Frederick the Great, that a monarch sucks the pomegranate and then flings away the empty rind. The saying was the Duke of Alva's. "But we must not let ourselves be sucked dry," he said, "we must not let ourselves be read through and through. Men fling aside a book they have read to the end*." They were talking once at the court of the possibility of conquering Portugal, and the good marquis de los Veles declared how much he desired it. Alva took a different view of the matter. "What asylum," said he, "would our children have left them, to fly to from a king?" He bethought him that the marquis was no friend to him. He had the face to relate this incident himself to the king. And yet he conquered Portugal: and yet he wished to see the immunities of the Aragonese suppressed; and yet he went to bring Flanders under the yoke†. For he had the aristocrat's inclination to help despotism, provided only he did not himself endure its pressure.

Such were the rival leaders of the privy council. If they had conflicting interests and pretensions, if their respective relations and friends stood aloof from each other, still it was principally by the antagonism of their own natures that they were alienated from each other. Their respective positions with reference to the king, are not badly expressed in the words Alva ventured to let fall in the royal antechamber, namely, that his rival "was not exactly qualified to give advice, but was a master in the art of humouring the one within there ‡." They implicated the privy council and the whole court in their strife; there was scarcely anything on which the two factions thought alike.

Did the king remain unaffected by this discord? Had it not an essential influence on his system of government, nay, on his own opinions and decisions?

He did not remain unaffected by it. As in the collisions that took place between them, he sided now with the one, now with the other; as he commended first Ruy Gomez, and then Alva also to an adelantado to which they both lay claim §, so he allowed them both a certain influence; and we find him limiting for the sake of the one, what he had conceded for the sake of the other. Ruy Gomez succeeds in having a Mendoza appointed ambassador to Rome; Alva contrives that he shall only be an extraordinary ambassador. After this Ruy Gomez procures a resolution that the post of ordinary ambassador should be conferred on Vargas; but Alva excites doubts as to whether Vargas was of sufficiently noble birth for so high a post; and the king joins in the doubt ||. Now if a stranger had any point to carry at this court he was

---

* At first this was done by the Ajutanti della camera. Tiepolo: "Li memoriali visti da alcuni suoi ajutanti di camera sono inviati al secretario di quel consiglio che ha questo carico d'espedir questi tali memoriali. Onde conviene che quello che negotia, anda a quel consiglio a qual è rimesso."

† "Rare volte sono mosse le deliberationi da S. M.—rare volte si parte dal loro conseglio."

‡ Cabrera, Don Felipe segundo, p. 184, 712, and elsewhere. Compare also Scipio di Castro, Avvertimenti respecting Sicily, p. 340; Molino's Report on Savoy; and above all the letters of Antonio Perez, the intimate friend of Ruy Gomez, particularly Carta a un gran privado, i. p. 75.

* Alva's words were, "Reyes usan de hombres como de naranja, que la buscan por el zumo y en sacandosele la arrojan de la mano." Perez, Segundas Cartas, p. 136.

† Relacione de Antonio Perez, p. 131.

‡ "Gran maestro de lo di aqui dentro." Alva's words as quoted by Antonio Perez. Cart. i. 75.

§ Lettera di Monsignore di Terracina, nunzio di Pio IV., MS. mentions this: "Come Sua Maestà è benigna e gratiosa e non può denegare il suo lavore a chi ne richiede."

|| Ibid.

driven to despair, seeing on the one hand how necessary it was to conciliate both leaders, since they both had influence with the king, and on the other hand how impossible it was to stand well with the one without losing the good will of the other. People thanked God when they were in such a position, that though they had not either decidedly on their side, yet they had neither decidedly against them [*]. It was only a Roman ambassador who succeeded in gaining the good will of both ; for had not the one just as much reason as the other to covet the pope's favour ? Here their strife put on a new shape, and they vied in proving each his own devotedness. And after all, Monsignore di Terracina, papal nuncio in Madrid, was obliged to promise both the victory in the affair of the adelantado; assuring Alva, who only demanded justice, he should have an impartial tribunal, and giving Ruy Gomez, who wished to be favoured, reason to expect judges inclined to his interests. It is easy enough to see how matters stood. Almost every affair was made subject of dispute between the two party leaders; both possessed undeniable influence, both sought to exert it to the utmost, and on all occasions; the consequence was, that the greater the importance of any affair the less likely was it to be brought to any definite conclusion, and that the tardiness in all official proceedings, which had already been noticed under Charles, now reached an intolerable degree [†]. So far then was this conflict of interests from being without influence upon the state. But would any one have imagined that it was not altogether unwelcome to the king? Yet such would almost appear to have been the case. Every occupation, Philip once said, has its rules, and so has that of a king as much as any other. Accordingly it was for good and substantial reasons he did not appear in the privy council. The presence of the sovereign is a bar to the free utterance of opinion, and makes every man speak as if he stood in a pulpit. But leave the members to themselves, then they fall into disputes, and when they are heated their opinions and their passions display themselves more in their true colours. Their mutual strife will afford the king the best advice, if he can only find a faithful reporter [‡]. He thought he could in no way gather better counsel than from the conflict of opinions. It is said that in the affairs of Flanders he sometimes had a sitting held in which Ruy Gomez only, and another in which Alva alone of the two rivals was present, so that he might fully possess himself of their several views [§].

In fact this monarch did not keep himself wholly independent either of the one or the other ; nevertheless he maintained a certain superiority over both. If I am not mistaken he had naturally a decided susceptibility for others' counsel, a decided need of it; but therewith so strong an inclination to be personally active, to carry out business with his own hand, and so lively a jealousy for his own supreme consequence, that though he did not indeed escape the influence of others, but underwent it perhaps unconsciously [*], still he well knew how to prevent its ever obtruding itself very manifestly. Nevertheless there can be no doubt that Ruy Gomez gradually acquired the upper hand, so judiciously did he comport himself towards his master, so much did he possess the art of bringing about his designs without letting them be perceived; so much was he aided by his office as *somiglier du corps*, which kept him always near the sovereign's person. In affairs of war indeed Alva always had a decisive voice; but Ruy Gomez gave the empire itself a pacific tendency; in doubtful cases he was always for peace. The finances, and the affairs of the home administration, were almost wholly in his hands [†].

While these two men thus strove with each other, whilst Alva saw himself ousted from the foremost place by a man of supple character, who was not particularly remarkable for his distinguished services, and whilst he was probably for that reason filled with the bitterness we note in him, it came to pass that a third candidate for the royal favour rose to eminence between them both.

A doctor stepped in between the prince and the duke. This was doctor Diego Spinosa, who had risen through the gradations of judicial offices to the dignity of president of Castile. After this, having now more frequent opportunity of approaching the king, he ingratiated himself with his majesty in the highest degree by his dignified appearance, the originality of his character, and the lofty intellect of which he gave token [‡]. He was indefatigable in his love of labour, even to jealousy of others. He managed almost alone the business of the council of Castile, and gave the other members as little as possible to do. But this was not yet enough for him. He furthermore took upon him the office of grand inquisitor ; he presided in the council of Italy ; he also took an active part in the privy council; and in all these occupations he was equally ardent and prompt. Couriers, who arrived in Madrid with the news of a vacancy which had just occurred in Granada, found him already in possession of the fact; they found the office about which they had been dispatched already disposed of through his intercession. When he rose at last to be cardinal, and the king consequently treated him as an equal, advancing to meet him before the door, uncovering to him, and offering him a chair, so great was the consequence he obtained in the eyes of the people that he was called the monarch of Castile. Many regarded him as a man designed by nature to reign.

I know not whether Ruy Gomez was aiding in

---

[*] Soriano : "Chi vuole il favore del duca d'Alva, perde quello di Ruigomez : cosi per contrario quel che cerca quel di Ruigomez, non ha quel del duca: et può ben ringratiar dio chi si governa in modo con l'uno et l'altro che non s'acquisti contrario a l'uno et l'altro."

[†] Soriano, where he speaks of the strife : " Donde è nato nasce e nascerà ogni desordine di questa corte : perche con questi dispareri si ritarda l'espeditione di tutte le cose et publiche et private, con pena et disperatione di chi le tratta."

[‡] Cartas de Antonio Perez.

[§] Tiepolo : "Conoscendo che per gli odii che sono tra il duca d'Alva et Ruigomez, in cose di tanta importantia, quando havesse seguito senza altra consideratione li loro consigli, haveva potuto divenir in qualche discordine, però a parte consigliava in questa mattina (materia no doubt) in absentia l'un dell' altro et poi deliberava quel che più credeva dovesse esserli utile."

[*] Soriano : "L'imperatore si governava in tutte le cose per opinion sua : il re per quella d'altri."

[†] Tiepolo.

[‡] Perez compares his favour to a flash of lightning : " Privó como relampago." Segundas Cartas, n. 48 a Francisco Lercaro. For the rest see Cabrera, Felipe II. p. 700 ; Strada, de Bello Belg. dec. i. lib. vi. p. 161, edit. Ratisb. 1751, fol.

the promotion of Spinosa; but Cabrera asserts that Spinosa stood by Ruy against Alva, whom they both hated alike. They belonged therefore to one party.

Such was for twelve years the state of things at the court of Spain; two factions engaged in continual secret war; the king rather more inclined to the one, yet without at all sacrificing the other; both actively participating in the administration. We notice them from the time of the king's accession. Soriano tells us, in the year 1558, how both parties exerted themselves for the honour and welfare of the king, but in different ways. In the year 1560, Monsignore di Terracina describes how these parties swayed the court more than ever *; and in 1567, Tiepolo says that no subject presented itself, on which Ruy Gomez and Alva were not at variance.

But afterwards, we find one leader after another supplanted. Alva first.

In the year 1567, the state of affairs in the Netherlands seemed to call imperatively for some attempt to set them at rest, either by mild means through the king's presence, or by force with an army. Ruy was for gentle measures, Alva for force. The king was for the latter course, and he committed the execution to Alva himself. He gave him an almost absolute authority, as the princes of that house more than once did by tried and approved commanders, such as Gonzalvo de Cordova and Pescara in former, and Spinola and Wallenstein in subsequent times †. He dismissed him with such authority, and it seemed a great mark of favour. For all that it was not prejudicial to Alva's opponents. They now enjoyed their influence in public affairs, untroubled by the interference of their detested rival; they controlled the state from its centre. Meanwhile, Alva perpetrated those atrocities in the Netherlands, which have brought down on him the execration of posterity; which were not satisfactory to himself, for he might at the same period have won in warfare with the Turks a better fame, after which his catholic heart thirsted; and which finally, as they failed at last of their purpose, did not advance him in his master's favour.

Spinosa was the second who fell. It was easy to resist an open and decided opponent, whose steps could be discerned; but it was hard to counteract the secret insinuations to which Philip's ear was always open. Spinosa, the very man who seemed to have least to fear from them, was the first to feel how dangerous they were. Was it, perchance, his multifarious activity itself that displeased the king, or the complaints made by the grandees of the pride and inaccessibility of the new cardinal, or other things which have not been revealed? It was Philip's wont to hearken long, and to hearken again, and long could he keep his thoughts concealed, till at last the measure of his wrath was full, and suddenly overflowed. Suffice it to say, as Spinosa was once addressing the king on a Flemish

affair, the latter broke out vehemently against him, and abruptly announced his disgrace. Strong and elastic as was the mind of Spinosa, it was not sufficiently so to endure this: he died that same year, 1571 *.

Had not the old favourite, Ruy Gomez, now reason likewise to fear. "Señor Antonio," he said to Perez, "believe me, I would gladly fly from this court, could I but do so †." He complained sometimes of the king, saying that a favourite felt more sensibly a slight scratch of the skin, than another would a wound to the bone. He dreaded those secret influences, from which, however, there was no withdrawing the king. He could never rest in full assurance of the royal favour. Accordingly, he was always on his guard; always striving to disarm his opponents by favours obtained for them, and at the same time to give them evidence of his power. And in fact, he was very adroit in these things. Unbending as was the character of Don Carlos, who hated him, and who felt himself affronted if people refused to communicate to him what had passed in private between them and the king, still he managed to subdue even him, and finally to gain him over to his interests ‡. By such dexterous caution, exerted without ceasing, he contrived to preserve his influence without any essential diminution till his death, on the 22nd of July, 1572.

But the party that had gathered round him was so well established, that even the death of their leader could not break them up. The princess of Eboli, the widow of Ruy Gomez, supported by the memory of her husband's services, and by powerful relations, maintained a great influence at court. The marquis de los Veles, now the queen's mayordomo-mayor, a man of whom Philip said he was wholly his own, so thoroughly devoted did he appear to the royal person, figured among the men as the head of this party. They saw their friend, Antonio Perez, making bold and rapid way, his influence being founded on the reports with which he furnished the king from the privy council, and not less on the entire devotedness he manifested to him in his efforts to court the royal favour §. The party, closely knit, held together for a considerable time. At last the events in the life of Don John of Austria decided their fortunes. We must give some account of him in this place.

3. *Digression respecting Don John of Austria.*

It may be supposed that Charles V. loved his natural son, Don John, the more, because he was the child of his old age, the offspring of an amour wrapped in the profoundest mystery. Nevertheless, he gave no heed to him, either during his life or in his will, but contented himself with recommending him to Philip. Was it from regard to the weal of the monarchy, as is supposed, or was it more probably from narrow-sighted love for the child, that he recommended his successor to have

---

* "Ho cercato d'informarmi con diligenza degli umori di questa corte et inteso primeramente che regna più che mai l'intrinseca discordia cominciata molti anni sono tra il duca d'Alva et il principe d'Eboli: onde non solo il consiglio di stato, ma tutta questa corte, è divisa in fattioni."

† Tiepolo: "Si risolve S. M. mandarlo in Fiandra con absoluta podestà, così nel conceder gratia, distribuir gradi et honori," etc.

* Cabrera.

† Cartas de Antonio Perez, i. 151.

‡ Tiepolo: "Odiava (il principe Carlo) Don Ruigomez, se ben il era maggiordomo maggior: ma è tale l'astutia con che procede, con la quale (a more than Latin construction) astringe hora ad amarlo."

§ See the Relaciones and Cartas of Antonio Perez passim, and Cabrera.

the boy brought up only with a view to clerical honours * ?

In this respect, however, Philip did not follow his injunctions, and probably he regarded it as not the worst act of his life, that he complied more with his brother's inclinations than his father seemed disposed to do. From his earliest years, John displayed a sanguine, lively, and intelligent character, decidedly more adapted to arms than ghostly exercises ; for the rest, modest, amiable, and good. In all the unhappy circumstances in which Don Carlos, who was his junior only by one year, and who had been brought up with him, was involved with his father, John manifested a fidelity so unassailable by force or persuasion †, that Philip resolved to employ him in war and statesmanship. The privy council failed not to perceive the unpleasant results that this resolution might have, and hesitated awhile before they acceded to it ‡. But did not the realm require a brave young leader, such as he promised to be, a leader of the blood royal ?

Accordingly, Don John was sent in the year 1569, against the insurgent Moors of Grenada, accompanied by men of experienced knowledge in war, and by a secretary, Juan de Soto, of the party of Gomez, in whom the most implicit confidence was reposed. The young man now evinced a courage and a talent for war, that forthwith opened to him a grand career in life. The progress of the Turkish arms was still a common source of alarm to all Europe ; the conquest of Cyprus was beheld as a general calamity ; and as, moreover, there was no war elsewhere, the eyes of all Christendom were bent on the league which, after long delays, was at last formed by some western powers against the enemy in the East. At the head of that league stood Don John, as leader of the combined fleets. What may have been his feelings when he won such a victory as that of Lepanto, a victory so glorious, complete, and decisive, as had never before been achieved by Christendom ; when, young as he was, he appeared in his own eyes, and in those of others, in the light of a hero and a champion, a very hope of Christendom ! But a change took place in him at this moment.

Don John was in the prime of youthful manhood. When he appeared among the ladies in the winter entertainments at Naples, whither he went after the victory; his figure of the middle size, and fairly proportioned ; his long light hair thrown back from his temples with a certain grace, after a fashion which his example brought in vogue § ; with the

most agreeable manners, and full of sprightliness and gaiety, it may easily be imagined whether he was a favourite with his fair friends. He was a capital rider; no one surpassed him in tournaments and in the use of arms ; after dinner he might be seen playing at ball for five or six hours together, and not sparing himself, for in this too he would be the foremost. But this was not enough for him. He knew well how valuable a thing it is to appear fluent in discourse, courtly, able, and well informed. He comported himself very discreetly with foreign ambassadors ; after having transacted business in the morning with secretaries and councillors of state, he often retired to his studies in the afternoon *. He won so far the praise he coveted ; but his heart was not yet contented. His whole soul, unsatisfied by the honours daily paid him, and by all he had already achieved, panted after still greater renown. He talked of nothing but deeds of war and victory. He averred that he would fling himself out of the window if he saw any one who made more way than himself on the path of fame. His maxim was, " He who does not push forward goes back."

How did it come to pass that he was no longer content to lend his arm to great enterprises, but that he wished—and this was the change that manifested itself in him—to become independent, to have a dominion of his own, and to be a sovereign? Was this a necessary ingredient in that honour he sought in the eyes of Europe ? Or did he feel that Spanish policy was no native element for him, and that he must look for some power of his own? Perhaps he was urged to this desire by the Spaniards themselves. Munificence was among the princely virtues he longed to make his own; he gave away 10,000 ducats on a pilgrimage to Loretto. His brother's privy council however thought him sufficiently recompensed by a grant of 40,000 ducats yearly. Moreover he was the son of an emperor. He often complained that his father had not enabled him to maintain any independent existence, and yet had recognized him †.

Such an independence he thought of working out for himself, and his grand aim was to win it in a Turkish war. The liga first of all gave him hopes, and he expected to render the Venetians such services that they would bestow on him an independent state. But the liga broke up before his eyes ‡.

The privy council of Spain itself now set a prospect before him, by commissioning him to conquer Tunis. Don John accepted the task with delight. Juan de Soto often spoke of the flourishing empire of Carthage, which had taken its rise in that very gulf of Tunis. The Lilybæan harbour was reno-

---

* Strada, de Bello Belgico, dec. i. lib. x. p. 259. Lippomano (Relatione di Napoli) calls John's mother " Madama di Plombeo," a Fleming, (the Blombergs deny the relationship)—" di notabile stirpe in Fiandria, la quale hora vive in Aversa con un marito, che le diede dapoi Carlo V. con X mila duc. d'entrada." MS.

† Original documents in Llorente, Histoire de l'Inquisition. Lippomano : " Essendo ben giovanetto non volse acconsentire a gli trattati del principe Carlo : anzi con gran pericolo della sua vita gli scoprì a S. M."

‡ Perez regards, as a peculiarly important secret, the division in the royal councils respecting the destination of Don John, " y los fines de cada vanda dellos." Segundas Cartas, 142.

§ Lippomano : " E di bellissimo aspetto et mirabil gratia ; ha poca barba et mustacchi grandi : è di pel biondo et porta lunghi i capelli et volti in su, chi gli danno grande orna-

mento, et veste sontuosamente et con tal attillatezza, in modo che è un stupore a vederlo. E poi agile et disposto compitamente, riuscendo senza paragone negli esercitii del corpo."

* Lippomano : " Molte volte sta fin a sera solo nello studio scrivendo di sua mano."

† Ibid. " Più volte ha havuto a dire con dolore, che havendolo publicato per figliuolo in vita doveva anco darli il modo da vivere in quella maniera che deve un figliuolo di così grande imperatore, senza rimetterlo ad altri."

‡ Ibid. " Hebbe pensiero che questa republica gli fusse per dar qualche stato nel Levante ; ma con la rottura della lega cessò per all' hora questo disegno."

vated and called the harbour of Austria *. On the same ground on which Charles V. had won his fairest victory, Don John was likewise victor; he took Tunis by storm, and Biserta surrendered to him. His hopes now rose higher; he requested his brother, through the pope, to nominate him king of Tunis. An unexpected, an appalling request for the privy council of Spain ! They had thought to employ the prince's talents for the aggrandisement of the Spanish empire, and now it appeared he thought of becoming independent. It had wisely determined that Tunis should be demolished, and the country defended only by the fortress of Goletta: how totally different would be the case if Tunis were erected into a kingdom. Philip thanked the pope for the good will he manifested towards his brother, but he rejected the request†. He went further. He persuaded himself that none but Juan de Soto was the deviser of such bold schemes ; to remove him from his brother he gave him another place, and sent Escovedo in his stead. Don John was now so discontented that he deemed it a disgrace to be already twenty-nine years of age, and not yet to have won any territory of his own. He would by no means let Soto quit him ; we find him employing both secretaries, and very soon Escovedo was filled with extraordinary projects more than Soto had ever been.

Now what do they purpose doing ? Would they provoke a war, in order to secure an opportunity they could not otherwise have? Don John expressed himself very peculiarly on this point. " When the *comite* says, Ave Maria, the sailors respond, Be she welcome: so will I do too, and wait my opportunity, not seek it ‡." Or since internal troubles might well afford him a chance of possessing himself of Genoa, would he take advantage of this, as was commonly talked of and desired by his whole court ? " God forbid," he said, " that I should ever be instrumental in stirring up war among Christians. My father often had Genoa in his power, yet would not subjugate it; my brother follows his example, and so will I." All his schemes were directed against the Turks. He devised a new and well contrived plan for this war, which continued uninterruptedly, and in which Tunis had just been lost again. The system of the Spanish monarchy against the Turks was altogether defensive; it cost from four to six millions a year, and yet the defence was in no place strong enough to withstand a vigorous attack. Don John suggested that this expense might be spared, and the amount employed in augmenting the fleet, so that it might command the sea, and render it possible to undertake offen-

sive measures on an important scale *. It was his ambition to have the uncontrolled command of such a fleet of three hundred vessels, or thereabouts. It was reasonable to expect that the Venetians, who had cause to apprehend from so faithless a neighbour the same fate for Candia and Corfu that had befallen Cyprus, would after all afford their co-operation. The Turks from being the assailants might then be made the assailed, and seeing the existing condition of their empire, the most brilliant results might be anticipated. But it was to no purpose he stated all this to the privy council. " Had it been advisable Charles V. would have done it," was their reply †. They took no heed to the difference between Soliman and his successors, or to the fact that in the days of Charles V. such a course as that proposed was forbidden by the interests of Doria. There was no moving these Spaniards to any innovation. Don John was forced to confess to himself how matters stood ; he was forced to admit the conviction that there was no hope of a well concerted enterprise on the part of Spain alone against the Turks, nor yet of a league: it has always been a prominent tendency of European policy to preserve the Turks ; at last he was constrained to turn away his thoughts from this favourite conception of his youth.

They were now entangled in the mazes of European intrigues.

Philip, weary at last of the war in Flanders, which Alva's violent measures had rather kindled than extinguished, now bethought him that the people of the Netherlands had always shown a certain partiality for Don John, who was born among them, and who so much resembled the father they held in reverence ‡. Why should he remain any longer in Italy ? Philip determined to send him to the Netherlands to allay the troubles there by amicable means. Don John, without hesitation, declared his readiness to undertake the office. He sent Escovedo to the court to procure what was necessary for his journey §.

But were his views directed only to the Netherlands ? It would doubtless have been an honourable renown to have reclaimed revolted provinces by gentle means, and to have assuaged the rage of angry passions: but he who would seek such a renown should not be a young man. He had other objects.

He had become acquainted in Italy with pope Gregory ‖, and with the Guises ; and these had

---

* Raggazzoni, Relat. di Sicilia, MS. " Don Giovanni d'Austria andando con l'armata al re Filippo all' impresa de Tunisi fece curar et aprir essa bocca et vi entrò dentro con l'armata predetta."

† Memorial de Antonio Perez del hecho de su causa, p. 188.

‡ " Non posso negare," said Don John to Lippomano, " di esser giovane et soldato, et soglio dire che chi non mira innanzi, a dietro torna: ma non voglia Iddio che io desideri mai che sia istromento di guerra tra Christiani. Contra il Turco sono dritte le mie speranze : pure alla fine in qualunque parte mi venga l'occasione di adoperare l'armi, dirò come si dice in galera quando il comite dice Ave Maria che ogni uno risponde Sia la benvenuta: così farò io, vendendomi l'occasione."

* Lippomano calculates thus : " Le 300 galere, como si potriano tenere armati colgono o sei mesi dell' anno solamente, così tenendo anco di 150 continuo con ogni sorte di provisioie et di genti da spada ancora non costeriano, per conto particolare che io hebbi da un principal signore, più che 2 milioni et mezzo d'oro l'anno, con facilità di fare quell' impresa che le Signorie Vostre Ecc. si possono imaginare."

† " Rispondendo S. M. et alcuni del conseglio di Spagna, che se il fare un numero grosso di armata et levar parte dei presidii fusse stato giudicato espediente dall' imperatore Carolo V., la M. S. l'haverebbe fatto."

‡ Lippomano: " Sendo di madre Fiamengha et il nome suo celebre in quei paesi bassi." Philip said he expressly sent him " para ser governador, no como en los principios de la guerra." Cabrera, 845.

§ Lippomano and Perez, 191.

‖ It is to be remarked that Escovedo was at the court of Gregory. " A Santità Sua ho mandato a dir a bocca per lo secretario Escovedo."

directed his whole attention to the affairs of England and Scotland, and to that lovely woman in her prison, to whom the crowns of both kingdoms seemed of right to belong, and who numbered so many adherents in both countries. John entered into these schemes[*]; they harmonized at once with his chivalric inclinations, his catholic feelings, and his thirst to win himself a kingdom. Only the consent of Philip II. was indispensable.

At last overtures were made to Antonio Perez. Assured of his silence, the parties interested applied to him in profound secresy to exert his influence in the matter[†]. The man they selected was able enough, had he only been more trustworthy. Perez went instantly and imparted the whole secret to the king.

How astounded and alarmed was Philip! He saw that Escovedo too was following precisely in the footsteps of Soto. So he forbore to dispatch his business, and he sent Don John no money. But far greater still was his alarm, when, contrary to an express command that he should without delay cross the Alps, and contrary to the order of Juan Idiaquez, Don John arrived in Spain on the 23rd of Aug. 1576, entered the roads of Barcelona with three galleys, and at once took his way to Madrid[‡]. Philip hardly knew how to measure out to him the marks of honour he should receive, without on the one hand offending him, or on the other encouraging his aspiring soul to greater ambition. Should he forbid his enterprise? In that case his zeal in the affairs of the Netherlands would be damped. Should he consent to it? He no longer trusted him: this would be still more dangerous. But Don John pursued his course so steadily, he proceeded with such perfect knowledge of the court and of his brother's temper, that the latter at last acquiesced in his design. He was at liberty to attempt it with the Spanish troops, which in any case were to be withdrawn from the Netherlands.

John arrived in the Netherlands provided with money, full of grander hopes and purposes than ever, and connected by new and closer understandings with the Guises. His first efforts were for the pacification of the country. The people too were disposed that way, and it was not long before an arrangement was come to on all but a few points. Who would have supposed that in those exceptional points the interests of Philip and Elizabeth, such bitter enemies, coalesced, and that the Netherlanders combated them both at once without being aware of it? The matter was, that the Netherlanders demanded the immediate evacuation of the country by the Spanish troops by land, and were inexorable in their determination that this should be so, whilst Don John thought of removing them by sea, and demanded three months' delay to allow of the fleet being equipped §. This frustrated the whole design, Philip's consent to which

had been specially given on the aforesaid condition. This was really a curious conjuncture of things. Elizabeth is freed from a great danger, of which she is perhaps unaware. The Netherlanders are her preservers, without their suspecting that they are so. What they do, they do to the delight of Philip, their own and Elizabeth's vehement adversary. But was all this indeed not so wholly accidental? Was there a natural connexion between these events, though concealed from the eyes of the public and of historians?

There was nothing more to be expected of Philip in this matter. The pope, indeed, interceded in the most urgent manner to press the execution of the design. He ordered his nuncio in Flanders, who was best informed respecting the affair, to proceed to Madrid, charging him immediately on his arrival to make "a spirited attack" on the king; and he wrote letter upon letter to the nuncio, always to the same effect. In truth, the nuncio displayed a zeal in stimulating the king, and in propitiating the ministers, which promised assuredly in the end to further an affair which he represented as a matter not of choice, but of necessity. Philip, moreover, willingly lent his ear to such representations; he listened with interest to more detailed discussions, and he even gave access once more to Escovedo, and communicated to him papers not before in his hands, which bore upon the subject. So far the nuncio had hopes. But if, as he says, he sought to entice the king further, if he would obtain from him a decisive word, the king retreated; "the affair," he would say, "was difficult; it needed further consideration." At first, this hesitation and evasion seemed probably chargeable upon the ministers; but the nuncio soon saw that the cause lay deeper, and that the king was filled with distrust against his brother. He wrote to Rome, that if they would have the design prosper, they must at least give up all thoughts of Don John[*].

Thenceforth things wore a darker and darker aspect daily for Don John. It is the nature of the soul, that when disappointed in its original purposes, it indulges in vague longings and projects, and gives itself up to far greater schemes, as though it would defy untoward fortune by the grandeur of its enterprises; doubly does it feel conscious of its repressed energies, but at the same time a gloomy discontent sits brooding in its inmost depths. In the first place, Don John became aware that he could not remain in the Netherlands. It was necessary to establish there a popular system of government, more suitable to the yielding softness of a woman, than to his temper and his youth; he was not made for the dull routine of such a government. Besides this, the presumptions against him were too strong[†]. Ere long we find him tormented with impatience to quit the country. He said there

* Strada, de Bello Belgico, particularly i. c. viii. 232.

† "Que haga officio," says Perez himself, "con su Magestad, para que su Magestad tenga por bien que si haga la empresa de Inglaterra y que el Señor Don Juan sea acomodado en aquel reyno." The pope refers his nuncio in the year 1577 to Perez, Ministro principale del re, che intendeva bene il negotio. MS.

‡ Cabrera. Particularly Memorial de Antonio Perez de hecho de su causa, 192.

§ Perez. Cabrera, p. 899, is silent on this point. Bor, Nederlandsche Oorlogen, i pp. 765. 841, edition of 1679,

states these things in detail. Even supposing him to have made use of Perez, as I think is probable, yet he has much special matter derived from other sources, The Justificatie der Staten tegens Don Jan, Bor, 159, is decisive. Wagenaar, Niederland. Gesch. iii. 382, follows Bor.

* Relatione compendiosa della negotiatione di Monsr Sega, vescovo della Ripa et poi de Piacenza nella corte del re catolico, MS.

† Brieven van den Heere Don Jan aen den Heere Antonio Perez van den 7 April, 1577. See a very important piece from letters seized in Gascogne, in the Byvoegsel van authentyke Stukken, Bor, 167. Also Bor's eleventh book.

was nothing he would not sooner do than remain there; he would be gone, right or wrong ; he would do so, though he should pay for his offence with his blood; he wasted there life and honour, nay, his soul was perilled by his desperation *. But after all, his mind was not decidedly made up. For awhile, he thought of attempting the English project in another way ; now he thought it more expedient to return to Spain, where, with the aid of his friends, he could have no difficulty in placing himself at the head of the administration; and now he requested permission to take part in the French war, as leader of an independent force of 6000 infantry and 2000 cavalry †. All these wishes had for their ultimate end a great dominion, whether in England, France, or Spain. In fact, the proceedings he engaged in, from motives of this kind, cannot have been perfectly inoffensive. It was known that he kept up intimate correspondences in Italy ; the Spanish ambassador in France noticed very distinctly, how frequently his envoys presented themselves to the Guises, and how often the Guises visited him in the Netherlands ‡. At last, well-informed persons spoke seriously of a league concluded between Don John and the Guises, ostensibly for the support of the two crowns, but in reality, for the purpose of subjecting both to their party. For what other object could such a league have ? The very thing of which the Guises accused Henry III., a lukewarm indifference in the affairs of the catholic faith, was at this time chargeable, with some show of truth, against Philip II., who was not to be moved to any decisive warfare against the Turks, who had only yielded a forced and reluctant consent to the enterprise against Elizabeth, and who had concluded peace with the people of the Netherlands.

Philip now knew enough to be filled with suspicion, and to fear what he knew, but still more what was unknown to him. He had found means to make himself acquainted successively with all the secrets of the party, through Perez, who was in their confidence ; and he even went so far as to allow the minister, for the sake of appearing more attached to them, to write disparagingly of his master, the king himself enduring to read the drafts of these letters, and to correct them with his own hand §. Such was the craft necessary to obtain a knowledge of Don John's designs. Now, what was Philip to think, when it was reported to him that Escovedo had let fall hints that all Castile might be mastered from Santander and Peña de Mogro ; and when Escovedo himself soon afterwards sent him in a memorial, requesting that Peña should be fortified, and that he should be put in command there ? Escovedo pursued all his affairs with an ardour intolerable to this deliberate monarch ; he was importunately eager for the despatch of his business. The theme of Don John's letters was continually, " Money and Escovedo, and more money."

Now as Escovedo seemed exceedingly dangerous, dangerous if he remained at court, still more so if he went back to Don John, Philip resolved to have

him put to death, but in such a way that suspicion should not fall on himself, but on others. Perez took upon himself to see that Escovedo should be killed. Some * say, indeed, that the king did not command the assassination, that he only did not disapprove of it ; but is not a king's approval in such a case equivalent to a command ?

This was the sorest blow for Don John. It is hardly possible that he should not have seen into the secret bearings of the case, and been sensible of his brother's hatred. The affairs of the Netherlands had taken a turn that promised tedious wars and odious difficulties without end, a turn moreover which was imputed to his impetuosity †. He was once more indeed victorious, but he felt the vigour of his life already broken. He now only dreamed of finding in a convent the contentment which the world denied him. He comforted himself with the bitter consolation, that he would devote himself, among the hermits of Montserrat, to the service of that God who was mightier, and more gracious than his brother Philip ‡. But even this was not vouchsafed him. Young as he was, his life declined as if bowed by age, and many feared that he was labouring under the effects of poison. He died in his thirty-third year, on the 1st October, 1578. His heart was found dried up, and his skin withered as if by fire. For the wretched remains of his mortal existence, of which so little other trace remained, that it was as though it had never been, he begged of his brother in his last moments a place near the bones of their father ; then would his services be well repaid §.

Such is this world. It tempts a man to unfold all his innate powers ; it stimulates all his hopes. He then thinks not of moderation or self-control ; conscious of his own energies, he presses onwards after the proudest prizes of honour or worldly fortune. But the world grants them not ; it closes its bars against him, and leaves him to die.

4. *The second ministry of Philip II.*

Whilst we follow the course of events, whilst we seek to explain them from their moving causes, in whatever these may have had their being, whether in the soul or in personal circumstances, or otherwise, we fall in occasionally with unexpected expressions, that suggest to us the presence of a secret element at work in the events ; expressions, on which it is very hazardous to build, while on the other hand it would seem negligent to overlook them. We meet with such an expression respecting the court and state of Spain, and belonging to the year 1578, of which we are treating. It is fully authenticated ; it is recorded by the imperial ambassador, count Khevenhiller, who is generally rather prone to suppress such things, and it is ascribed to the almirante of Castile, a man of the fullest information, who lived in the midst of public affairs. The almirante complained to the count that Philip's government was a government not of justice, but of revenge : the children of those who had taken part in the war of the comuneros

* Carta del Señor Don Juan de primero de Março de 77 a Antonio Perez. Perez 195.
† Carta de 3 de Hebrero de 77, Perez 196.
‡ Ragguaglio delle pratiche tenute con il re di Spagna dalli Signori di Guisa nella lega di Francia in tempo del re Henrico III. Inform. xvii. No. 11, MS.
§ Perez, Memorial.

* Cabrera. Perez from the king's letters, p. 200.
† Negotiatione di Mᵣ Sega : " Restando il re mal satisfatto dalla sua ritirata in Namurco, dalla quale pareva che fossero procedute le perdite di tante piazze et provincie intiere."
‡ Strada, de Bello Belgico, x.
§ Cabrera, Felipe segundo, lib. xii. cap. xi. p. 1008.

against king Charles and the nobility, were now at the helm, and their aim was to revenge themselves on their opponents [*]. Can it have been, we ask, that in spite of so totally new and altered a condition of the state, the old Castilian factions still subsisted, and continued to wage secret war with each other? And if a man of such note and so intimately acquainted with the existing state of things made this assertion, can it have been that no other traces appeared of this continuous strife?

It seems that such traces did exist. Those animosities, which had formerly divided the Spaniards between Ferdinand and Philip I., still endured under Charles. We recollect it has been asserted that Chievres leaned more to the one party, Gattinara more to the other. Navagero tells us, with reference to the year 1525, that all Toledo was divided into the factions of the Ayalas and the Silvas [†]. The Ayalas had adopted the side of the comuneros, the Silvas that of the king. It seems however that Charles had contrived to retain both parties in his service. On the accession of Philip II. they make their appearance again. Cavallo tells us that Philip II. bestowed such high favour on the condestable, a leader of the party of the nobles and of Philip I., that the consequence would necessarily be the decline of the house of Alva [‡], a house that had always been against this party, always on the side of Ferdinand the Catholic, and frequently on that of the towns. May there not have been some connexion between these facts and the enmity between Alva and Ruy Gomez de Silva, who was very closely connected with the first houses of the grandees? Cabrera does not conceal the fact that the old parties still subsisted in the time of Philip II. in Plasencia, Truxillo, Xeres, and Seville; and he extols this sovereign for the ability he showed in preventing the outbreak of their mutual hatred [§].

Now if those dissensions among the Castilian nobles, which displayed themselves so violently in the war of the comunidades, were in fact not yet allayed, it remains to be asked who were those powerful sons of the comuneros of whom the almirante spoke? There may possibly have been a greater number, but unquestionably I find at this time at the court only two chiefs of the comunero party, but those two from the capitals of the realm, Toledo and Madrid. The Ayalas in Toledo and the Zapatas in Madrid were at the head of the insurgents against the king. In the year 1578 we find a Zapata, Francisco count of Barajas, mayordomo-mayor to the queen, and an Ayala, Pedro count of Fuensalida, mayordomo to the king; the latter so much in favour with Philip, that after the death of Alva he succeeded to all the latter's court preferments. May we suppose that the influence which Alva still maintained after his return throughout numerous vicissitudes [||], the influence

of Chinchon de Bobadilla, of the house of Cabrera, which had once been in the position of that of Alva, and the high consideration enjoyed by Almazan, were regarded by the almirante as effects of the power of the comunero party? Thus much is clear, that this party had much to do with the final overthrow of that of prince Ruy Gomez, and that the before-mentioned Zapata in particular had much share in the downfal of Perez.

The prince's party belonged by all means to the opponents of the comuneros; and so in a remarkable degree did the Mendozas, the family of the princess. The wife of Perez was of the family of the Coellos, who adhered so strenuously to the emperor's party in the insurrection that their mansion in Madrid was demolished by the Zapatas [*]. We will not however take upon us to affirm that nothing but the old quarrel set on the enemies of the house of Eboli. Other causes may also have co-operated to this end. It is enough to say, that enemies there were, and that they were powerful.

The princess, Veles, and Perez, at this time the sole remains of the Eboli party, were soon aware of this among themselves. The princess felt most sensibly the diminished favour with which her house was regarded. When the president of Castile repeatedly refused her privileges which had before been conceded to her, and which were still constantly enjoyed by others, she addressed herself to Philip as her king and as a knight. "The president," she said, "fortified himself with the royal name. Was this the gracious reward for her husband's long services? Was her house wholly to lose all that remained to it, the credit and consideration it had hitherto maintained [†]?" What Veles most felt was the unhappy contest with a violently incensed party, which there was no hope of overcoming, since they had a thousand holds upon the king. He felt this so keenly that he preferred to quit the court; that in his exile he consoled himself with the reflection that he had escaped the outbreaks of this enmity; nay that he even thought of fleeing to Peru. "They oppress thee," he exclaims, "even when they do not possess the king's favour; let them once obtain that, and they will take away thy honour and thy life [‡]."

Lastly, Perez felt the preponderance of his antagonists as a personal mischance. Antonio Perez belonged in every respect to the number of those Spaniards of former times, who combined with a gravity, that became with them a second nature, a passionate eagerness to enjoy the world, with profound pride a still more profound craft, and with much external religion a policy regardless of all principle. He was at once a statesman and a courtier; the fortune of a royal favourite was the aim

---

[*] Khevenhiller, Annales Ferdinandei I. fol. 41.

[†] Navagero, Viaggio in Ispagna, p. 354.

[‡] Cavallo: "Ha grande inclinatione al contestabile di Castiglia, di modo che questo farà anco che il duca d'Alva et la casa di Toledo non continuerà in favore come è al presente."

[§] Cabrera, 273. The Peticion xlviii. of the Cortes of 1558 may also refer to this, where it says, "En los pueblos hay opiniones enojos y enemistades."

[||] Negotiatione di Mr Sega of the year 1577. "Il segretario Antonio Perez, con quale concorrevano l'arcivescovo di To-

ledo, il marchese de los Velos, il Escovedo: ma dell' altro canto il duca d'Alva con altri che lo seguitavano. Questa diversità di pareri era non solo in questo negotio (d'Inghilterra), ma anco negli altri più importanti di Fiandra."

[*] For the "grandes enemistades entre los padres y abuelos del Conde de Barajas y de Doña Johanna," see Perez, Relaciones, 119. Perez adds, in the later editions of his Memorial, p. 217, "En verdad, algunos ministros de las persecuciones destas personas eran descendientes de los comuneros."

[†] Carta de la Princesa d'Eboly al Rey, in Perez, Relaciones, 15.

[‡] Carta del Marques de los Velez, 26 Jan. 1579, in Perez, Relaciones, 12.

of his endeavours. For this he ventured to play the perilous game of sharing the confidence of two enemies, and betraying one of them; for this he looked even on crime steadily and unflinchingly; " he needed no other theology than his own, which allowed him this * ;" with such a sort of ingenuous simplicity did he habitually practise these principles, that he tells all these things without reserve or apology. When he lent the king his hand in so serious a matter as the murder of Escovedo, he no doubt thought that he should thereby gain another step in the royal favour. Soon after the deed Philip conferred on him the place of prothonotary of Sicily, with a revenue of 12,000 ducats; he also gave him the office of secretary to the council of Italy, by virtue of which the greater part of the affairs of that country were also placed in his hands. In the enjoyment of this favour, still young, in the full possession of bodily and mental vigour, alert and spirited,—had Perez reason to fear for himself † ?

The hostile party was in such good condition that they ventured to assail even him without hesitation. They made use of the assassination of Escovedo, the suspicion of which he had brought on himself. They particularly employed against him a man like himself, a cabinet secretary of the king's, named Matteo Vazquez. This man had acquired his master's entire favour, and great influence with him in the discharge of his office, which consisted in sorting the memorials sent in, distributing them among the several functionaries to whom they appertained, receiving their opinions thereon, and laying them before the king for his final decision. The count de Barajas and the king's confessor were his patrons, the princess and Perez hated him ‡. He returned their hate. He went so far as to append with his own hand a lampoon against them both to a document addressed to Perez from the royal cabinet. Could it have been supposed that Philip should have caught up the lampoon with curiosity, read it, recognized the handwriting of his secretary, and yet not punished him ? At first the king excused himself, saying, that " the man had matters of too much moment still in his hands." Afterwards he exacted from Perez, nay, even from the princess, a reconciliation with Vazquez, and he was indignant when this was not complied with. Whilst he now continued to write to Perez, whilst he consoled him for the loss of the marquis de los Veles, who died on his journey, telling him that he, the king, would not fail him, he had nevertheless resolved on his fall §. On the 28th of June, 1579, an alcalde put Antonio Perez in arrest in his chamber, and on the same day the princess of Eboli was carried off to the fortress of

Pinto. So ended the prosperity of the party of Ruy Gomez *.

It is not necessary to examine further how the affair of Perez, the chief feature of which was the prosecution for the murder of Escovedo, carried on by a relation of the murdered man, terminated after being repeatedly suspended, and taken up again, after reiterated promises and deceits, in close imprisonment, torture, and flight. It is very remarkable of Perez, how the devotion to the king, implanted in him from his youth upwards, was not to be shaken by any indignities; how even in his exile in France, he was always discreet, betrayed no secrets, uttered no unseemly accusations, contenting himself with mere self-defence, and saying nothing worse than that he could tell more if he would ; how moreover he lived on solely in the recollection of his court favour and fortune, till at last he made it his task to lay down rules for princes and favourites; rules that really display deep penetration, though I know not whether they ever proved more useful to others than to himself †.

What is most important to our subject is the change effected in Philip's ministry on the day of the arrest of Perez. On that same 28th of July, 1579, Granvella and Juan Idiaquez entered Madrid, the former called to the presidency of the council of Castile, the latter in opposition to the king's express command. But that express command had been given at the instance of Perez, who feared the influence of Idiaquez with the king. Probably the latter was well aware how slight was the hold Perez had on Philip. He followed the advice of Granvella, and went to Madrid in spite of the prohibition; the arrival of the two was fatal to Perez‡. Though I cannot distinctly show the connexion between these events, it is nevertheless manifest that there was a very intimate association between them.

From that time Granvella and Idiaquez took the helm. The potency obtained by the former, though never much talked of, nor ever placed in the same conspicuous light as that he had exercised in the Netherlands, was perhaps the most important he ever possessed. Idiaquez was in high favour with the king. There was soon associated with these two a third, named Christóval de Moura, who secured to himself a still greater share of Philip's favour. However great may have been the influence occasionally obtained by others, it was these three, and after Granvella's death the two remaining favourites alone, who managed the machinery of the Spanish empire.

A general remark presents itself to us touching

---

* Copia de un villete de Antonio de Perez para S. M. respondido en la margen de su real mano : the king replies, "Segun mi theologia yo entiendo lo mismo que vos." [According to my theology, I think as you do.] Memorial, p. 198.

† Contarini, 461 : " Questo Antonio Perez fu intimo et confidentissimo segretario di S. M. et maneggiava li più importanti et segreti negotii dello stato, onde dalla gran confidenza che in lui mostrava il re, cominciò ad assumersi maggiore autorità di quello che si conveniva."

‡ Cabrera, 971. Perez speaks of a " Liga del amistad del conde de Barajas contra la amistad de los Veles y de Antonio Perez."

§ Palabras singulares del Rey, in Perez, 179.

* We find (e. g. in Leti) complicated stories of the amours of the princess of Eboli with the king and with Perez. Let the reader take into consideration that the princess was already in years, and had lost an eye, that the wife of Perez, doubtless not devoid of Spanish jealousy, gave proof of enduring passion for her husband ; after this, let him believe such late rumours if he has a mind to do so.

† A MS. essay, " Discorso bellissimo di quello devon fare i favoriti," affords us indications of the applause obtained by these Cartas : " Con tanto e così continuo applauso ! Mi fu," says the author, " al fine data questa lettera per cosa unica e singolare, et chi me la diede, come pretiosissima gioia me la porse." The letter is from the Cartas.

‡ A letter of the king's at the moment of Granvella's arrival. Memorial, 205. Cabrera, 1047 —copious respecting Moura.

E

their policy. During the first twenty years of his reign, Philip's efforts were directed to the maintenance of peace, and to the preservation of things as they were. If he waged war in Flanders, he had there to do with a rebellion, which he had provoked indeed, but a rebellion it was. War was in this case only a means to the maintenance of his authority, and of the Catholic religion. But elsewhere Philip engaged in those years in no extensive schemes; he did not sow dissensions in foreign countries, nor had he any thoughts of universal monarchy. From the very first he plainly lacked the ambition, and the bold projects of his father. This was especially what Don Carlos regarded as censurable, and unworthy of their ancestors. The Venetians, on the other hand, and the Italians, thought this very thing highly laudable. Whichever judgment was right, the fact at least was admitted on all hands *.

That which properly brought on this monarch the world's hatred, which has so long clung to his memory, belongs to his last twenty years. It was within this period he conquered Portugal, and sent out the armada against England; it was then he had a hand in all the internal commotions of France, and sought to bring the crown of that realm into his own house; it was then he waged incessantly vehement and successful war upon the Netherlanders, and then too he destroyed the freedom of Aragon, and exhausted and ruined the resources of his kingdom.

Whence proceeded so striking a change? It may perhaps be imagined that the spirit of the times drove him upon a different path from that on which he had set out ; for if I am not deceived, about that same period all Europe assumed a far more warlike aspect than it had previously worn. But it is very plain that this new impulse proceeded for the most part from the Spaniards and from himself. Furthermore, if we consider that the party of Ruy Gomez, which had hitherto ruled the state, had always leaned to pacific measures; that the grandees, who adhered to that party, had invariably insisted on a peaceful accommodation even of the disturbances in the Netherlands, particularly in opposition to Alva's adherents; that it was not till the fall of the Gomez party, and the formation of a new ministry, that the new principles came in vogue; it will then appear in the highest degree probable that it was not so much a new modification of Philip's character that caused this altered policy, as the change of ministers, and if any thing besides this, nothing more perhaps than casual opportunity.

We have no difficulty in pointing out the transition by which Philip's earlier policy passed into that of his later years. Whereas there was nothing that sovereign had more dreaded than the schemes of the Guises, which embraced at once England and Scotland, France and the Netherlands, and the confederacy we have mentioned as subsisting between them and Don John; it was now that very same confederacy which his ministers adopted in his name, and those same schemes were now taken up by himself †. Europe now dreaded alike his ends, and the means he took to gain them; it feared

the means, those subtle deceitful arts of which every one believed him guilty whether he practised them or not; such, for instance, as his writing that letter, in which he, the most Catholic of sovereigns, was said to have offered money to the Protestant princes of Bearn to induce them to attack Henry III., a dispatch in which the hand of Idiaquez was recognized: it feared the end he aimed at, the establishment of an universal monarchy. The idea of the balance of power had taken a peculiar shape about this time. It was wished that two great powers, tolerably equal in strength, might stand over against each other, so that the smaller powers might always find protection from the one or the other *. The destruction of such an equipoise seemed destined to lead directly to universal monarchy. It came to pass that Philip gradually became hated and dreaded by all Europe, by those he immediately attacked, and by those who were remotely threatened by him.

Thus we perceive how important was the new ministry. Moura was so especially; he was, as a Relatione says, the soul of Philip. Whilst Philip could not sufficiently extol him, declaring, "he had never found a man so deserving of trust in the weightiest affairs, so loyal to God and his king, so free from ambition and avarice † ;" the rest of the world beheld him with wonder, amazed to think how he had contrived by his services and his moderation to acquire such complete control over this monarch, who in his later years was almost inaccessible to every one ‡. Next to him a considerable influence was permanently maintained by Idiaquez, who had the talent to play even the second part, and who was given credit for shrewdly shaping his course by the prevailing wind §. Contarini drew no bad parallel between these two men in the year 1593. "Idiaquez," he says, "having seen much of the world, knows how to content those who transact business with him. Moura, a Portuguese, having never been beyond the Peninsula, is more austere and intractable. The former, who long filled the office of secretary of state, is much better acquainted with foreign affairs; the latter, who did good service in the conquest of Portugal, is a greater favourite with the king. The former is recommended by long service and great experience; it is the advantage of the latter that he is placed in his majesty's chamber, and is frequently about the royal person ||. It is common to them both that it is only in urgent cases they importune

---

* Discorso al Sʳ Landi, MS. "Essendo questo regno pervenuto nel presente re di Spagna tanto amico e desideroso della pace et particolarmente d'Italia."

† The embassy of Alonso de Sotomayor to France, Cabrera 1009.

* Perez: "Que se conserven en ygual peso para balanças, en que los demas se ygualen y contrapesen para su conservacion.

† Philip's words, reported by Gonzalo Davila, Felipe III. p. 13.

‡ Cabrera, 1045: "Muchos servicios y su moderacion le conservó siempre bien visto."

§ Davila, Felipe III. p. 36.

|| Contarini: "L'uno che è Don Giovanni, è Biscaino; l'altro è Portoghese. Quello ha la cura delle cose d'Italia: questo di Portugallo e delle Indie. Quello per essere stato per il mondo da maggiore satisfattione a i negotiante: questo per non essere mai uscito di Spagna è più austero e difficile. . . . . Quello per la lunghezza della servitù è più stimato: questo per godere l'officio della camera di S. M. ha più spesso occasione di trovarsi (appresso): quello per le lunghe esperienze è più adoperato. . . . . Il consiglio di stato e gli altri consigli di S. M. non hanno alcuna parte nelle cose importanti che alla giornata occorrono, ma solamente li sono delegate alcune di poco momento."

the king with anything novel, and that they procrastinate all business, all weighty decisions, as much as possible. By so doing they please his majesty. He gives them proof of this, not only by his munificence towards them, but above all, by the exclusive confidence he reposes in them. Only trivial matters are now laid before the privy council, and it has no power. Every thing of moment is discussed and settled by these two."

5. *Philip III. and Lerma.*

Now if it is probable that a sovereign so busy, self-willed, and alive to his own interest, as Philip was, so dependent on his ministers, that with a change in these his whole policy underwent an alteration, what must have been the case under his son, who was neither efficient, nor shrewd, nor had any will of his own ?

Philip II. died in great despondency. He witnessed the delivery by Moura of his key of office to the prince's favourite. The last order he reluctantly gave was to that effect. The dying monarch was not spared; he was forced to see the transference of power to that man whose influence he most feared [*].

It requires a sort of self-denial to resolve on being in all respects the follower of one's predecessor. Commonly princes form for themselves a system of action that suits their nature, long before their accession to the throne; and this they continue, not making their own lives a mere sequel to their fathers'. Had not Philip II. done this ? He too had committed the management of the state to the court assigned him for the service of his person. So likewise had his son, and so do all monarchs.

When Philip II., some years before, designing to form a court for his son, looked about him for persons of good birth and good reputation, yet not self-sustained and independent, he fixed his eyes on the count of Lerma, a courtier who with little property contrived nevertheless to content his creditors [†], to marry his sisters well, and to sustain a character for liberality. He placed him among the rest, but the count soon overtopped his fellows. The marchesana de Vaglio [‡], and Muriel, gentlemen of the bed-chamber, both of whom were in favour with the prince, rendered him services. He contrived to help the prince out of his little embarrassments. It was observed that when the latter had promised a new suit to the court fool, and could not give it him, whereupon the fool importuned him with many a biting jest for the fulfilment of his promise, Lerma failed not to satisfy even the fool. But the main thing was that the count exercised a direct personal influence over the prince, for which there was no accounting on extraneous grounds. It was to no purpose that the king banished Lerma to the Vireynat of Valencia ; his very exile, his secret correspondence, and now and then a pretty present, only stimulated the prince's regard for him, and when he returned he was the declared favourite. When Philip III. ascended the throne there was no doubt as to the future.

His first act of royalty was to receive Lerma's oath; his first order, an unparalleled one, was to the effect that Lerma's signature should be as valid as his own. His first favours were conferred on Lerma; on the day the old king died it was made manifest that Lerma was all in all with the new sovereign [*].

Don Francisco Gomez de Sandoval y Roias, first count, and afterwards duke of Lerma, was one of that class of men who have the art of seeming. No man could bestow more care on his outward appearance, on his hair and beard. He was already advanced in years, but he did not give token of this. He had not much real knowledge, yet he seemed to have mastered all branches of study, both theoretically and practically. He perfectly understood the wonted tactics of statesmen high in office, to send away contented all who appear before them, and even those who were most aggrieved he dismissed best satisfied [†]. He appeared open-handed and sumptuous, and in his manners and habits there was a certain royal magnificence.

His power in the state was based chiefly on the consulta, that most private council in which all the resolutions of the various functionaries were examined, and either adopted, or modified, or rejected, and from which initiated all grants of royal favour. Lerma transacted business in this consulta with the king; and this council, which had formerly been the focus of royal omnipotence, was now that of ministerial despotism; all its decisions depended essentially on Lerma.

So potent was the personal influence he had acquired over the king. Restlessly, carefully, and jealously, did he labour to retain it without a rival. He was apprehensive at one time of his sovereign's Austrian consort, at another time of the sister of Philip II., who was still living in Madrid, and who was scarcely his friend. He would not allow the two to converse together alone, or in German, and it is supposed he removed the court to Valladolid for the purpose of parting them. He went so far as to enjoin the queen never to speak to her husband on affairs of state, not even in bed; so that miserably restricted and circumvented as she was on all sides, she often wished that she was cloistered in the convent of her native Grätz, rather than queen of Spain [‡]. Even Muriel, and the marchioness de Vaglio, seemed to Lerma not sufficiently trustworthy ; in the end, he thought it best to remove them. He trusted no one but the father confessor, fray Gaspar de Cordova, a man who went about in

* Davila, Felipe III. lib. ii. p. 40.
† Khevenhiller's report of 1606: How Lerma avoided "pleito de accreditores." Annal. Ferdin. vi. 3040.
‡ Khevenhiller: the Marchesa della Valle "die nit klein Ursach dass er in dieser Privanz."

* Relatione della vita, etc. " Niuno si dubitava d'altro se non che havesse d'essere potentissimo, et così fu tanta la moltitudine della gente che concorse a visitarlo et a servirlo, che bastò per isbigottire li altri pretensori."
† Ibid. " La piacevolezza del privato è così grande che quel che Tito diceva, ' neminem e conspectu suo tristem discedere,' fa al proposito, che a chi con l'opere non si può dar sodisfattione, si dia con le parole." Khevenhiller interweaves with his German the following Spanish words respecting him : Lerma, he says, is " sospechoso, codiciosissimo, y para sacar un gusto suo no mirara cosa alcuna," p. 3041 [suspicious, very covetous, stopping at nothing to gratify any desire of his]. We do not however put implicit faith in Khevenhiller.
‡ Imprimis Khevenhiller, vi. 3040. Rel. della vita, etc. " Con l'imperatrice, che sia in cielo, hebbe S. E. alcuni dispareri : . . , . ma sendo egli così gran potente e quella principessa lontana del mondo, li fu agevole il tutto vincere."

a ragged cowl and torn shoes, and who had neither talent nor inclination for affairs of government; and this man was entirely devoted to him *. Then he had in his house a young page, aged twenty, named Rodrigo Calderon, indefatigable, clever, subtle, and wholly his own. He promoted this young man to the gold key, and to the daily society of the king, and gave him the secretaryship of the consulta. Rodrigo, arrogant, full of effrontery, and greedy of gain as he was, nevertheless contrived to ingratiate himself completely with the king; but he was a man who needed a master; he was nothing but a subtle servant, without loftier views; he always employed his position for Lerma's advantage. The other persons about the king were likewise more devoted to Lerma than to himself. It is incredible to what a degree he was under subjection to the favourite. It was observed once, that he made up his mind to make a little resistance against Lerma; but upon the very first attempt to do so, he was seen to tremble all over. He could not keep any secret from him. Lerma was charged with the use of magic arts †.

The favourite next filled the most important places with his own creatures ‡. If Loaisa, archbishop of Toledo, was guilty of the villainy imputed to him, of having brought up the king with the hope and intention of making him his tool, he was now bitterly repaid for this, when Lerma announced to him in the Escurial, that the king had quitted the cloisters, but that he, the archbishop, might remain in them to consecrate an altar or two. He saw his own work turn to his destruction in the hands of his enemy. He died soon afterwards, from mortification of mind as it was supposed. After this, Lerma likewise removed the grand inquisitor, Portocarrero. He bestowed the two vacant offices, of which the one was regarded with deference and submission by the clergy for its time-honoured dignity, the other for its real power, on his uncle Bernardo de Sandoval. The presidency of the council of Castile, and with it the control over the civil affairs, was lost by Rodrigo Vazquez, who had so long held the office. Lerma gave it to Miranda of the house of Zunica, a man who had acquired a name by the part he took in Don John's campaigns; fortune, by a prosperous marriage, which no one would have predicted for him, for he seemed a mountain of flesh; and consequence, even in the eyes of Philip II., by the way in which he had made his functions subservient to the support of the royal prerogatives. Lerma brought him entirely into his interest by a marriage between their children. Miranda allowed Lerma to interfere with the business of his own office, one of the hardest things for a man to submit to who covets distinction §; but

his wealth daily augmented, and his splendour grew every day more and more dazzling!

The next thing to be done was to purify the privy council. Moura was made viceroy of Portugal, and soon took his departure for that country *. Juan Idiaquez was as compliant as ever, and the king and the favourite willingly allowed him to retain some of his consequence for the sake of his name. Probably Francesco Idiaquez, the brother of Juan, was not so tractable: or was it, that his office was thought of such moment that it could only be entrusted to a person of implicit devotedness? Lerma removed him. Now, while he was looking about for a fit successor for him, it happened that a certain Franchezza was trying every art to ingratiate himself with the potent minister. This man stood high in the estimation of the world in general, from the great Indian wealth of his wife †; he was recommended to the government functionaries by his prominent activity in the cortes of Aragon and Catalonia, and his support of Lerma's interests in those assemblies won him the goodwill of the minister. Lerma bestowed the secretaryship upon him, and found in him a man of unwearied industry, and inviolably devoted to him. He himself took Moura's place.

There is no telling the multitude of other changes Lerma found necessary. He treated even those he put down with a certain generosity; he left them their titles and their incomes, but he did put them down and remove them. Above all, he exalted his own family. His brother was made viceroy of Valencia, Lemos, his brother-in-law, viceroy of Naples. One of his sons in law was appointed general of the Spanish galleys, another president of the Indies, and his uncle, Borja, was president of the council of Portugal. He very soon allied himself by marriage with the families of Mendoza and Guzman: one of the former was made president of Italy, and another was admitted into the king's chamber; the post of grand-master of the horse was given to a Guzman. No sooner was an infante born than he was committed to the care of Lerma's sister. Gradually, too, he began to advance his sons to high dignities. The most important offices in the state were shared among this house, like a family property.

How rapid and complete was the change in this court from what it had been under Philip II. There was now a favourite invested with royal authority, a great noble family at the head of public affairs, and access to the king was thrown open to the grandees.

We shall see how the grandees lost their independence, lapsed from their warlike tendencies, and confined their ambition to leading a life of sumptuous display. They came back to the court vying with each other in this display. We find heads of families never making their visits but with twenty

---

* Relat. della vita, etc. "Credesi per acquistare la gratia del duca sotto ombra et colore di santità fusse instrumento di persuadere al re cio che il duce desidera et vuole."

† The serious opinion of the younger Khevenhiller.

‡ Relat. della vita, &c. "Ha saputo il duca così ben fare i fatti suoi che ha mutato et ritornato da alto a basso tutti i creati del palazzo et ha posto intorno al re huomini che del tutto son sue fatture: et se qualch' uno de creati vecchi, come Don Henrico Guzman, è rimasto di essere con S. M. famigliare, è molto certo che cercò prima et ottenne il favore del duca."

§ Ibid. "Vero è che alcune et molte volte il duca s'intromette nelli negotii con poca dignità del conte."

* Khevenhiller as to the years 1599—1602, p. 2584, etc.

† Relatione: "Figliuola di un calzettaro di Alcala de Henares, che era tornato dall' Indie con molta robba.—Le prime occasione che hebbe di farsi conoscere furono del 1585 nella corte di Monzon, ove come più vecchio protononotario di Aragona fu impiegato in quei negotii et mostrossi huomo da molto.—Partissi poi (1599) il re di Valenza et andossene a Barcellona per tenervi i corti di Catalani, et il duca di Lerma introdusse in quel negotio il segretario Franchezza, come pratico che n'era et conosceva li humori di Catalani. Di tutto diede al duca buon conio et molta sodisfattione."

carriages, and escorted by troops of gentlemen *. The ladies are accompanied each by their equerry on foot, and by all the gentlemen of her house †. The mutual reaction of the court and of the grandees produced a strange mixture of ceremony and luxury, which long continued predominant in all the courts of Europe, but which is particularly deserving of notice at the court of Spain. It has an immediate connection with Lerma's position and character.

What a singular ceremony was that by which every departure of the court from place to place was announced. On the day before the general move, a part of the establishment set out, preceded by trumpeters; the kings of arms, the German and the Spanish guards, began their march, along with many others on horseback and on foot, forming the escort of the great seal. After the kings of arms, and immediately after the keepers and the lord high keeper of the seal, followed two mules bearing a frame covered with green cloth, and surmounted by a canopy adorned with the arms of Leon and Castile : on the frame lay a crimson velvet case, and in the case the great seal ‡. Next followed four macebearers with their maces, and then the soldiers of the guards. The principal persons, however, of the escort, turned back to be present likewise at the departure of the king. This singular kind of parade was never more strikingly exhibited, than when the king or the queen ate in public. At the queen's table stood three ladies, with napkins neatly arranged over their shoulders. If the queen had a mind to drink, she made a sign to the first of these three ladies, she to the second, the second to the third, and the third to a mayordomo. The mayor-domo made a sign to a page, and the page to a servant in the room : the servant called out in a loud whisper, "Without there," and then the page and he went out to the sewer. The page came back from him with a full covered goblet in his right hand, and a gilded salver in his left. The servant accompanied him as far as the door, the mayor-domo went with him to the dais, and lastly the lady knelt with him before the queen. The lady tasted the beverage, having first poured some of it into the cover, and taking care not to touch even that with her mouth. The queen then drank; the lady and the page rose from their knees, and the former gave the goblet and the salver to the latter, which he carried back to their place.

But with all this formality and stiffness, the thing had still its lively and pleasant side. Grandees and knights stood lounging on one side of the room; the queen's ladies were present, the gentlemen accosted them, and a lively conversation was kept up. Even the three ladies in waiting were not so engrossed with their functions, but that they could salute their admirers *. It was this that made them so fond of the court journeys : the cavalier escorted his lady to her carriage, mounted his horse, and rode by her side, entertaining her with conversation by the way.

The luxury practised by this court was often ill directed; but again, it was allied with a better impulse towards literature and art. If Cervantes had at last the enjoyment of learned leisure, he owed it to Lerma; and it was to a great man of this court he dedicated his Don Quixote. But above all, the theatre was an object of passionate predilection. The king had for himself and his grandees two companies, whom he paid 300 reals for each performance ; refreshments were distributed during the entertainment; it was with extreme reluctance this amusement was foregone on occasions of mourning, and during Lent. As Calderon de la Barca resided at this court from 1619, from his eighteenth to his twenty-fourth year, that most plastic period of life, when the character usually acquires its peculiar bent; as it was in such scenes he unfolded his fine talents ; and as the court supplied him not only with spectators, but doubtless also with most of his dramatis personæ, and frequently with the subject of his dramas, we may fairly assert that we owe to this court, and pointedly to its fresh and original constitution, one of those few poets who have become European. The whole nation participated in this taste. To be sure, it was not permitted for any company to give representations without a license under the king's own hand †, and the permission was only granted because three fourths of every giulio paid for admission were handed over to the hospitals, and only one fourth to the players: still it was granted. In the year 1611 there were thirteen companies at the court, and in the country; and how far were the comedies, which began with the Cælestina, from the gravity of the court regulations !

We return to Lerma. Whereas, by his entire sway over the king, by means of the highest functionaries who were his instruments, by placing his relations in important offices, and with the aid of the grandees and nobles, whom he drew to the court, and on whom he bestowed favours and presents, he had made himself the centre of the state, he likewise conducted the foreign policy of Spain on new principles. His views at first were for peace, and to this indeed he was impelled by necessity. However strong the resistance he encountered on the part of the priests, who wished to see English protestantism extirpated ‡, on the

---

* Bassompierre, Journal de ma vie, p. 536; of Ossuna.

† Relatione di 1611 : "Le signore per servitio loro tengono le donne che vogliono : ma sempre hanno quattro o sei gentilhuomini, che non servono ad altro che ad accompagnarle fuori et assistono alle visite, non ostante che menano ancora seco *tutti gli altri gentilhuomini* officiali di casa, come maggiordomo, mastro di stalla et gli altri. Tengono ancora per servitio loro due palafrenieri et almeno quattro paggi. Per uscir di casa tutti hanno sedie e cocchio."

‡ Ibid. "Vanno dietro li 4 re d'armi con li loro habiti: seguitano le guardie del sigillo, con il guardiamaggiore : et poi una cosa come una lettiera, che portano due muli coperta di tela incerata verde, con baldachino foderato, con l'arme di Castiglia et di Lione dipinte, che porta dentro una cassa di velluto chremesino con l'inchiodature indorate, dentro la quale va detto sigillo reale; quale accompagnano ancora li 4 mazzieri con le loro insegne, et guardie d'Alemagni et di Spagnoli."

* Ibid. "Ragionano di quello che vogliono, con grand' allegrezza ; il che si permette in tali occasioni ; et l'istesse che servono, di quando in quando salutano li loro inamorati."

† Ibid. "Nessuno può far commedie publicamente nella corte senza licenza del consiglio reale, il quale da licenza alli commedianti sottoscritta dal mano del re, come si fusse cosa di gran consideratione. Et al presente sono 13 compagnie in tutta Spagna, et si comporta che rappresentino nella corte et tutta Spagna per l'utile che viene alli hospitali, perche ogn'uno che va a vedere li commedie da di limosina le tre parti di un giulio et la quarta parte alli commedianti." See also Bassompierre, Journal de ma vie, an. 1621, i. 537.

‡ Davila, speaking of the year 1603, relates, that in order

part of all those who claimed as it were for themselves a portion of the supremacy belonging to the king in the Netherlands; from the jealousy that had subsisted for many a year against the French; still he carried out his views; he concluded a peace with England; he recognized the independence of the Netherlands, and he effected a double alliance by marriages between the infantes of Spain and the children of the king of France. This helped him to success in another point. The Austrian family compact of the house of Habsburg, to which all other alliances had previously been postponed, was now pushed aside. Spain separated her own interests from those common to the whole house. The imperial ambassador lost the influence he had before possessed ; count Khevenhiller was among the number of the superseded and the malcontent. Lerma maintained in politics also the same opposition which he offered to the German influence at court. So closely were these things linked together, the most important items in the impulsive forces affecting the affairs of Europe, and considerations of so very personal a nature.

And here we cannot forbear from a general summing up of our observations.

Antonio Perez states that he knew the man who then held the helm of the state, he knew Lerma from his youth up; a young Rojas, a first cousin of the latter, had been brought in the house of Coelles along with his wife, and he had himself been visited by Lerma when a prisoner. This is in itself enough to draw our attention to the early position and connexions of the favourite. But Perez affirms furthermore, that the individual of whom he speaks had been a partisan of the prince Ruy Gomez. We are aware that the Guzmans, the Mendozas, the Sylvas, and other houses, which constituted the party of Ruy Gomez, now rose once more, and that the policy of the two ministers, the prince and the duke, was directed to peace with Europe. Is it too bold a surmise that the Eboli party was revived in that of Lerma? If this could be distinctly authenticated it would exhibit to us the policy of the Spanish minister in a new bearing. As we saw the pacific Eboli maintain the tranquillity of all Europe, Flanders excepted, over which his enemies had obtained influence; as we afterwards saw a warlike party driving out his, setting all Europe in confusion, and exhausting Spain; so we should now have grounds for concluding that after the old king's death the second party declined, and the first rose again and carried its pacific views into effect. At all events the heads of the Lerma party were in immediate connexion with those of the Eboli party. We might even follow out this clue further. We might see reason to conclude that the party of Ruy Gomez was one of an aristocratic character, that which followed it popular, and the new one again

aristocratic; that the efforts of the grandees, of the aristocrats, was for peace, those of the popular party for war.

Lerma did not succeed in maintaining himself in this position till his death.

Setting aside all the few extant narratives on this subject, with which inquisitive readers are entertained on the authority of Vittorio Siri *, I find two, decisive as to the dismissal of the favourite. In the first place, it was not so certainly the work of the confessor Alliaga as of Cordova. Alliaga allowed clerical complaints to reach the king's ears. " The wretched condition of the poor people was, after all, attributable ultimately to Lerma. How could it fare well with the catholic kingdom, if people granted peace to heretics, sanctioned the rebellion, and acknowledged the sovereignty of heretics ?" Religion was just the point on which the king was accessible, and through this he was acted upon by Fray Juan de Santa Maria Recolete, and brother Geronimo, a jesuit. " Even the lamb will sometimes utter a cry when too hardly dealt with." In concert with Alliaga, they made an impression on the king. They persuaded him that he acted unjustly in committing the realm entirely to his favourite †.

Next it befel, that a new union of the two lines of the house of Habsburg arose out of pretensions, which seemed destined to sever them for ever. Nothing is more important with regard to the whole body of policy, however little it be known. Philip III. laid claims to Hungary and Bohemia in full earnest, as a grandson of Maximilian II. Now this claim was not admitted by the archduke Ferdinand, afterwards emperor of Germany, who was regarded as the rightful heir to these possessions; but he promised under his own hand, in deep secresy, and with the privity only of his most confidential favourite Eggenberg, and of his chancellor Götz, that if he attained to the government of those kingdoms, he would consent to resign the Austrian provinces in Suabia, to Spain ‡. The designs of the Spaniards on the Valtelline, their enterprises against the Palatinate, the aid they afforded Ferdinand II. for the re-conquest of Bohemia (matters all of them so momentous with regard to the commencement of the thirty years' war), are hereby, and only hereby, placed in their true light. There appeared a prospect of founding a compact Spanish hereditary dominion, which should directly link together Milan with the Netherlands, and so give Spanish policy a necessary preponderance in the affairs of Europe. These were schemes altogether different from Lerma's pacific views ; in the first place they cemented the union between Austria and Spain as closely as ever; they also exhibited themselves as rigorously catholic.

---

to hinder a peace, proofs were adduced that the English treated the sacraments with contumely. But nothing can be more illustrative of the subject under consideration than the " Breve relacion de la vida y muerte y pios exercicios de Doña Luysa de Caravajal, que en estos dias (1605) murió en Inglaterra." Following the example of the female converters of the heathen, she went to heretical London. The narrative is to be found in " Oracion panegirica es a saber exortativa y consolatoria de la muerte della illustr. Doña Isabel de Velasco y de Mendoza." 1616. 4.

* Carta de Antonio Perez a un señor amigo, Cartas, i. p. 64; after the death of Philip II.

* Del Mercurio overo Historia de correnti tempi di Vittorio Siri, tomo terzo, Lyon 1652. He mentions these things, the " privanza del duca di Lerma combattuta dal figlio," on the occasion of the fall of Olivarez, p. 187. But we do not find where he got his information.

† The main points of all this matter are to be found in Gonzalo de Caspedes y Meneses, Historia del Rey Felipe IV. a history composed as early as 1631, by a man who had an opportunity of learning the truth, and who could venture to speak it.

‡ On this point only Khevenhiller, Annales Ferdinan. viii. 1099.

Lerma gave way before both these influences. He quitted the court on the 4th of October, 1618. He had one more quite private audience with the king for two hours. As he passed through the garden the prince met him to bid him a friendly farewell. About five o'clock Lerma stepped into his carriage. He looked out once more up to the windows of the apartment where he had so often talked and transacted business with the king, and he made the sign of benediction. Just at that moment the convent bells tolled in memory of one of the deceased queens *.

He withdrew, but not, as we see, in disgrace. On his journey he received affectionate letters, and a present of game hunted by the king himself. Philip III. was as much attached to him as ever; only he had been persuaded that it was sinful in him to give himself up to a favourite.

This event produced a conflict in the king's own mind that embittered his life, and especially his last moments. He exclaimed, "O who would not regret to have been a monarch!" and yet he was so habituated to the splendour, the imposing majesty, and the supremacy of royalty; he was heard to inquire, "Where is the prince? What is he doing? He will begin to exercise the functions of royalty; I shall no longer stand in his way." He did not wholly conceal how loth he was to part from the pleasing habit of monarchical authority. He was above all tormented with the fear of incurring eternal punishment for his abandonment of the duties of a ruler and his promotion of favourites. And yet these acts of favouritism were after all so natural to him, so strongly prompted by the constitution of his mind! At this very moment he sent and had Lerma called to him, and he bestowed on Uzeda, Lerma's son, who succeeded to his father's offices, a favour which he did not venture to accept †.

Before Lerma arrived Philip had died, in a state of dependence on the men he condemned, yet could not forego; in dread of that divine tribunal, before which it had been his serious purpose to stand clear, but under the sentence of which he fell by necessity through the consequences of that almost involuntary dependence; a man whom nature had made too good, and too weak, and too pious, for his station.

CHAPTER III.

Of the Provinces and their administration.

THE mode of investigation we have adopted, beginning from the centre and gradually embracing remoter circles, has carried us from the kings and those immediately about them, to their ministers and councils, and now places before our eyes the administration of the several provinces. Now this was no peaceful administration, the calm growth of time and of events, but one whereof the origin and the progress were marked with continual strife. The provinces often set themselves in vigorous opposition to the central power. The struggle be-

tween the two is the precise object of our consideration.

No question is more important for the whole history of Europe, for an understanding of the current moment as well as of the century just elapsed, than the question, how came the old Romano-Germanic state to be converted into the new? The matter may be put in general thus. Whereas the old constitution was based on individual and corporate immunities, which sought carefully to repel every incursion of the central power; whereas this central power was more acted on than active, and even by the natural course of things grew weaker from epoch to epoch; whereas, finally, the constitution was not yet shut in within itself, but saw its clergy dependent on a foreign supreme head, and its nobility and its citizen classes so much at variance that each body clung more to its co-equals in other countries than to its fellow subjects at home,—how came it that in the succeeding times the central authority restricted or overthrew the liberties that opposed it, hedged in the state more closely, and raised itself to intrinsic strength and power?

This could not have happened every where in like manner, nor any where without sharp contests.

The struggle in the Spanish empire is interesting for this reason, that we see the central authority engaged at once with very diversified constitutions. The Aragonese, though it was their boast that they were more faithful to their kings than any other people, had yet possessed themselves of such peculiar rights, that although the king's prerogative was often asserted, yet it never was allowed free scope for action. Similar rights were also shared by Sicily. Castile and the Netherlands did not present such close barriers to their sovereigns; but the time was not very long past since John II. had been kept a prisoner in the former country by the barons, and Maximilian I. in the latter by the towns. But little active power to enforce their wishes remained to the sovereigns. The state of public affairs in Naples and Milan allowed the kings more influence; but in Naples there were inveterate factions, threatening imminent peril every moment from their dissensions, whilst in the neighbourhood of Milan there was a strong enemy always on the alert to take advantage of every discontent in the country to establish a footing there. Now seeing that not one of all these provinces was much disposed to recognize or further the royal authority, how came the possibility of establishing over them all a vigorous and uncompromising central authority, strong without and within? Charles found himself in great perplexity shortly after his accession. Aragon made difficulties about recognizing him; Sicily expelled his viceroy; Castile broke out into complete insurrection. Naples vacillated at this moment, and the greater part of it deserted him when his enemy's forces appeared on the frontiers. He was forced to conquer Milan with arms, and to keep it with arms. The insurrection of Ghent showed how little the Netherlands were habituated to obedience. What means then had he recourse to, and what means did his successors adopt to secure themselves from insurrections, and to give more stability to their authority?

The question we see is twofold. First, were

---

* Chiefly from Cespedes. Some particulars from Khevenhiller, ix. p. 1245.

† See Bassompierre, Khevenhiller, and particularly Davila, ad an. 1621.

measures successfully taken to deprive the nobles of the influence over the rest of the state, to make the clergy independent of Rome, to diminish the customary immunities of the towns? Secondly, how far was it contrived to unite in the king's hands the legislature, and the judicial authority, and the force of arms? In a word, how was the old constitution assailed, damaged, or destroyed? How was a new one established?

The question is identical for all the provinces; but as they were in themselves so various it will be best to examine them one after the other.

I. Castile.

So long as Castile was under the sway of native kings, or of kings naturalized by length of time, no country ever suffered more from intense distractions and violent civil wars. It fell under the dominion of foreign sovereigns in the sixteenth century. How extraordinary that from that moment it enjoyed profound internal tranquillity! Nor let it be supposed that this was a consequence of the spirit of the times. The passions were hushed in this country whilst most others were rent by violent intestine wars. Even under the worst rulers we find among the Castilians no trace of anything but quiet and allegiance.

Now to have a clear perception of how this came about, we must recollect that all the old Castilian dissensions merged ultimately in the conflict between the grandees and the towns. This was the strife that during the fourteenth and fifteenth centuries kept all the nations of Europe in a continual state of warfare, always subsisting though sometimes latent, and breaking out only from time to time. The main subject of this quarrel in Castile was that the nobles had possessed themselves of the domains, and that the burthen of meeting the public wants out of their own property was thrown upon the towns. It was brought up upon every occasion; but when could a more likely occasion arise than when the succession to the throne became disputed after the death of a king? After the death of Henry IV. the towns sided with the party of Aragon, the nobles with that of Portugal; the towns were victorious, and by their aid Ferdinand and Isabella became the sovereigns of Castile. After Isabella's death the towns again declared for Aragon, for the widower; but the nobles, who were now of the Austrian party, sided with the son-in-law of the deceased queen. The nobles carried their point, and Philip I. ascended the throne. After the unexpected demise of this young monarch the old strife broke out a third time. The nobles went so far as to offer the government to Philip's father, the emperor Maximilian; it was not without vehement opposition on their part that Ferdinand, the Catholic, returned to the sovereignty of Castile; it was in spite of them, and only through the support of the towns, that he kept his ground; many powerful persons went in defiance of him to the Netherlands to attach themselves directly to the house of Austria. Was it likely that these factions should disappear when Ferdinand died? The minority of Charles V., and the mistaken measures of his ministers, caused the old ill-will of the towns to break out in open insurrection. That insurrection was decisive.

For a while the nobles looked on it inertly, for they too were somewhat offended by the predominance of the Netherlanders at the court. But when the towns brought up the old subject of quarrel, when they bethought them of demanding a restoration of the domains, the nobles seized their arms. They conquered at once for themselves and for Charles. His interests and theirs were most closely associated; they re-established the authority of the king. The grand question now was, how would Charles use this decision of the strife. Both parties were dependent on him, the nobles as his own party, the towns as defeated rebels. The question was, would he allow the former a share in his authority, and the latter opportunity to re-establish themselves; or would he find means to hold both in dependence, to keep the one party down and the other at least in abeyance.

The Nobles.

It was decisive for the position of the nobles in latter times that there was no longer war to wage within the limits of Spain. They had been used to keep bodies of troops in their pay, and to retain in their service beneath their banners a multitude of hidalgos who had no property. This greatly enhanced their consequence. But now the kings carried on their wars far from Spain; and the nobles were exempted from taking part in these, as well by their privileges as by the wishes of the kings, who did not choose any longer to have armies in which the formula for giving orders ran, " Such is the command of the king and the condestable *."

It was furthermore of great moment for the position of the nobles, that they could no longer make their way good at court, or in the higher offices of state. Charles hardly ever kept his court in Spain, and Philip II. contrived to hold the nobles aloof. It was a maxim with both to entrust important offices only to men like Alva, whose fidelity was beyond all question, and to none besides †.

Thus withdrawn from war, and from affairs of state, the nobles were likewise excluded from the national deliberations. This was in consequence of the proceedings of the national assembly of 1538. When Charles represented his necessities to the assembled cortes, and made known his intention of introducing the excise, he did not look to experience so much opposition from his confederates and friends as from the other members. But the nobles pointedly resisted him, the condestable Velasco most conspicuously, though he was a decided adherent of the house of Austria. Velasco insisted upon it that to bear burthens was in Castile the portion of the peasants, and that the least tax robbed the gentleman not only of all the immunities won by the blood of his forefathers, but of honour itself. He brought it to pass that Charles was addressed with the unwelcome and almost insulting advice to mend his affairs by staying at

* Relatione delle cose, etc. " Il contestabile nelli bandi mandava a dire: questo comanda il re et il suo contestabile: il che si è cominciato in Spagna ad imitazione di Francia."

† Contarini, MS. " I grandi sono dal re tenuti bassi, et non dà loro alcuno carico d'importanza in Spagna: et se li ne distribuisce alcuno fuori di questa provincia, sono brevi et spesso tramutati: onde non possono acquistare molta autorità. Sono admessi rare volte alla presenza del re per non dar loro reputatione."

home, and keeping himself within bounds. Had Charles persisted in his intentions, there would have been reason to apprehend an insurrection *. Seeing, however, that his demands were refused, he resolved at least, as Sandoval says, never again to assemble such powerful persons. This was the last general assembly of the estates that was convoked.

And now whereas the condestable had asserted that the nobles were bound to serve with their persons, but not by pecuniary contributions, they henceforth did neither the one nor the other, but became mere passive inhabitants of the state, cut off from all participation in public life. They fell back upon the enjoyment of their wealth in their country seats, and their somewhat Moorish palaces, almost windowless towards the street, built in the form of a quadrangle round a broad court-yard planted with trees †. According to an apparently very trustworthy enumeration of the year 1581, the heads of the Mendozas and Enriquez, the Pachecos and Girones, that is the dukes of Infantado, Medina de Rioseco, Escalona, and Ossuna, possessed in those days each 100,000 ducats yearly income, and the duke of Medina Sidonia, a Guzman, 130,000 ‡. Many of them had severally 30,000 families subject to them. They maintained a royal expenditure on the strength of this opulence. Each had a kind of courtly establishment, a master of the household, of the hall, of the chamber, of the horse, a mayordomo, an accountant and secretary, and a crowd of pages and retainers. Many had sumptuous body-guards of two hundred men, and they were particularly careful to have well-appointed chapels. Contarini describes these as incredibly fine, and rich beyond description. With what pomp was the lady of the house waited on! Her women tendered their services on their knees; the page who handed her the cup remained kneeling till she had finished the draught; even the knight of the highest blood whom she addressed, bent the knee to her as she sat §. The nobles vied with each other in pomp like this, and laid aside the warlike habits and feelings of their forefathers.

Noting then, how the nobles were naturally inclined to the king, and to his party; how they gradually disarmed themselves and their subjects by the adoption of a wholly pacific tenor of life; how they next, by applying their ambition to luxury and pomp, ruined their circumstances and fell into debt, we shall clearly understand how they would

necessarily begin to fear the king, they who in former times had made kings fear them*.

The nobles of subordinate rank could now no longer expect honour and advancement in their service. Cervantes mentions a proverb of those days ; " Choose the church, the sea, or the king's house." Many of the hidalgos, who used to serve under the banners of the grandees, now betook themselves to the Indies; others began to study in order to fit themselves for clerical offices ; others sought service under the king, in the field when there was war, in the palace when there was peace. As the king had the patronage of the three knightly orders, and had so many benefices in his gift, they could look to him for a suitable provision for the remainder of their days †.

And thus was actually accomplished the purpose of circumscribing the class of grandees, and destroying its influence over the rest of the state. When Lerma threw the court open to them again, matters were in a very different position from that in which they had formerly stood. Their ambition hardly went beyond the right of being covered in the king's presence, or in his chapel, of obtaining for themselves the cup out of which the king had drunk, or, for one of their ladies, the dress worn by the queen at Easter. They looked up to the king as so exalted above them, that their own elevation above the rest of the nation seems to have consisted in their eyes chiefly in the trivial marks of honour he vouchsafed them, and the services he permitted them to discharge ‡.

The Towns.

If such was the fate of the victors in the before-mentioned conflict, it may be asked, how fared it with the vanquished party—the towns ?

All the power of the towns rested on the cortes, and in it on the rights of granting taxes and stating grievances, rights that were very closely connected with each other, since no taxes were granted unless grievances were remedied.

The earlier kings had striven to bring the cortes into a state of dependence. The royal corregidor long exercised a legalized influence on the elections. Henry IV. made an attempt directly to nominate the deputies of Seville §. Ferdinand the Catholic established the rule that the cortes should swear to keep everything secret that was committed to them, and his secretary of state, Almazan, had a predominant authority in the assembly of 1505. But little, however, was definitely and permanently effected till the times of Charles V. If Charles treated his rebellious subjects with clemency in other respects, still he was resolved to break down their legitimate power. He set about this without the least hesitation or pause, and he

---

* Soriano, Relatione di Spagna: " Tutti li signori non hanno altro obligo che servire il re alla guerra a sue spese *per la difesa di Spagna* solamente: et quando Carlo V. ha voluto rompere li suoi privilegii, hebbe tutt' i grandi contrarii et il Velasco gran contestabile più di tutti, si ben era affettionato a S. M. et quello che più d'ogn'altro le fosse grato. Se non si metteva silentio a questa novità, seguiva gran tumulto nel regno." Cf. Oracion del condestable a la junta de grandes. Sandoval, ii. 362.

† Navagero, Viaggio fatto in Spagna, 350.

‡ Nota di tutti li titoladi di Spagna con le loro casate et rendite che tengono, dove hanno li loro stati et habitationi, fatta nel 1581 alle 30 di Maggio in Madrid. Informatt. Polit. tom. xv. n. 11. MS.

§ Relatione delle cose, etc. " Parlandosi con alcune signore se si sta a sedere, li cavalieri, ancorche siano più nobili, s'inginocchiano.'

---

* Contarini: " Se ben sono ricchissimi, hanno però infiniti debiti, che gli fanno perdere il credito. Temono S. M. dove quando si governassero prudentemente, sariano da essa per le loro forze temuti. Sono superbi et altieri oltre ogni credenza, vivendo otiosamente."

† The Cortes of 1560 complain that the grandees cease "de tener y mantener en su casa parientes pobres y honrados." (Peticion 94.)

‡ Relatione delle cose, etc. "In tutti gli officii maggiori della casa del re sogliono servire titolati, ancorche sia scopatore maggiore, acquator maggiore et sono tenuti degni di qualsivoglia gran cavaliere."

§ Marina, Teoria de las cortes, tom. i. 190.

employed, generally speaking, four decisive measures to effect his purpose.

After the victory of the grandees, after his return on the 28th of May, 1523, Charles summoned the towns to a meeting in the Cortes. " But," he says in his warrant to the corregidor of Burgos, " in order that the credentials granted by this city may be complete, and not different from those of the other ciudades and villas, you shall take care that in every case they be conformable to the draft annexed hereto *." In short, he took upon him to prescribe to the towns the nature of the authority they were to grant their representatives. What then was this authority ? There is extant one of the credentials drawn up in accordance with his draft. It empowers the procuradores " to vote the servicio, to treat what shall be laid before them by his majesty, to do what his majesty shall command, so far as it may be for God's service and his majesty's †." This was the first measure he adopted. This cortes met, furnished with no other documents but such as conferred on them unlimited power, with none but such as were approved of by the king.

The only remaining inconvenience now arose from that other right of the cortes, which restricted even the unlimited plenipotentiaries through the old established routine of not granting the taxes till grievances had been removed. Charles commanded positively, that money should be voted first, and grievances discussed afterwards. Though the assembly of 1523 insisted on it that he should immediately, and in the very first place, reply to the remonstrances addressed to him, and provide for what was required by the condition of the realm; though they even showed symptoms of a purpose to dissolve their sittings, still he persisted stedfastly in his determination to hear nothing, and to receive no remonstrance till the servicio had been voted; and he carried his point. This was his second measure. The custom he introduced now became a precedent, and precedent always becomes law when public circumstances long remain unchanged. Charles consented that attention should be given to grievances, not however, as previously, before the grant of supplies, but only before the close of the cortes ‡.

This extinction of all influence on the part of the constituents, was not even yet enough for him ; he thought also, how he might keep the deputies themselves in awe, or voluntary submission. He effected the one purpose, by not suffering any discussion to take place, except in presence of his president, whereby every expression hostile to his interests became more dangerous to the deputies, than to himself §. The second purpose was effected by favours, either granted, or held out to expectation, which the president himself did not scruple to mention. It thus became a profitable thing to have a seat in the cortes ; and we find as early as 1534, a deputy paying 14,000 ducats for this advantage ||.

These then were the four measures to which

Charles had recourse, in order to subdue the assembly ; they were, as we see, unambiguously and openly directed to this end, and they perfectly effected it. From the year 1538, there was no cortes except this of the deputies of the towns ; they assembled every three years, and they always granted what was demanded of them *.

The successors of Charles drew the reins he placed in their hands somewhat tighter. In the year 1573, the cortes themselves complained that courtiers, judicial functionaries, and other persons in his majesty's pay, were elected, persons whose freedom was small, and the only effects wrought by whom was dissension among the assembled members. In 1598, Philip III. summoned the procuradores to Madrid, in order that, as he said in his writ, they might consider and discuss, grant, admit, and resolve, whatsoever it should seem good to resolve in that cortes †. The only uneasiness entertained was, lest they should bring with them any secret instructions from their constituents ‡. They were to swear before God and the blessed Virgin, on the holy cross and the four gospels, that they would place in the president's hands every instruction, whether already in their possession, or to be afterwards received by them.

Henceforth everything was mere ceremony. First, the procuradores went to the castle to kiss the king's hand ; the latter then appeared in person in their hall of assembly ; after he had seated himself, and bidden them sit down, he stated to them first in his own words, and afterwards at more length through a secretary, why he had convoked them. Burgos and Toledo contended, according to immemorial custom, which should be the first to reply. The king said, according to immemorial custom, " Toledo will do as I command; let Burgos speak." Burgos then begged for time to reflect. This was the first sitting. The second began with a call to the royal scribes to withdraw, and ended with a resolution to petition the king for their removal. In a third, of course the king did not grant the petition, the deliberations were held in the presence of the scribes, and the servicio was voted. Thereupon they went to announce the grant to the king, who was gracious on the occasion, and gave each member his hand to kiss. And now nothing remained, but that a committee should present petitions affecting the community, each town those especially relating to it, and each member such as personally concerned himself. These were all laid before the royal council; some were granted, others not; till at last the president appeared, thanked the assembly in the king's name for the grant of the servicio, and to save the towns from incurring further expense, declared the cortes terminated §.

Digression respecting the range of action of the later cortes.

Thus were the vanquished in the war of parties kept in their condition of subjugation. The cortes

---

* Convocatoria para las Cortes de Valladolid de 1523 dirigida a la ciudad de Burgos por el Rey Don Carlos. Marina, Teoria, iii. c. i. 177.

† Carta de procuracion o de otorgamiento de poder que el ayuntamiento de Burgos dió a sus procuradores." Marina, ibid.

‡ Transactions reported by Marina, i. 300.

§ Marina, Teoria, i. 258, note.

|| Don Pedro de Salazar y Mendoza; Marina, i. 213.

* Ordine della casa : " Le corti di Castiglia si fanno con molta sodisfattione di Sua Maestà. Ottiene ogni tre anni ogni volta cento mila ducati."

† Convocatoria a la ciudad de Toledo para las cortes de Madrid. Marina, iii. 195.

‡ Carta de los procuradores a su ayuntamiento, 1599. Marina, i. 236.

§ A treatise " Como se hacen las cortes," in Marina, Apendice, iii. n. 35.

had lost their old independence; they had no longer the strength to offer any real resistance; they were subdued.

But I would not take upon me to say that they forthwith became useless. Representative institutions, when once they have struck root in a nation, frequently display, even under circumstances of impaired independence, an inward vitality that still works beneficially. There was left indeed to the cortes of Castile no right save that of presenting petitions on the fulfilment of which they could not insist; but they made use of this right in such a manner, that hardly in the transactions of any delegated assembly of that century shall we find more good intention, more comprehensive and provident zeal, than was shown here.

They were by no means backward in admonishing the king. How often did they remind him of what the welfare of the country demanded, of what it was entitled to by its services. If they petition him to diminish the cost of his household and his table, they call to mind the existing dearth of money*. In their desire to persuade him they sometimes produced old pledges and written promises, made to them on former occasions of granting money†. They did still more. When he made alienations they put him in mind of the duties by which he was bound as king and liege lord‡. They appealed to his royal conscience that he should appoint none but persons of high qualities as gobernadores and corregidores to watch over the conduct of his officers §.

Their attention is peculiarly directed to the functions of the magistrates, and to the proceedings of the courts of justice. They make it matter of complaint if the members of the supreme courts are either too old, or loaded with extraneous business, or inaccessible ‖ ; they are anxious that no family alliances should engross the audiences, that no oidor for instance should employ his son or his son-in-law in a commission, or promote him to advocations ¶. They take it amiss if ever an alguazil breaks into the closed house of a peasant, or any other servant of a tribunal is guilty of violence of any kind. They require that the local councillors should inquire every first of the month into the conduct of their several courts, and if need be report their misconduct. They take pains to put an end to the collision between different jurisdictions, between the civil jurisdictions and the cleri-

cal or military. If they will not suffer that the secular court shall molest a church, on the other hand they insist that every spiritual tribunal shall be subject to the king's pre-eminence *. Besides these things they make it their business to resist sometimes the inroads of the royal councillors of finance on the rights of the estates, sometimes the domiciliary visits of the farmers of the royal salt-works, sometimes the extortions of the officers of the Mésta. In every way they labour to defend freedom and custom against every assault of arbitrary power.

In fact they have always before their eyes the whole condition of the state, its public economy, and its general welfare. They are not unobservant of the importance due to the affairs of the forests, the pastures, and the tillage lands. If they disapprove of the practice of burning down heaths in order to have better pastures†, neither will they sanction the breaking up of pasture lands for tillage. They go very minutely into these matters. They wish to prevent the stripping off the bark of oaks and cork trees. There are meadows on the tops of lofty mountain ridges to which cows cannot be driven; they take care that the grass shall not be lost. Innumerable are the ordinances they demand on behalf of trade and commerce. They note with displeasure the increase of luxury and the augmenting dearness of all articles. The extravagance of the grandees and the courtiers in dress and furniture, the introduction of carriages and litters ‡, which it required a considerable fortune to keep, the disorders of the lackeys, the gambling with cards and dice that brought forward people who were seen strutting about in silk clothes with gold chains, though they had no fortune, had never filled an office, or been in any one's service,— with all these things they express themselves most strongly dissatisfied. The artisan already went so fine that he set an insufferable price on his work.

They, on the other hand, directed their care to more real wants. They desired that there should be in every town a father for the orphan children that were left to roam about like vagabonds §, and that a guardian should be appointed for the poor who should give them work. They wished also that in every town two good men should every week inquire into the state of the prisons ‖ ; it incensed them that orphan girls should be refused shelter and education in nunneries. They turned their thoughts to facilitating travelling by means of guides and better appointed inns. In this sedulous regard to things of every kind they do not overlook the

* Cortes of 1560, Petic. iii. " Los gastos de vuestro real estado y mesa son muy crescidos, y entendemos que conviniera mucho al bien destos reynos que Vra M. los mandasse moderar asi para algun rimedio de sus necessidades como," etc.

† Cortes of 1558, Petic. vi. " Especialmente mande V. M. guardar la cedula que la Magestad imperial dió en las cortes de Toledo."

‡ Cortes of 1560, Petic. v. " Suplicamos a V. M. que considerando la obligacion que tiene como Rey y Señor de todo," etc.

§ Cortes of 1560, Petic. xiii. " Asi conviene al descargo y sosiego de la real consciencia de V. M."

‖ Cortes of 1552, Petic. i. " Las personas que residen en el vuestro consejo real, quando alli vienen, son ya viejos y enfermos, y con sus indisposiciones y vejez no pueden despachar tantos negocios como al vuestro real consejo ocurren."

¶ Cortes of 1552, Petic. iii. " Las partes reciben gran daño en que los oydores de vuestras chancelierias tengan hijos y yernos abogados."

* The same, Petic. lx. " Al juez ecclesiastico no se haze agravio en mandarle que otorgue y embie el processo, para que se vea, si haze fuerza: y esta es la preheminencia real de los Reyes de España."

† Cortes of 1555, Petic. lxvii. " No contentos con los pastos que hay en los montes, les ponen fuego para tener mas y acaece quemarse tres o quatro leguas de montes en que se recibe notable daño."

‡ The same, Petic. cviii. " Para entretener o sostener un coche o una litera es menester una hazienda particular."

§ Cortes of 1552, Petic. cxxii. " Muchos mozos de estar mal vestidos y mal tratados ninguno se quiere servir dellos —y se andan perdidos, porque no hay quien tenga cuydado dellos." They wish to have " una persona diputada que recoja los tales mozos y los haga yr a trabajar."

‖ Cortes of 1560, Petic. cii. " Cada semana o cada mes se nombren dos regidores, los quales se hallen a la visita de la carcel."

smith who has the effrontery to demand 25 or 25½ maravedis for a light horseshoe, not so good as the old one which he keeps; nor the servant for whom his master pays the cruzada and who runs away from him thereupon; nor the young girl whom her cautious mother leaves shut up at home, but who goes meanwhile and sits down to the reading of Amadis, and fills her imagination with a disordered appetite for the strange incidents narrated there*. As for them, like men of sense they are more inclined to real than to fictitious history. They wish that above all the valour of the Spaniards should be known throughout the whole world, that the heroic deeds of their forefathers should be held up as examples to existing and future generations. Never perhaps was a historian more urgently commended to his sovereign than was Florian de Ocampo commended by them to Philip II.†

Nor can it be said that their suggestions passed unregarded. The king often replied to them, " We hold what you require to be just," or " Our council shall weigh the matter," or " We have given orders that your advice be acted on." Often the petition was forthwith converted into law. Philip II. probably ratified but too often the plans thrown out in such documents respecting trade and commerce ; but it was not so with respect to his prerogatives, his revenues, and the augmentation of the taxes. His answer to the supplications of the cortes was very frequently that the existing law was satisfactory ; no innovation was admissible.

And so the assembly of the cortes may be regarded as a council which the towns, in remembrance of older and more important rights, sent every three years at their own cost to the king, that it might help to repeal abuses, and to exercise control over the state functionaries; that it might take cognizance of ancient custom and make proposals for the general good. Care was taken that this should not in any way prejudice the supreme power; all decisions rested solely with the king. He was not a little helped, however, by this institution in keeping his officers in check, and in maintaining a complete authority over them.

The Clergy.

We return to the circumstances of the three estates. The cortes were now instrumental in making the nation bear the burthen the king thought it good to lay upon it. Two main pillars of the ancient constitution were overthrown. Did the king succeed in prostrating the third, the clergy ? Or did the profound reverence for the outward forms of worship displayed by these kings, a reverence which made it with them the first of duties to spread abroad the sway of the pope, did this enable them

to allow the clergy a certain degree of independence ?

The clergy by all means enjoyed an easy and even a pleasant existence. In Toledo they enjoyed such ample revenues that they were not only proprietors of the first houses, but were besides tantamount to lords of the city; they fared every day of the best, and no one found fault with them. The monks of Guadelup derived alms to the amount of 150,000 ducats yearly from their miraculous image. Their convent was surrounded with beautiful gardens ; they had excellent wine-cellars excavated, some for earthen, others for wooden vessels; their residence was provided with all the comforts of life, and they wanted nothing from without. The convents were above all frequently remarkable for their beautiful and delightful situations. Navagero is full of enthusiasm about the Carthusian monastery of Seville. How beautiful was its site, at the foot of the most charming hills clad with orange groves; in the midst of gardens full of pomegranate trees, whence the breezes wafted the good fathers the sweetest perfumes all the summer through; before it the great river, and all around the most luxuriant fields. " These brethren," he says, " have climbed a good step in advance on the way hence to Paradise *."

But it does not follow from this that the clergy possessed independence, or an influence of their own proper strength on the government. The very foremost consideration with regard to their relation to the state is, in whose hands lay the right of collation to benefices? Ferdinand the Catholic had obtained from the popes, for the kings of Spain, the privilege of nominating their own clergy †. So unlimitedly did Philip exercise this right, that he devised his own maxims of ecclesiastical administration. He made a distinction as to districts. He placed theologians in the mountains of the Asturias and in Galicia, for there doctrine was wanted ; to Estremadura and Andalusia, where the people loved litigation, he sent canonists ; and he sent monks to the Indies, because these men usually did the most effective service in converting the natives. In the disposal of appointments he looked by all means to birth, and to the recommendations of his ministers and of approved men ; but his usual practice was, to try his men first in humbler employments before he advanced them to higher ; and above all, if he anywhere discovered a poor monk distinguished for erudition and irreproachable conduct, or a bold man, like that Quiroga who would rather be excommunicated than receive bulls of the pope that were contrary to rule, he was sure to promote them. The one class gave his administration credit in the eyes of the people ; the other lent it intrinsic energy. He made Quiroga the first ecclesiastic in the kingdom, viz. archbishop of Toledo. And as in all these matters he

---

* Cortes of 1558, Petic. cvii. Illustrative also of Don Quixote. " Como los mancebos y las donzellas por su ociosidad se principalmente ocupan in aquello (leer libros de mentiras y vanidades), desvanecense y afficionanse en cierta manera a los casos que leen en aquellos libros haver acontescido, anzi de amores como de armas y otras vanidades : y afficionados, quando se offrece algun caso semejante, danse a el mas a rienda suelta que si no lo huviessen leydo."

† The same, Petic. cxxviii. " Movido de su natural inclinacion ha escripto veynto y ocho años en la chronica de España. Con gran trabajo de su persona y espiritu las ha recopilado et teniendo lugar las sacara a luz : de que a estos reynos se seguira notable beneficio."

* Navagero, Viaggio, 353—359.

† Contarini : " Ha il re il nominatione di tutti i beneficii di Spagna et li distribuisce a chi più li aggrada, tramutando anco uno istesso da un vescovado a l'altro a suo beneplacito." See, above all, the law of Philip II. of the year 1565 : " Por derecho y antigua costumbre y justos titulos y concessiones apostolicas somos patron de todas las iglesias cathedrales de estos reynos, y nos pertenesce la presentacion de los Arzobispados y Obispados y Prelacias y Abadias consistoriales de estos reynos, aunque vaquen en corte de Roma." Nueva Recopilacion, lib. i. tit. vi. ley i. p. 36.

proceeded entirely after his own good pleasure, it was satisfactory to him to have this acknowledged, to see the clergy, after their nomination to an appointment, present themselves before him and return thanks [*].

Under these circumstances, it was not possible but that archbishops, bishops, and the whole clergy should hang upon him to whom they owed all they enjoyed, and to whom they looked for their future fortunes. Instead of adhering to Rome, which they could not support against the king, they clung to the king, who had the power and the inclination to support them against Rome. They were their master's most obedient subjects ; they bore their part cheerfully in the burthens of the state. It was the common opinion that no clergy in the world was more burthened than they [†]. It was affirmed in 1629 that a full third of the ecclesiastical revenues fell into the king's hands, and that a single prelate contributed to the king as much as 2000 peasants or 4000 gentlemen [‡].

New Constitution.

We see the third pillar too of the old institutions broken : let us now inquire how far the kings succeeded in founding a new constitution on the ruins of the old.

Now we have already perceived how the elements of the old state co-operated to the formation of the new one. The removal of the grandees from affairs of state, and from war, obliged the inferior nobility to attach themselves entirely to the king. As the nation had no other organ through which it could express its feelings than the procuradores of the towns in the cortes, the subjection of these men became a matter of great moment with regard to the general obedience of the subject. The clergy, who were linked to the king as they had previously been to the pope himself, now laboured as strenuously for the former as they had done for the latter. From the self-same three estates, which had of old offered resistance to the kings, that servility and that impassibility now originated which so distinguished Castile in this century.

But the king had still other and wholly different means for effecting and securing this state of things. The new constitution was based essentially on three things, the standing army, the judicial functions, and the taxes. The first gave the central authority plenary power against its domestic and foreign enemies; the second kept the people in dependence unawares; by means of the third, the whole course of private life, every property and calling, were rendered subservient to the community or to the sovereign. The subject of the taxes involves the consideration of the whole administration, and of the condition of the people, and will be treated of in a separate section : the character of the cortes shows at once, that the taxes were to be paid by the people. The standing army was supported by these

funds. Though these kings had such considerable armies in their other territories, and frequently in the field, that they might have considered themselves abundantly secured by them, still Castile too was filled with troops of its own. First of all, hommes d'armes were introduced after the precedent of France, and after the immediate example of the Burgundian house. The twenty-two companies of these, with the 5000 light horsemen [*], rendered necessary by their peculiar constitution, formed the guards of Castile ; a body of soldiers deemed so important, that it was thought hazardous to entrust the command of them to a private individual, and that even so unwarlike a monarch as Philip sometimes bestirred himself to review them. It was frequently no slight burthen to the several localities to furnish the contributions in aid of the pay of these men, or to afford them quarters [†]. Besides these, there were 1600 horsemen with targets and javelins, who continually patrolled the coasts of the Mediterranean, to ward off all danger of the corsairs. Fuenterrabia and Pamplona, the four mountain towns on the sea, Cadiz, Carthagena, and other places, had their garrisons. The king had body guards round his person, a German, a Spanish, and a third, after the manner of his ancestors, composed of Burgundian nobles. This force, perhaps not strong enough to repel a foreign foe, (Philip II. established in addition a militia of 30,000 men,) was yet sufficient instantly to smother every attempt at resistance from within.

The administration of justice likewise contributed not a little to the preservation of tranquillity. I will not enumerate the tribunals and audiences which depended on the council of Castile, nor detail the manner in which the executive and the superintendence of the judicial institutions were combined in the latter. Strict equity was insisted on, and the meanest man could disarm his oppressor with the words, " I will go to the king." The chief thing we have to treat of is the tribunal most peculiarly Spanish, the court of the inquisition.

The Inquisition.

Llorente has given us a famous book on this subject, and if I presume to say anything that contravenes the opinion of such a predecessor, let my excuse be, that this well-informed author wrote in the interest of the afrancesados, of the Josephine administration. In that interest he disputes the immunities of the Basque provinces, though these were hardly to be denied. In that interest too, he looks on the inquisition as an usurpation of the spiritual over the secular authority. Nevertheless, if I am not altogether in error, it appears, even from his own facts, that the inquisition was a royal court of judicature, only armed with ecclesiastical weapons.

In the first place, the inquisitors were royal officers. The kings had the right of appointing and dismissing them [‡] ; the kings had among the vari-

---

[*] Cabrera, lib. xi. cap. xi. p. 890.

[†] Contarini : " Tutti i prelati sono obedientissimi a S. M. sì per lo debito della gratia come per la speranza delle future. Quando hanno bisogno di qualche ajuto, non ricorrono a Roma, ma a S. M.; et così anco fanno quando da Roma sono molestati di qualche cosa, che ricorrono subito al re, che gli protegge et favorisce : onde gli è facile di cavar buona somma de danari da tutti quei prelati."

[‡] Moro, Relat. della Spagna, MS.

[*] Contarini : " 5000 cavalli obligati armati alla leggiera di lancia et targa, che nè per esperienza nè per la qualità de cavalli (che per il più sono debili et tristi) è di molta considerazione."

[†] Transactions of the Cortes in 1619 in Davila, Felipe III. ad h. a.

[‡] Bull of incorporation, Llorente, Histoire de l'Inquisition, i. 145.

ous councils at their court, a council likewise of the inquisition; the courts of the inquisition were subject, like other magistracies, to royal visitors * ; the same men were often assessors therein, who sat in the supreme court of Castile †. It was to no purpose Ximenes scrupled to admit into the council of the inquisition a layman nominated by Ferdinand the Catholic. "Do you not know," said the king, "that if this tribunal possesses a jurisdiction, it is from the king it derives it ‡." If Llorente speaks of a suit attempted against Charles V. and Philip II. themselves §, still it is plain from his own statement (for to this we always refer for our information), that Paul IV., then in open war with the emperor and the king, proposed some such experiment,—but not that the suggestion was put in force, or that such an attempt was ever made.

In the second place, all the profit of the confiscations by this court accrued to the king. These were carried out in a very unsparing manner. Claim was laid even to the presents which had been made by the condemned long before their trials, and to the portions they had bestowed on their daughters ||. Though the fueros of Aragon forbade the king to confiscate the property of his convicted subjects, he deemed himself exalted above the law in matters pertaining to this court ¶. It was calculated in the year 1522, that the property of those alone who had voluntarily pleaded guilty of heresy, had even in the short period since the accession of Charles brought him in upwards of a million of ducats **. The proceeds of these confiscations formed a sort of regular income for the royal exchequer. It was even believed and asserted from the beginning, that the kings had been moved to establish and countenance this tribunal more by their hankering after the wealth it confiscated, than by motives of piety ††.

In the third place, it was the inquisition, and the inquisition alone, that completely shut out all extraneous interference with the state: the sovereign had now at his disposal a tribunal from which no grandee, no archbishop, could withdraw himself. Foreigners were particularly struck with this fact. "The inquisition," says Segni, "was invented to rob the wealthy of their property and the powerful of their consequence." As Charles knew no other means of bringing certain punishment upon the bishops who had taken part in the insurrection of the comunidades, he chose to have them judged by the inquisition. Philip II., despairing of being able to punish Antonio Perez, called in the aid of the inquisition. For open heresy was not the only question it had to try. Already Ferdinand had felt the advantages it afforded, and had enlarged the sphere of its activity. Under Philip it interfered in matters of trade and of the arts, of cus-

toms and marine. How much further could it go when it pronounced it heresy to dispose of horses or munition to France * ?

Accordingly, as this court derived its authority from the king, it directed it to the advantage of the royal power. It was a portion of those spolia of the ecclesiastical power, by which the government was made mighty, such as the administration of the grand masterships, and the appointment of the bishops. It was in spirit, and tendency above all, a political institution. The pope had an interest in thwarting it, and he did so as often as he could. But the king had an interest in constantly upholding it †.

Now if the inquisition did mischief enough, as there is no denying, this is not to be ascribed solely to the government. Peculiar propensities of the Spanish mind particularly favoured the establishment and the perversion of the inquisition.

First, there were the prejudices with regard to the distinction between pure and base blood, which had taken hold of the Spaniards to an extent unequalled in any other nation. Proof of pure blood was required of candidates for most offices, and it was even thought a great mitigation, when the search was not carried back further than to the fourth generation ‡. But, besides, the continual wars with the Moors, and the hostility to the Jews who were particularly numerous in that kingdom, had so blended together the pride of birth and a certain religious pride, that the two feelings seemed but one. Not to be of pure catholic faith seemed to this people as much a vice of blood as of mind. Hence the value they attached to pure blood (limpieza); hence the contempt that was mingled with their hatred of unbelievers and heretics ; hence are to be explained the caste-like distinctions they introduced into America, and the religious wars to which they applied themselves in Europe. Now, as the inquisition was, as it were, a weapon of the pure blood against the tainted, of the children of Germanic and Latin Christians against the progeny of Jews and Moors, it found the strongest support in the feelings of the nation. The sons of the convicted had no claim to a place in a royal council, or in a town corporation; no, nor even their grandsons §. Nay, the man who had been merely accused before the inquisition was by the very fact dishonoured; no good Spaniard would have given him his daughter in marriage ||.

This peculiarity of the nation was undoubtedly

---

* For an example see La Nuza, Historias de Aragon, ii. p. 11.

† The Cortes of 1560 complained of this : "Y otros del dicho real consejo son assessores y consultores en el consejo de la santa inquisicion." Peticion vii.

‡ The king's words in Llorente, ii. 498.

§ Ibid. ii. 183.

|| Fragment d'un ouvrage espagnol : Del regimento de Principes, Llorente, App. iv. 409.

¶ Lettre de Jean de Lucena au roi Ferdinand; ib. 376.

** Lettre de Manuel à Charles quint, Llorente, i. 399.

†† Literæ Sixti IV. ad Ferdinandum et Isabellam, Llorente, App. iv. 354.

* Segni, Storia Fiorentina, 335. Llorente, i. 402 ; ii. 397 ; iv. 123. We learn from the Lettres du Nonce Visconti, an 1563, ii. 282, that Rome attributed to the introduction of the Spanish inquisition "gran diminuzione dell' autorità di questa santa sede."

† Tiepolo : "L'inquisitione in questi luoghi è il maggior mezzo di tutti li altri di contener quel regno in quiete, cosa che conosciuta dal Signor re, per essa tende quanto più può non solo a conservar, ma ad ampliar quanto è possibile la giurisdittione di quel tribunale."

‡ Petition of the Cortes of 1532, in Davila, Felipe III. 211.

§ The Cortes of 1522, Petic. liii. complain that this law was sometimes violated. "En lo qual," they say, "la republica recibe gran detrimento et es cosa rezia que tales personas tengan tales officios."

|| Sometimes an inquisitor held another office, and it was sure to be the case that he made his arrests in the former capacity. The Cortes complain of this : "Ainsi se infaman muchas personas." Even this was considered an infamy. The same, Petic. lix.

mightily subservient to the introduction of the inquisition, and to its early efficiency.

But if we take into account the abuses that grew out of the statute of limpieza,—how enemies attacked each other before the tribunals with false testimony respecting their ancestors, so that Gabriel Cimbron says *, there was no such thing as noble birth or pure blood in Spain, save such as consisted in having good friends or malicious enemies;—we shall then find it easier to explain also the abuses connected with the inquisition. In that court the custom had been introduced in the beginning to conceal the names of the witnesses, in order to protect them from persecution, when the persons accused were rich and powerful. Thus were the most convenient opportunities afforded those whose desires were to be gratified by revenge, and above all by secret revenge. How frequently did it happen after the supposed culprits had been long condemned and executed, and their children robbed of their inheritance and reduced to beggary, that their accusers confessed, on their deathbeds, they had borne false witness.

If such an institution could hardly be established in any nation without the utmost danger, assuredly it was surpassingly perilous in a nation, the families of which bore to each other a rankling, inveterate, and immemorial enmity, and scorned no means of doing each other the utmost mischief.

Thus did the inquisition, by its secret proceedings, by the severity of its measures, by the extension of its rights over persons of every rank, and over cases of the most diversified kinds, by the religious pomp with which it surrounded itself, and by the gratification it afforded to the passions of petty souls, become a tribunal of terror that invested him in whose control it was with immense power over the nation.

The obstacles removed, which the old constitution had presented to the sovereign, the royal power firmly established by means of taxes and soldiers, it was after all the inquisition by which the unconditional authority of the government was completed.

II. *Aragon.*

But had the inquisition singly the power of establishing despotism?

It was likewise introduced into Aragon, and yet that kingdom preserved its original freedom unimpaired, though so neighbouring to Castile, and though so closely connected therewith by the original unity of the nation, and by the existing unity of the government.

Old Constitution.

The fundamental principle of the constitution of Aragon was that the king was entitled to exercise only a very trifling influence on internal affairs. He was not at liberty to delegate his authority to any but a native. When he would hold the cortes it was indispensable that he himself, or at least a prince of the blood should be present, to open the proceedings and to close them again with the solemnities of homage†. Nevertheless, his part

in the cortes was very limited. His proposals could never stand good if there was but a single vote against them *. Individuals could always arrest the course of the proceedings by presenting a memorial of grievances, or as they were called *greuges*, a word of fear for the Aragonese sovereigns; and till these grievances were remedied the sittings could not be closed. Especial care was taken to render the administration of justice independent of the royal will. There were royal tribunals indeed, and Philip II. established a new criminal court, but these were subordinate to the others; first to the Justicia and to its *lugartenientes*, whose duty it was, at the words " Avi fuerza," to aid all who thought themselves dealt with by might rather than right, and who were bound to hear the appeal of a condemned man, though the rope were actually round his neck. It was their office to investigate the proceedings of the former court. The justicia again was responsible to four inspectors, who heard complaints against it, and to a representative body of seventeen†. The whole constitution was secured by an express law that no foreign soldier should be permitted to set foot on the soil‡. Aragon was a republic, detached and shut up within itself, having at its head a king, but a king with very limited prerogatives.

It was inevitable in the period before us that this state of things should have been productive of numerous disputes. The king saw the supplies, for which alone he had any interest in holding a cortes, swallowed up immediately by the expenses of his journey, and of the long stay to which he was obliged in consequence of the *greuges* §. For a long while Philip II. forbore from holding cortes ; the Aragonese paid no servicio ; under these circumstances it was almost as though the country was without a king; the laws were administered without him, and civil affairs proceeded in their usual course. It is true indeed that no proper national peace obtained in the kingdom; we find count Martin of Aragon engaged in a sanguinary feud with his county of Ribagorza, which had expelled him and emancipated itself ; we find the Montaneses of the Tena valley in arms against the Moriscoes of Codo: but the king did not interpose in these matters, even admitting, as some asserted, that he encouraged the Ribagorzans; nor could he do so, his hands being tied by the constitution ||. The inquisition met with peculiar resistance in this kingdom. Persons could escape from the authority of this as well as of every other royal court by manifesting, as the expression was, that is appealing for aid to the justicia. That aid was readily granted ; the national court sometimes assigned the whole town of Saragossa as a prison to those who seemed already within the clutches of the inquisi-

---

* Gabriel Cimbron de Avila, quoted by Davila, 212.

† Blancas, Modo de proceder en Cortes, ciii. "Quien puede llamar Cortes."

* Geronymo Martel, Forma de celebrar Cortes, c. ii. "Es necessario que concuerde la voluntad del Rey con todos los que intervienen en cortes, sin que falta un solo voto."

† Blancas, Rerum Aragonicarum Commentarii, ap. Schott, Hispania illustrata, i. 747.

‡ Fuero segundo, De generalibus privilegiis regni Aragonum. Perez, Relat. 88.

§ Sommaria dell' ordine, MS. " Sua maestà avanza poco, perche si danno 600,000 ducati, quali spende prima che si parta, nè viaggi et perche convien stare molto tempo."

|| Blasco de La Nuza, Historias ecclesiasticas y seculares de Aragon desde 1556 hasta el 1618, tom. ii. lib. i. cap. xx. cap. xxxvi.

tion, and they were to be seen walking about in freedom as though nothing were the matter. Upon this the inquisition would excommunicate the *lugartenientes* who had robbed it of its prisoners ; but the Aragonese did not give way for all that. They sent to Rome, and did not spare 30,000 ducats to procure a revocation of the excommunication : what a triumph for them to obtain it ! Still they were incessant in their complaints of the usurpations of the inquisition, and in the cortes of 1585 they forced the king to promise them a speedy inquiry into the matter *.

Much as the Aragonese boasted of their position with respect to the king, proudly as they dwelt on the words of Peter III. †, " If there be vassals faithful to their lord, it is you; for you are not under a tyrannical dominion, but endowed with many immunities; I can distinguish you from other vassals," —words which they maintained were still applicable to them; nevertheless there existed an antagonism between the government and the estates, which only waited for an occasion to break out into open strife ‡. Queen Isabella is stated to have said in her day she only wished the Aragonese would rebel, that there might be an opportunity of having recourse to arms against them, and changing their constitution. When disputes again arose between the royal functionaries and those of the kingdom, the duke of Alva exclaimed, " If the king would give me only four thousand men, four thousand of those I have myself disciplined, I would soon lay low the immunities of Aragon §."

Revolution.

While things were in this inauspicious state the affair of Antonio Perez occurred. As a native of Aragon he took refuge under the immunities of the Aragonese constitution, and they protected him. But was the king to allow his rebellious subject an asylum in the midst of his own dominions, where he could not but be irksome to him? He left no means untried to obtain the condemnation and surrender of Perez. When all failed he had recourse to the inquisition, which then arrested on a charge of heresy the man who might in case of the worst be tried for treason. Upon this the people of Aragon called to mind all the injuries they had sustained at the hands of that tribunal ; " Besides it was accepted only for a hundred years, and they are now elapsed :" accordingly they broke into open insurrection and rescued Perez ‖. If the king thought himself justified in putting down the insurrection by force of arms, the people on their part thought they were justified in resisting force with force. The Aragonese banner of St. George waved once more in the field. But whether it was from want of experience, or from cowardice, or from treachery, their resistance was almost no-

thing *. The Castilians marched into Saragossa almost without a check. The justicia, that bulwark of Aragonese liberty, now met its doom; the chiefs of the people perished in prison, many fled the country. The king summoned the cortes to Tarragona, in order to modify the constitution, whilst the terror of arms still prevailed.

Spittler has said, and many have repeated it by rote after him, that the Aragonese immunities were left untouched on that occasion. But this opinion cannot rest on a general view of the facts; they are too plain and unambiguous.

The cortes proceeded in violation of the law. They were not opened either by the king or by any one of royal blood, but by a Chinchon, archbishop of Saragossa, to whose family was justly imputed a certain share in the measures adopted by the king. The Aragonese were vanquished, terrified, prostrated ; they dared not contradict him. As if it had been purposely intended to set an example of the breach of the law, the archbishop suspended the proceedings in the midst, and held a court of homage to confirm what had been so far done. Things were pushed still further. The king was consulted by letter in dubious cases, and his decision was adopted. " A thing never heard of, a thing never deemed possible," exclaims Martel ; " the king was not only not in the cortes, but even not in the kingdom. From the Hieronymite convent of our Lady of Estrella, in Castile, the king issued his orders, which were solemnly communicated to the officers of the justicia, and enrolled in the records †. The maintenance of other immunities was now not to be thought of, and the thirty-first article of the resolutions of the cortes expressly declared that for the future it should free to the king and his successors to nominate viceroys, whether native or alien ‡.

Next those laws were overthrown which bore upon the king's influence over the cortes. A definite time was fixed for hearing grievances, after which no more were to be listened to §. The force of an opposing vote was abolished with respect to most cases, and the voice of the majority declared valid. " The majority of every estate constitutes the estate; even if a whole estate be wanting, this shall have no influence upon the course of the cortes, provided the same shall have been duly summoned according to law ‖." This was the more important as the king possessed great and legitimate rights with regard to the convocation of the assembly. Only eight titled houses of the grandees, not a single one of the lesser nobility or of the hidalgos, could claim to possess a seat and a vote; the king summoned them at his pleasure ¶. Some of the towns had an unconditional right; but the king

---

* Llorente.

† Molinus (Blanca's Commentarii, p. 763) appears in error when he names Martin

‡ Tommaso Contarini: " Quando per avventura il re procurava moderare alcuna di quelle leggi (Contarini charges the Aragonese nobility with 'infiniti sforzi,' and 'cose monstruose,') tutto il populo et tutti li grandi si sollevano sotto pretesto di voler difender la libertà loro."

§ Soriano, Relatione di Spagna, 7.

‖ See the account given by Perez himself,

* " A pena furono a vista dell' inimico, che senza essere assaliti si voltarono tutti in fuga. . . . . Forse sariano anco restati superiori, se fossero stati così bravi nel defendersi como furono arditi nel ribellarsi. . . . . Hora S. M. ha scemata et riunata la libertà loro, castigando tutti i loro capi con bandi, con prigione perpetue, con torgli la vita."

† Martel, Forma de proceder en Cortes, c. vi.

‡ La Nuza, Historias, p. 325, where there are also some limitations.

§ Fuero: " El tempo dentro el qual se han de dar los greuges." Martel, p. 56.

‖ Fuero: " Que en las cortes la mayor parte de cada braço haga braço." Martel, c. ii.

¶ Martel: " Los hidalgos no pueden alegar possession de aver de ser llamados," etc.

might add as he pleased to their numbers. Now if the old *fuero* was based upon this usage, for without it it would have been absurd to make complete unanimity an indispensable condition of every measure, it is likewise plain that the validity of the majority of votes involved in it a kind of command. For this reason the practice was still retained, for certain cases, of requiring an unanimous vote.

The tribunal was next taken in hand. Philip did not indeed change its form, but he changed its essence. The independence of the court sprang from the manner of appointing the lugartenientes of the justicia, and their acting deputies, for they themselves were usually gentlemen not versed in legal studies. These functionaries were nominated by the cortes directly, or in such a way that out of those proposed to him the king selected those who were to fill the existing and the future vacancies respectively. Philip still continued to allow them a certain part in this choice, but such a one as was almost ridiculous. He settled that he should himself put nine eligible persons in nomination; from these the cortes made a selection no doubt, but a selection of eight, so that they had only the right of rejecting one; and of these eight the king appointed five to act at once, and three to fill up vacancies *. This was in fact no whit better than though he had named his own men absolutely. He also suffered the four inspectors to continue, and the court of the seventeen, though he diminished the number, and he took them alternately from the four estates, but the real nomination was entirely with himself †. The independence of the courts was wholly destroyed; and as they were thenceforth all royal courts just like the inquisition, there were few collisions afterwards between them and the latter ; they and it had but one common interest, and that was the king's.

To perfect these arrangements Philip converted the Alfajeria, near Saragossa, where the inquisition was established, into a fortress commanding the town ‡.

Thus the king successfully made the most decisive inroads upon the old rights of Aragon. The national tribunal was subjected to him, the legislative assembly exposed to his influence, the country opened to his soldiers, wider scope given to the inquisition, and great rents made in the compact body of the old constitution. But everything cannot be done at once; there still remained many privileges unimpaired, and the old unanimity of all the members of the cortes was still required even for the grant of new taxes. The Aragonese had still before them, for a future day, another open struggle against the new constitution.

III. *Sicily.*

The example of Sicily shows how arduous such a struggle continued even yet to be for the royal authority.

There the king had two thousand five hundred Spanish troops; there the inquisition was in operation; the administration of justice was for the most part under the king's control; he was therefore further advanced by two important aids to despotism, than he had been in Aragon previously to the late events there : yet was he far from being absolute; no where was the situation of his viceroys more difficult.

For, although the new system of government had gained some footing in Sicily, still the old feudal constitution subsisted in unbroken strength. The towns boasted that they had accepted the Aragonese kings voluntarily and by treaty, nay that they had paved the way for them to the kingdom. Messina deduced its rights from the first arrival in the island, not of the Normans merely, but of the Romans* ; and in fact it possessed, in the opinion of competent judges, greater prerogatives than any city in the whole world subject to a sovereign. Those of Palermo were not much inferior; but besides these it was proud of its then flourishing condition, and of the residence of the viceroy within its walls: it laid claim to paramount consequence in the kingdom†. If these two cities were sometimes jealous of each other, they were both still more so of the supremacy of the Spaniards. How often did Messina point its cannons against the ships in which Spaniards were approaching it ! How often did Palermo revolt against the inquisition ! If the towns had opened the country to the kings, the barons had helped them to conquer it. Capmany gives a list of fifty baronial families of Sicily, all of Catalonian blood ‡. They clung with jealous pertinacity to the claims to which they were thus entitled ; they were also strong through armed feudal service. Lastly, the clergy were rich and powerful; many of them were Spaniards, and these were so much the prouder. The circumstances of the *Monarchia Sicula* (for the Sicilian kings asserted that they were the pope's born legates), to the pretensions of which the pope yielded, but with reluctance, made him their natural protector, and they had frequently just grounds for appealing to him in consequence of the abuses made of the royal rights §.

Now, when these three estates, severally so powerful, assembled in parliament, which happened in their case as well as in that of the cortes of Aragon and Castile, only that they might vote a servicio ||, it was no very easy thing for the viceroy to obtain this. The barons indeed were very ready to vote what they were not liable to pay; their vassals paid for them, and remained in consequence only so much the weaker and more submissive. But the prelates who were called on to open their

---

* Martel, p. 90: "Nominacion de personas per lugartenientes del justicia de Aragon."

† La Nuza, Historias, p. 319.

‡ Contarini : ". . . . Citadella che si edifica nel luogo dove era situato il palazzo della inquisitione, dal quale per essere in luogo eminente si dominerà tutta Siragossa."

* Ragazzoni, Relatione della Sicilia : " Messina adduce li privilegii che gli furono concessi dal Senato Romano." Roger's Charter to Messina, an. 1229, in Raumer's Hohenstaufen, iii. 435.

† Ragazzoni : " Per la verità Palermo per la grandezza di popolo, che fa intorno 100,000 anime, per ricchezze et per nobiltà, habitandovi quasi tutti li signori del regno, et per la continua quasi residenza della regia corte in lei et per il trafico et negotio è la principale che sia in detto regno "

‡ Capmany, Del establecimiento de varias familias ilustres de Cataluña en las islas y reynos de Aragon. Memorias sobre la marina, tom. ii. Apendice de algunas notas, p. 37.

§ Scipio di Castro, Avvertimenti al Sᵣ M. A. Colonna quando andò vicerè di Sicilia." Tesoro politico, tom. ii. p. 350.

|| Breve Clementis VII. ad Carolum V. anno 1531, ap. Rainaldum, Annales Ecclesiastici xx. 624.

purses frequently resisted. The viceroys made it their study to have among them some more obsequious adherents, such men as were disposed to make themselves acceptable to the court, on account perhaps of some lawsuit. They even adopted the petty stratagem of holding the assembly in the worst season of the year, so that the superior spiritual princes rather than attend in person might be inclined to send proxies, who were sure to be more easily managed. It was a special advantage that the principle of making even the vacant places pay had been definitely established; the royal treasurer voted on behalf of those places. Thus the viceroys after all usually obtained what they wanted of the clergy. But the towns still remained to be dealt with. These had commonly to impose a tax on themselves to make up the amount of the donative; they therefore chose for their representatives the most obstinate of their citizens, those who were most injuriously affected by the tax, and who were most independent of the viceroys. It seemed necessary to the latter to get their own officers among them in some way or another, and indispensable to gain over to their interests the prætor of Palermo, who gave the first vote, and whose example was usually followed by the other members. They did not open the assembly till they had first struck an accurate balance between the favorable and unfavorable votes, and assured themselves that they possessed a majority [*].

Thus there was associated, and in constant relation with the viceroy, a power really very superior to his, a power the preponderating influence of which he strove to get rid of by all manner of contrivances, but which continually threatened him from the background.

His most important functions concerned the administration of justice. The government had indeed succeeded in getting the remains of the baronial jurisdictions into the hands of doctors of law; it had placed presidents in the supreme court instead of the *maestro giustitiere* and the *luogotenente* [†]; nor was it possible to find men more obsequious to the viceroy than the majority of the ministers of justice; nevertheless, these functions of his were coupled with the greatest difficulties.

The main thing was, that all the real active powers of jurisdiction belonged to the functionaries, whilst all the responsibility was heaped upon the viceroy, and he could appoint none to judicial offices but native born Sicilians [‡].

Three evils were remarked in the class of judicial functionaries, and all three seemed incurable. In the first place, Sicily, like Italy and Spain, abounded throughout in private feuds, feuds so widely ramified that the judges in any important cause were seldom free from the bias of personal interest, and so rancorous that no effort of force or kindness availed to allay them [§]. Secondly, the members of the tribunals had no fixed salaries, but depended

on the fees upon suits. These fees being technically known by the name of candles, it became a standing joke to say, that the litigant was sure to win who lighted most candles for his judge, so that he might the better discern the truth. Shameless bribery prevailed. Thirdly, the two superior tribunals, called the Great Court and the Holy Conscience, were constituted by functionaries appointed only for two years, who made it their utmost endeavour to please the viceroy, so that they might be again employed by him at a future time.

Whilst all these judges were thus more intent upon their own advantage than upon justice, they were dexterous enough to conceal this from the viceroy, to prevent his perceiving the truth, and to cozen him with their unjust judgments. The biennial judges exerted every effort to appear such as they thought he wished them to be : they did not only whatever pleased him, but whatever they fancied would please him, and strove to read in his countenance the decision it imported them to pronounce. But what would be the consequences, so soon as these dangerous motives of interest found footing in the viceregal house itself ? There were instances of persons, who to gain the goodwill of a public officer of high station and to make use of him for petty ends, contrived by extraordinary hints and suggestions, to fill him with flattering anticipations that resulted in nothing but confusion. There were women, whose property was more in expectation than in actual possession, and who sought to ally themselves in marriage with some of the viceroy's ministers, in order to strengthen their interests. Accordingly, the viceroy was sometimes in the condition of the duke of Messina, who had sometimes five law-suits at once in his house. His chamberlain was engaged in litigation with a commune, his most confidential favourite, Pietro Velasquez, with a duke; his auditor and his secretary laid claim each to a barony, and his son's chamberlain even to a county. These claims became entangled in the ramifications of the general feuds, and clashing with each other made his house seem a hell [*].

In this state of things the tribunal was an institution for injustice, an arena for private feuds; the most iniquitous verdicts were inevitable. What could the viceroy do ? If he would delay judgment he was hated like death. If he did not show himself upon the tribunals, all the faults committed were charged upon his absence, and he was censured for neglect of his duty : but if he made his appearance the sentences were ascribed to his influence. If his house had but the most remote interest in the affair in question, the most righteous decision was forthwith set down as being a work of partiality.

Herein was manifested the natural character of these Sicilians ; submissive, crouching, and seemingly born to be slaves, so long as one could promote their advantage, but who started up the instant their rights and privileges were in the least invaded, and maintained them with the utmost vehemence [†]. The number of the malcontents was

* Scipio di Castro, Avvertimenti.

† Buonfiglio Costanzo, Historia di Sicilia, ii. lib. viii. p. 595.

‡ Ragazzoni: "Alcuno non può esser giudice che non sia dottore et cittadino del regno."

§ Soriano, Relatione di Spagna. "Partialità sono fra loro le quali se bene Don Ferrante Gonzaga et altri vicerè hanno cercato di comporre, non hanno però potuto far tanto che basti, perche la discordia invecchiata è come una infermità venenosa sparsa per tutt' il corpo."

* All this is from Scipio di Castro, Avvertimenti : "dell' artificio de gli ufficiali," p. 371; "dell' interesse de servitori," p. 377.

† Avvertimenti : "della natura de Siciliani," 346. Ragazzoni.

presently swelled by the functionaries appointed for life, who, in direct contrast with the biennial functionaries, were always in opposition to the viceroy, and ascribed to their own influence whatever good he did, and all that was bad to his neglect of their counsel. Next came those of the powerful landed proprie'ors, who had some cause or another of complaint. Their resistance, which appeared never to be directed against the king and the law, but always against abuses and the viceroy, affected a very legitimate character.

And thus we have here this singular spectacle; a governor endeavouring to circumvent the natives by stratagem, to get money from them, and the natives again besetting the governor with a thousand intrigues, with the effect, if not with the intention, of getting rid of him.

For what was this or that viceroy to the court? We know this court, where an enemy was to be found for every man; where slander opened a sure road to the royal ear; where to be doubted was to be ruined. The conflict was speedily transferred from Sicily to Madrid. The viceroy and his antagonists made themselves each their party in the council of Italy. Their struggle lasted for awhile; but by and by the complainants usually gained the upper hand, particularly when they backed their complaints with presents. Then followed first of all reproofs, and next investigations called *sindications*, and lastly condemnations, for the sindicators acted in accordance with the will of the king, who had by this time lent his ear to the complaints. There was no help for it; the viceroy was obliged to retire, or if he remained in office it was with obloquy and disgrace.

The strife that convulsed Sicily was in reality carried on between the royal authority and the rights of the several classes of the native inhabitants. But the whole hatred which the island might in such continuous strife have bent upon the king, became personal and fell upon his viceroy. The latter was then abandoned by his sovereign, and the battle began anew.

And hence it was, not one of these viceroys ended his career with honour *. Juan de Lanuza in vain sacrificed his own son to the claims of justice; Ferdinand the Catholic, said that his virey did the deeds of a Roman, but from stupidity, and he deposed him. Don Ugo de Moncada was expelled in an insurrection by the Sicilians. Though the duke of Monteleone was old and weak, he was compelled to go to Spain to justify himself. Don Ferrante Gonzaga was accused of mal-administration of the corn revenue, and subjected to a very severe sindication. Juan de Vega experienced one no milder, having been implicated through his father-in-law in the internal quarrels of the Sicilians. The duke of Medina was forced to witness the punishment of those confidants who had thrown his house into confusion, and then to quit office. Don Garcia de Toledo was overthrown by his enemies at court. It was in vain the marquis of Pescara kept himself aloof from every private interest; his most confidential minister committed the faults he himself avoided; the strong reprimands addressed to him would infallibly have been followed by his dismissal, had not his death anticipated this. Though Marc Antonio Colonna, having

* Cabrera: " Sicilia fatal a sus virreyes."

had all these cases urgently put before him, profited by the warning, and on the whole conducted himself very well, still even he did not escape suspicion on the king's part. Upon the strength of some letters found in the inventory of a baptized Jew at Messina, Marc Antonio Colonna was recalled, and his accuser made president of the kingdom *.

So stood matters in Sicily. This strife between the two powers was never brought to a definite decision. The Spanish kings found themselves constrained to limit the privileges of the inquisition, and when they re-established it, to bind the inquisitors to greater moderation in the discharge of their office †.

IV. *Naples.*

If the towns and barons of Sicily derived a greater degree of independence from the fact, that they had rendered services to the royal house; those of Naples could compare with them in this respect. There the Aragonese faction of the barons had thrice proved victorious for their king, and obtained a distinguished position in consequence. The first occasion was on the arrival of Alfonso V., and in the wars connected therewith, waged by Ferrante the elder, against his rebellious subjects. The second was on the conquest of the kingdom by Ferdinand the Catholic, when Gonsalvo de Cordova portioned out no few possessions of the vanquished among the chief persons of his army. The third was at the successful defence of Naples by Charles V. against Francis I., when eleven of the most eminent men of the defeated party were punished with the confiscation of their property, six others with confiscation and death, and many other persons of inferior station were implicated in the mischance; the property of all these persons was transferred to the victors. The prince of Orange was almost too liberal in disposing of it. The burghers of Naples took a lively part in all these conflicts, and on the same side. In the third greatest peril of Ferrante the elder, and of Ferrantino, they were their main supporters. On the first arrival of Gonsalvo de Cordova, with whom they had long kept up an understanding, they opened their gates to him. In the siege of 1528 they displayed a pertinacious fidelity that determined the issue of the war. Notwithstanding all this, there was in Naples nothing like independent strength, on the part either of the nobility or of the towns; the viceroy was there free from the difficulties encountered by his compeer of Sicily. The condition of Naples excited the wonder of politicians, still more than did that of Castile; they saw the government despotic, the subjects proud; the former hated, and the latter disposed to revolt; yet the former firmly established, and the latter obedient ‡.

* Buonfiglio Costanzo, Historia di Sicilia, p. 658.

† Llorente, ii. 125, limited by the words of Scipio di Castro, p. 371: " Li padri inquisitori, i quali hanno potuto conoscere che alla maestà del re catolico è stato più grato colui il quale nel suo procedere ha usato maggior modestia, doveranno guardarsi da rottura."

‡ Al Sr Landi, MS. " In vero, consideratosi il governatore et il governato, quello imperioso et altiero, questo superbo et indomito, quello odiato per la repentina grandezza et per la natura insupportabile da molti, questo inclinato alle rivolte et perciò atto a poter essere sollevato et favorito da diversi interessati, essendosi quello talmente stabilito nel

Thus we come again to the old question; how was the feudal system humbled ? How was a new constitution established on the basis of the royal prerogative ?

The nobles and the towns.

In the first place, the nobles were divided among themselves. Often as the Aragonese faction had prevailed, it could never altogether put down that of Anjou; hence it was never possible for the nobility to combine in any united effort against the government. The nobles used to assemble in the *Seggi* of Naples, and there they exercised some rights affecting the general interests. There was no need of disturbing them in the exercise of these. The majority possessed by the government party was so strong and so much to be relied on, that Thomas Campanella advised the king to establish similar institutions in his other states, as certain instruments for securing allegiance *. No additional member could be admitted into these *seggi* without the king's express permission †. To prevent the possibility of unanimity ever occurring in these assemblies, the king bestowed the vacant fiefs on persons of the burgher class, or on foreigners, such as Genoese merchants ; and these new men claimed all the privileges of the others, but naturally incurred the mortification of not being recognized as equals by their fellow members.

Secondly, the king of Spain contrived to bind the ambition of the Neapolitan nobility to his own cause. There was no baron so petty that he might not aspire to the rank of count or of duke ; the kings of Spain even bestowed the title of prince, which had always before been withheld. Now this did not merely attach the recipients of favour to its dispenser; the shrewd politicians of those times noticed also an effect of a totally distinct kind resulting therefrom. All the people of rank in the land flocked to Naples, where, as their natural emulation gathered strength from the concourse of numbers, each strove to outdo the others in splendour, and every man endeavoured to live at least in a manner suitable to his rank. But as their titles alone rose, but not their incomes, this was not always possible, and most of these ambitious persons ruined their fortunes ‡. From the affluence which would have sufficed to maintain them in consideration and importance, they fell into debt, poverty, and that embarrassed condition that cut them to the quick. If they then retired to their estates to retrieve their affairs, they still needed the indulgence of the king. He left their hands free as to their manorial possessions ; he did not

stand in the way of their assumptions against the clergy as he might have done; how often did these nobles appoint needy priests to benefices, who contented themselves with a small portion of the income of their cures, leaving the rest to their patrons! On these occasions the royal tribunals often enough shut their eyes to the abuse.

But there was another still more direct way to humble the nobility, viz., the exercise of impartial justice in the city. The better to understand the advantage of this, we must call to mind the relation in which the nobles stood to the people of Naples. This was the same relation of jealousy, of hatred between class and class, of secret or open dislike, which has shown itself more actively in Germany than in any other nation in the world. This cannot be more strongly exemplified than by the circumstances that accompanied the attempt of the Spaniards to introduce the inquisition into the country. Pietro di Toledo made little account of the first movements, and of the isolated resistance offered by the several ranks; but when both united in arms, and nobles and burghers flocked together at the sound of the tocsin, took hands and marched two and two, a noble and a burgher together, to the church, shouting, " Union !" as they went, then the viceroy was alarmed *. He called to him, to Puzzuolo the old *eletto* of the people, Domenico Terracina, the consultores, and the chief people of the different localities. There he represented to them that it was he who made the burghers and the nobles equal ; he would now grant them something which he had not granted the nobles when they stood alone, nor now when they had at last united with the burghers; he would grant it to the latter, and to them alone. He gave them a written assurance that there should never be any question of the inquisition, nor of any prosecution to be begun on account of those proceedings †. So urgent did it seem to the greatest viceroy Naples ever had, to keep alive the hostility between the two classes.

But how, we ask, could he boast of having made the burghers equal to the nobles ?

When Pietro di Toledo departed from the imperial court at Ratisbon, to assume the government of Naples, and reflected by the way on the condition and the disorders of that kingdom, he made up his mind to a rigid and unbiassed administration of justice. This man, who gave the city a new form, did as much by the state. Under his government marquises, dukes, and princes, were seen committed to prison for their debts; their causes were tried before judges of plebeian extraction ; in criminal prosecutions they were not spared the rope, but were punished even capitally‡. In this

possesso et nel regimento che questo non possa così facilmente nè scuotersi nè ricalcitrare,—si deve ammirare et stupire di così fatto successo."

* Campanella, Monarchia Hispanica, c. xiv.

† Beaumont, Statistics of Naples and Sicily, chap. vi. of the six seggi of the city of Naples.

‡ Alla Santità di Paolo V. MS. c. 2. "Come quelli che si pascono assai di fumo et belle apparenze, cominciarono a pretendere diversi titoli, intanto che ogni minimo barone si procurò titolo di duca, principe, marchese et conte : il che facilmente essendoli stato conceduto dal re, che sempre hebbe mira di tenerseli grati, ... et per mantenimento di essi titoli essendoli stato necessario spendere largamente, mentre hanno voluto far residentia in Napoli. et conseguentemente essendosi indebitati, sono stati forzati a ritirarsi nelli loro stati, dove si cominciarono a dare in preda tutto."

* These particulars are from the MS. "Delle scritture del Sigᵉ Hettore Gesualdo, commissario per Sua Maestà nella causa delli romori dì Napoli." Informatt. vol. xxxiv. and in particular from the Relatione di detto Sigᵉ Hettore di detti romori a Sua Maestà : I have not found them elsewhere.

† From the same Scritture, " Eccettione presentata per la città." Pietro di Toledo assures the citizens, " che l'haveva egualati con li signori principi di questa città et regno ;" moreover, " che voleva più tosto fare detta gratia al popolo solo che a tutta la città insieme."

‡ Lippomano: "In Napoli, massime nelle cause che si trattano innanzi al vicerè, veramente si fa giustitia, et non si permette che huomo per grande che sia opprima le persone basse, perche si procede contra di loro, benche siano marchesi, duchi et principi."

way the old disorders were put an end to. The nobles and the burghers were made equal before the law. The rebellious necks of the former were bent ; the latter were inspired with a lofty feeling of self-esteem. The passions of this people were made use of to keep it in allegiance. New food was given the secret hate it cherished against the nobles, by appointing a man of burgher rank to judge the offences of the princely transgressors, and in point of fact that judge gave free course to a certain spirit of vengeance.

Complaints were now raised by the nobility, and that not by the Neapolitan alone. The Venetian nobili also, to whom we owe our Relationi, were dissatisfied with these things. Had not nature and fortune established an ineffaceable difference between the two ranks * ? Were people to imitate the Turks, among whom all were equally slaves ? Besides the noble would be reduced to despair, finding himself debased, and the burgher would become arrogant when treated like a noble.

Pietro de Toledo however knew very well what he was doing; he knew that by the course he pursued he kept the two ranks apart from each other, so that neither could now attempt anything without the other †. He saw that by this means he tranquillized the kingdom, and so he pursued his way unswervingly, and the greater the rigour of the judges, the greater were in his eyes their claim to promotion and titles. In this way he broke all the remaining strength of both these classes. They had still the right of granting the donative, and at times we see them assembled in what were called general parliaments ; but these are not to be compared even with the Castilian cortes in their last aspect ; the influence of the Sindico gave them their determinate bias, and they vied in granting all that was demanded of them. Their existence was almost overlooked ‡.

The Clergy.

But there remains yet a third estate to be considered, the ecclesiastical, and this was more important in Naples than any where else, in consequence of the peculiar position of that kingdom.

The popes, we know, never made upon any other country such strenuous or such successful claims of complete supremacy ; here they had immediately in their own hands the patronage of most ecclesiastical places; and were not all clergymen natural allies of the pope ? The Neapolitan clergy carried into actual instantaneous operation those decrees of the council of Trent which the king rejected, those namely that had reference to the jurisdiction of the church over the laity. The famous bull In Cœnâ Domini, which pretends to limit the right of the temporal sovereigns to impose taxes on their subjects, met with their entire approval. Though the viceroy strongly prohibited its promulgation, six bishops and an archbishop of Naples did not hesitate to threaten with excommunication those who should endeavour to exact taxes *. The close connexion of the clergy with Rome was on every occasion very dangerous to the whole state.

The viceroys however derived advantage from the fact that the higher clergy of the catholic church are actuated by a twofold interest. The one interest is in favour of the fulness of ecclesiastical authority, and, in as far as this is directed against the laity, is by all means in opposition to the welfare of the state. But it has another interest in conflict with the absolute supremacy of the pope, which falls too heavily upon its own body. It was under the influence of this feeling that the great councils were held; it was for the same reason the clergy had recourse to the royal authority against the ecclesiastical, against the supreme bishop. This last named interest was very prominently exemplified in Naples.

It may be that the Roman curia often set up very unjust pretensions; but at times it really had very well founded causes of complaint. If the Neapolitan bishops demanded extraordinary fees for every act of their office, though this was otherwise amply remunerated; if they required compensation even for the completion and execution of papal dispensations to marry, this might possibly have been excused; but was it to be endured that upon bestowing small benefices they should demand half the income of the first year, and besides this higher fees than the papal dataria and chancery ? that to secure these profits they never troubled themselves as to whether the benefices were reserved to the pope or not, but even looked out for pretenders to the right of patronage, and uniting with them, proceeded at once to fill up the appointments † ? Many other things besides were complained of by the papal nuncios. The bishops had empowered the apostolic chamber to fix at a certain tariff the tithes accruing to it from the kingdom, and to leave the collection of the amount to them; but upon this they not only arbitrarily augmented the rate, but they also established collectors' places, the burthen of which fell upon the tithepayers, and disposed of them by sale; and yet for all that they paid the papal chamber badly. The camera had also compounded with the chapters for its right to spolia; the bishops collected the specified sums in this case also; but here again they increased the amount, they appointed collectors unduly, and they were equally dishonest in their payments to the apostolic chamber. Thus they at once oppressed those beneath them, and defrauded their superior. The council of Trent had enjoined the establishment of seminaries for the education of young persons without fortune, and directed that the expense should be defrayed, first, by contributions from the clergy, and next, by the combination of smaller benefices. Now the Neapolitan bishops levied contributions at first, and then they united benefices; but no matter how many of these they put together, they never desisted from levying the

---

* Tiepolo : "Una diversità che non si può mutare chi non muta la natura et li costumi di tutt' il mondo."

† The author of the Ragionamento del re Filippo II. al principe suo figliuolo, MS. " I popoli godono mirabilmente di questa giustitia, col mezzo della quale ponno vedere i conti loro contra lor baroni, et i baroni senza il popolo sono capi senza membro."

‡ See some particulars in Parrino, Teatro de' Vicerè, from which Giannone has taken almost all he communicates on this subject. Both are very unsatisfactory.

* Giannone, Istoria Civile di Napoli, lib. xxxiii. c. iv.

† Relatione alla Santità di Nro Signore Papa Paolo V. "Per avidità di guadagnare l'emolumenti delle espeditioni delle bolle hanno conferito detti beneficii indifferentemente, non havendo riguardo se sono affetti o riservati alla sede apostolica. Et in caso che sono riservati,—pongono in campo che siano di juspatronato, et operano che li figurati pretendenti del juspatronato ricorrono in Napoli."

contributions *, and no matter how much they raised from both sources, they never admitted into the seminaries any but persons who could pay. They were at constant variance on these and other subjects with the papal chamber, with the nuncios, and the visitators of the Curia. What could have been more to be dreaded by them than a strict control and supervision such as Rome had in view ?

Now if the first purpose which we noticed in the clergy, namely that of extending their jurisdiction over the laity in concert with the popes, was attended with inconvenience, nay with danger to the government, though the latter always contrived to avoid the danger by means of its relations with Rome and new treaties,—this second tendency of the clergy to counteract the apostolic see was on the other hand of extraordinary utility to the government. For to whom could the ecclesiastic have recourse ? He was always obliged to take refuge with the government; he was forced to appeal to the interest it had in putting bounds to the church's jurisdiction, an interest which on other occasions he himself warmly opposed.

Thus it was that the Neapolitan clergy surrendered to the laity among other things the administration of its seminaries, and if the pope desired to have these inquired into, the clergy obtained a declaration from the government that no sort of authority over the laity should be conceded to a papal commissioner, and they contrived that the pope's instructions should be refused the *exequatur* †. Again, what an easy matter it was to uphold and confirm before the royal chamber the claims of those pretenders to the right of patronage before mentioned. It was plain that a patronage once in lay hands might, from the peculiar circumstances of the country, fall one time or another into those of the king, but that this could never occur so long as the patronage was acknowledged to be vested in the church. This was a principle of frequent recurrence in other cases besides. An alliance grew up between the government and the ecclesiastical order ; an alliance directed in the first instance against the encroachments of Rome, but one by which the temporal power of the clergy was necessarily limited, and the power of the crown over the body greatly enhanced.

New constitution.

Here, as in Sicily, the contest was carried on with arts that cannot be justified ; the consequence in Sicily was that the viceroy became impotent and his credit unstable, whilst in Naples the government grew strong, nay unlimited. It availed itself of the ambition of the barons, of the antipathy of the burgher class to the nobles, of the craving of

the clergy for wealth and enjoyment, to divide and humble them all. But perhaps it would not have succeeded in this if it had not at the same time contrived to establish its strength securely upon the basis of a rigidly defined hierarchy of officials, devoted troops, and considerable taxes. The destruction of the old constitution, and the creation of the new, proceeded always hand in hand. We separate them only that we may set the various points of the matter in a more distinct light.

Relation to the Pope.

Let us then confine our attention in the first place to the point already touched on, the securing of the country against the machinations of the pope, who, as feudal lord, asserted here a twofold claim to legitimate influence. The palladium of the kingdom, the true bulwark against all papal encroachments, was the royal *exequatur*. The catholic kings of Spain were not so catholic as to allow of this being wrested from them. Ferdinand indignantly commanded a courier of the pope, who had entered the kingdom with a brief, and without an *exequatur*, to be arrested and hanged *. Charles V. laid it down as his most decided will that no decree should be published in the kingdom without his permission † ; no one was to contravene this who valued his favour and service. Philip II. gave orders to punish any one who should have the audacity to publish any decree in the kingdom without his own approbation ‡. These kings adhered firmly to these principles, notwithstanding all the vehemence with which the popes protested that they were in contradiction to the clauses of their investiture. A *capellano maggiore* had been appointed, only to determine whether a decree was of purely ecclesiastical import, or whether it bore on secular matters; the papal adherents complained however of that officer, that his pretended independence was only apparent, and that the decisions he pronounced were in every instance dictated by the royal councils. This position of the kings was however the easier to maintain, inasmuch as all the three orders, not only the clerical, of which we have spoken, but the two others likewise, had a great interest in getting rid of the pope's influence. During the troubles with which the kingdom was constantly afflicted, the nobles had received a vast deal of church property from the archbishops and bishops, at first perhaps on lease or by way of pledge, or for safe keeping, and this they had afterwards retained as their own. They had therefore

---

* Alla Santità di Paolo V. " Molti vicarii hanno uniti beneficii semplici più di quello che saria bisognato al vitto et sostentamento di detti seminarii, et molti altri n'hanno uniti in buona parte, il, nondimeno seguitano d'esigere tutta detta tassa, quale incorporano con l'entrata degli ordinarii."

† Alla Santità di Paolo V. " Il commissario, Carlo Belhuomo, ancorche molto tempo facesse instanza per havere l'Exequatur regio, mai potè ottenerlo, poiche li vicarii secretamente fecero intendere a li regii officiali che non lo dovessero concedere, asserendo che saria stato interesse alla giurisdittione di Sua Maestà, essendo che l'administratori di detti seminarii erano tutti laici et non dovevano essere astretti a render conto a giudici ecclesiastici."

* Ferdinand au viceroi de Naples, Burgos, 22 May, 1508. Spanish and French Lettres du roi Louys XII. i. p. 109. Afterwards given to the press by Van Espen, Lünig, and Llorente.

† Edict of Charles V. of April 30, 1540, in the Relatione "alla Santità," &c. not known, as it appears, to Giannone. " Perche sono le regie pragmatiche nel regno, che qualsivoglia provisione che venghi fuori del regno non si può esseguire senza nostra scienza e licenza, le quali sono in viridi observantia, ... per questo ordiniamo che così le debbiate esseguire et far esseguire : e se si facesse il contrario con li notarii et altri laici vi assecurarete delle persone loro, et se fossero clerici, gli ordinarete che ne venghino a dare informatione, perche si possa da noi procedere come si conviene."

‡ Philip's edict of the 30th of Aug. 1561. Ibid. Already known.

the utmost reason to fear the pope, who was always intent on the recovery of alienated church property. Fortunately for them the papers, by which the church might have proved its priority of possession, had been lost in the troubles; still a multitude of lawsuits were continually going on about these matters, and the nobility were incessantly in need of protection on the part of the royal against the clerical authority. In no less degree must the burgher corporations, which would never tolerate the exemption of the clergy from the public burthens in their towns, have wished to keep out a power, the influence of which would have upheld or restored the exemptions. And thus the three orders cooperated with the king's decided will to restrict the operation of the supremacy of Rome to such a degree, that it brought in to the pope little more than the white palfrey every Peter and Paul's day. Those who inclined to the papal interests dreaded they should see a counterpart to the Monarchia Sicula arise in Naples.

Functionaries, the Army, Revenues.

In this way the viceroys had the kingdom so much the more freely at their disposal. The old dignities indeed still subsisted ; there were still to be seen at times the supreme judge with his banner of justice, the grand prothonotary with his honorary emblem the book, the high chancellor with his doctor's laurel, but all essential power had passed away from them to the presidents and councillors of the royal courts. At the head of the real effective judiciary was the holy council of Santa Chiara. Even the native inhabitants were content to see five Spanish councillors sitting in it besides ten Italian; it seemed to them that one set would be free from the party feelings prevailing in the country, and that the other would be furnished with adequate knowledge of local circumstances, so that the two together would co-operate the more efficiently to the ends of justice*. Appeals were referred to this court from all the others of the kingdom, particularly from that of the vicaria, and the seven other tribunals of the city. It enjoyed so much the more consideration, because it formed an exception to the rule affecting all the other courts, inasmuch as its members could be removed, either not at all, or only with extraordinary difficulty. It was well known that the president could be more serviceable to his friends than many a prince ; and it was remarked that even the king, by whom he was appointed, gave him the title of Serene. This court is fairly comparable with the great council of Castile †.

* Littera Scritta al Card¹ Borgia. " Gli uni, spoliati come straniere dell' affetto del sangue et dell' amore et dell' odio che nell' istessa patria sugliono alterare li animi nostri, vengono a far contrapeso alii altri colleghi talvolta ingannati da queste passioni ; gli altri come pratiche nel paese delle inclinationi, fini et interesse della gente, dan molto lume alla discussione delle cause." According to Lippomano it had, as early as 1575, fifteen members, a thing which is left undetermined by Tapia. Jus regni Neapolitani ex constitutt. etc., Naples, 1605, p. 146. The number was augmented in the year 1600.

† Lippomano. " L'ufficio del consiglio detto, nel quale si riducono quasi tutte cause d'importanza concernenti la roba et la vita degli huomini, è di grande autorità. Gl' ordini stabiliti et le leggi di quel regno in questi officii sono mira-

Only those matters however belonged to its jurisdiction which did not appertain to the king's patrimonium ; all these latter were disposed of by the Sommaria della Camera. The Davalos still filled the office of grand chamberlain, but they had to content themselves with carrying the crown in procession on occasions of solemnity ; even the show of their connexion with the exchequer was put an end to, when this was removed from the palace. As matters concerning the taxes and feudal tenures were under the control of the Sommaria, it may in some degree be likened to the council of finance of Castile.

There was over both a council immediately connected with the viceroy, called *conseglio collaterale*, his own consulta, consisting of two Spanish and one Neapolitan *regent*. It assembled daily in the viceroy's palace, and finally determined all cases otherwise left undecided. The Cappellano Maggiore made his reports to this council : Lippomano calls it the papacy of the doctors; it was ̦the centre of all public business.

Under these magistracies there was a whole hierarchy of subordinate functionaries. The manner of nomination was that each college proposed three or four candidates, and the viceroy appointed one of these. The court of Madrid never ventured to promote any one in opposition to the viceroy's will ; it left his hands perfectly free. The best places fell to the lot of the Spaniards. The most favoured after these were those who were of mixed Spanish and Neapolitan blood, and who were called by those who disliked them, janissaries. They formed as it were a colony sent out to exercise dominion; they hung very closely together; they were almost all equally proud, impetuous, harsh, and inaccessible ; they devoted themselves above all things to the extension of the royal and the viceregal power*.

By the side of this host of functionaries there was a standing army consisting chiefly of Spaniards, ready to execute their commands, and to quell all attempts at resistance. The viceroy was attended in war and peace by a hundred gentlemen splendidly mounted and armed, called the Permanents, a picked body, half Spanish half Italian. Besides these there were sixteen companies of Huomini d'Armi, five Spanish and eleven Italian, each always led by officers of its own nation, and four hundred and fifty light horsemen. This was the whole cavalry of the kingdom, for though the barons were still bound by law to do feudal service, the practice had been wholly discontinued †. The main strength of the army was constituted by four thousand Spanish infantry quartered in the heart of the kingdom, and one thousand six hundred others employed in garrisoning the castles and towers extending in an uninterrupted chain from Pescara to Reggio, and from Reggio to Gaeta. These troops were all under the orders of the viceroy. The time had been when the constable was the first person

bili, causati forse dalli disordini delli ufficiali et della malitia delle genti."

* Lippomano: al Signor Landi; al Cardinale Borgia; in several places.

† Lippomano. " Nè altra cavalleria si trova nel regno. E ben vero che li baroni sono obligati a servire in tempo di guerra a difesa con le proprie persone. Questi per quanto che ho inteso per nota cavata della summaria, erano l'anno 1564 da 600, et hora il numero e poco alterato."

in the kingdom, and sat on the king's right ; but now he was of no account ; a *maestro del campo* was next in command under the viceroy. A general arming had also been provided for here as well as in Castile, and at a still earlier period. Every hundred hearths were required to furnish five men, who were bound to serve for five years, and the number of troops thus raised was computed at 24,078 men. They were mustered from time to time, and the captains were empowered to dismiss those that were inefficient *.

Now all this together, the functionaries, the army, the fortresses, the previous debts, and the king's necessities, rendered heavy taxes inevitable. I will treat in the succeeding chapter of the style and character of the administration, and the way in which it worked. For the present it will be enough that I state the amount and the gradual augmentation of the taxes, so far as I have been able to make them out. Under Ferrante the Elder the royal revenues amounted, according to the calculations of his son Federigo, to 800,000 ducats †. To this I will subjoin two other statements. Whereas Giovanbattista Spinello computed that, all drawbacks deducted, there remained to the king only a net income of 450,000 ducats, it agrees very well with this, that Alfonso II., Ferrante's eldest son, calculating his father's outgoings for all the necessities of the state, for salaries and the expenses of the household, found the whole to amount to 342,780 ducats ‡. Thus there would have remained a net 450,000 ducats at king Ferrante's disposal. This sum could only have been brought together by so rigorous a system of administration that it would seem as though the king was bent on being the only merchant in his kingdom. This income must have been much diminished in the wars after his death, particularly as Ferdinand the Catholic bought off the opposition of the Angevine barons partly with the royal estates; in short, in the year 1551, it had not risen much higher than it had been in 1490. Cavallo estimates the combined revenues of Naples and Sicily at a million and a half. But from that date they began to rise under Philip II. In the year 1558, Soriano sets down the income of Naples alone at 1,770,000 ducats. Tiepolo reckons that in the year 1567 it amounted to two millions. Only seven years later Lippomano reports 2,335,000 ducats, and in 1579, the estimate was two millions and a half. The augmentation went on in the same ratio. We find this revenue enlarged to five millions of ducats in the year 1620 §. Without any increase in the prosperity of the country, without the addition of one foot of land to the kingdom, we see its public income augmented six or sevenfold within a space of sixty or seventy years.

A more palpable proof could hardly present itself of the total subjugation of the country.

* Al Signor Landi : "Questi sono nominati dagli eletti di ciascuna terra, pero se non piacciono a i capitani, bisogna trovare degli altri : questi sono armati sufficientemente et atti più al patire che al guerreggiare, et è chiamata questa gente la fanteria del battaglione. Et questi se ben non sono pagati son se non servono,—i capitani però et gli altri ufficiali hanno le provisioni loro ordinarie."

† Zurita, Anales de Aragon, lib. iv. fol. 187.

‡ Ib. vol. i. p. 338, and Passero, Giornale, p. 340.

§ Cavallo's Relatione respecting Charles V. ; Soriano's and Tiepolo's respecting Spain ; Lippomano's to Sigr Landi and to Cardl Borgia respecting Naples.

Thus it appears that the Spanish court observed a different line of policy with regard to the representation of royalty in this province from that it employed in Sicily. In Sicily the exasperation against the viceroy, if not guarded against, might have turned into revolt against the sovereign; but here this was not so readily to be apprehended. Here they were but slow to listen to complaints; here the authority of the viceroy was upheld as long as ever it was possible. When the king sent him out from Spain, he declared, "He took him from his right hand, and sent him as his other self into his kingdom of Hither Sicily; he gave him high and low jurisdiction, pure and mixed lordship, and the power of the sword; he endowed him with the right of remitting punishments, legitimizing natural sons, dubbing knights, granting fiefs and bishoprics, and even doing that wherein of right the king's own presence were requisite *." He was upheld in the exercise of this authority, even when he abused it to the prejudice of the country,—if so he only did not turn it against the interests of the king.

V. *Milan.*

Lombardy acquires an interesting character with reference to general history, from the fact that so many wars, important to all Europe, were fought out on its plains. We may look upon it that Charlemagne achieved there his supremacy over the Germanic nations. There the German emperors gained so much of the country as was destined to be theirs, and what Otho I. won on that soil, was lost upon it again by Frederick II. In Lombardy was decided the old conflict between the houses of Burgundy and Valois, in which all Europe was implicated. Even the French revolution first achieved a complete preponderance over Europe in these plains. So important is the possession of these, and of the mountains at whose feet they extend, to the establishment and maintenance of a commanding position in our quarter of the globe.

Never, perhaps, was there a more obstinate strife waged for the possession of Lombardy than in the first half of the sixteenth century. How often was it the battle ground where met Italian and foreign arms, Swiss and German, French and Spanish. How often was the country taken, lost, and taken again ! How many treaties were concluded about it and broken ! How many bloody fields were fought for its sake !

When the Spaniards were at last masters of Milan, they saw clearly how important it was to them; how Italy, now for the first time surrounded by their power, could best be kept in check from that position; how their relations with Germany and Switzerland were now, for the first time, secured by this acquisition; how serviceable it was towards connecting the rest of their empire with the Netherlands; and what a bar it was to the ambition of their neighbours the French †.

Nevertheless they could not venture at once to deem themselves quite secure. No sincere abjuration of their own claims was ever to be expected of the kings of France. Never were the neighbour-

* The viceroy's patent in the time of Charles II., Parrino, Teatro de' Vicerè, tom. i.

† All this was fully perceived by Soriano in his day.

ing powers to be implicitly trusted *. What fears were felt at the designs of Pierluigi Farnese alone! The Swiss, it was asserted, might still be heard saying in the second half of the sixteenth century, in the spirit of their forefathers of old, that it was not right he should ever want bread who had steel in his grasp, that they must look out for the lands where corn was to be reaped †. There were Milanese exiles whose hatred to the Spaniards was compared to the rage of infuriated bulls ‡. In the interior, the old factions were by no means extinguished.

It was found so much the more necessary at once to secure the country, and to keep it in subjection by means of an armed force, by a standing army and fortified places.

Above all, care was taken to fortify the capital. Here they had that castle which even the French admitted to be the most complete in the world, and to lack nothing but a French garrison §. But, besides this, Ferrante Gonzaga strained all the resources of the state to surround the whole circumference of the city with excellent walls and bastions ‖. Pavia had a castle that more resembled a palace than a fortress, but the defence of 1525 gave it reputation and credit. Cremona could not trust to its walls, which were somewhat decayed ; but its castle was very strong, and there were in the city itself two companies of huomini d'armi. Como—not from any apprehension of danger from within, for no town was truer to its allegiance, but for defence against any possible attack on the part of the Swiss—Lodi, Tortona, Novara, Alessandria, six smaller fortresses on the most exposed points of the frontiers, were not less carefully strengthened and garrisoned. The infantry quartered in them constituted the Terzo di Lombardia; they were all Spaniards. It was only among the cavalry, the eleven companies of huomini d'armi, armed half with lances half with arquebuses, that Italians were admitted. The government scrupled to introduce here even that infantry militia, which was formed from the native husbandmen throughout all the rest of Italy, Naples not excepted. In the infantry, as we have said, none were employed but Spaniards. They had the reputation of being very apt proficients in military duty, and in moments of peril the most expert among them were sent to the wars in Flanders ¶.

* Juan de Velasco al Rey nuestro Señor, MS., calls Milan, "provincia di tantos confines y en que tan de ordinario suele bullir la guerra."

† Avvertimenti et ricordi di Scipio di Castro al duca di Terranuova, MS. "Sperando che una morte (di Filippo II.) possa apprir loro qualche grande occasione."

‡ Mémoires du Sieur de Villars. Coll. univ. 38, p. 23.

§ Voyage du Duc de Rohan fait en Italie, etc., en l'an 1600; in the duke's memoirs, Paris, 1665, tome ii.

‖ Leoni, Relatione di Milano e suo stato nel 1589, MS., makes some remarks respecting the walls, which are not without interest as regards the art of fortification in those days : "Ha molti e spessi bastioni o piatteforme, le quale se si fossero andate convertendo in alcuni più rari baloardi, saria forse maggior fortezza et minore spesa. Resta la mutaglia imperfetta per li parapetti et per qualche altra cosa che le manca. Non ha di fuora quelle spianate che haver sogliono le buone fortezze al meno d'un miglio intorno. Ma ha ben provisto per dentro alla sua securità con larghe et spatiose piazze, nelle quali, quando anco la muraglia venisse a perdersi, haverebbono li difensori grande agio a bastionarsi."

¶ Leoni : "Sogliono anco a tempi convenienti farsi le

If, according to all this, Milan was to be regarded chiefly as a military post, equally well situated for defence and for aggression, the country was likewise governed on the principle of keeping it sufficiently obedient to supply all that was called for by the continuous state of warfare.

Upon this principle the commander of the troops was also placed at the head of civil affairs. For we must by all means admit that the power of the governor in this duchy was founded upon military force, and that he was before all things captain general of the forces maintained therein. His rank was neither more nor less than that of a field marshal, whom Charles V. associated with the administration of the last Sforza. When the race of Sforza was extinct, and both the civil and military authority fell into the hands of the king of Spain, an attempt was made to separate these, and to establish a civil government independent of the military commander. It was twice essayed ; but the bad understanding between the two leaders showed soon how impracticable it was. In fine, the civil government devolved upon the commander of the forces *.

He was not counterbalanced by any clergy numerous enough to constitute a distinct order in the state ; there was no superior nobility, or next to none; he had no cortes to contend with. Would it not seem as though the general, at the head of an imposing force, restricted by no privileged orders, was free to exercise a purely arbitrary authority ?

There were no magnates, yet there existed a senate with distinguished rights ; an united order of clergy was unknown, but so much the more prominent were the pretensions of the archbishop, who represented in his own person, and exerted, the entire ecclesiastical authority ; if the towns did not assemble in regular parliaments, they nevertheless, each for itself, and all privately, looked to their own rights. There existed a state of things, for which there were analogies in other states, but which was peculiarly modified by the special history of this country. At first the archbishops had possessed great power ; afterwards the towns had formed themselves into independent communities; and, lastly, a monarchical government was established. Every thing of a self-sustained character that had survived these three mutations, now set itself in opposition to the Spaniards. The governor fell into a distinct position with reference to either party.

The Senate.

When Louis XII. conquered Milan, the supreme authority was exercised by two ducal councils, a privy council and a council of justice. That monarch, who won for himself an equally good name among his Italian as among his French subjects, would not govern the duchy despotically, but in accordance with law; he combined the two councils into a senate on the model of the French parliament, with the right of confirming or rejecting the royal decrees †. Thenceforth the senate appeared as the protection and bulwark of the country. It contri-

scelte di più veterani di tutti li soldati de presidii per mandare in migliori occasioni o in Fiandra o altrove."

* Ripamonte, Historia Urbis Mediolani, lib. x.

† The jus decreta ducalia confirmandi et infirmandi. Verri, Storia di Milano, ii. 104.

buted not a little to the fall of the French authority, that Francis I. undervalued the senate and disregarded its privileges, and that his representative made encroachments on the course of justice, and took upon himself of his own good pleasure to publish decrees not ratified by that body. For this reason Charles V. was careful not to commit similar offences. In the year 1527 he renewed the privileges of the senate through the constable Bourbon *. No doubt he reserved to himself a certain influence by means of the nomination of its members, and by filling three places with Spaniards†, but the members retained their seats for life, so that this precaution was not decisive; they were expressly pledged to regard nothing but law and reason. The articles of Worms, a fundamental charter of this state granted by Charles V., enjoin the senate to care for no bye-considerations, and not to suffer themselves to be misled from observing the law by any royal edict, even though it concerned the exchequer, much less by any order of the governor's‡.

With the senate was associated a twofold magistracy, an ordinary and an extraordinary, on which devolved the administration of the revenues, the superintendence of the subordinate functionaries, and the decision of all disputes affecting the royal exchequer; it was a remnant of the administration as it had subsisted under the Visconti and the Sforzas, retaining even a certain pretension to independence§. But as it was usual for a senator to be associated with the members of this magistracy, on such terms that his weight was equivalent singly to both theirs together, it is plain how great a preponderance remained to the senate. Much depended on this, and on the relations between the latter body and the governor.

Now, if the governor had the right of appointing to all places which were retained for two years, all podestaships, vicariats, captainships, all inferior judgeships, all commissionerships, refendary's places and fiscalates, the senate on the other hand had the right not only of rejecting, if necessary, the candidates elected, but above all of instituting the strictest inquiry into their conduct, on the termination of their offices, through a sindication. The governor indeed could modify the resolutions of the senate, and even pardon condemned persons; but it rested with the senate to admit or reject these acts of grace. The governor represented the supreme authority, the senate right and law. As the governor had but a transitory position, but the senate a permanent one, it was hence the more easy for the latter to effect whatever it pleased: there was always a living interest at hand to withstand any despotism on the part of the supreme authority, while at the same time the governor exercised a wholesome control over the senate.

But a radical discordance was thus produced between the two sections of the magistracy, which often led to bickerings and contention. When

* Rovelli, Storia di Como, iii. 1, from a Diploma nell' archivio di stato, dated Jan. 1, 1527.

† Leoni · " Il senato di Milano consiste solamente nel presidente et dodici senatori dottori, tra quali ne sogliono essere tre Spagnuoli."

‡ Ordini di Vormatia, in the work, Ordines Senatus Mediolanensis, p. 26.

§ "Il magistrato ordinario consiste in sei persone, tre togate et altrettanti cappe corte, che hanno cura dell' entrate ordinarie della camera et delle spese ancora."

Ferrante Gonzaga governed Milan, he suffered himself to be induced by his private secretary, Matrona, to pardon without consulting the senate, and to fill up places without concerning himself to know its wishes on such occasions. Upon this the senate enforced its own rights; it opposed the acts of grace and commissioned sindicators over the governor's functionaries, men capable, so to speak, of finding a hair in an egg. But Gonzaga was not dismayed. He procured himself an unlawful influence over the senate through secret understandings with some members, and by various acts of annoyance and compulsion. Even his wife Hippolita succeeded in accomplishing her own whims. Nothing then remained but complaints at court, and open strife *.

In this strife Charles V. sided with the senate. There were few men perhaps to whom he was personally so much attached as to Guasto and Gonzaga. Nevertheless, at the entreaty of the senate, he resolved to commission sindicators over them, who dealt so severely with the former that he is said to have died of vexation, and removed the latter from all participation in public affairs. Such was not the temper of Philip II. Possibly, too, the senate may have overstrained its rights in its elation at the advantages it had won. At any rate there is extant a paper of Philip's, full of violent invectives against the senate. He says it forced matters before its tribunal upon which it was not competent to judge ; that it violated decrees and constitutions ; it recognized no law but its own arbitrary will; it punished small offences with severity, and overlooked great ones; its justice was excessively slow. Philip determined to curtail its rights. He forbade it its open protestation against the governor's acts of grace, alleging that it was derogatory to the royal authority. He made the magistrates more independent of the senate ; all complaints against the former should be addressed directly to the governor. He forbade the senators to interfere with the marriage of wealthy heiresses ; if any interference was requisite in such cases it should come from the governor alone. " This," he concludes, " shall be an inviolable law, command, and decree; as such it is given, as such shall it be accepted, held, and executed †."

Thus did Philip give judgment in the contest in favour of the governor, though not so as to render the power of the latter unlimited. The right of issuing arbitrary decrees, or of directly interfering with the tribunals, was not conceded to him ; the Milanese continued quietly to enjoy the protection of their laws, and of their senate.

The Archbishop.

But it came to pass that a third power rose up beside these two, which obstructed them both, and against which they made common cause. This was the archbishop.

We are familiar with the archbishops of Milan, who claimed the first place in the general councils

* Scipio di Castro, Avvertimenti. It is remarkable that William of Orange in his " Verantwoording," ascribes Gonzaga's mischance to the envy of Granvella.

† Ordini dati nuovamente di Sua Maestà Catolica al Senato Eccelentissimo di Milano, of the 17th April, 1581. Originally in Spanish. Italian Ordines, p. 109.

on the pope's right hand *; who were so influential from the very first in their own city, that very many persons refer to them the whole growth of the duchy's greatness † ; and who, when they happened to be men like Heribert, and like those two Visconti, Otho and Giovanni, by whom the whole greatness of that house was established, might easily attain to really princely dignity. Was it likely the Spaniards should regard the renewal of so influential a power within the walls of Milan as a thing to be desired? No doubt it was a very welcome circumstance to them, that archbishop Hippolito d'Este never took up his residence in the city. They contrived too to keep his successor Archinto away from Milan up to the day of his death. But Archinto's successor, Carlo Borromeo, was far more to be feared. What if that man, backed as he was by the renown of a life blameless to sainthood, should avail himself of the personal credit he enjoyed, to restore the fallen grandeur of the archiepiscopal see ‡ ? What if he should turn to account the general tendency of his times to tighten the reins of church discipline, a tendency, originally indeed created by the protestants, and first fully realized in Geneva, but which had now extended among the catholics likewise,—what if he should apply this to the end of bringing the laity into complete subjection to the Church and its jurisdiction?

If we reflect that nothing was so well adapted to counteract such an influence as the Spanish inquisition, for the very reason that it was of a kindred nature with it, while, at the same time, it was so totally dependent on the king; and, moreover, that Philip made the attempt to introduce it just at this time, namely, in the year 1563, we may well ask, was he indeed disposed to make use of it against the authority of the archbishop?

The attempt failed however. When the duke of Sessa, the then governor, published the names of the first inquisitors, a tumult broke out, nearly in the same way as in Naples. The people shouted, " Long live the king ! Death to the inquisition !" They had on their side their senate and their bishops, and even the fathers of the council of Trent, the cardinals, and the pope. The duke and the king found themselves obliged to withdraw their institution §.

Two years after this Carlo Borromeo arrived in Milan, and at first he appeared to be on the best terms with the governor, who received him with solemnity ‖. But when, not content with reforming churches and churchmen, monks and nuns, he proceeded to curtail the public amusements, to

insist on a stricter observation of the fasts, and to keep watch over the sanctity of marriage, in a word, to direct his attention to the lives of laymen as well as of ecclesiastics ; when he clung with the most unyielding pertinacity to his jurisdictional 'rights, published new laws, and provided himself with an armed force to give them effect, a violent opposition instantly arose ; the royal functionaries complained that their orders were brought into contempt ; they caused servants of the archbishop to be arrested and punished with the cord, and his palace to be surrounded with soldiers ; Borromeo on his part encountered them with ban and curse *.

Borromeo was the victor in this conflict. It demands a certain strength of mind to march with so firm a tread in the warfare between spiritual and secular pretensions, that the combatant feel not at last some scruples of conscience. The duke of Albuquerque, the then governor, had no such force of mind ; he was reduced to tne extremity of beseeching pardon of pope Pius V. He only obtained it upon presenting an explanation, respecting which he neither consulted his privy council nor the senate, and which he did not venture to record in the public archives; an explanation which satisfied the ecclesiastical functionaries, and tied up the king's hands †.

But the matter did not end here. The new governors began the contest anew ; sometimes it was provoked on the part of Spain ; the pope and the king interchanged unfriendly letters. But there exists in a moral tendency truly and deeply implanted in the mind, a power that not only vanquishes foes, but even calms them. It was found after all that Borromeo devoted himself wholly as a true bishop to his spiritual duty ; he was seen day and night, whilst the plague was raging, rendering at once bodily and spiritual aid in the streets, and in the dwellings of the poor, stripping his house bare and giving up his own bed‡ : the conviction was felt that he had no merely secular purposes in view, that his only desire was to renovate his church and to gather together his scattered flock. Towards his opponents he invariably displayed a fatherly good will, and he inspired them with reverence even in the heat of contest. Hence matters already assumed a certain state of equilibrium during his time, and in that of his successor, Gaspar Visconti, all strife seemed ended.

But Frederick Borromeo, the next archbishop

* Antonius Saxius, Archiepiscoporum Mediolanensium Series, p. 423.

† Leoni: "Si può dire che dalli arcivescovi cominciasse la grandezza del dominio."

‡ Leoni says of him, "Paragonando la pietà Christiana alla grandezza temporale, si può dire che non minor riputatione habbia conseguito questa sede archiepiscopale dalla volontaria povertà, di questa devota memoria del Cardinale di S. Prassede, che da quanti la resero mai con li maggiori titoli di potenza et d'autorità secolare."

§ Llorente, Histoire de l'Inquisition, ii. 193. Thuanus, lib. 36, p. 719. For the senate's proclamation, see Natalis Comes, Historiarum lib. 14, p. 312. For the best and most authentic information, see Pallavicini, Histor. Concil. Trident. lib. 22, cap. 8.

‖ Ex literis Borromei, Verri, ii. 376.

* Laderchii Annales Ecclesiastici ab anno 1566, p. 103. Natalis Comes, lib. 24, p. 531. Rippamonte, Historia Urbis Mediolani, p. 815 : the best authority. Saxius, 1047—superficial.

† This very important point, not known to other writers, not even to Catena (Vita di Pio V. p. 144), whose purpose it would have suited, is mentioned by Don Juan Velasco alone (al Rey nuestro Señor, MS.). He tells how the people made a punning epigram upon the duke, whose Christian name was Gabriel, and on two of his councillors, Gabriel Casato and Herrera, on whom they laid the blame of the affair:
" Du' garbui ed un error
Faran perd el stad al nost signor."

‡ The special ground of his canonization. It is especially dwelt upon in the Votum Smi D. N. D. Pauli V. in the MS. "Vota seu suffragia Illmorum et Revmorum DD. S. R. E. Cardinalium, Patriarcharum, Archiepiscoporum, et Episcoporum, super canonisatione Beati Caroli Cardinalis Borromei olim Archiepiscopi Mediolanensis, celebrata Romæ in Basilicâ S. Petri primâ Nov. 1610."

after Visconti, who seems to have stood to Carlo in the relation of an imitator to his original, more intent upon externals than the latter, more obstinate and narrow-minded, and destitute of the conciliating blandness of genius, provoked the slumbering discord again. He found in the post of governor Juan Velasco, a Spaniard, proud of the name of a Christian cavalier, of his descent from the first grandees of Castile, and of his position in the service of his king. Velasco has very characteristically expressed this in his own words. " By God's grace," he says, " I am sprung whence I am sprung, was brought up where I was brought up, and serve whom I serve. In how many works of piety, how many endowments of hospitals and convents, has the munificence of my ancestors been illustriously displayed ! There is not a hill nor a valley in Castile where my ancestors have not shed their blood for the catholic faith." Was a man like this, so singularly imbued with the religious, the ancestral, and the personal pride of the Spaniard, likely to bend to the archbishop ? Would he take it quietly when the latter denied him the customary place of honour in the church, or had meaner cushions laid for him on occasions of religious solemnity ? They were soon hotly at war with each other. The archbishop would not tolerate any dancing in the country on Sundays, or any theatrical performances in the city. The governor insisted that the poor peasant, who toiled through the week in digging and ploughing, could not dispense with the one, nor the citizen with the other, unless he would neglect his business on working days*. The archbishop would have the agriculturists on church estates freed from the services to which others of the rural population were liable : the governor made the magistrates proceed with all the rigour of the law against the recusants. Whilst Frederick Borromeo evoked before his tribunal all suits in which either a clergyman was concerned or an ecclesiastical law infringed, and filled his prisons with laymen, Velasco issued proclamations threatening the violators of the secular jurisdiction with arbitrary punishment, proclamations so severe and peremptory that the subjects, almost of their own accord, desisted from appearing before ecclesiastical courts. The priests then had recourse to personal measures. The vicar, Antonio Seneca, who took the most active part in these proceedings, excommunicated the president Manoquio, an otherwise irreproachable old man. Borromeo himself grappled with the governor. He appointed prayers to be read similar to those offered up during Diocletian's persecution, and the priest of a church, in which Velasco made his appearance, placed himself near the governor and chaunted the prayer in a particularly audible voice. Borromeo summoned his synod, had resolutions passed against the governor, and caused threatening remonstrances to be addressed to him. But Velasco was quite impracticable. In vain monks passed backwards and forwards day and night, between the two palaces, to reconcile the incensed rivals. At last the archbishop's monitories, threatening the governor with excommunication, were seen one morning posted up at the street corners and on the churches.

The whole country was now in commotion. No other subject was talked of in the public lounges and assemblies, and in public despatches. Velasco boasts of the fidelity displayed in this matter by Milan, " a city as devoted to the king as any of the most faithful in the whole empire *." To be sure its loyalty was put to no very trying test, when it was considered a proof of attachment to the royal cause to play a showy part in the celebration of the carnival. But the excitement was so considerable, that some old antagonists of the Spanish dominion already conceived hopes of a political change, and entered into correspondence with France. Did it not seem indeed matter for grave reflection, that the clergy removed from some places the portraits of the principe and the infanta as being too profane ?

The governor suddenly put an end to all this. He too, as well as Albuquerque, turned to the pope, but the latter was no Pius V., and Velasco had no thought of soliciting absolution. His king had already interceded for him. Velasco says, that through the gracious hearing accorded his envoys by Clement VIII. and his nephew Aldobrandino, through the support of the duke of Sessa, then at Rome, but above all, by force of the truth which these mediators defended, he succeeded in dispersing the mists and bringing forth the bright sunshine of justice. Two days before the threatened excommunication was to have taken effect, letters arrived from Rome to stop the act. And now, Velasco boasts a year afterwards, his holiness is satisfied, his majesty is served, and the city and state of Milan are edifyingly administered; justice takes its free course.

Such was the struggle in this province between the spiritual and the secular power. At last a compromise was concluded between the two in the year 1615, but I cannot say that it appears to me to have been of a satisfactory nature†. In any case, the independence of the archiepiscopal see must have proved a continued source of division, and have thwarted and impeded the growth of an unlimited power.

The Communes.

A strange form of constitution in truth was that of Milan, in which public liberty was not secured by regular institutions, but by the antagonism between the superior powers. Nevertheless, the communes, which constituted the real body of the state, still retained some remnant of those immunities for which they had once shed so much of their blood.

Up to the beginning of the Spanish rule, the communes were so independent of each other, that in no district could real property be acquired by a freeman of another district ‡. The communes still retained a considerable share in the administration of justice within themselves in these several dis-

---

* Don Juan de Velasco al Rey nuestro Señor. He dwells particularly on theatrical performances. " Por bandos particulares han dado a los farsantes los Governadores convenientes ordenes respecto de los vestidos, subjectos, palabras y movimientos, mandando que en las quaresmas, viernas y pasquas del año no si represente."

* Velasco al Rey. " La ciudad estava muy escandalizada y offendida : la nobleza, ciudadanos y todo el pueblo. Juntaron su consejo general, y en voz comun se resintieron con el cardenal con palabras vivas." The rest is from the same report.

† Concordia jurisdictionalis inter forum ecclesiasticum et forum seculare, c. x. Ordines Sen. Med.

‡ Novelli, Storia di Como, iii. c. ii. 15, from an edict of 1539.

tricts. Every half year there were elected by lot four consuls of justice from the two colleges of native doctors and causidici, of the former of which there were twelve, of the latter fourteen, about the year 1550, at Como. These consuls went in their togas every day to the tribunal in the palace to hold their judicial sittings *. Every year in May a judge travelled, by order of his commune, through the highways and byeways of the district, to see to the repairing of the roads, bridges, and embankments by the villages and localities upon which that duty devolved. It was left to the towns to collect the mensuale in the manner they found most convenient. In contrast with the general body of the state, they held fast by the unity of a close corporation. They were not content with sending one of their number to Milan as often as their affairs required it; they had also their regular representatives, their oratori, there, who were bound, in consideration of the salaries they received, to act as the advocates, attorneys, and solicitors of their respective towns, and who were wont, when any general question was to be discussed, to assemble in a congregation under the presidency of their Milanese colleague. This congregation no doubt occupied but a subordinate position, but still it always enjoyed a certain consideration; for instance, in the year 1548 the mensuale was not imposed till the congregation had first been satisfied of its necessity. But not unfrequently even single towns, particularly Cremona, offered obstinate resistance to the governor. The Cremonese never looked to the example of any other town ; they always acted upon their own devices; they never yielded in any point to the governor or the Spanish settlers. In the year 1585, the duke of Terranuova had come to a tolerably satisfactory arrangement with the other towns respecting a new donative, but he never could gain the consent of Cremona. " They were their sovereign's most faithful vassals; they were ready to serve him with their lives and substance; but they were not minded that the governor should ingratiate himself with their king at their cost, and without their receiving any credit for the same." They contrived to prevent the donative, and they enjoyed so much consideration, that the other towns on all occasions made it their first business to see what Cremona would do †.

Now if there is obvious herein undoubtedly a remnant of municipal independence, the question is, who were they in whom this was specially invested? We still meet repeatedly with the democratic name, Conseglio Generale ; was this general council identical with the old one ?

We must confess it was not so ; the fact is evident from the example of Milan. There we see the still somewhat democratic element giving way

with extraordinary rapidity to a completely aristocratic system. When the general council assembled in the year 1512, on a green between the market and the new gate, it certainly did not consist of a great popular multitude, but it still numbered nine hundred members. Even then it appeared indeed that the resolutions adopted were dictated by the few rather than by the many *. But who could have foreseen, that but six years afterwards, this council should have dwindled down to a sixth of what it then numbered? An election of the general council took place in the year 1516 ; twenty-five members were chosen for each of the six gates, in all one hundred and fifty. And yet even this council was thought too numerous by the French. On the 1st of July, 1518, Lautrec, governor for Francis I., in Milan, named sixty persons of noble blood to constitute the conseglio generale †. To these was transferred all the power that belonged to the communes.

Something similar took place in the other towns likewise. We find a general council in Como also. It assembled at least every Monday and Friday under the presidency of a podesta. Every man was at liberty to speak his sentiments in his turn, and that even twice. The votes were taken by means of balls differently coloured, and the majority decided ‡. But there are two points to be remarked on this head. In the first place the number of this council was continually made less and less. In the beginning of the sixteenth century there were a hundred ordinary and fifty supernumerary decurioni. These hundred and fifty were reduced in the year 1534 to seventy-five, in the year 1583 to sixty, in 1614 to fifty, and lastly, in 1638, to forty §. The more important affairs were managed by a committee of twelve, presided over by a doctor of noble birth. Secondly, it was noticed that the decurionate fell entirely into the hands of certain families. The fact of being a member of the general council was often advanced as a proof in corroboration of the evidences of nobility called for on many occasions ||. This abuse was the more incurable, inasmuch as the council filled up the vacancies in its own body.

The same thing happened in other towns, as in Milan and Como. Leoni tells us, in the year 1589, that every town in the duchy had usually a council of sixty members for the management of its internal affairs (that of Como just then consisted of this number), but that the chief controul was exercised by twelve of their body, whom he names distinctively decurioni.

Now, this remnant of municipal independence had an important bearing on the whole state. The towns possessed a power, not merely defensive, but even actively influential on the conduct of the government. The chief places succeeded in filling the senate with their own citizens. In the year 1547, Como, desiring for itself a firm footing

---

* Ibid. iii. c. ii. 66, 227, from the Ordinazioni of the city. For the consuls of justice in Milan, two from the college of doctors, four from the college of notaries, see Statuta Mediolani, cap. 55. The colleges proposed the candidates, the sovereign nominated them.

† Leoni: "Il popolo di Cremona di bravura tra ogni altro dello stato Milanese pare che tenga il primo vanto. E constantissimo nelle sue risoluzioni le quali pretende et si sforza di far maturamente, et però è quello che nell' occasioni, o particolari della città o publiche dello stato, fa sempre testa nè si lascia tirare dall' autorità nè di Milano nè d'altro luogo."

* Arluni de Bello Veneto, v. 204. In the Statuta Mediolanensia, p. ii. cap. iii. under the title De Consilio Nongentorum Virorum Communis Mediolani, published in the year 1502, it is stated, that the Nine Hundred were chosen by the sovereign " de melioribus et utilioribus."

† Verri, Storia di Milano, from MSS. ii. 170, 171.

‡ Novelli from the Ordinazioni of 1567, iii. c. ii. 75, 76.

§ Ibid. iii. c. i. 472 ; ii. 109. 153. 181.

|| Novelli from the Ordinazioni of 1577, 1588, and 1591, iii. c. ii. 117

in the senate, appealed to the example of the other towns, which were already in the enjoyment of that advantage. Accordingly, for a century and a half from that date, we always meet with a citizen of Como in the senate. In the year 1560 that city had also a place of quæstor in the magistracy, occupied by one of its own people *. Leoni informs us that a place in the senate was accorded to every chief town in the duchy, not by virtue of any law, nor even by virtue of any very ancient usage, but in consequence of a certain sense of convenience. Now this must have been of vast advantage to the towns, seeing what a considerable portion of the whole government was in the senate's hands.

While such were the mutual relations in this state between governor and senate, associations and communes, soldiers and inhabitants, there was also a court in which both elements were combined, namely, a consulta connected with the governor. This privy council, consisting of the superior officers of the troops and of the presidents of the tribunals, was in reality invested with the care of both interests. The soldiers required to be fed and paid; the citizens desired the maintenance of their lawful condition. Both objects were effected. Much as the citizens complained of the taxes, single and double, imposed upon them, and of the light and heavy cavalry required of them, they still paid their dues. Their independence did not reach the length of enabling them to refuse this. But so much power at least they had, that though their rights and laws might not be preserved utterly inviolate, at any rate not in every individual case, or when especially persons of inferior consideration were concerned, still they were on the whole maintained and enforced †.

So it was at least under Philip II. But how, when these frontiers were directly approached with arms in the seventeenth century, when war was levied against Savoy, against the Valtellina, and to settle the disturbances in Montferrat, and lastly, when the country became entangled in all the perplexities of the thirty years' war? The military element then gained the ascendancy over the pacific ; the royal court neglected the practice of inspecting and controuling the provincial administration ; the Spaniards assumed in Milan, as elsewhere in Italy, an oppressive predominance ; to scarcity and disease were added the intolerable burthens of military contributions, and the quartering of troops on the inhabitants. Many a Milanese then wished that Don Philip II., of blessed memory, might rise again from the dead, and live as long as the world stood ‡ !

VI. The Netherlands.

All things considered, it cannot be said that the Netherlands enjoyed particular freedom under the house of Burgundy, and under Charles V.

Monarchical Authority.

Here too we have to deal with the three estates. The clergy who filled the higher places were nearly all nominated by the sovereign, as was likewise the case with the majority of the inferior clergy. Without his permission they durst neither admit any command from Rome, or acquire a new property any where *. The lord had only restricted rights over his vassals, more restricted than those directly exercised by the sovereign †: he served the latter in peace and war; how then should he have been independent ? Lastly, we must admit that the sovereign exercised an influence also over the internal administration of the towns. Antwerp, which pretended to be very free, was not at liberty for all that to nominate its own schoeppen, or local justices ; a council consisting chiefly of the senior justices proposed two for each place at the yearly nomination; but the selection and the nomination were left to the sovereign. Even the burgomasters were elected in conformity with the sovereign's views. Now, if we reflect that upon these burgomasters and schoeppen, the choice of the presidents of the *wicks*, and that of the fifty-four presidents of the guilds, was so far at least dependent that they decided on one out of three candidates, we shall see how deep down the influence of the government could extend ‡. In Brussels the court yearly nominated the seven schoeppen out of the seven septs ; in most of the towns there were old colleges of councillors, called Breede Raade or Vroetschappen, which proposed two of their members as candidates for every schoeppe's place ; the nomination rested with the court. The court had influence likewise over the college of councillors in Rotterdam; it caused three names to be presented to it for each vacant place, and selected one of them §. The consequence of the insurrection in Ghent, in 1539, was that on the 10th of May, every year, the court put whomsoever it pleased into the twenty-six places of the schoeppen ‖. As far as I can discover, there was but one place, Valenciennes, which still possessed a general assembly, but I do not find that it was of much importance. Such then was the composition of the estates ; clergy named by the king ; nobles in his service ; burgomasters scarcely ever chosen without his interference.

This state of things paved the way—it could not have been otherwise—for the establishment of the new constitution in this country. The supreme authority had no little influence on the judicial body, high and low. It nominated the schoeppen in the towns, by whom justice was locally administered ; and it appointed and deposed at pleasure the schultheissen or bailiffs connected with the former, whose duty it was to look to the sovereign's rights and the laws, the prosecution of the guilty,

* Novelli, iii. c. ii. 28, and in other places.

† Leoni: " Patiscono come possono al meglio la signoria de Spagnuoli, all' humor de quali per la lunga assuefattione hanno di maniera accommodato l'animo, che da quel desiderio impoi ch' è natu: ale in ogni popolo, di veder mutatione, si può dire che vivono non in tutto mal contenti sotto il governo del re di Spagna.—Sono governati con qualche dolcezza maggiore che li Napolitani, conoscendo che la natura Lombarda più mansueta che la Napolitana ha anco bisogna di minor asprezza."

‡ Li vasalli della Maestà del re catolico nello stato di

Milano alla santissima et gloriosissima vergine Maria, MS. An essay not so prolix as its title.

* Guicciardini, Descriptio Belgii generalis, Amsterdam, 1660, p. 85, and Compendio degli Stati e Governi di Fiandra, Informatt. i. p. 95, MS.

† Ibid. Descriptio Belgii particularis, p. 256.

‡ Ibid. p. 171.

§ De Laet, Belgii confœderati, Respublica Hollandia, cap vi. p. 83. 88. Cf. Philip a Zesen, Leo Belgicus, p. 148.

‖ Additamentum ad Guicciard. Descriptionem, p. 343.

and the execution of judicial sentences [*]. The provincial courts, such as the council of Flanders, the chancery of Brabant, and the court of Holland, courts not only of appeal, but charged also with some portion of the duties of government, received from it their functionaries and their salaries. Here and there it was even allowed to admit foreigners to seats on the tribunals; two at least in that of Brabant, and in that of Friesland all the members but four might be foreigners [†]. Over all these tribunals Charles the Bold had established a supreme one in the great court of Mechlin, which he called a parliament. Before it the knights of the Golden Fleece were tried. This court was likewise wholly dependent on the sovereign. With whatever violence the question was agitated elsewhere, whether the members of the supreme courts should be appointed by the sovereign or the estates, that right was here exercised without dispute by the sovereign. He had here too a standing army. Some native infantry were always maintained, in addition to which Charles V. set apart one hundred and eighty thousand ducats a year for six hundred lancers, each with five horses [‡]. Whilst these armaments afforded the means of keeping the nobles employed, and of retaining them in a sort of ambitious dependence on the sovereign, Charles devised the plan of dividing them into unequal companies of thirty, forty, or fifty, by which means the occurrence of every vacancy gave him an opportunity for bestowing favour and promotion that cost him nothing. This was an institution which Marino Cavallo thought especially worthy of imitation [§]. Lastly, Charles was in the receipt of considerable taxes. Soriano estimates the income of a few years at twenty-four millions of ducats; William of Orange computes the contributions to a single war at forty millions [‖].

Provincial Rights.

Now, if the estates were under the controul of the sovereign, if they left the administration of justice in his hands, paid him taxes, and maintained troops for him, wherein consisted the freedom of which they boasted?

No doubt the supreme power has its influence in every state, but it always encounters a resistance in the local interests. If the sovereign chose the schoeppen, on the other hand every town, Ghent alone excepted after the insurrection, prescribed to him those from among whom he was to choose them. Though the before mentioned college of councillors had little else left it to do than to take the necessary steps in the elections, nevertheless the actual government was usually linked with that body; all the officers elected were necessarily members thereof; besides which other members, charged with the protection of local rights, were in many places associated with the schoeppen [*]. In Zieriksee there were two burgomasters, one for matters pertaining to the jurisdiction of the sovereign, the other for those belonging to that of the town; the former was selected from the schoeppen, the latter from among the other councillors [†]. Moreover, though the sovereign had a share in the concerns of justice, still he could not alter the laws, and every province clung jealously to its own; the North Hollanders to their Asingish law of inheritance; the Groeningers to their peculiar laws of debtor and creditor, and the men of Guelders to their peculiar feudal usages. Lastly, if he could exercise an influence over the domestic administration of the provinces, still he was every where met by some privilege. Flanders boasted of being the freest lordship in the world. Brabant had seven invaluable privileges, the last of which was, that if the sovereign broke through the rights of the country, and did not listen to its remonstrances, it should then be absolved from its oath of allegiance [‡]. Mechlin was free from all imposts for subsidies upon the real estates of its inhabitants. Holland and Zealand relied on the great charter granted them by the daughter of Charles the Bold. Just about the middle of the sixteenth century the provinces took up the question of their privileges with renovated zeal; they brought forth the genuine documents dispersed through registries, chanceries, and convents, and put them in better order; they hesitated in disputed cases to impart the originals to the court [§]. They aimed at no unconditional authority; they had no desire for unrestricted freedom; but their privileges seemed to them a property, as much so as any material possession of the community, and they would not part with them.

When these estates assembled at the sovereign's summons, they listened in common to the proposals laid before them; but when the time was come to discuss these, they separated province by province, each deputy mindful of the privileges of his own. Now, many of these committees were only empowered to hear and to report at home; others demanded a gratuity for their assent, and it was always some extension of rights they required: others again were flatly resolved on opposition. They were agreed only on one thing, that, unless confirmed eventually by a general vote, no assent previously given was at all binding. The governor had often to treat with the several states, with the several towns, and it must be admitted that the example of the consenting majority had a certain influence on the recusants. Sometimes however the governor found himself compelled to grant some new immunity; sometimes he had even to forego his plans [‖].

---

[*] An excursus on this subject in Addit. ad Guicc. Descr. p. 429.

[†] Ubbo Emmius ap. De Laet, Belgii confœderati Respublica Frisia, c. 8.

[‡] Cavallo, Relatione: "Computati li suoi condottieri et officiali a ducati 140 per huomo d'arme et 120 per leggieri."

[§] Cavallo: "Con la vacanza senza accrescimento alcuno di nuova spesa s'accresce dignità o utile a tre o a quattro condottieri: il che saria benissimo fare la Serenità Vostra."

[‖] Soriano: "L'imperatore ha potuto cavare in 24 millioni d'oro in pochi anni."—Verantwoording des Princen van Oranje, ap. Bor.

[*] Decretum ordinum Hollandiæ et Westfrisiæ de antiquo jure reipublicæ Batavicæ, in the work entitled Respublica Hollandiæ et Urbes, Lugd. 1630, p. 148.

[†] Additam. ad. Guicc. tom. iii. p. 171.

[‡] Among others Meter, Niederl. Historie, tom. i. p. 68.

[§] Wagenaar, Allg. Geschichte der Vereinigten Niederlande, tom. i. p. 548.

[‖] From the Examples of the transactions of the estates in Wagenaar, Giucciardini Descr. gener. Hugo Grotius de Antiquitate Reipublicæ Bataviæ, p. 62. Soriano: "Si tratta prima con li principali delle città et degli stati et poiche questi sono persuasi, chi con parole, chi con promesse et altri con premii, son seguitati dagl' altri. Così sono stati aggravati da' sussidii li paesi bassi."

Balance of the Constitution.

Upon this antagonism between the central and the local authorities, an antagonism so characterized that there was, if not constant strife, at least perpetual jealousy between the highest courts and those of the provinces, between the latter and the schoeppen of the towns, between the schoeppen and the sovereign's schultheiss on the one hand, and the common councils on the other, and lastly, between the councils and the guilds and communes ;—upon this antagonism, and, above all, upon the natural opposition between the state authority and the provincial rights, rested the balance of the constitution. The sovereign usually obtained the money he required, but it cost him pains to procure it ; he could not conceal from himself the fact that the subject had the power of refusing it. Charles V. was used to say he would concede liberties and immunities to his territories, but they should not chaffer with him. Upon this the country would answer, that it would support him with ample supplies, but of its own free will; only he should not arbitrarily burden it. They, both the sovereign and the country, had their respective rights; the act of homage consisted in their swearing reciprocally to these. The sovereign swore "truly and sincerely to observe all statutes, privileges, briefs, exemptions and immunities, all justiciary and manorial rights, all town laws, land laws, water laws, and all customs of the province, old and new." The inhabitants swore "to be, in consideration thereof, good and lawful subjects to him, to guard him from hurt, to provide for his advantage, and to preserve his sovereign authority *." They swore to uphold each other's rights and claims ; but whereas the monarch was given two titles, viz. sovereign prince and natural lord; the former was more pleasing to the monarch, because it seemed to infer a more absolute right; the latter was more acceptable to the people, because apparently involving the idea of a limitation founded on custom and prescriptive rights. Even the small towns of Holland were used to close a petition with the words, " Thus doing your imperial majesty will do right †."

Misunderstandings under Philip.

In such a state of equilibrium was the administration of the Netherlands in the times of Charles V. Philip II. however resolved to give the sovereign's authority the preponderance.

Wherever Philip II. looked around him he saw his authority in his other dominions based chiefly on a considerable addition of Spanish, or rather Castilian material, to the old stock of government. He had there Spanish viceroys with their own privy councils, independent of the respective countries; he had along with them Spanish troops and Spanish functionaries; he had there the inquisition, which acknowledged a supreme head in Castile. True, these means and instruments of dominion had not been fully introduced into any country.

Sicily preserved itself from Spanish functionaries ; Milan and Naples succeeded in keeping out the inquisition : but either of these was singly enough to keep a country in perfect allegiance.

What, then, if the attempt were made to effect similar measures in the Netherlands too ?

There can be no doubt that Philip entertained this purpose. Contrary to all the laws of the country, he designed to leave the Spanish troops there during peace, the presence of which had been rendered necessary by war *. When he committed the government to his sister Margaret, he appointed indeed with her a council of state consisting chiefly of native nobles ; but he crippled the powers of that council, not only by establishing along with it an independent privy council under a president who could be implicitly relied on, Viglius van Zuichem, but he also instructed Margaret that in difficult cases she should only consult and hearken to the most trusty members, especially Granvella, bishop of Arras, taking their advice in a privy consulta, such as was usual at the king's court, and those of the viceroys †. Finally, if he still avoided putting forward the name of the Spanish inquisition, still he made so many innovations in ecclesiastical affairs, he so rigorously enforced and aggravated the old edicts against heretics, that every one was persuaded he would introduce that institution, and a rumour that he had already obtained a bull to that end from Pius IV., gained unhesitating and entire credence ‡.

Whilst the king thus resolved to reduce the Netherlands to the same footing of obedience as his other provinces, was it likely the country should second his purpose with alacrity ? The leading men of rank, men whose fortunes had been founded in the civil and military service of Charles V., set themselves against it.

Three things seem more particularly to have determined them. Whereas, in the beginning of the reign of Charles V., nobles of the Netherlands had ruled the whole empire, and had afterwards been forced to share at least with Castilians all the influence accorded them by the sovereign, it now turned out, as every one must have expected from Philip, that he excluded the men of the Netherlands from all participation in the government of the empire. The Castilians had rebelled against the Belgian administration under Charles V. Egmont could fairly compare his services in the field and in the cabinet with those performed by Alva. Count Hoorn had formerly stood as high at the court of Philip as Feria ; they both commanded body guards of his, the former the archers, the latter the Spaniards §. But now Alva and Feria sat in the king's council of state ; Egmont and Hoorn were of little account. Spaniards and Ne-

---

* Oath taken at Antwerp and Valenciennes on the occasion of tendering allegiance to Philip, in Guicciardini. Eed gedaen en Gröningen un Byvoegsel van autentyke Stukken, Bor, Nederlandsche Oorlogen, ed. of 1679.
† Wagenaar, ii. 537.

* Tiepolo, Relatione di Spagna. "Il re fece gagliardissimo sforzo, perche si contentassero i Fiamenghi, che restasse nelle fortezze più principali per guardia di esse 3000 Spagnuoli."
† Strada de Bello Belgico, Vienna, 1754, i. p. 25. The same thing is mentioned by Burgundus.
‡ Tiepolo : " Oltre che havevano per cosa sicurissima che Sua Catolica Maestà haveva ottenuto da Pio IV. un breve col quale voleva mettere la inquisitione in quei stati per ridurli in quella stretta obedienza che le sono Spagnuoli. Da che venivano essi, a perdere totalmente l'autorità et la libertà solita et gli antiquissimi privilegii suoi."
§ Sandoval, Carlos V. lib. xxx. p. 657.

therlanders had been equal and alike jealous of each other in the service of Charles ; but now the Spaniards were granted a predominant considera- tion *.

But this was not all. The people of the Nether- lands not only saw themselves excluded from pub- lic affairs, but beheld their own country threatened with a foreign administration. When Montigny was afterwards despatched to Spain, he did not conceal what it was the nobles of the Netherlands most dreaded. When they became aware that the barons in the Italian provinces were reduced to a condition of mere insignificance, they feared that the Spaniards would fain bring them too to the same footing ; they saw, too, every preparation taken by the king to that end; hence, Montigny owned, proceeded the whole discontent of the nobles †. Here that peculiar propensity of the Netherlanders for local exclusiveness came in play. In like manner as each several province claimed to be governed only by its own natives, a claim occasionally indeed, but only occasionally disre- garded, so they would not have any foreigner, any Spaniard, admitted to a place in the general go- vernment of the provinces at large. This was so vehemently insisted on, that the king is said to have exclaimed, " I too am a Spaniard; do they mean to reject me also ?"

Lastly, personal connexions also produced in this case their natural result, particularly those of the prince of Orange. When it was first discussed to whom the administration of the Netherlands should be entrusted, the prince of Orange wished to see it in the hands of Christina, duchess of Lorraine, niece of the deceased emperor, a neighbour, and one familiarized with the national habits. He hoped to make her daughter his wife, whereby he would have been sure of obtaining the greatest in- fluence over the government. But others probably feared this as much as he desired it. Granvella and Alva were for the emperor's natural daughter, Margaret, who had lived upwards of twenty years in Italy, and who was regarded as a more trusty Spaniard. This party prevailed ; it caused Mar- garet to be appointed governess, and even pre- vented the marriage which the prince was seek- ing ‡. This was enough to put Granvella and Orange at open enmity. But soon after the prince brought home a wife from that Saxon house which had dashed the emperor's fortunes ; and thence- forth a bell was heard at the court of Brussels summoning to the Lutheran worship §. The ill- will between the parties was aggravated, not only in consequence of the fact that Granvella, as a bishop, approved of all measures that were rigor- ously catholic, but also because the princess was the grand-daughter of the landgrave, whose family ascribed to Granvella everything untoward that

had befallen their head, and hated him therefore with all their hearts. It must, moreover, have stirred up ill-blood when Granvella let fall the ob- servation, that the distinguished position of the prince in Brabant was not consistent with the king's dignity *. Was the prince to endure pa- tiently that all the power to which he thought himself entitled as a native prince, should pass into the hands of an alien, and his enemy ? that he should be put off with an empty title without real authority ? Charles V. had thought otherwise, and had reposed a more affectionate confidence in the prince than in the bishop.

Perez asserts that he was acquainted with the direct causes of the Flemish troubles, and could point them out as distinctly as any one could indi- cate the unquestionable sources of a river †. It seems to me not improbable that he alludes to these and other similar personal circumstances.

Putting all this together, we find, in the first place, that the king's designs involved him in open war with his province. He wished to make it as submissive as the others; the province, on its part, wished to maintain the freedom of which it saw itself plundered. He wished to hold the ecclesias- tical and the secular administration in more com- plete obedience, through the instrumentality of functionaries exclusively devoted to himself, and of new bishops : the province desired men who had a home interest to be at the head of affairs, and it thought the old church constitution more convenient. The king desired to leave foreign soldiers quartered in the country ; the people were incensed at the sight of arms after peace had been restored. Then we see that the superior functiona- ries of state, by whom the allegiance of the country should have been cultivated and confirmed, were led, by the position of the empire and of the court, to adopt the cause of the people instead of that of the king. It was the good fortune of the country that they but indifferently administered the cen- tral and sovereign authority which they should have represented, or rather that they looked to the advantage of the province. They were the very persons who most opposed the king. Let us con- sider the course their opposition pursued.

The Troubles.

First, they set themselves against what was cer- tainly the most alarming thing of all, the leaving behind of the troops. The prince of Orange hastened home from France for the express purpose of pre- venting that design, and he actually succeeded in exacting a promise from the king. But how was the latter to be brought to fulfil his promise ? Long after the term he had himself assigned was expired, he set the shrewd wit of the governess to work to gloss over the delay ‡. The natives were resolved to force the removal of the troops. The Zealanders threatened to break down their dams, and to let the sea in upon the country, rather than endure the presence of the Spaniards in it. The districts refused to contribute subsidies; they refused to pay back the money that was taken up in their name ;

* Soriano: " I popoli mal contenti per assidue gravezze et perche il governo d'ogni cosa che soleva essere in mano sua è tutto in mano de Spagnuoli."

† Hopper, Recueil et Mémorial des troubles des Pays bas du Roy, chap. ii. 8, makes this remark in the very begin- ning of the troubles. Montigny (Hopper, iii. chap. 3, § 100) calls it "la vraye ou au moins la principale cause de ces maux et altérations."

‡ Bentivoglio, Relatione delle provincie unite di Fiandra, lib. ii. Relationi del cardinale Bentivoglio; Venetia, 1667, p. 21.

§ Cabrera, Don Felipe segundo, p. 284.

* Vita Viglii ab Aytta Zuichemi in Hoynk van Papend- recht, Analect. Belg. i. n. lxx.

† Perez a un cavallero amigo. Segundas cartas, n. 115, p. 143.

‡ Strada, de Bello Belgico, iii. p. 49, from the king's letter.

G

nay, they would not furnish the pay of their own troops till the Spaniards were gone *. Seeing, therefore, the imminent peril of ruin to the finances, and pressed by the open resistance of the towns, and by a mutiny among the native troops, the king gave way. Reluctantly, late, and on compulsion, he recalled the troops.

But another urgent danger manifested itself at this moment (1561). At that period the Netherlanders saw all the remonstrances they addressed to the king, all the arts of policy they tried with the pope, to prevent the purposed introduction of new bishops remain of no effect. This in itself was alarming with regard to the freedom of the country, and the old constitution. One of the three estates, the ecclesiastical, was injured in its property, for it was intended to provide out of this for the new bishops; but all three were threatened, because the new clergy, more numerous as it was, and wholly devoted to the court, would easily sustain its pretensions to superiority in future assemblies †. But it was a still more formidable consideration, that the new Flemish churches were to be formed into a hierarchy, at the head of which was to stand that same hated foreigner, who was invested at once with the primacy of the bishoprics and with the cardinal's purple. He was already the actual wielder of the state council's authority; Viglius his friend, nay dependent, managed the privy council according to his views; and now he was becoming the head of a clergy which had in old ecclesiastical laws strong weapons against all who displeased them. All the powers of the administration, of justice, and of the church, were subservient to him, and in his hands; the distinguished rank of a cardinal seemed calculated infallibly to exalt him above every assault ‡.

The greater the fortune designed for Granvella, the greater was to be the resistance it provoked on the part of his antagonists. Orange and Egmont, who had previously not been on very good terms, hastened to renew their mutual connexion; they were joined by Hoorn. And, first of all, they tried what their combined credit could effect with the king. They declared to him that the affairs of the country could never go on well as long as they were all, in the aggregate, in the hands of Granvella; that he was too much detested, his life was not adapted for the edification of the people, the country would be ruined under him. But these remonstrances, and those they addressed to the governess, were all in vain §. They resolved to go further. Tiepolo confirms expressly, and with more accuracy of detail, what others besides have hinted at. First of all Orange, Egmont, Montigny, Hoorn, Bergen, and

Megen, united together, nearly in the manner of German potentates, and formed a strict league for mutual defence against all who should attack any one of them, a league to which they admitted others also, and to which they pledged themselves by solemn oaths *. A sound of perturbation now filled the country. It was alleged for certain that Granvella had said there was no hoping for quiet in the provinces till some heads should have fallen ;—that it were well the king should come, but with a strong army, and with a predetermination to bind the necks of the people by force. It was currently reported that Granvella had serious designs against the prince's life. What a talk there was then of foolscaps and and of arrowsheaves on liveries ! What a multitude of satires and caricatures were circulated ! At last, when not only the three opposition leaders declared they must abstain from attending the council of state so long as Granvella sat in it, but the estates too refused to enter upon their proceedings so long as Granvella was the mouthpiece of the government †; when a formal resistance to the prime minister appeared then organised, Margaret likewise bethought her, and yielded to her feelings of discontent at being obliged thus to play as it were a secondary part: accordingly the king at last consented to the removal of the cardinal.

Thus the Flemish lords had obtained their first and their second objects. They had got rid of the troops that threatened their freedom; they were quit of the foreigner who had both domineered over and threatened them, and whom they had hated and feared. What were the means by which they obtained this success? Let us mark the facts well. They petition, they make remonstrances: nothing is done. But when they begin to offer resistance, when the king has reason to apprehend an insurrection, then their desires are complied with.

After Granvella's removal the lords returned to the council. They applied themselves with the greatest diligence to business; they were at their posts from an early hour till evening; whilst endeavouring to instruct Margaret, they succeeded also in gaining her over to their cause; standing on the best terms with the estates and with the people, they hoped to free the country entirely from the Spanish influence, and to be able to govern it upon their own principles ‡.

New difficulties however occurred. While they were striving with Granvella the new bishops had been introduced into no few places, and invested with that ecclesiastical authority so commanding in those times, and which they had themselves such good reason to regard with jealousy and alarm. Was

---

* Arcana Gubernatricis Epistola; Strada, iii. 51.

† For the manner in which this fear was expressed, see Hopper, Recueil, chap. iii. § 8. Viglius calls it "nubecula in serenitate." Vita, n. 77.

‡ Tiepolo: "Si accrebbe il sospetto che il Re non havesse intentione di soggiogarli a fatto, vedendo esser del tutto escluso il consiglio loro nelle cose di stato et non esser messo in alcuna consideratione di Madama, la quale si adheriva a quello del cardinale Granvella et voleva anco che fosse con molta severità esseguito, con che si conveniva distruggere la autorità sua."

§ For this letter in the shape in which it was finally drawn up, Lettre par diverses fois réformée et corrigée, see Hopper, chap. iv. n. 10. The extract in Bentivoglio's Historia della guerra di Fiandra, i. c. i. p. 48, is but dubious.

* Tiepolo. "Si strinsero insieme il principe d'Oranges, li conti d'Egmont e Horn, il marchese di Berges morto, Monsignor di Montini et il conte di Mega, conseguiti da molti altri grandi per l'autorità et dipendentie grandissime che havevano quelli signori, et conclusero una lega contra'l cardinale predetto *a difesa commune contra chi volessero offendere alcun di loro*, la qual confermarono con solennissimo giuramento; nè si curarono che se non li particolari fossero secreti per all'hora, ma publicarono questa loro unione fatta contro il cardinale." Hopper also, chap. vii. n. 19, mentions the "confederation avecq serment tres estroict." Wagenaar says the tenor of this league was never divulged; iii. 49. Tiepolo gives some information though not complete.

† Vita Viglii, n. 82.

‡ Hopper, Partie seconde, ch. i. n. 20.

not Granvella, even though removed, still arch-bishop and primate of the national church? More-over, the court of the privy council was still swayed in the same spirit as had prevailed under Gran-vella's rule. Their foe's administration had struck such deep root that its influence was not to be annihilated at once by the mere removal of the leader. If the nobles would avail themselves of victory they had won, it was incumbent on them to get rid of these obstacles.

They endeavoured to effect this sometimes di-rectly, sometimes by a variety of indirect means. They brought it about that the president of the privy council should no longer make his official communications directly to the governess, but only in the sittings of the council of state, a device by which a wholly new share in public business was necessarily secured to themselves. It is alleged that they prevented the introduction of the new bishop, where it had not yet taken place; that they favoured every refractory disposition towards the judicature of the church and of the privy council; that they filled up offices at their own pleasure, nay, for money; and that they deliberately post-poned the dignity and consideration of the gover-ness to their own [*].

But whatever means they might employ, these never fully sufficed to compass their ends. They resolved to apply directly to the king. If the decrees touching religion were mitigated, and the penal orders repealed, there was no ecclesiastical power which could cause them either alarm or obstruction. They resolved to petition first for the mitigation of the decrees in question. The number of the new religionists, they argued, was so great that it would be impossible to inflict the punishments prescribed without exciting a rebellion. Next, they complained that the partition of business amongst independent councils only impeded its progress. It would be well, they said, formally to render the other coun-cils subordinate to the council of state [†]. They lost no time in sending count Egmont with these petitions to the king. Egmont had frequently private audiences with the monarch. Philip treated him with peculiar marks of honour, and in the answer he gave him he afforded encouragement to hope for the fulfilment of both requests [‡].

But Philip's government was doubletongued, and its motto was "From afar." On the very day the instruction was made out for Egmont, the king wrote to Margaret that he did not think fit to increase the power of the council of state [§]. After this, when some bishops and divines, whose opinions were consulted, did not even pronounce in favour of a mitigation of the penal ordinances, as it might well have been guessed would be the case, Philip declared their opinion to be true as truth itself: heresy, he said, grew by neglect; who could think of diminishing a punishment whilst the crime for

which it was ordained was growing [*]. He granted therefore neither the one petition nor the other. The privy council pronounced his determination wise and holy. The decrees of the council of Trent were everywhere proclaimed. The king's new orders were sent into all the provinces. The magistrates were called upon to aid the inquisitors.

How fiercely, says Hopper, did the fire now blaze up that had hitherto smouldered under the ashes! The higher nobles thought themselves especially perilled. Granvella could assail their estates, nay, their lives, under cover of the proclamations [†]. Hatred to him mingled intensely in all their common views and feelings.

What then did they do to secure themselves? We find that the nobility of the second class here-upon joined in the famous compromise. It is true indeed that the most eminent chiefs did not per-sonally unite in this league. But their brothers, their nearest friends, and the retainers of their houses, belonged to it. Can there be any serious question that they were themselves privy to it [‡]? When the country was now thus brought into a state of open ferment, when civil war seemed actually broken out, when all the elements of strife were already in motion, the two petitions before men-tioned were once more addressed to the king. Was it not to be expected that in a moment of such imminent danger he would give way a third time, as he had done once and again before? They declared that if he would abolish the inquisition, mitigate the stringency of the proclamations, and grant them a general amnesty, tranquillity should be restored in the country; if not, he should not see them take horse to put down those who were in rebellion against him. They had not miscalcu-lated; they knew their sovereign well: he now pro-mised them actual abolition of the existing inquisi-tion, moderation of the proclamations, and am-nesty [§].

When he did this, the time was already past when the concession could avail. The impatient confederated nobles held armed meetings; the iconoclastic storm swept the land from end to end; there was open insurrection. The lords had only wished, as Tiepolo says, for an alarm of rebellion, but not for the thing itself. But it fared with them as with a man who leads a canal from a river to irrigate his field, but finds the whole force of the current desert the main bed, burst through the canal, and inundate his whole property.

The iconoclastic mania split the confederates them-selves into two parties; it put weapons into the hands of the governess, and the catholic party; it snatched the reins from the hands of those who had hitherto been the leaders in these movements. The first result was that the king actually acquired the complete mastery. He sent an army of Spaniards

---

[*] Respecting these purposes and proceedings, see chiefly Viglius himself in his Vita, n. 87 : also Hopper, and Cabrera, Don Feiipe segundo, lib. vi. c. 17, p. 335.

[†] See, above all, Hopper, p ii. ch. 3. n. 126 The last point was laid to Egmont's charge as a special crime. "Tenor sententiæ capitalis in Egmondanum." Schardius, Rer. Germ. tom. iv. pp. 83. 85.

[‡] Instructio earum rerum quas tu princeps Gauræ, etc. exponere meo nomine debes sorori meæ : Extracts in Strada, lib. iv. 88.

[§] From the king's letter, April 8, 1565. Strada, ibid.

[*] L'apostille mise en marge de l'Ecrit des Evesques, Hopper, n. 64.

[†] Hopper, Partiç. iii. ch. 1. n. 88.

[‡] Tiepolo: "Se bene li più principali cercavano di dis-simular, però avenne che quattro nobili, non però di molta consideratione, ne della lega, si scoprirono per capi a popoli, che altro non aspettarono che questo." He alludes undoubt-edly to Brederode and counts Nassau, Berghe and Eulen-burg, of whom Hopper says, n. 92, "Tous amis de la ligue des dicts seigneurs." It strikes me Hopper too comes under the category, "et de la ligue d. d. s."

[§] All this from Hopper, particularly n. 113.

G 2

and Italians into the country, and there was none to venture on opposing it; he appointed as governor, the general of his army, with almost unlimited power; he established a council which far outdid any inquisition; and that all this might be irrevocable, he had castles built commanding all the chief towns.

Fortunately, however, matters did not take the course he expected. When things had arrived at the highest pitch, they took a change. The local interests once more asserted their force in opposition to all encroachments of the supreme authority. The triumph of those interests constitutes the revolution of the Netherlands. Tyranny for once had freedom for its result.

CHAPTER IV.

OF THE TAXES AND THE FINANCES.

1. *Under Charles V.*

THERE is on record a curious conversation of Charles V. with a peasant of Toledo. The emperor fell in with him as he was roaming about the woods in pursuit of game, and entered into discourse with him. Upon the peasant saying that he had seen five kings in his time, Charles, who was unknown to the man, asked him which of the five was the best, and which the worst. Upon this he had to hear what could hardly have been very agreeable to him. "The best," replied the peasant, "was Don Fernando, who was rightly called the Catholic; and the worst—well, I do think the one we have got now is bad enough." "Why so?" said Charles. The peasant objected that the king was always leaving wife and child, and setting off for Germany, for Italy, or for Flanders; that he carried off with him all the wealth he drew from his rents, and the treasures he derived from the Indies, enough to enable him to conquer the world, and that not content even with all that, he ruined the unfortunate husbandman with taxes [*].

The feelings expressed by the peasant were in fact those of most Castilians, nay, of most subjects of Charles throughout his dominions. They found fault with him precisely for what he was most forced to by the condition of his empire, and by his position in the world. Each of his states would care only for itself, and not for the whole; he alone had a comprehensive feeling for the whole, by the combination of which the wars and the expenses complained of had been occasioned. Hence, from the very first, Charles found himself under pecuniary embarrassments, which exercised the greatest influence on his public life, and on the condition of his states. On both accounts it is necessary to take into consideration the financial position of this monarch.

It was common to all his states that the royal domains in them were greatly reduced in value. Isabella had not recovered nearly so much as she could have wished from the vast donations of former sovereigns; and even what she retrieved was again much diminished by Philip I., and Ferdinand the Catholic, whose lot it again was to be under

the necessity of courting the favour of the grandees. In Naples, too, Ferdinand the Catholic was obliged to satisfy the French party, and the exiled Anjevines, out of the royal demesnes. In Milan they reckoned nineteen alienations made by the last Visconti, sixty by the first Sforza, seventy-four by Louis the Moor, all out of the ducal possessions; how much could the remainder amount to * ? It is asserted with regard to the Netherlands, that the old possessions of the dukes and counts were found in the time of Charles V. to have been for the most part alienated.

The monarch no doubt had other sources of income altogether distinct from the proceeds of real estates. There were customs upon foreign and domestic commerce, there were tolls, and regalia had been enforced.

In Castile there existed, at least in its main features, that system of taxation which continued there down to modern times. First of all the country was inclosed all round within custom lines. These did not comprise Biscay, the Asturias, and Gallicia [†]. Whatever was landed in Biscay and Guipuscoa, and in the four mountain towns on the sea, Laredo, Santander, Castro, Urdiales, and San Vincente, and took the road thence to Castile, had to pay the sea tenth in Orduña, Vittoria, and Valmoseda. Goods from the Asturias paid in Oviedo; those from Gallicia, in Sanabria and Villafranca. From these points, extended westward along the borders of Portugal, eastward along the frontiers of Aragon, Navarre, and Valencia, those so called dry ports, which separated those kingdoms from Castile, after they had been united with it, as fully as before. It was only in the south that Castile stretched with reference to the tolls as far as the sea. No new partitions had been made in that quarter, but the almoxarifazgos of the Moors had been retained in the ports. In Seville, besides the general custom-house (almoxarifazgo mayor) there was also another exclusively for the American trade [‡].

The internal trade of the country was no less liable to duty than the external. Here the *alcavala* applied. This impost, by virtue of which every seller was bound out of every ten maravedis of the selling price, to pay one to the king, and which extended even to barter, an impost from which the law declared that no town or village, no royal, ecclesiastical, or manorial place, no knight or squire, no judge, or civil functionary was free [§], and from which there were in fact but few exemptions allowed, furnished, after all deductions, very considerable proceeds, particularly after the *tercias*, a portion of the ecclesiastical tithes conceded to the government, had been reckoned in with it. Its obstructive, nay, fatal operation, was in some degree evaded by the merindades, towns and villages combining to make a composition with the govern-

---

* Verri, Storia di Milano, ii. 121.

† Gallicia, at least, not since 1558. Cortes of 1558, Pet. 47.

‡ Printed tables of the Spanish imports at this period are given in Laet, Hispania, Lugd. Bat. 1629, p. 387; Rehfues, Spanien, Bd. iv. p. 1246; and Les estats, empires et royaumes du monde, 1616, p. 322. Llorente, Provincias Vascongadas, t. ii. gives lists of the old and new duties arranged alphabetically.

§ Three laws respecting the Alcavala in the Recopilacion of 1545, vol. ii. pp. 617. 623; all three by Ferdinand and Isabella, an. 1491.

---

* Sandoval, Historia del Emperador Carlos V. lib. xxiv. p. 569.

ment, and raising among them the specific sum agreed on, called *encabezamiento* *. The new encabezamiento too, which came in force under the administration of Ximenes, instead of a tenth did not amount to a twentieth †. It was renewed from time to time. When the appointed years were elapsed, the first and most earnest petition of the cortes was sure to be for a continuance of the rate to a further term ‡. But the alcavala was not the only burthen on the domestic industry of the land. Special dues were levied on Granadan silk at Granada, Murcia at Almeria. When the flocks migrated to Estremadura, the farmers of the royal servicio y montazgo sat down in the passes of the country, reckoned flock by flock, and demanded the money, or the cattle per hundred or per thousand, due to them §. Salt was a monopoly. Fines, confiscations, the rents of the grand masterships, and smaller contingencies were added to these regular sources of revenue.

Altogether I find the income in the times of Charles V. calculated at 920,000 ducats ‖; but if we may judge from not much later accounts, it may have reached a million. It was founded, as we have seen, chiefly on commerce ; over this, above all things, the government had acquired a complete control.

It aimed at the same result in the other provinces likewise; but it was not successful in all. Sicily was the freest of them all from taxes, as well as from other interferences on the part of the central authority. The custom houses in Messina and Palermo could yield but small returns, seeing how inconsiderable was the commerce the kingdom carried on with foreign countries. Sicily had but one important branch of commerce, the corn trade; Sicilian wheat continued still to be consumed in Valencia and Malta, Genoa and Lucca, and even in Venice since the Turks had begun to annoy that state. The government kept this trade completely under its own control. The proprietors having conveyed their superfluity to eight places on the sea-coast, where the corn was received by a royal storekeeper, and kept till a purchaser was found, the viceroy had the power not only of determining how much should be allowed to be exported, but also at what price. The government received some tari on every salma. It was not the easiest part of an office encompassed with so many difficulties to arrange these matters. It was necessary to have a near-guess calculation of the probable proceeds of the whole harvest, and it was only when this exceeded 800,000 salme, that exportation was allowed. Then if a great profit might be realised from some advance of price, it was necessary to employ the utmost caution in the matter. Instances had been known of an advance of four tari the salma sending away purchasers to Provence or

Alessandria. The prosperity of the citizens depended on this trade ; as soon as exportation stopped, they could neither clear off their debts of the past year, nor make provision for that ensuing. The tranquillity of the country depended upon it ; for a slight dearth was enough among these men, naturally so intent on their profits, to cause a great rise of price, and consequently multiplied evils, nay, dangers. The government itself depended on the trade for its best source of income, and so it may easily be imagined what care it exacted with regard to it *. The sovereign was here the real merchant ; he fixed one price for the buyer and another for the seller ; the difference between the two was his profit. But as the buyers did not pay more here than elsewhere, it needs little penetration to perceive that this arrangement was a real tax upon the country. This source of revenue rendered somewhat about 250,000 ducats, and this was nearly all the Sicilians suffered to be extracted from them. The remainder of the revenue, some time after the reign of Charles, was computed at 160,000 ducats. I do not believe that the government in his day collected more than between three and four hundred thousand ducats.

The Netherlanders ranked next to the Sicilians in point of freedom and immunities. In fact they submitted to still fewer burthens on their trade, on which their existence and their fortunes depended. The government did not receive much more than 200,000 ducats from the Antwerp customs †. But another impost, called for by the wants of the state, was facilitated by the prosperity of the province, a duty, namely, on articles of consumption, particularly wine and beer. By means of this and other dues the regular income of the Netherlands was raised even above that of Castile, to the amount of 1,250,000 ducats.

If trade was taxed in Sicily, and in the Netherlands a portion of the consumption, we find the government in Milan the possessor, in addition to these sources of profit, of the monopoly of salt. It imported yearly some 330,000 staja of salt, and sold it to the inhabitants. We find the regular income of the duchy in the time of Charles V. calculated at 400,000 ducats ‡.

No other country perhaps ever suffered more from financial measures than Naples. The harsh policy of the emperor Frederick II. is well known §. Much as the Anjous hated him, they nevertheless followed his example in this respect; much as they, in their turn, were detested by the Aragonese, they were nevertheless imitated by the latter in their extortions. Charles V., too, went greater lengths here than any where else. Not only were export and import, internal trade and consumption taxed, and that so rigorously that even the herdsmen driving their cattle in winter from the mountains to the plains of Apulia, were bound to pay a considerable toll to the custom-house of Foggia; but what particularly distinguished the Neapolitan administration was, that since the collections of the Normans and of Frederick II. a direct tax on hearths had been

---

* Estimated in Ulloa, Restablecimiento de las fabricas y commercio Español, p. 20.

† Origen, progresos y estado de las rentas de la corona de España, por Don Francisco Gallardo Fernandez ; Madrid, 1805, tom. i. lib. ii. artic. ii. p. 164.

‡ Cortes of 1558, Petic. v. " De dar el dicho encabezamiento perpetuamente en le precio en que estava, a lo menos prorogacion por otros veynte años."

§ Nueva Recopilacion, lib. ix. tit. 27. ley vi.

‖ Marino Cavallo : " De datii et altre entrate ordinarie di Spagna 800,000 : dalli gran mastri, che tutti sono nella persona dell' imperatore, 120,000 ducati."

---

* Ragazzoni in the Avvertimenti di Don Scipio di Castro.

† Cavallo, and a list appended to the otherwise useless Compendio degli stati, etc. Informatt. i. f. 96. MS.

‡ From the Sauli contract with Francesco Sforza II. in Verri, Storia, ii. p. 190. Likewise Cavallo and Leoni.

§ On this subject, see Von Raumer, Hohenstaufen, Bd. iii. p. 548 ; Schlossers Weltgeschichte, iii. 21, p. 415.

introduced, which bore with particular severity on the poor [*]. From all these different sources the country contributed, in the times of Charles V., about a million of ducats.

All this put together, we find that Charles V. derived some four million ducats regular income from his European states collectively,—for the provinces of the crown of Aragon administered their own revenues, and in such a manner that no surplus was left. The special object contended for by his subjects was, that he should make that sum suffice for his expenditure. The towns of Castile affirmed, in the year 1520 [†], that so enormous a sum of maravedis were collected from the regular sources of income before mentioned, that they should be amply sufficient without new taxes, without, as they said, laying new loads on the royal conscience, to uphold and enlarge the realms belonging to the crown.

They meant, of course, on condition that the sovereign arranged his measures in accordance with his income. They complained of the introduction of the Burgundian court establishment; they calculated that Charles, though unmarried, required twelve times more for his court than his grand parents had expended, including the prince's 12,000 maravedis daily, and the 150,000 maravedis daily for the numerous grown-up daughters [‡]. They called for economy. But when we find the same author setting down the regular expenditure of Castile at 250,000 ducats more than the regular income [§], it must seem to have been almost impossible to rectify the balance by economy alone. Certain it is the rectification was not effected, either in Castile, or in the other provinces; there was not one in which the expenditure did not more or less exceed the regular income.

Hence it came to pass that the mere internal administration of every province indispensably required pecuniary aid from the estates. Nor was there one in which this was not supplied. Castile granted every third year a servicio of 300 cuentos (the hundred cuentos for each year make 267,300 ducats) a sum about equivalent to the deficit in the revenue. Sicily granted a donative of 75,000 scudi [||]. Naples, though already burthened with a direct impost, was by no means excused from the donative; reckoning that it paid in the seventeen years from 1535 to 1552, 5,185,000 ducats [¶], this donative amounted yearly to something more than 300,000 ducats. Milan contributed about as much. The towns paid 25,000 ducats monthly. They gave their grant the name of *mensuale*. It was the same thing as what was called in the Netherlands the *Schildzahlen*. The latter tax brought in 500,000 ducats. The urgent necessities of the state induced the Aragonese kingdoms also to afford some aid; they

agreed to pay 200,000 ducats yearly; but they found means nevertheless to pay little or nothing.

This tax is important with reference to the constitution in a twofold point of view. In the first place it was the means of keeping up the assemblies of the estates in Castile, Sicily, and the Netherlands; and even in Naples it kept up an assembly resembling these, though but remotely. In the second place the nobility for the most part excluded themselves from liability to the tax. This was usually portioned out among the communes, which were required to furnish the sum voted from their incomes, their estates, or from individual contributions. It was only in case the vassals of the nobles were hard pressed [*], that they too were allowed to put in a word on the occasion of the grant.

But all the money thus raised, served after all, as is plain in the case of Castile, for little more than to meet the domestic wants of the administration, and to defray perhaps the expenses of the royal household. What remained for the general government, and for extraordinary contingencies? The provinces were compelled to furnish extraordinary supplies. From the time the Castilian cortes in the year 1538, just at the period the grandees displayed such obstinacy, granted in the first instance fifty cuentos, and as much in the next sittings [†], they continued every year to pay the king something over 400,000 ducats. The Sicilians too submitted to extraordinary taxation for the building of bridges, palaces, and fortresses [‡]. The donative of Naples, and the mensuale of Milan gradually augmented in amount. The Netherlands were the hardest plied. They contributed, though not without continual negotiation, one year with another, 400,000 ducats, extraordinary taxes [§].

In all the proceedings connected with these matters, each of these provinces appeared in its own peculiar character. The three Aragonese kingdoms kept themselves quite apart, and almost without any participation in those burthens. Sicily resisted, but granted after all just as much as was unavoidably necessary. Milan certainly gave more, but it stood out successfully against exaggerated demands. It was only in Castile that the king, and in Naples the viceroy, effected more perhaps than was wholesome for the country. In those provinces the habit gradually grew of looking more to the wants of the sovereign than to the resources of the country. The Netherlanders unquestionably occupied the worthiest position. On every occasion they paid the largest sums, but they paid them voluntarily. They were so rich that they were not ruined thereby; they enjoyed so well-grounded a freedom, that they were not thereby reduced to servitude.

---

[*] Lippomano, Relatione. Cavallo.

[†] Capitulos del reyno, Tordesillas, Oct. 20, 1520, in Sandoval, i. 316.

[‡] Remonstrances of the Cortes in Marina's Teoria, ii. 426.

[§] The several items of the taxes enumerated by Cavallo amount together to 1,188,000 ducats; he reckoned the receipts at no more than 920,000 ducats, so that there appears a deficit of 268,000 ducats.

[||] Raggazzoni, "Angaria antica et ordinaria, di 7500 scudi instituita per la spesa della persona del re, et si chiamano donativo ordinario."

[¶] Parino, Teatro de' Vicerè, i. 156.

[*] Speech of the Condestable Velasco, of the year 1538, in Sandoval, proves this for Castile; Castro's Avvertimenti for Sicily; Leoni for Milan.

[†] Carta de Carlos I. of the year 1542, in Marina, iii. n. 28. It was not quite gratuitously they did this. Charles gave them in return a written promise, "que no le esentaria ni apartaria ninguna volta ni lugar de su jurisdicion." Cortes of 1558, Petic. vi.

[‡] Ragazzoni: "Donativo straordinario per la spesa delle gallere della guardia del regno scudi 5000; per le fabriche delle fortezze 16,666, delli ponti 8000, de palazzi 6666," besides quasi donatives, a duty on flour 100,000, and a duty on the trade of Messina 62,000 scudi; these were of late origin.

[§] Cavallo "Delli paesi bassi per ordinario 500,000 ducati, sussidio straordinario 450,000."

We return to the sovereign. Besides all we have enumerated, he had turned to account his close connexion with the church. The pope not only allowed him now and then imposts on ecclesiastical estates, but also afforded him a continual and not inconsiderable source of income, through the sale of the cruzada bull, which allowed the eating of eggs and milk on certain days, and which every Castilian was forced to buy whether he chose to make use of it or not. But in spite of such various resources, the remains of the old demesnes, the imposts on commerce, the two subsidies, and, lastly, the ecclesiastical aids ; in spite of the difficulty of getting all these together (how many assemblies was it necessary to hold in order to obtain some two and a half million ducats of the extraordinary contributions !) Charles was yet far from making these means suffice for his expenditure. In extraordinary cases he was always forced to have recourse to extraordinary means. To enable him in the year 1526 strenuously to resist the assaults of Francis I., who had broken the treaty of Madrid, he required the rich dowry of his Portuguese bride. Yet what a little way did this reach. His army was without pay in the year 1527, and marched off to take the pay the emperor was not in a condition to give it from his enemy the pope. In the year 1529 Charles was only enabled to undertake his journey to Italy by surrendering to the Portuguese the Castilian pretensions to the Moluccas for a considerable sum *. But it was not on every occasion he had a dowry to receive, or dubious claims on remote regions to dispose of. His wars on the other hand, and his journeys, went on unceasingly. Nothing was left him but to have recourse to loans.

But to raise loans was a thing attended in those times with two difficulties. One consisted in the pledges which it was still the rule to exact, the other in the usurious and extravagant interest demanded by the creditor. Now, as Charles had not much left to pledge in the way of real estates, he was forced to hand over to his creditors the produce of the taxes in his dominions (the *juros*, of which mention is so often made), and his direct sources of income. The right of levying taxes was regarded as an estate, the administration of which was alienated till payment should be made of the sum lent. This operation was the more easily effected, as the amount of the taxes was nearly defined by the encabezamientos of the communes. When he adopted this course he usually got off with 7⅔ per cent †. But he had frequently occasion to borrow without pledges, and then, notwithstanding the strictness with which Charles used to abide by his engagements, public credit appeared so insecure, the scarcity of money so great, and the wants of the moment so pressing, that he paid not only from 10 to 20, but 20 to 30 per cent. interest ‡.

Now, these loans had a very depressing effect. The first kind forthwith consumed the revenues indispensably requisite for the current expenses,

and thus swept away the ground on which the whole economy of the state was founded. The second kind made new and extraordinary efforts necessary within a brief period. The former swallowed up the taxes before they had yet come into the treasury, the latter anticipated those of the succeeding year. It was plain, that if this system was not pursued with the greatest moderation it would infallibly ruin the whole state.

Charles was well aware of this. Often did he complain of it loudly and bitterly. "To keep war away from his realms, to withstand the Turks, and to meet the wants of the kingdom, he had been forced to expenses not to be covered by the royal rents, nor by the servicios, which were but trifling, nor by what the pope granted out of the ecclesiastical revenues; but he had been constrained to raise large sums by the sale of his hereditary estates, so that these were no longer nearly sufficient for the maintenance of his royal household ; besides this, he had taken up so much on interest that the remains of the royal revenues could not possibly defray that interest, much less suffice to pay back the capital *."

Now, as his loans were principally contracted on account of the wars he was forced to wage, the latter were attended with this serious result, that whether their issue was prosperous or not, they necessarily produced a diminution of the royal revenue, a loss in the rents previously enjoyed by the crown. No war waged by Charles terminated with such startling and complete success as that of Schmalkalde. Nevertheless it was a question weighed by the enemies of the house of Austria, how much that war had impaired its circumstances †.

We may here fitly institute a comparison between the oriental and the western strategy of those times. In order to raise an army, Soliman handed over his estates and his revenues to others; and so did Charles. Soliman made the transfer to soldiers, who thenceforth fought all their lives beneath his banners, and did him gallant feudal service. Charles surrendered his property to mercantile men, who gave him money instead, but that only once, so that he was enabled indeed to raise troops, but only for a very short time. The obligation of the one class of soldiers was personal, permanent, unconditional ; that of the other was always dependent on pay, it had to be renewed from month to month, and never afforded the monarch full security.

Charles was constrained by his continual wars to employ such pernicious means without remission. Cavallo calculates that there were pledged in the year 1550, 800,000 ducats of the 920,000 regular income of Castile, 700,000 of the 800,000 Neapolitan and Sicilian, the whole 400,000 of Milan, and the larger part of that of Flanders. Whereas in the year 1567, they calculated at thirty-five millions of ducats the sum for which so many properties of Philip II. were pledged, by far· the greater portion of that amount was chargeable to the account of Charles ‡.

---

* Sandoval. Gomara. Soriano.

† This was the rate of interest sanctioned by the Cortes, 1552, Petic. cxi.

‡ Cavallo: " E gran cosa, nelle guerre passate hanno pigliato da x fino a xx et xxx per cento l'anno, nè mai ha voluto l'imperatore mancare alli mercanti della parola sua, di modo che se bene ha sentito qualche incommodo ha pero conservato talmente il credito che per guerra grande che potesse havere li mercanti non mancheriano mai a lui."

* Proposicion de las cortes generales de Toledo de 1538, Sandoval ii. 355. Carta of 1542, Marina.

† Relatione della casa d'Austria, MS.

‡ Tiepolo speaking of Philip II. " E solecito quant' ogn' altro al accrescimento del denaro : et certo ha grandissima ragione di farlo, essendo impegnate le entrade sue per 35 millioni d'oro."

But if we call to mind those loans which were not founded on pledges, it must appear obvious that the state revenues were hardly sufficient to pay the interest on its debts[*]. Hence the extraordinary servicios, destined for extraordinary contingencies, were necessarily applied to meet the current expenses; hence war, and every new enterprise, continually required new loans. How rapidly the consumption of the public wealth proceeded is proved by a calculation Philip II. caused to be laid before the estates of the Netherlanders. According to that document, the remains of the regular income derived by Charles from the Netherlands amounted, in the year 1551, to 927,960 gulden; but even this was so encumbered in the year 1557, that there remained little more than a net 18,000 gulden.

From all this it appears, that though there was some exaggeration in the expression attributed to Ruy Gomez de Silva, that the reason why the emperor abdicated was very simple, namely, that he did not know how to manage the affairs of his crown any longer; nevertheless there was at bottom a certain degree of truth in this. Charles saw his means exhausted. It is very possible that this exhaustion may have had some share in bringing about his determination.

Income from America.

As we ponder over all this, and sympathize with the painful feelings which so embarrassing a condition must have created in the mind of an active monarch, we turn as to a welcome relief to the thought of the Indian wealth, the treasures of the Incas, and those mines of Potosi and Guanaxuato, the deepest, the most extensive, and the richest in the world, which were then in the possession of the Spaniards and their sovereign. For a long time language seemed at a loss to express the magnitude of the revenues that already, in the days of Charles V., flowed into the royal treasuries from that source. There are authors of the seventeenth century, who estimate the sums of money registered for importation into Spain between 1519 and 1617, at one thousand five hundred and thirty-six million pesos; others make the whole amount received, during the first one hundred and three years after the discovery of America, two thousand millions of pesos[†]; so that the quinto due to the king must, allowing for all deductions, have certainly averaged three millions yearly; and later authors have found this calculation very moderate[‡]. In fact, Don Diego Sandoval asserted in the year 1634, that the mines of Potosi alone (he was procurator there) brought the king in yearly four million pesos in the middle of the sixteenth century[§].

How fortunate for Charles had this been so! But how happens it that we find not the least trace in his European finance of such ample supplementary supplies?

[*] Cavallo: "Di sette millioni di ducati (thus high Cavallo estimates the revenue in the total) the several items given make up together only six and a half millions. Soriano too, in the year 1558, reckons only "6 millioni e più" regular expenditure and income) l'imperatore non avanza, quando siano pagate tutte le obligationi d'assignamento, 500 o 600 mila ducati l'anno."

[†] Ustarez, Teorica y practica de comercio, c. iii.

[‡] Robertson's History of America, ii. 449.

[§] Quoted by Ulloa, Entretenimientos.

It is well known that these bold assertions, put forward by Spaniards, and taken up on credit by the English and the French, received their first successful contradiction from a German. Alexander von Humboldt was the first who brought to light the genuine accounts of Potosi, which, far from setting down the quinto at four millions, make it fluctuate for twenty years after 1556 between a quarter and a half million. Its maximum in that interval was 519,944 pesos; but it often fell much below this, sinking even to 216,117 pesos. Are we to suppose that the earlier years, since the discovery of these mines in 1545, were so vastly superior in their returns? To cut off even this evasion, Alexander von Humboldt has directed attention to a report by Piedro Cieza de Leon, which sets down the royal quinto of Potosi at betwen 30,000 and 40,000 pesos weekly, 120,000 monthly, and at 3,000,000 within the four years, from 1548 to 1551. This account, though, as we see, somewhat fluctuating, and not in accordance with authentic computations, nevertheless confutes the extravagant statements above mentioned. Proceeding then to a closer examination of the gains made by the Spaniards, Humboldt comes to the conclusion, founded partly on facts, and partly on conjecture, that the annual import of the precious metals from America amounted, from 1492 to 1500, to somewhat about 350,000 piastres; between 1500 and 1545, to 3,000,000 piastres; and that after this it may have risen between 1545 and 1600 to 11,000,000 on the average[*].

We should scarcely expect to deserve the thanks either of this distinguished and profound writer, or of the public, did we content ourselves with a mere repetition of his conclusions. On the contrary, may it not be possible to discover yet other facts which shall further restrict the range of conjecture? There actually exist documents—some of them in our manuscripts—which, if I mistake not, throw new light on these matters.

In the year 1526, thirty-four years after the discovery of America, and five after the conquest of Mexico, Andrea Navagero was residing in Seville. He was the friend of that Rannusio who collected the Travels, and he was expressly commissioned by him to collect information for him respecting the New World. He learned at Seville, that the royal quinto from the American treasures usually amounted to 100,000 ducats a year[†]. In the year of the conquest it might possibly have been higher, but certainly not much. In the year 1550, five years after the discovery of the mines of Potosi, the whole revenue from America was estimated at no more than 400,000 ducats[‡]. Eight years afterwards it was perhaps increased, but not to any great extent. Soriano, who composed his Relatione in the year 1558, says, they talked indeed of

[*] Humboldt, Essai politique sur le royaume de Nouvelle Espagne, iv. 174. 183. 259.

[†] Lettere di Navagero a M. G. Rannusio. Opera Navagerii, 315: "Ci è qui in Seviglia la casa della contrattazione delle Indie, dove convengono venire tutte le cose che vengono da quelle parti; nel tempo che arrivano le navi si porta a detta casa molto oro (till 1525 hardly anything but gold was brought from America, Humboldt, iv. 260) del quale si battono molti doppioni ogn'anno, ed il quinto è del re, che suol essere quasi sempre intorno a cento mila ducati."

[‡] Cavallo, MS. "Dalle Indie, non è cosa certa, ma si pone d'aviso, per conto di S. M. 400,000 ducati."

millions of pesos, but in reality the king did not receive more than from 400,000 to 500,000 scudi *. It is not till after the year 1567 that Tiepolo definitively sets down 500,000 scudi for the yearly returns, and it is not till after the year 1570 that a statistical list by Huygen van Linscoten gives a sum of 800,000 ducats.

These accounts, which are the more worthy of credit, because, though independent of each other, they furnish a very consistent scale of the Indian revenues of Spain, not only confirm Humboldt's arguments against Robertson, Raynal, and all the earlier writers, but they show that even the qualified statements of those authors admit of further qualification ; they oblige us, if I am not mistaken, to settle the amount of money imported from America into Europe, as not much more than half a million about the year 1525, and not more than from two to three millions about the year 1550 †.

Let us now see how far these accounts agree with the most trustworthy testimonies proceeding specially from America. This inquiry must first be directed to Peru, the richest of the new provinces.

When the first booty arrived in Spain from Peru in the year 1533, an immense one, as it was said, and surpassing all expectation, the royal quinto, according to accurate accounts, did not exceed 155,300 pesos of gold, and 5400 marks of silver, that is to say, not much more than 200,000 scudi ; for the peso is equivalent to 13½ reals, the scudo to 12, the ducat to 11, and the mark of silver to 67. For ten years from that period the royal officers in the provinces gave in no accounts : affairs were in too confused a state when Charles V., in the year 1543, appointed Don Augustin de Zarate chief collector in Peru and Tierra Firma ‡. How could he possibly have fulfilled the duties of his office in a province where the viceroy himself, to whom he was subordinate, was openly attacked with arms § ? Gonzal Pizarro enjoyed all the royal dues. It was not till Pedro de la Gasca had won, on the 8th of April, 1548, that victory which recovered Peru for the emperor, that a thought could be given to calculating the revenue. Zarate then found that since the conquest there had been delivered to the royal officers in all 1,800,000 pesos of gold, and 600,000 marks of silver ‖. Even if we assume that the first booty not be included in this, we find on dividing this sum by the fifteen years elapsed since the date referred to, that the average of each year was not much above 360,000 scudi. But it was far from being the case that all this passed into the hands of the Spanish government. How much of the amount was consumed by the viceroys ! The war carried on by Gasca cost alone nearly a million of scudi. Even the civil administration required extraordinary expenditure in that country, where every thing was sold at an extravagant price. Out of all the royal dues, out of the confiscations and fines which were largely inflicted every year, Gasca did not bring more than 1,300,000 pesos to Spain. This sum, however, was so unusual that Gasca had to set out in person to secure its safe transit. In this he barely succeeded.

Reconsidering all this, we find three authorities agreeing together. The estimates of Potosi, published by Von Humboldt, prove that the produce of the mines there still remained at a much later period between 200,000 and 600,000 pesos; and we certainly cannot assume that it was greater at first, since the increase in it did not take place till the mines were begun to be worked on a better system than that practised by the Indians. Zarate's reckonings show that the amount of all the royal dues of Peru between 1533 and 1548, averaged 360,000 scudi. It must certainly have been more considerable in later than in earlier years, and may possibly have risen to more than 500,000 scudi. But as much of it was consumed in Peru itself, and as this was no doubt the case likewise with the other branches of the American revenue *, we may well credit the testimony of the relationi, that little more than 400,000 scudi a year reached the king's hands. If, indeed, we were to put faith in common report the thing was far otherwise. Even contemporaries tell us how every one of several thousand Indians gathered some marks of silver weekly, and how a great number of bars of silver had been thrown overboard, yet, nevertheless, millions were delivered to the king †. But who would put faith in rumour, notorious as it is for exaggeration ? None knew the amount of the treasure, but he who had the control of it ; error began on the outside from the very doors. Cieza was in Potosi, yet he did not see the accounts, and unquestionably he exaggerates greatly when he tells us that three millions passed thence into the royal treasury in the space of four years. But succeeding writers did not stop short even at that statement. Acosta, who lived at a period not long after Cieza's day, reports a million and half of pesos annually. The writers who followed went on swelling the error, and in Sandoval's hands the supposed sum was already grown to four millions.

It needed not such vast sums to produce astonishment in those times. Gomara says, " Within sixty years the Spaniards have discovered, conquered, and overrun the country ; the gold and silver they have won there is not to be told ; it exceeds sixty millions ‡." At first scarcely more than a quarter of a million, and for a long time after scarcely more than half a million can have been imported. The amount may possibly have been three millions in 1552, the year in which Gomara wrote.

---

* Soriano : " Il quinto di tutto quello che si cava è del re: ma poiche l'oro e l'argento è portato in Spagna, la decima di quelle che va alla zecca s'affina e si stampa in modo, che vien ad haver il quarto di tutta la summa e non passa in tutto 400,000—500,000 scudi, se ben si conta a millioni et a million di pesi." I leave these round sums in various coins as I find them. To reduce them would only tend to produce a false impression, as they are only given approximatively.

† This estimate does not disagree with Humboldt's so much as it may appear. His average sum must be equally great, as the importation received such an extraordinary increase towards the end of the century.

‡ Herrera. Robertson, ii. note 39.

§ Zarate, Conquesta del Peru, iii. 23. French Translation, p. 100.

‖ Gomara, Historia general de las Indias. Anvers, 1554, p. 257. He says that Almagro, Castro, Blasco Nuñez, Pizarro, and Gasca all made use of this treasure.

* According to an authentic computation in Robertson's Notes and Illustrations, 101, the yearly expenditure of the government amounted in 1614 to more than the half of the then incomparably great income.

† Cieza, Cronica del Peru, c. cix.

‡ Gomara, p. 300.

Philip II. at a later period saw indeed very different amounts arrive to him from the Indies. But Charles V. had to content himself with those we have stated. If that monarch was not reduced to absolute bankruptcy, he owed his preservation more to the aid he received from the Netherlands, than to that from America. Holland, neither the largest nor the most compliant of the seventeen provinces of the Low Countries, paid almost every year two contributions, each amounting to between 400,000 and 700,000 carlsgulden. The Netherlands often paid nearly five millions of gulden, that is, two millions and a half of ducats *. What were the 400,000 from America in comparison with these? There, says Soriano, in the Netherlands, are those treasures, mines, and Indies which have rendered the emperor's wars possible, which have upheld his realm, his dignity, and his credit†. In this we must really agree with him.

2. *The Finances under Philip II.*

Hardly ever did monarch ascend his throne under more disadvantageous circumstances than Philip II. Whilst his old enemies were reinforced by the accession of a new one whose hostility he most deprecated, by a pope who deemed himself born to annihilate the Spanish power; whilst he was threatened with formidable wars simultaneously on the Flemish, the Milanese, and the Neapolitan frontiers, he found all the resources of the state exhausted, the fountains of the regular revenue dried up, the land laden with debt, the rate of interest crushing, credit tottering ‡. Might he hope to retrieve his desperate circumstances? Might he even hope to rally the energies of his state to a vigorous defence?

If ever there is an excuse for uncompromising measures, it is on the occasion of an accession to a throne. To escape from such painful pecuniary embarrassments, unquestionably only one of these three means is practicable. Either the monarch endeavours to augment his solvent powers in a decisive degree, as has been done in many a state by the sale of public property; or an attempt is made to get rid of the claims of creditors, which can only be done by a national bankruptcy, or declaration of insolvency; or the liquidating medium, the value of money, must in some way or other be changed.

We observe that king Philip's counsellors proposed all these means one after the other.

First, they suggested the sale of the repartimientos in America. To secure the Indians from the cruel oppressions of the Spanish settlers, and at the same time to keep the latter in continual dependence on the crown, the enormous fiefs bestowed on them had for the most part been granted only for life. Royal commissioners saw to it that they exacted only a fixed tribute, only prescribed tasks from the natives. What an advantage for the Spaniards if their fiefs were declared freehold! A great part of the American gold was in their hands; they offered it for such a concession. They had already offered eight millions for it to Charles.

Humanity, however, and prudence were alike opposed to the measure; humanity, for what was to be the fate of the Indians, if their masters were empowered to regard them as serfs; and prudence, for distance and independence combined would have tempted too strongly to revolt. The old emperor exerted all the influence that remained to him after his abdication to prevent the adoption of such a measure *. The united interests of the Indians and of the crown proved a bar to it.

Hereupon some counsellors had the courage to propose direct bankruptcy to their sovereign. They pressed two points upon his consideration; first, that he was not bound to acknowledge his father's debts; secondly, that the creditors were abundantly paid by the inordinate rate of interest. They would have Philip neither pay back the capital nor continue to discharge the interest upon it. But mature reflection rejected this counsel likewise. What was to become of public credit? Were the debts at all personal? Were they not the debts of the state? And how were the exigencies of the moment to be met amidst the confusion which such a resolution would be sure to occasion? This scheme too was rejected †.

To think of adopting the third means must have appeared almost wild and visionary in an age when paper money was unknown; and, indeed, had it been known it could hardly have been applied in this case. Soriano's narration to his Signoria borders almost on the incredible. For who could imagine that he who was owner of the mines of Peru, not satisfied with genuine silver, should conceive the design of fabricating false? Yet Soriano assures us, with all his usual colour of credibility, that this not very honourable, closely concealed, and most extraordinary device had been entered upon since the year 1556. An attempt having been persisted in for a while to introduce it into circulation under the form of coin, it was only a misunderstanding between the contractor and the king's confessor, who had a hand in the matter, that put a stop to the experiment. We are told, however, that a German soon after made his appearance in Mechlin, who produced a mock silver, capable of enduring the test of the touchstone and the hammer, but not of the fire. The idea, it is said, was seriously entertained of paying the troops in that metal; and it was only given up, though not without liberally rewarding the inventor, because the estates of the kingdom had come to know of the project, and had set their faces against it, on the ground " that very possibly good and genuine money might be thrown away after the spurious." Incredible as all this sounds, Soriano, nevertheless, avers that this invention was known to some of his auditors, the Venetian nobili ‡.

---

* Soriano: "Benche molti delli principali per il bisogno grande che si havea de danari per la guerra, lodassero questo partito, S. M. Cesarea non ha mai voluto accettarlo, per non far torto all' Indiani di sottometterli a tanti tiranni et per non mettersi in pericolo d'una rebellione universale. Questa è una delle cose (forse sola) che sia stata regolata secondo il parere d'imperatore dappoi che questo re è al governo."

† Cabrera, Don Felipe II. p. 41.

‡ Soriano: "Oltre queste vie n'è un' altra straordinaria, la quale, perche è poco honorevole, è tenuta secreta. Questa è un' industria che è principiata gia 2 anni e più con titolo della zecca, *ben conosciuta d'alcuni in questa città*, ma non

---

* Wagenaar, ii. 535.

† "Questi sono li tesori del re di Spagna, queste le minere, queste l'Indie.

‡ Ruy Gomez said to Soriano that the king was "senza prattica, senza soldati, senza danari."

These measures, so perilous or so visionary, so intensely extravagant in their aim, were at last abandoned. Philip, making up his mind to endure the burthen that lay upon him as his father had done, and to entangle himself still more in these uneasy circumstances, thought of nothing but how he might supply the wants of the moment, and effect the measures of defence most immediately and urgently demanded. Though he put the resources of all his dominions in requisition to this end, he turned his chief attention to Castile. He sent Ruy Gomez de Silva thither with full power not only to pledge, but also to sell whatever could be pledged or sold, and with injunctions to raise money, no matter by what means *. The princess Juana was constrained to sell the yearly pension of ten cuentos assigned her out of the alcavala; wealthy private individuals were compelled to lend on parole security; Indian goods were begged of the king of Portugal that they might be turned into money in Flanders; and lastly, 300,000 ducats were taken up at usurious interest, on the security of the fair at Villalon. By such means the king certainly obtained considerable sums from Castile. But the Netherlands were strained far more severely. In the year 1558 Philip demanded a loan of twenty-four tons of gold from that country, and the money was raised; in the same year, he demanded an annual tax for nine years of 800,000 gulden, and it was granted him; in the same year, lastly, Holland not only voted on its own account smaller sums for the payment of certain troops, but besides this it undertook to pay an extraordinary tax of 300,000 gulden, a tax which the other provinces likewise must unquestionably have submitted to (for Holland was always the least forward in such cases), and which upon that supposition must have amounted to more than a million and a half. These states granted the king in one year five millions of gulden, about two and a half millions of ducats, a sum much beyond the amount contributed by Castile, particularly if the Indies be excluded from the estimate †.

By these intense exertions of all the powers of his dominions the king was enabled to recruit that army which conquered at St. Quentin and Gravelines, and which brought about the exceedingly advantageous peace of Chateau Cambresis, after all the painful embarrassments of the Spanish realm.

But after the peace there was nothing more pressingly requisite than to do away, if by any means possible, with this perplexed and debilitating system of finance, which had been left as an heir-

fu continuata, essendo occorsi certi dispareri fra lui et il confessore, per la cui mano passava tutta questa pratica. Si trovò poi un Tedesco a Malines, che la mise in opera et con un oncia di certo suo polvere et 16 d'argento vivo fa 16 oncie d'argento, che sta al tocco et al martello, ma non al foco. E fu qualche opinione di valersi di quella sorte d'argento in pagar l'esercito, ma li stati non hanno voluto acconsentir."

* Micheli, Relatione d'Inghilterra, f. 79: " Havendo detto Ruigomez commissione amplissima, non solo ad impegnare ma a vendere et alienare officii et entrate et di concludere ogni sorte di partiti, per metter insieme quella maggior somma di danari che potrà." They reckoned upon " il partito dell' Indie, i danari dell' ultime flotte intertenuti in Seviglia, l'imprestito del clero, gli ajuti particolari." See also Soriano and Cabrera.

† Wagenaar, from the Resolutien von Holl. ii. 13. How important this seemed to the people of the Netherlands, appears from the Reply of William of Orange.

loom by the emperor. There seemed perhaps some reason to hope that the evil might be remedied in years of tranquillity with the help of better economy, and of due use of the resources offered by such numerous, wealthy, and flourishing provinces. It must be owned that Philip devoted particular attention to this branch of his duty. It wore, however, very strongly the complexion of his times.

The fact was, there existed as yet no true science of state economy; there lacked even that subsidiary knowledge requisite for a comprehensive system of finance. Instead of this, individuals came forward with schemes worked out by themselves, of which they made a mystery, and which they would only communicate for a reward. These men, who were like the forlorn hope preceding the numerous host of fiscal functionaries and their subordinates, were for the most part Florentines. Pre-eminent among them was a certain Benevento, who had already made offers to the Signory of Venice, saying, that " he would considerably augment its revenues without burthening the people or requiring any innovation of importance; all he asked was 5 per cent. on the profits he effected." The emperor Ferdinand called this man to his court; he also appeared at that of Philip. To the latter he offered a really advantageous suggestion. By his advice Philip bought back the right of manufacturing salt in Zealand from the proprietors, and thereupon, without raising the price of the article, or inconveniencing any one, he farmed out the privilege to the Genoese house of Negro de Negri. The 200,000 ducats paid by that house were thought no trifling gain *. It is very likely that something of the same sort was at the bottom of the changes which we find taking place after this in the salt trade in Milan and Castile. The duties on beer and wine in Holland had shortly before been farmed out in like manner with advantage. The characteristic of this first essay at a new system of state economy was the endeavour to enhance the revenues of the sovereign by artificial contrivances applied to some single branch or another, usually under condition, and with the intention that the burthens of the people should not be aggravated. This, however, was but seldom possible. We find Philip soon obliged to burthen his people with new taxes.

Proceeding now to examine his financial system more in detail, we have to remark in the first place, that all the provinces did not leave his hands free in this respect. There was absolutely nothing to be had from the crown of Aragon before the war of 1592. Sicily presented so compact a front to the king, that, except an increase of its servicio to some 200,000 or 250,000 ducats, nothing else was to be extorted from it. The Milanese towns were certainly far less free. They suffered their mensuale to be raised once by cardinal Trent, and another time by the duke of Sessa † ; and though we find

* Soriano : " E novamente comparso nella corte un Giovanni Leonardo· di Benevento, il quale ha raccordato al re una provisione nova sopra il sale che non è d'alcuno danno alli popoli.—Questo è quel Benevento che s'offerì gia d'accrescer l'entrata di Vostra Serenità." He also appeared at the court of Pius V., who however put no faith in his devices. Catena, Vita di Pio V.

† The list of taxes given by Soriano mentions, " 1, il mensuale, che è il sussidio imposto a quel stato; 2, l'augmento imposto dal cardinale di Trento; 3, l'augmento imposto dal duca di Sessa."

them vehemently resisting the attempt of the duke of Terranuova to establish a new donative, still it appears that their taxes had risen in the year 1584 to 1,183,000 scudi. But though they contributed ever so much, all was consumed by the troops quartered upon them. The expenditure was estimated at the same period at 1,166,696 scudi [*]. The same reasons which caused their immunities to be respected, made it necessary at that time to abstain from adding to their already excessive burthens. And thus the only provinces their king had left, capable of at all supplying his existing exigencies, were the Netherlands, Naples, and Castile.

What heavy blows then to the empire were first the revolt and afterwards the loss of the Netherlands! We have seen that in the times of Charles V., and in the early years of Philip's reign, they had borne the chief part of the public burthens. But now this was reversed. In the very beginning of the troubles the king was forced to send the governess Spanish money.

Nothing remained to him therefore but Naples and Castile. We have seen in what manner the revenues of Naples were raised more than fivefold; the three taxes paid there, the fiscal, the servicio, and the trade duties, rose in the same degree. The first of these had advanced from five to fifteen carlines, but even this was not thought enough. A new increase was made for the defence of the frontiers, another for the construction of roads, another for the maintenance of a watch in the interior of the country, and lastly, a very considerable one for the quartering of troops: all these items amounted to several ducats [†]. The natives now complained, that "even the old principle of law, that no obligation should be of force which was counteracted by poverty, was not admitted in this case; for even he, whose only property was the breath of his body, was forced to contribute eight or ten ducats yearly [‡];" but their complaints were all in vain. In the next place the servicio was immoderately raised by the viceroys, who wished to gain the credit of improving the royal revenues. We find that they generally carried their point, and the towns were forced to pay them the several sums exacted of them, though they could not do so without borrowing. The consequence was that they became inordinately involved in debt, and the tolls they raised within their limits were no longer applicable to their internal administration, or to the payment of their tribute, but had to be applied in liquidation of the interest on their loans, and hardly sufficed for that. Now, in this critical state of things, a hand was also laid on their trade. The viceroys imposed a carline on every pound of silk, wrought or raw, exported from the the kingdom. The effect of this was soon felt by the inhabitants of Naples, four-fifths of whom, it has been asserted, had hitherto gained their livelihood by this trade; there was reason to fear that this improvement in the royal income would not long continue to appear an improvement. Oppressive as these means plainly appeared, yet the exigency was so strong and inevitable, that they were adopted. Such was the course of things in Naples.

Administration of Castile.

But our chief attention must be directed to Castile.

The main grievance of the Castilians in past times had been, that they were deprived of the presence of their sovereign. "That was the reason so much money went out of the country; a dearth of gold was already discernible, and silver too was becoming scarcer." How often had they solicited Charles to return to them, or to remain among them. But now Philip was king. He complied with their entreaties; he came to Spain, took up his residence at Madrid, and declared Castile the first of his provinces [*]. Now, if this change was connected in many other ways, as we have seen with this monarch's position, still it is also thought that he remained in Castile in order to turn its wealth to better account than did his father [†].

In fact, his foremost endeavour was to improve his income. To this end Ruy Gomez had founded for him a council of finance, in which Francisco Eraso took a leading part among other distinguished members. To this end the king was surrounded, as Cabrera says, with those shrewd men of arbitrary principles, those adroit schemers, who were continually devising new imposts.

It is to be regretted that Tiepolo feared a more laboured exposition of Philip's several measures would weary his hearers, and preferred inviting to his house those persons who wished for more detailed information. He had no idea that so long after his day people would look for information to his report. The consequence is, that we are compelled to have recourse to scattered notices.

Now, on putting together those that present themselves to me, I notice five conspicuous points in the general range of Philip's financial administration.

First, the beginning, which if difficult as regarded the monarch, was distressing to the nation in an extraordinary degree. How oppressive were those measures which Philip introduced or sanctioned during his residence in Flanders, each successively more grievous than the preceding. Wool, it is well known, constituted in those days a main branch of the Castilian trade. Under the pretence that the merchants were fairly liable to share in the cost of maintaining the fleets by which the sea was kept clear from corsairs, Philip exacted for the export of Spanish wool by native Spaniards one ducat the saca, when the wool was destined for Flanders, and two ducats when it was to go to France or Italy; whilst foreigners had to pay in the former case two ducats, in the latter four [‡]. The cortes opposed this with all their might. They stated that they were sufficiently burthened with

---

[*] Rovelli, Storia di Como, iii. c. ii. 111, very authentic, but not minute in its expositions.

[†] Al Mr Landi: 'Grani 3! per gli alloggiamenti della gente d'armi: grani 7 per la guardia delle torri: grani 9 per l'acconciamento delle strade: grani 5 per li barigelli di campagna."

[‡] Lettera: "Coloro che non hanno altro al mondo ch'il commune respirare con li animanti, hanno da sodisfare ogn' anno otto o dieci ducati."

[*] Representacion al Emperador Carlos, para que no dejasse salir de España al principe D. Felipe: Marina, Teoria de las cortes, iii. 183. The Cortes of 1558 petition Philip to return to his Spanish dominions: " Pues esta entendido, que residiendo en ellos puede V. M. conquistar y ganar los agenos y defender y conservar los suyos."

[†] Tiepolo.

[‡] La princesa governad. en Valladolid, 30 Abril, 1558. Nueva Recopilacion, libros ix. tit. 32, ley i. Pragmatica, i.

the alcavala and almoxarifazgos, with the land and sea dues of various kinds, and with the servicios ; they represented that it was not on the merchant the weight of taxation fell, but on the sheep breeders, who now received smaller payments from the former ; they appealed to laws of the realm opposed to these impositions, laws which the king was bound to respect *. Philip's answer was, that however all this might be, he was constrained by necessity. He had the boldness to make a still more violent inroad upon custom, law, and equity. The conversion of direct into indirect tenure by the introduction of middle men is a measure that has always been looked on in Castile with abhorrence. The cortes complained in the year 1558 that he had disposed of hamlets and villages, vassals and jurisdictions, and numerous commons, and separated them from the towns to which they had previously belonged. They did not fail to remind him of the charters, the written promises, and even the oaths that were contrary to such proceedings ; but however urgently they remonstrated, however pointedly they set forth the cheerless condition of those who were now fallen under the hands of private persons, still they obtained no more from the king than promises for the future. Meanwhile Philip had already gone much further. Cabrera complains that the king had now made sale of commendaries, and rights of nobility, of places of regidores, alcaldes, and secretaries, all of them properly rewards of merit. We find that he gave away commendaries worth 18,000 ducats yearly to satisfy his creditors †; and that shortly afterwards he solicited permission of the pope to sell those estates too on which the clergy had rent-charges, saying that he would indemnify the clergy out of his juros ‡. But unquestionably the harshest measure of all, and one that was a real violation of the rights of private property, was that the king laid his grasp on the money brought by merchants and travellers from the Indies, giving them instead a lien for interest upon his revenues. The loss did not fall alone on those from whom the money was taken; it was felt of course almost more severely by those who should have received payment out of it. Numbers became bankrupts, and a general stagnation of trade ensued. To our amazement we learn that this was repeated almost regularly from 1555 to 1560 §. It was not till 1560 the king gave orders it should not again occur.

This was the beginning of Philip II.'s adminis-

tration. We have remarked that he certainly avoided measures of the utmost extreme of harshness ; we see nevertheless how harsh were those he actually adopted. It is not necessary to enumerate them all, his increase in the rigour of the custom regulations between Castile and Portugal, his exaction of heavy subsidies from the clergy, besides a multitude of minor innovations ; neither indeed is it possible for me to recount them all; we shall dwell only on the most important points.

Another matter of great consideration was the arrangements of the year 1566. Philip introduced them with expressions of regret, that the duty incumbent upon him of defending Christendom and religion, and of preserving his realms in peace and safety, forced him to devise new means of augmenting his revenues. He went on to say, that having consulted with his ministers he found the object could be effected in the least objectionable manner by increasing the export and import duties. Accordingly he issued three decrees to that purport on the same day, May 29, 1566. Not content with his first ordinances respecting the exportation of wool, he now exacted four ducats absolutely for every saca of wool destined for France, or for another division of the peninsula, whether exported by natives or foreigners. But this is a trifle compared to the increase of tolls he laid on the almoxarifazgo mayor of Seville. Formerly the export duty on silk, dried fruit, sugar, wine, and oil, had been two and a half per cent. ; he now demanded seven and a half. He ventured to go further with jewels and pearls, cochineal and leather, claiming ten per cent. instead of the previous rate of two and a half. But the manner in which the almoxarifazgo of India was dealt with was the most remarkable of all. The original freedom of trade appointed by Ferdinand and Isabella, between the mother country and the colonies, had been damaged by Charles. It was completely shackled by Philip. He ordered that all goods shipped for India should pay five per cent. in the Spanish ports, and ten in the American, but wines were all alike to pay twenty per cent *.

Was he satisfied with these sources of revenue ? There can be no doubt that it was for the Flemish war Philip provided them. Therefore it was that he spoke of religion, and of public tranquillity when he called for them. But they did not suffice him for that purpose. True, he had also raised the price of salt about this time by a third ; true, he obliged the communes to pay a certain price to the exchequer for the use of the public lands †, and his Castilian revenues increased to the surprise of foreigners (the Venetians, who had estimated them at a million and a half in the year 1558, found them three millions in 1567 ‡), still his necessities were very far from being supplied. Tiepolo asserts, that at this period Philip kept back 800,000 scudi

* Cortes de Valladolid del año de 1558, Petic. ix. " Lo qual es novedad y cosa no acostumbrada y en gran daño y perjuyzio de estos reynos y de los subditos y naturales dellos y del estado de los cavalleros hijosdalgo dellos y otras personas esentas y contra sus libertades." They then mention the "impuiciones prohibidas por leyes y pragmaticas, las quales de justicia y honestidad deven guardar los Reyes et mas V. M. que todos."

† Cortes de 1558, Petic. vi. Soriano : " L'anno passato consegnò al centurione una commenda in Spagna di 18,000 scudi d'entrata l'anno a conto de suoi crediti, et questo anno ha venduto il secretariato di Napoli per ducati 12,000."

‡ Lettera di Mula amb. Venet. Roma alli 28 di Giugno 1560. MS.

§ Cortes de 1555, Petic. cx. Cortes of 1558, Petic. xxxiii. " Por haversi tomado para las necessidades de V. M. el oro y plata que ha venido y viene de las Indias, estan perdidos los mercaderes, tratos y tratantes destos reynos, y ha cessado la contratacion en ellos, de que se han seguido y siguen grandes daños e inconvenientes."

* Nueva Recopilacion, ix. 32. Pragmatica, iii. ix. tit. 22, lei i. ix. tit. 26, lei ii.

† Tiepolo: " I popoli si chiamano offesi per il pagamento del sale, che è stato accresciuto un terzo di quello che si cavasse prima, et per esser stati privi di buoni comunali goduti da loro per il passato a discretione, bisognando hora, chi ne vuole comprarne dalla camera per pochissimo precio."

‡ Ib. " Ha causata la residenza di S. M. in quelli regni et la diligenza che ha usato, che ha accresciuto tanto l'entrada di quelli regni che hora ne cava più di tre millioni d'oro all' anno, et se continuerà in esso, la farà maggiore."

annually of the money that arrived from India, on account of private individuals, paying them five per cent. interest for the same *. He reverted to the most iniquitous of his former measures.

The Castilians now found what were the fruits of the fulfilment of their supplication that the king would remain among them. All the burthens occasioned by the general administration of Philip's realms, all those rendered necessary by new contingencies, all the exigencies formerly supplied by the Netherlands, and all the expenses created by the war against the latter, now fell on their shoulders. In return, they had the consolation of being the head of his empire, and, as they thought, of all the world. Might but the burthen remain endurable!

Between the years 1575 and 1578, however,—this is the third main point we distinguish—it seemed likely to increase beyond bearing. Whatever may have been the cause of the king's embarrassments, whether the effects of his extraordinary efforts in the war of Cyprus (for that the cost of this was very great appears from a computation of the Sicilians, who had paid out 1,300,000 ducats, chiefly for provisions such as biscuits, wine, and cheese, supplied by them to the fleet from May 1571 to November 1573 †), or the expenses of the Flemish wars, or the intolerable burthen of usurious interest, or whatever else it may have been; suffice it to say, we find him in such urgent want of money that he was ready to grasp at every expedient; that he even approached those high-handed measures from which he had at first receded.

In the year 1575 appeared an edict against the state creditors, suspending all their assignations upon the royal revenues. Next, it was proposed to alter the contracts made since 1560; it was proposed not only to lower the interest, but also, if I am not mistaken, to deduct from the capital as much as should appear to have been overpaid, according to the new rule of computation, and to give the creditors new securities in that proportion‡. Now, if we reflect that there was perhaps no important commercial place in the south and west of Europe where some great house had not this king's name in their books for large sums, we may easily guess what confusion must have been produced in the whole range of money matters by the sudden stoppage of the payments in question. In fact, there was hardly a house in Rome, Venice, Milan, Lyon, Rouen, Antwerp, and Augsburg, that was not hard upon the verge of bankruptcy. The greatest sufferers were the Genoese, who had placed a great part of their wealth in the hands of the king of Spain, and who were then consuming their own strength in the revolt of the lesser families

against the greater. The disruption of commercial credit began first with them. Yet, after all, this was but a stoppage of the payment of interest; what was to be the consequence, if capitals too were diminished, and if the right proclaimed by the edict was acted on, namely, that every house might deal with its own debts as the king did with his?

We know that the towns, above all in the cortes, insisted on the most decisive and severe measures on this head*. They called for another additional one. This was in those years in which, as we saw reason to think, the communero party acquired a new share in the conduct of the state. At any rate we hear forthwith a repetition of this party's old complaints against the grandees. They talked of the numerous alcavalas, revenues, and vassals acquired by the latter from the kings; of the embarrassment in which they had plunged the crown; of the wills of Isabella and of Charles, which it was desirable that Philip should now carry into effect. In fact, Philip made preparations to that end. He called on all the grandees to produce the titles by which they claimed their possessions, and the exchequer forthwith assailed the chief among them, such as the Velascos, dukes of Frias, and wrested from them the sea-tenths they had so long enjoyed. Universal alarm seized on the grandees †.

But it was easier to threaten and to attack one by one the proprietors of the land, namely, the grandees and the owners of capital, viz. the state creditors, than to do them any serious hurt in the mass. They held too strong a position for this. Perhaps the grandees availed themselves of the claims given them by their services to the house of Austria, perhaps Philip himself recoiled from making so great an innovation; at any rate he did not carry his intention into execution; he contented himself with letting the suits take their course as far as regarded some vassals who wished to belong directly to the crown.

And now the capitalists also found an escape. The king, who saw the Flemish war instantly renewed in spite of the perpetual peace, required new loans. The Genoese at last laid aside their quarrels and sent embassies. When two parties have need of each other they readily come to an understanding. The king consented to leave the capitals ostensibly inviolate; the commercialists acquiesced in a reduction of interest, as Thuanus says, from 7⅓ to 4⅓. If we may venture to surmise a slight error here, and read 7⅐, 4⅛, the result would then come out, that whereas, supposing the purchasing price of an annuity of 1000 ducats to have previously been, as in fact it usually was, 14,000 ducats, it now amounted to 24,000 ducats‡. But as this arrangement was retrospective for some years, as the king now paid no more interest for 24,000 than previously for 14,000 ducats; as the commercialists dealt in the ratio of this reduction

* Ib. " E ben vero che ne riceve commodità (da India), perche si serve ogn'anno di 800,000 scudi de particolari con pagarli cinque per cento."

† Raggazzoni, Relatione della Sicilia, adds: " Di maniera che non havendo supplite l'entrate ordinarie, hanno convenuto quelli ministri vendere a diversi quello che hanno da scuodere da qui a un anno et più con interesse di 14 o 16 per cento l'anno: onde il re in quel regno si trova molt' esausto de' danari."

‡ Cabrera: "Con facultad de pagar las deudas que por razon de los asientos hizieron, al mismo precio che el Rey pagaba a ellos." Coligny asserted, in a memorial laid before the king of France in 1572, that German houses had been driven from their just demands by the terrors of the inquisition. Thuanus, lib. 51, p. 1062.

* The Cortes insisted, as early as the year 1560, on a reduction of the rate of interest: " Que luego se trate de moderar y limitar los dichos interesses y cambios de manera que para adelante cessen; pues los interesses que han levado hasta aora han sido tan crescidos que con ellos solos se podrian muchos de los que los han levado tener por contentos y bien pagados de las deudas principales y interessos justos."

† Cabrera, Don Felipe II., ii. 955.

‡ See besides Cabrera the circumstantial account by Thuanus, also Laet, De principibus Italiæ, p. 139.

with their own creditors, which were frequently petty houses, it is easy to see, not only what confusion must have ensued, and how many a house must have broken down without any fault of its own, but also, that as in this case there was no hope of the return of the principal, but only of the interest, the affair was a state bankruptcy yielding a dividend of a little more than 58 per cent.; only that it did not extend to the whole bulk of the capitals, and that it wore the form of a voluntary compromise.

At the same time it does not escape us how very inadequate must have been the result even of such extreme measures. In fact, the king was again obliged to press hardly, above all, on those from whom he had least resistance to apprehend. First, the clergy. Every thing depended on his gaining the pope over, who, though he often resisted, always ended with letting himself be talked over. Philip had already augmented his income from ecclesiastical property in an extraordinary degree. Not only did Pius IV. once grant him the half of the proceeds of the ecclesiastical estates *, but he afterwards conceded to him permanent dues for the galleys he was to keep up against the Turks. After long struggling Pius V. allowed him a renewal of the *escusado* (a tithe upon the ecclesiastical estates), and of the *crusada* †. This revenue was always on the increase; whereas it amounted in 1575 to 1,200,000 scudi ‡, it was computed at one million and a half by the papal nuncios in 1578. But even this did not satisfy Philip. He demanded back from convents the vassals assigned them by his ancestors, to deal with them far differently from their monastic lords. He wished to have the escusado, which had hitherto yielded 250,000 scudi, augmented to 420,000 scudi, the sum to which the money for the galleys amounted. However great the difficulties attending such a further increase, Gregory XIII. was nevertheless induced to grant him a new ecclesiastical impost of 170,000 scudi for three years, as a subsidy for the Flemish war §.

Thus Philip laid hands on all he could, grandees, clergy, and state creditors ; was he to be expected to spare the commons ? They had done very right indeed to direct his attention to other resources; but when these proved insufficient they were themselves burthened with new taxes. The king now first fixed the alcavala actually at ten in the hundred ; he also made playing cards, quicksilver, and corrosive sublimate articles of the royal *reservas ;* and he proceeded from his first encroachments on the estates of the communes to open sale of them ||. It being the opinion of those days that burthens on foreign trade were the least oppressive of all, he not only imposed new duties on the importation of

Florentine cloth and Flemish goods, but also on the already so much burthened exportation of wool ; and he raised the duties at Seville.

Hereupon the cortes began to complain. They petitioned the king in 1576 not to impose new taxes, but rather to repeal those already established. In 1579 they complained that their petitions were not attended to, but that the distresses of his majesty's subjects were daily growing. In 1586 they admitted that they were bound to do every thing requisite for the defence of the crown, but, on the other hand, it should be left to their judgment to determine how that might best be effected; but now not only were new taxes daily imposed contrary to every pledge, although the old ones ought much rather to be remitted, but besides this, means the most prejudicial to proprietors were adopted for collecting them *. The wretchedness and misery endured from the new taxes were, they said, intolerable.

Their petitions and their complaints were vain. Castile was not yet near that pass to which it was destined to be brought by Philip. Had he not to prosecute the Flemish war ? to aid the French League ? But besides this he had in view the enterprise against England.

This enterprise marks the fourth chapter in Philip's financial administration. Its bearings were as important on the internal as on the foreign relations of Spain. In the first place it exhausted the country through the extraordinary efforts with which it was prosecuted. Not only large sums of money, but also heavy contributions in kind were raised †. Andalusia alone furnished along with many other necessaries 120,000 quintals of biscuits ; Seville gave with many other things 6000 vessels of wine ; Galicia 6000 quintals of salt meat ; every province did its very utmost. But the mischievous operation of the enterprise was far greater in consequence of the new efforts which its total failure and its unfortunate re-action rendered necessary. If the king contrived to console himself, the kingdom had good reason to be inconsolable.

In the very next year, 1589, Philip found himself obliged to call for the harshest of all his taxes, the *millones*, a tax similar to the servicio, inasmuch as it took its name from its amount being fixed at eight million ducats in six years, but which was a real excise, inasmuch as it was laid upon the most indispensable necessaries, wine, oil, meat, and so forth ‡. The cortes stood out a long while, and it was necessary to have recourse even to the imperial ambassador, count Khevenhiller, in order to prevail upon them ; at last they passed the grant §. After all it was as though nothing were done. We find the king in the year 1590 busied with three new extraordinary means. He demanded a donative, opened a loan, and sought to anticipate the millones. The grandees granted him the donative; being but little affected by most of the mischances of the community, they were able to raise about three millions and a half of ducats. The greater

* Mula in the above mentioned letters.
† Catena, Vita di Pio V. p. 184.
‡ Lippomano, Relatione di Napoli.
§ Negotiatione di Monsʳ Sega, MS.
|| Cabrera is classical on this head : " Ayudaba al Rey muy bien el frudo *dela nueva imposicion de la alcavala de diez por ciento, y lo* que procedia de las rentas del estanco o reservas reales de los naipes, açogue, soliman salinas :" decisive against Gallardo Fernandes, Origin de las rentas de España, tom. i. which fixes the first imposition of duty on playing cards at '1636, poco mas o menos.' " The same author too does not sufficiently define the final augmentation of the alcavala, p. 165.

* Remonstrances of the Cortes in Marina's Teoria, i. 304; ii. 394.
† List of the contributions in kind in the papers, "Dell' apparato della guerra quest' anno, 1588," printed in the Tesòro politico, i. 67.
‡ Gallardo Fernandez, Origin de la Comision de los servicios de millones, in Origin, etc. de las rentas, 47.
§ Khevenhiller, Annales Ferdin. tom. iii. p. 772.

part of the loan was probably furnished by foreign commercial houses; it reached about 850,000 ducats. But the towns, though so very ready with their services, though pledged speedily to furnish the sums they could not instantly pay, nevertheless could not supply 250,000 ducats of anticipated taxation *.

It now happened very opportunely that richer fleets arrived from America. Contarini estimates Philip II.'s American revenues for the year 1593 at two millions of scudi, which is certainly not too high. Potosi alone yielded for fifty years after 1579 a quinto of more than a million of piastres †. The employment of quicksilver in the reduction of the ore had been introduced there about the year 1574‡, and to this improvement the increased produce of the mines had undoubtedly been owing. The fleet brought home extraordinary wealth in the beginning of the 17th century, upwards of ten millions of ducats in 1613 and 1615, upwards of eleven in 1608, 1612, 1614, and 1616, and actually upwards of fourteen in 1620 and 1624 ; of these sums above a million and a half was always for the king, more usually between two and three millions, and once four millions §. The receipts cannot have been much less towards the close of the sixteenth century ; only such was the king's financial economy, nay that of the country itself, that it was spent before it arrived. Castile seemed to receive this money only to pass it away forthwith. The fact seems incredible, yet it rests on the positive assertion of a trustworthy man, Gonzales Davila, that in the year 1595, which must have furnished the collective produce of some three years, thirty-five millions of scudi in gold and silver crossed the bar of San Lucar, and that of all this wealth not a real remained in Castile in the year 1596 ‖.

At the same time the state in which things stood, and the sort of system pursued in matters of finance, may be inferred from the official documents of this year, the fifth that strikes us as peculiarly important. The king, who had once more commissioned his counsellors to inquire into the causes of his bad circumstances, began now to complain, that whereas nothing remained to him from his rich and powerful kingdoms and the pope's gratuities, and whereas his treasury was clean emptied, all this was attributable solely to the heavy interest with the payment of which he was burthened. He had recourse anew to the measures of 1575. He decided that the pledged revenues, rights, and possessions, and the assignments made to the state creditors, should be withdrawn from them, and placed under the royal administration, and that more reasonable interest should be paid out of their proceeds. Hereupon the old panic was renewed in Spain, Italy, Germany, and the Netherlands, and bankruptcies already began. The Florentine houses alone lost several millions. There was no commercial man in Pisa and Florence who was not a loser ¶. Long and vainly did the state creditors exert every influence in their power with the king's ministers, with the clerical persons who

had his ear, and with himself : at last they procured a mitigation, but by what means ? Only by consenting to grant new loans. They promised a loan of eight millions of ducats, but on such terms that they were only to pay down 7,200,000 ducats, and that within a period of eighteen months, whilst they were to receive back the whole eight millions within four years out of the extraordinary servicios up to the year 1600, out of the Indian revenues of the years 1598 and 1599, out of the proceeds of the cruzada of 1599 and 1600, and finally a whole million from the sale of places, and from "other revenues yet to be devised." They had then, on the whole, the moderate profit of ten per cent. for four years; still it is evident that the main receipts of the following years were anticipated and consumed by this loan *.

In fact, every year ruined that which succeeded it. In the year 1598, the king had to send round from door to door in quest of a new donative, which Davila calls downright an alms. This author adds, that what was lost in reputation on this occasion was of more moment than the money scraped together.

Here we have then the strange spectacle of a king exhausting his dominions to the utmost of his ability, yet always having his coffers empty ; all the gold and silver that augmented the existing stock in Europe passing into his hands, and never remaining a moment his own ; enormous sums raised, yet not a real squandered. Next to the expenses of his wars, it was chiefly the system of finance inherited from his father, which he suffered to go on as he found it, and against which he would not employ any radical remedy, that ruined him as it had ruined Charles.

Meanwhile Castile went on paying its taxes with difficulty. Contarini states that it yielded thirty millions of scudi during the four years he resided there †. It was with sore murmuring it paid these sums. Those who were inscribed in the new encabezamiento, say the cortes of 1594 (for the millones was raised like the servicio, and with it), were incapable of defraying the sums imposed on them. It appeared, they said, from the papers delivered into his majesty's exchequer, that many persons had farmed out their incomes, and that the sums they received were not equal to those demanded of them. Upwards of two hundred ciudades, villas, and localities had not acceded to the encabezamiento; they preferred enduring all the oppressions of the collectors. His majesty had indeed remitted a million, but it was as impossible to raise the reduced sum as the whole ‡.

---

* Ib. p. 870.
† Table given by Alex. von Humboldt, iv. 175.
‡ Ulloa, Entretenimientos, German translation, ii. 40, with Schneider's annotations, 226.
§ Laet, Hispania, p. 400.
‖ Davila, Vida y hechos del Rey Felipe, iii. p. 35.
¶ Galuzzi, Istoria del Granducato di Toscana, tom. iii. p. 285. Lettres du cardinal d'Ossat, n. 82.

* The king's decrees, and circumstantial accounts in Khevenhiller of the years 1596 and 1598. Thuanus, Historiæ, lib. cxvii. tom. iii. p. 777
† Tomaso Contarini, Relatione di Spagna. " Nei 4 anni che io sono stato a quella corte, gli fu fatta una imposizione straordinaria di 6 millioni da pagarsi in 4 anni et un altro donativo di 2 millioni in due anni, di modo che in 4 anni S. M. ha cavato di quel regno 30 millioni d'oro, la qual somma è altro tanto vera quanto pare incredibile : onde per queste insopportabili gravezze si sono grandemente afflitti et estenuati quelli popoli." He computes the yearly revenues of the whole monarchy at 14,560,000 scudi ; certainly too low. Milan, which yielded about 1,200,000 scudi, is here set down at 900,000, and Naples, which gave more than two millions and a half, at 1,200,000. It is always exceedingly difficult to state general amounts with certainty.
‡ Memorial del reyno en principio de las cortes aº 1594. Marina, Apendice, 189.

The answer was, that his majesty's notorious necessities did not allow of his attending to these remonstrances. In fact, whilst Contarini remarks that the taxes paid by the people were extravagant, that it had been and would be ruined by them, and with the best volition would probably not be much longer in a condition to pay them, he is yet obliged to confess that it was quite impossible to remedy the evil, since even such great imposts were not adequate to the necessities of the state *. Such was the manner in which Philip II. administered the public wealth in Castile and in the rest of his empire. Castile may be compared to a lake from which more water was drawn for works of various kinds than the sources which fed it could replace ; endeavours were made to enrich it with a new influx, but before this reached the lake, the waters in its own channel were also consumed.

3. *Finances under Philip III.*

Castile exhausted itself of men in order to keep the Netherlands Spanish, to bridle Italy and hold it in obedience, and to maintain the ascendancy of the catholic faith. For the same ends it exhausted itself of money : the interest to be paid entailed on the current year the expenses of its predecessors ; pensions were bestowed to uphold a party ; the expenses of war went on continually. There was in this case no lavish profusion at home arising out of the personal qualities of the sovereign, as was the case in France under Henry III. ; the foreign relations of the country, in the shape they assumed in the course of time, wasted and consumed its energies.

Lerma therefore had almost a more difficult problem to solve than Sully. Could he withhold the payment of interest ? The old king's example showed what fruits were borne by such a measure. Or could he suppress the pensions ? They were indeed very considerable. For instance, in order to gain the duke of Urbino, though a man of no great weight, Philip II. had granted him 12,000 scudi for his table, and pay for four colonels, twenty captains, one hundred heavy, and two hundred light cavalry, and two companies of infantry †. But as the Spaniards had everywhere incurred enmity, and called up opponents ; as France was powerful enough to rally all these around her, it would have been very rash to alienate the friends of the monarchy by withholding from them the usual gratuities. In the year 1600, Spain actually maintained in the states of the church not only the duke of Urbino, but as many barons as ever it could ‡, Orsini, Cesarini, Gaetani, and besides these no few cardinals. Sarpi asserts in 1609, that there was not a town in Italy in which Spain had not paid retainers §. It kept up a party of its own by

the like means in Switzerland, in Germany, and in England. One thing, however, Lerma did, which was by all means necessary ; he gradually gave peace to the empire. But whilst he did this, he began to spend in the interior as much as Philip II. had done in war ; he introduced habits of profusion at home.

How much was he himself enriched from the public wealth ! He was able to spend on the occasion of the king's marriage 300,000 ducats, and 400,000 on the betrothal of the infant of Spain and madame royale of France ; and according to the accounts of his own house, 1,152,283 ducats on pious foundations alone. His relations and retainers lived in the same sumptuous style; Miranda collected a great stock of jewels ; Calderon was incredibly rich. The salaries of the officers of state were soon advanced a third higher than under Philip II. But besides this, what sums were required for the frequent festivities, the high play, the change of abode of the court, the journeys, and the gratuities bestowed on the grandees who had flocked back to the capital ! The king's marriage cost him 950,000 ducats, about as much as the conquest of Naples had cost Ferdinand the Catholic *.

Thus in spite of peace the embarrassments of the empire only grew more distressing ; recourse was had to still more extraordinary measures than under Philip II. The king issued an edict in 1600, stating, that " foremost among the causes of the public need he found the manufacture of silver into articles of daily use. How much better were it that it should be in circulation ! To put a stop to so great an evil he desired to know the quantity that existed, both white and gilded. Therefore he commanded a declaration of all silver plate to be made within ten days,—he the king." What could have been the intention of this ? Was it to despoil private persons of their silver plate ? Or was it the fact, as some asserted, that the pope had lent the king the half of that which was in the churches ? The clergy were refractory ; the monks preached against the measure ; even the king's confessor was against it; and so the end of the matter was, that the government had to content itself with the voluntary contributions made by some bishops and cathedrals, in accordance with the examples set by the bishops of Valladolid and Zamora †. But the new government had shown what arbitrary measures it was capable of ; and speedily it gave further proof of this in a still higher degree.

In the year 1603 two members of the royal council of finances and of the council of Castile proposed an alteration in the value of the coinage. So intense were the embarrassments of the state, that this extravagant measure was caught at as "a suggestion from heaven." The value of copper was raised from two to four just as though Castile were a commercial state compact and complete within itself. We may imagine what profit was reckoned on, when 6,320,440 ducats worth of copper were coined at this rate.

---

* " Le gravezze sono cosi esorbitanti che hanno consumato et tuttavia vanno consumando quei popoli et specialmente quei di Spagna, onde in breve tempo non corrisponderanno quella eccessiva somma de danari che al presente contribuiscono. In tutto che l'impositioni siano eccessive, di gran lunga non suppliscono alla grandezza del bisogno."

† Lettre du cardinal Bellay; Ribier, Mémoires et lettres d'estat, ii. 760.

‡ Delfino, Relatione di Roma, MS. " Quanti più possono non solo valendosi di colonelli dependenti, ma di molti altri."

§ Litteræ Sarpii ad Leschassenum. Le Bret. Magaz. i. 501.

* Davila, Hans Khevenhiller in Annal. Ferdin. vi. 3035. Relatione della vita, etc.

† Edict of Oct. 29, 1600. Relatione della vita, etc. " Se bene alcuni s'acquietarono, altri però nol fecero nè volsero obedire a questo comandamento." This Relatione mentions a brief, " accioche potesse pigliar l'argento lavorato per servitio degl'arcivescovi, vescovi, prelati e cavalieri degl'ordini militari," with a condition of restoration within eight years; the provisions of the brief however were not enforced.

H

But neither can there be any difficulty in guessing what was the actual result. The traders of half the world hastened to transport their copper to Castile, where that metal bore so high a price. The Castilians too were gainers by this exchange; it was carried on with extreme rapidity in Cadiz, San Lucar, Puerto de Santa Maria, Malaga, San Sebastian, and Laredo. Silver soon became so scarce that a premium of 40 per cent. was paid for it at court, and the common people were no longer able to pay in silver the two reals which the cruzada bull cost. On the other hand it was computed that there were 128,000,000 ducats worth of copper in Castile. What a state of things! Every year the fleet brought in ten, eleven, twelve millions of silver, and there was not one silver real in the whole country *.

Now, as such expedients gave temporary relief, but inflicted permanent mischief; as commercial duties to the amount of thirty per cent. on foreign trade either ruined that trade, or strongly promoted smuggling, and consequently diminished rather than augmented the state revenues; as the merchants too would advance no more loans, what was to be done? It was always necessary to fall back on the grants of cortes. That body was not in a condition which should have enabled it to make any serious resistance or to give a decided refusal.

When, after the lapse of other grants, the imposition of the millones was called for in the year 1600, at the rate of 3,000,000 a year for six years from the 1st of Jan. 1601, eight towns indeed for a while offered a certain opposition to the measure; but they were soon forced into compliance †. But could the excise, which ten years before did not yield a million and a half, be now forced up to as much more? It was soon found necessary further to increase the rate of duty imposed on wine and oil. For the suppression of smuggling three orders of courts were established, a first in each town, a second in each chief place of a district, and a third consisting of a junta of the towns that had the right of voting; each of the two inferior courts was subject to the permanent inspection of those above it. Did these measures attain the end proposed? Of the tax which should have been paid in full on the 1st of Jan. 1607, a large part had to be remitted in 1608 ‡.

It might have been expected that experience like this would have taught the government to moderate their demands, and the cortes to be more chary with their grants. But no. On the 22nd of November, 1608, the cortes again granted 1,750,000,000, payable within seven years. And though they diminished the demands on the excise on this occasion by about half a million yearly,

still they agreed in the same year to raise a loan of 12,000,000 on the revenues of the communes, in order to help to extinguish the king's debts with their own *. They continued to pursue the same course on subsequent occasions. In the year 1619 they again granted 18,000,000. Their alacrity in voting money cruelly contrasted with the condition of the people. The less capable was the people to pay, the more ready were the cortes to grant supplies.

But what could they do? It was no secret how matters stood. The council of Castile computed with amazement and dismay, in the year 1619, that the king had been granted since 1598, in the new taxes alone, fifty-three millions and a half, that he had drawn another hundred millions from his dominions, and that every thing was nevertheless mortgaged, all the sea-tenths, all the almoxarifazgos, alcavalas, and tercias, and all royalties however rigorously extended and increased, and that nothing was left but those immediate payments which the country was hardly in a condition to make. The king too complained with keen grief, that the head of his realms, the mother of so many illustrious sons, who had gained renown in peace and war, who had conquered new worlds and tamed barbarous nations, that Castile was so deeply fallen †. Still they could not break through the old system of procedure, or shake off the habits of thinking on which it was founded. Even at this moment the king resolved on calling for new taxes that could but augment the misery he deplored; even in this moment of pinching want the council of Castile did not forego the thought of supremacy over the world. Whilst it told the king that with the money he had received he might have become master of the world, it subjoined its belief that all hope of that kind was not yet lost, and it owned that it still cherished the wish. And in fact the Spanish policy strenuously resumed its old warlike tendencies. It is not blindness, it is not unconsciousness of their situation, that ruins men and states. They do not long remain ignorant of the point whither the path they are treading is to lead them. But there is an impulse within them, favoured by their nature, strengthened by habit, which they do not resist, and which hurries them forward so long as they have a remnant of strength left them. Godlike is he who controls himself. The majority see their ruin before their eyes, and yet go on to meet it.

CHAPTER V.

NATIONAL CIRCUMSTANCES.

1. *Castile.*

WE have now made ourselves acquainted with one aspect of Castilian affairs; we have now discussed the influence exercised on them by the government.

But does the public weal of a country depend solely on the administration? In the Spanish empire this was but one and the same throughout; it had every where the same views and every where adopted analogous measures; yet were the results very

---

* For details see Davila, s. a. 1603, and for further explanations, Cespedes, Primera parte de la historia di Don Felipe, iv. p. 583. All the gold and silver left by a Chilian bishop who died in Spain were seized, and when the papal camera laid claim to the spolium, it was promised copper instead. Cagioni che condussero S. Santità a levare la nuntiatura al Monsignor di Sangro, MS.

† Relatione della vita, etc., the best authority on this subject. "Avenga che molti et gravi inconvenienti se presentassero, il papa Clemente concedè un breve, accioche per questo tributo contribuisse tanto il stato ecclesiastico quanto il secolare." This throws light on a somewhat obscure passage in n. 274 of Card. Ossat's letters.

‡ Gallardo Fernandez, Origen, etc. i. 49.

* Khevenhiller, Annal. Ferdin. vii. 117.

† Manifesto of the king and the Gran Consejo de Castilla, Davila, Felipe III., p. 218.

different in the several provinces. A sovereign can only promote, he cannot create ; he may impede, but never can he singly destroy.

A peculiar reciprocal re-action between the character of the administration and that of the nation, is evident in Castile.

People have sometimes possessed themselves with the notion that Castile was very flourishing, populous, and industrious in the beginning of the sixteenth century. But there is no proof of this. In the year 1526, when Peru had not yet begun to allure adventurers to America, and when the dominion of the Burgundo-Austrian kings could not yet have begun to exercise the disastrous influence ascribed to it, the Venetian traveller, Navagero, describes the country in a manner quite corresponding with the state in which we find it at a later period. He speaks of Catalonia even as stripped of inhabitants, and poor in agriculture ; Aragon deserted and little cultivated, except where its rivers produced a little more animation ; the old water courses, which were indispensable to comfort and prosperity, in a state of decay, even about populous towns such as Toledo ; in the rest of Castile many a long tract of wilderness, in which nothing was to be met with except now and then a venta usually uninhabited, and more like a caravanserai than an inn. It was only in Valladolid, Seville, and Granada, that some trade flourished *. It is in vain, too, that we look into commercial books of the middle ages for the names of trading towns in Castile. When exportation is spoken of in the royal decrees, the only articles mentioned are raw materials, corn and silk, hides and wool, iron and steel ; but when importation is in question foreign manufactures are mentioned †.

This was not a decay of the nation ; it was rather its natural condition, and was in keeping with its most peculiar institutions.

It is indeed highly deserving of attention, that the distinction so long subsisted which grew up on the recovery of the country between the liberators and the liberated, between those who descended from the mountains with arms in their hands, and those who were found by them cultivating the soil. This was the distinction between hijosdalgo and pecheros. The hijosdalgo owed their rights to arms which it was their vocation to bear. " They must be treated with favour," said Ferdinand and Isabella, " for it is with them we make our conquests ‡." It was the hidalgo's privilege that neither his house, nor his horse, nor his mule, nor his arms, should be taken from him for debt, much less that he should be curtailed in his personal freedom. He was exempt from the application of torture §. But what, above all, distinguished him was the right of not being liable to pay taxes. The pecheros on the other hand paid taxes ; trade and agriculture were their vocations, as war was that of the hijosdalgo. They too undoubtedly had their honour, and the king called them good men ; they asserted moreover their right of portioning out among themselves the

taxes they had to pay without the interference of a hijodalgo *, and they frequently filled most of the public posts in the pueblos †. But, in fact, and how should it have been otherwise, the hidalgos were regarded as the right hand of the nation. The offices of state were committed to them ; the towns took it amiss when any person engaged in trade was named corregidor over them ‡; the cortes of Aragon would not tolerate among them any one who had to do with traffic ; in short, public opinion declared in favour of the order of hijosdalgo. Every one would fain have passed his life like them, in high honour, and exempt from wearisome toil. Numberless persons made just or spurious claims to the privileges of the hidalguia ; so numerous were the lawsuits on this subject, that Saturday was always set apart for them in every court, and frequently was not enough for the business in hand §. It naturally followed from all this that a general aversion grew up against mechanical employments and traffic, trade and industry. And is it really so absolutely excellent and laudable a thing to devote one's days to occupations, that although intrinsically insignificant, yet consume a whole lifetime for the purpose of gaining gold from others?— Good ! But be sure that all is right and honourable in the occupations you prefer to these. Be sure that the likings and dislikings you encourage do not run into extravagance and absurdity. Above all, it is necessary that the balance be so adjusted that the welfare of the nation be not perilled.

A balance seems to have existed still under Charles. Undoubtedly he afforded the amplest food to the warlike propensities of the nation ; Europe opened to its campaigns ; Asia just then in most hostile contrast with it ; the African coasts often filled with its arms ; besides this a new world to conquer and to people. Now if the people was found to be martially disposed, it was also found sober and temperate. The sons long obeyed their fathers ; the daughters sat long by their mother's side, and wrought their marriage outfit. They married late ; the men not before the thirtieth, the women not before the twenty-fifth year. Luxury was still within bounds. Some sought renown in arms ; others lived on the produce of their lands and their cattle ; others on the interest of their Indian wealth ‖. The false tendencies perhaps existed, but they were kept in check by the patriarchal ways of the land. Trade too had received an impulse from the recent events ; the new connexion into which Spain entered with the world at large under Charles V. had also thrown open a wide field of enterprise to the pecheros. The attraction of wealth and gain unquestionably approaches near in force to that of arms and aristocratic advantages. The Indian trade flourished especially in Seville. " God be thanked," says Charles, in the year 1543 ; " it has always grown, and still grows daily. So vast is the quantity of

* Navagero, Viaggio, 346. 349, 350. 370.

† Capmany, Memorias sobre la marina, comercio y artes, iii. l. iii. capitulo 2 : " Si la industria y las artes de España han igualado en alcun tempo a las estrangeras."

‡ Don Fernando y Donna Isabella in Toledo, anno 1480. Nueva Recopilacion, tom. ii. p. 10.

§ Don Alonso's law of 1386, confirmed verbatim by Philip II. 1593. Ibid, ley 13, p. 12.

* The Cortes of 1552, Petic. lxxxviii. were against this, and also a law ; yet it took place.

† Cortes of 1552, Petic. lxxxvi. "Como son mas los pecheros que los hidalgos, quedan (los hidalgos) excludos de officios." They were dissatisfied with this, and required, that where there were six hijosdalgo resident, they should fill half the offices.

‡ Complaints in the Cortes ; Marina, Teoria, ii. 417.

§ Cortes of 1555, Petic. cxvi.

‖ Cabrera, Don Felipe segundo, i. c. ix. p. 43.

goods of all kinds, and the articles of subsistence conveyed thither, and imported thence into our realms, that the merchants derive a very great profit therefrom *." In Granada, the decay of the silk culture, which Navagero had prophesied from the inquisition, had nevertheless not taken place. In the year 1546 the government declared that the silk trade had been and still was constantly on the increase; that silk stuffs were woven, and wrought, and sold, that had previously not been woven, or sold, or exported from the country †. Care, too, was taken that the Granadan mulberry should not be transplanted out of the country, not even into Valencia. It can hardly be taken as a proof of the decline of the cloth manufacture, to find it remarked that too much fine cloth was made ‡. In short, if we cannot just say that extraordinary industry prevailed here, still we must own that some trade subsisted and flourished.

But it gradually declined. Two false propensities particularly gained ground among the pecheros; the oné was to pass for nobles, the other to live in the cloisters; both of them coinciding in this, that they withdrew men from the active pursuits of plebeian life, and aimed at the enjoyment of the good things of life without exertion. Both were seconded in a peculiar manner by the government, though not intentionally.

It was a matter of no slight influence in this respect, that the royal rents, which had been transferred for the most part to foreign creditors of the state, gradually passed into native hands. When we consider the great danger that threatened all capitalists, especially in 1575 and 1596, we cannot wonder that they gladly got rid of their Spanish securities. Now, the result of this was, in the first place, that the proceeds of the royal revenues passed very much from hand to hand. We discover with some astonishment from a mercantile ledger § of the year 1590, how Antonio de Mendoza, a trader in Seville, purchased now from one, now from another of his fellow citizens, among other property, rents which they drew from the royal almoxarifazgo in Seville. He tells the price that Donna Juanna received in the year 1555, 14 for 1,14,000 ducats capital for 1000 ducats annuity, so that, in fact, he lent his money at 7¼ per cent interest. But a second consequence of still greater moment ensued. The Spaniards eagerly caught at opportunities of securing themselves fixed annuities based upon the royal revenues. It frequently happened then that when a dealer, or an artisan, had got together an annuity of 500 ducats, for which he required to have some 7000 ducats capital, he secured it inextinguishably to his son by creating a majorat for him. The son now thought himself immediately elevated to the rank of nobility. His brothers too, as brothers of a majorat, began to be ashamed of the low occupations from which their little fortune was derived; they all desired to be styled Don, and they disdained labour ‖. Perhaps the sudden success of the Spanish soldiers in Italy, who,

as pope Paul IV. said, from grooms in the stables, became lords of the land, or the still more rapid advancement of the Indian adventurers, had some influence on producing this state of things. Suffice it to say, that the number of those who laid themselves out to enjoy an easy life by means of their annuities, the number of those knights, such as they are presented to us in Lazarillo de Tormes, who lived rather upon their imaginations than upon their wealth, increased beyond measure, and we may well assert that the proceedings and the peculiar character of the government seconded the national inclination in this respect.

The same thing was further induced in another manner. What strange forms does human ambition put on ! Because king Philip founded the Escurial with so much pomp that he was called the second Solomon, the grandees thought it no less becoming them to found convents ; for had they not states and vassals, courts and subjects, as well as the king * ? Their ambition then, and their emulation, were turned in this direction. They esteemed it an advantage to their estates to have convents upon them. Every place in the realm saw new ones spring up, and in none of them was there any lack of monks. What an easy life, free from all care, and yet by no means without weight and consideration, did the convents offer ! What strong temptations to this manner of life were created by the grammar schools, which were established in the smallest spots, and which filled the abler heads with an inclination for the ecclesiastical order at least, if not for better things. The families esteemed it a sort of wealth to have one of their members in the cloisters, and in fact they did thereby acquire certain exemptions. Thus the king and his grandees founded schools of indolence (Philip III. and his consort did so to a still far greater degree than Philip II.), and the people were eager to enter them, particularly those who could entertain no hopes of being ennobled. It was when it reached to this extent that the monastic system became truly pernicious †.

Possibly the conclusion might be admitted, that the development of both these tendencies arose naturally out of the position of the monarchy. Its growth ceased under Philip II. If there had formerly been hot wars in Italy, on the Spanish frontiers, and on the coasts of Africa, the garrisons in those regions now remained quiet, and their existence too was in some sort like the enjoyment of a benefice. The Indian discoveries were completed; the galleons sailed quietly from the Canaries to Vera Cruz, from Acapulco to Manilla ; the wars with the natives were ended ; peace had long prevailed throughout the whole empire, with the exception of Flanders. Accordingly, when quiet and enjoyment were seen throughout the whole range of the empire, taking the place of the ceaseless commotions and the mighty efforts that had formerly pervaded it, the same result took place likewise in private life in the interior of Spain.

Now, if such became the diminished inclination of very many Spaniards for the pursuits of industry, the government, if I am not mistaken, participated in another way in bringing this about, and that rather by excess than by deficiency of care.

---

* Pragmatica, etc. Nueva Recop. ii. 678

† Nuevo Arancel, etc. Nueva Recop. ii. 702.

‡ El Emperador Don Carlos en Bruselas. Ibid. 283.

§ " Manuel del libro de caxa de mi, Antonio Mendoça, commençado en esta ciudad de Sevilla en primero de Setiembre de 1589 años, que sea para servicio de Dios y de su bendita madre, Amen." Madrid 1590.

‖ Navarrete, Conservacion de monarquias, Capmany, 363.

---

* Well explained by Davila, Felipe III. c. 85.

† Diego de Arellano, Consejo.

Striving to aid commerce by a host of laws, restricting importation at one time, exportation at another, they did mischief after all to the object of their solicitude. They had passed a law against the importation of goods from Barbary ; but as the country could not dispense with the hides, the Cordovan leather, and the drugs from that region, the consequence was, that foreign ships took in cargoes of these articles in Barbary, carried them to Spain and sold them there at a very high price *. In the year 1552 the exportation of all cloth was prohibited, whether coarse or fine, both frisas and sayales, and also that of all wools, spun and combed : the consequence was, that many manufacturers of cloth abandoned their business, and shut up their premises. It was found necessary, no later than 1558, to repeal this prohibition, at least in respect of the districts along the confines of Portugal †. These prohibitions on exportation were what above all characterized most peculiarly the commercial legislation of Spain. The great object aimed at was, to have the goods in question cheap in the country. The kings enjoined that no one should export corn or cattle great or small from the kingdom, on pain of forfeiting all his property ; for the same was prejudicial to their service, and entailed scarcity upon their subjects and vassals ‡. The exportation of leather had long been forbidden, and the cortes further insisted that no special licence thereto should be granted, since foot clothing was then so dear, and even more so than all other articles of dress. They complained, that notwithstanding the great number of mules and asses raised in the country, the price of those animals had become doubled, and they required that the prohibition against exporting them should be rigidly enforced. Nay, they went so far as to propose that the importation of foreign silk should be permitted, and the exportation of home made prohibited, because the article would then be cheap, and the profit would be considerable §.

In its peculiar anxiety to have goods cheap, the government applied itself with particular earnestness to restrict the trade in raw materials even in the interior of the country. There was a law that no one should buy corn to sell it again. Another forbade the trade in live stock, another made it penal to buy up unwrought hides, with the intention of selling them again in the unwrought state. All these measures appeared to the cortes well conceived and advantageous ‖. They strongly recommended, that if any one bought up wool to

dispose of it again, it should be allowable for the woolworkers in the same locality to appropriate the half of the quantity so purchased at first cost. They advised that no one should be at liberty to purchase woad or madder, except the cloth-makers themselves who made use of them, besides a multitude of other suggestions in the same spirit *.

Now there can be no doubt that this officious guardianship over trade in its pettiest details must have crippled the energies of all concerned, and that the continual enactment and repeal of impracticable laws must have been anything but serviceable to traffic ; and it would often perhaps have been desirable that the government had not hearkened so much to the cortes. Too frequent meddling and attempts at official regulation will always be noxious to commercial industry.

In this instance, at least, the result was, that the commerce of the country passed for the most part into the hands of foreigners. When those Germans and Italians, from whom Charles took up loans, came to Spain to take possession of the localities assigned them by way of security, they were soon found engaging in other branches of business. The Fuggers enhanced the value of quicksilver in Spain to such a degree that its price became tripled †. If I am not mistaken, the connexion of foreign capitalists with the sovereign was productive of this further disadvantage to the country, that it helped the former to obtain special licenses for exporting all those things which native subjects were prohibited by law from exporting. Certainly they monopolized the exportation of Spanish wool, silk, and iron. Moreover, the great desire that was felt to encourage cheapness in Spain, was beneficial to them in the way of importation. We find that for a while every one who took twelve sacas of wool out of the country, was put under an obligation to bring into it in return two pieces of cloth, and a fardo of linen ‡. It was not long indeed before the disadvantages of this system were perceived. Complaints began in the year 1560, that silken and woollen cloths, brocades, and tapestries, and weapons, were imported from abroad. There were materials for all these at home, nay, the foreigner manufactured them out of Spanish materials, and then set an exorbitant price upon them §. Proposals were made for remedying this ; proposals which were innumerable times renewed, but always in vain. The evil rather increased continually, from the preference given by luxury to foreign productions. People wore English short coats, Lombard caps, German shoes, and furs from Saona. Though the silk spun by worms fed on the black mulberry leaf, which was cultivated in Granada and Murcia, was far superior to every other kind, the preference was given to Italian and Chinese silk. Dutch linen was worn, and even the embroidery of collars became an article of luxury, which was taken notice of by the council of Castile. Plain or figured, and frequently damasked table

---

* Cortes of 1552, Petic. cxiv.

† Suspension de la pragmatica sobre el passar paños en Portugal, printed in 1559 on a separate sheet with other suspensions, mentions the " Carta firmada y sellada que no se saquen destos reynos paños ni frisas ni sayales ni xerguas ni cosa hilada ni lana ni cardada ni peynada ni teñida para labrarlos." But it tells likewise the result · " Han dexado muchas personas, que hazian los dichos paños, de los hazer."

‡ Nueva Recop. vi. tit. 18, ley 27. By Henry IV. and the emperor Charles.

§ Cortes of 1560, Petic. xxviii. of 1552, Petic. lxxxii. and lxxxiv. " Vuestra Magestad sea servido mandar que libremente se puedan meter en estos reynos seda en madeja y de qualquier manera que sea, para que aya mas abundancia, y que la seda destos reynos non salga fuera dellos, pues con esto abaratara y será grande el provecho."

‖ Cortes of 1558, Peticion xxiv. and elsewhere.

---

* Cortes of 1560, Petic. xxxiv.; of 1552, Petic. cxlvii. " Ninguna persona compre pastel ni ruvia ni rassucas ni los otros materiales necessarios para el obrage de paños sino las mismas personas que la labran."

† Cortes of 1552, Petic. cxxix.

‡ Pragmatica, mentioned by the Cortes of 1555, Petic. lxxxiii. and repealed because it was impossible to carry it into effect.

§ Cortes of 1560, Petic. lxxxiii.

cloths, were imported from Antwerp; Brussels carpets were laid on the floors, and writers sat at tables brought from Flanders. If any one was curious in dress, he had Florentine brocade; if he chose to pray, he used handsome rosaries of French make; and when he slept it was within bed curtains wrought abroad *.

The people of the Netherlands joyfully reckoned up how much profit they derived from this traffic; they counted the ships that left their ports with such goods for Spain; they calculated the numbers who derived their subsistence from this source †. Intelligent Spaniards beheld the matter with dissatisfaction. Above all, they were incensed against the French, who exposed for sale in all the shops in the streets their trumpery toys, their chains, dolls, and knives, and had them hawked about by pedlars; who obtained high prices at first for their strings of false stones and coloured glass, as long as they had the advantage of novelty, and afterwards brought down their prices to such a degree as plainly testified the worthlessness of their wares. "Were they Indians, that people should bring them such gewgaws? Must they squander upon such useless things the gold they had brought with toil and danger from India ‡?"

Not only were handicraft trade and traffic, particularly in the most indispensable requisites of luxury, in the hands of foreigners; they had also become farmers of grand masterships and commendaries, of bishoprics, and of the manorial rights of the grandees; their dealings extended to corn, and every necessary of life §. The country was even dependent on them as regarded war. "Would you know," says Villalobos, "what is required merely for artillery? A fleet must come from Flanders with wood and powder, another from Italy with metal and workmen, both to cast the guns and to make the carriages ||." It was not till after the loss of her Italian territories that Spain established cannon foundries of her own.

While matters stood thus, while the Spaniards conducted themselves like the proprietors of an estate, who leave its management to others, contenting themselves with drawing a small annuity from it, and devoting their attention to other pursuits; while foreigners got into their hands five-sixths of the home trade, and nine-tenths of the Indian trade, it came to pass that the government engrossed and used up, so to speak, all the disposable resources of the nation.

This took place first of all by means of the exorbitant taxes, of which we have already spoken. The cortes of 1594 complained on this score ¶. "How is any one to carry on trade if he must pay 300 ducats tax on every 1000 ducats of capital? The capital is eaten up in three years. If any one will still be a trader he must raise his prices in such a manner as to cover his own private losses

at the expense of the public; he must ruin himself and his customers. But few are inclined to this. People prefer retiring with what they may have, in order to live upon it, as long as the times will let them, though in the narrowest way. However low the contract may be, no contractor can hold out; either he throws up all he has got and flies the country, or he takes up his permanent abode in prison. Where formerly 30,000 arrobas of wool had been wrought, hardly 6000 are used now. In consequence of this, and of the duty on wool, the number of flocks is also on the decrease. Thus agriculture and grazing, manufactures and commerce, are prostrate; already there is not a place in the kingdom where there is not a dearth of inhabitants. Many houses are seen shut up and uninhabited. The realm is going to ruin."

Secondly, the result was brought about through the arbitrary conduct of the civil functionaries. Contarini asserts that Philip II. was served in the most dishonest manner; that no one felt afraid of the consequences, since Philip, at all events, did not punish such offences capitally, and if he were to do so he would not find a soul to undertake the management of his revenues *. The cortes complained that the costs of collection sometimes equalled the whole amount of the taxes. The despotism that began from above grew but sterner and harsher through all its subordinate degrees. How was the poor peasant tormented with a tariff prescribed him, appointing how he should sell the corn he reaped, with executions often inflicted upon him for his unavoidable debts, whilst his corn lay yet on the threshing-floor, and frequently was he taken away from his labours, and cast into prison †. Here it was that the mischief arising from the sale of offices most strongly displayed itself. Philip III. boasted, indeed, that in his auspicious days justice flourished as vigorously as ever it had done ‡; but Khevenhiller assures us it was really become venal, and that every litigant was thrown entirely on the power of his gold §. And how should it have been otherwise, since the worst examples were beheld at court in the persons of Franchezza and Calderone, and the municipal appointments, even to the four and twenty, and the regidores, were disposed of by sale || ? New places were sometimes created for the purpose of selling them. Instead of young persons, such as used formerly to be commissioned by the courts, and who sought to commend themselves by the legality of their conduct, it became the practice, after the year 1613, to send out a hundred receptores appointed for money, men who had no prospect of promotion, nor any other ambition than to realize the interest upon their purchase

---

* Luis Perraza, ap. Capmany. Guicciardini, Descriptio Belgii. Arellano's Consejo.

† Houder, Declamatio panegyrica in laudem Hispanæ nationis, ap. Capmany.

‡ Peticion xvii. de las Cortes de 1593. Capmany.

§ Cortes of 1552, Petic. cxxv. "Estrangeros arriendan y tratan en todo genere de mantenimientos y hasta el salvado ha havido estranguero tratante in ello, y buscan generos y maneras nuevas de tratos."

|| Villalobos, Problemas naturales, 1534, ap. Capmany.

¶ Memorial de las Cortes de 1594; Marina, Apendice.

---

* Contarini: "Tutte queste entrate sono maneggiate da persone macchiate d'infedeltà et che hanno mira più all' interesse proprio che al beneficio comune, et se S. M. volesse venire al castigo universale di tutti, non troveria poi chi volesse prenderne l'assunto sopra di se, et se alcuna volta ne castiga qualch' uno, la pene non si estende mai alla vita, ma si ferma nel bando et confiscatione de beni."

† Consejo.

‡ Proposicion que S. M. hizo 1611, ap. Marina.

§ Report, vi. 3035.

|| Relatione della vita. "I ministri sono così interessati et ingordi che non se ne ha mai espeditione se non se li ongono molto bene le mani: et questo è caso di molta importanza, perche chi compra, vende; et di qui nascono molti inconvenienti contra il servicio di dio et del regno."

money, and who proved a sore burthen to the people from their continual litigation and their exorbitant fees *. This evil pervaded the whole state.

Lastly, the mischief in question was fostered by the court establishment of Philip III. which gathered all the grandees and nobles to Madrid. These magnates had consumed their wealth in the rural districts during the last reign; they had however thereby, at least, kept alive a certain activity in the local trade attached to the vicinity of their petty courts. But now nothing remained to the provinces but to send their incomes to Madrid, where they were squandered in luxury that did not profit the country. It was not long before this was felt by the chief places in every province †.

In this way did the court gradually absorb all the resources of the country, partly through the natural action of its own composition, partly through the rapacious functionaries it sent out, and partly by the taxes it extorted. As the court drew its necessaries from abroad, as its wars were prosecuted abroad, and as its chief creditors were foreigners, its exactions never returned to the country, but this was every year more and more exhausted. We cannot conceive how it could have continued to subsist without the Indian supplies.

The state of things was notorious under Philip III. Spain was seen filled with ecclesiastics. They counted 988 nunneries, all well occupied; Davila reckons up 32,000 monks among the Dominicans and Franciscans alone, and he computes the number of the clergy, only in the two bishoprics of Pamplona and Calahorra, at 20,000 ‡. Every one saw the evil; people complained that if this went on so, the clergy would get possession of the whole kingdom by donation and purchase §; no one could devise a remedy. Most of the other Spaniards lived idly; some under the name of gentlemen, others in the rags of beggary. Madrid above all was filled with beggars, but Valladolid, Seville, and Granada, had also their share. Vassals were seen starting off, as the expression was, with house and family, and betaking themselves to the beggar's profession. Every kind of labour devolved on foreigners. In the year 1610 there were counted in the territories of the Castilian crown alone 10,000 Genoese, and altogether 160,000 foreigners, who engrossed all traffic, as well as the petty employments which were disdained by the Spaniards. "These men," says Moncada, in the year 1619, "have completely excluded the Spaniards from the pursuits of industry, since their productions are more suited to the taste of purchasers, or are cheaper than those of the native workmen. We cannot dress without them, for we have neither linen nor cloth;

we cannot write without them, for we have no paper but what they furnish us with." "They gain," he adds, "twenty-five millions yearly *."

Whilst the Castilians were sending out colonies not only to the Indies, but also to Sicily, Milan, and Naples, for war and dominion, they were thus receiving colonists into the bosom of their own country, who absorbed all its trade and its wealth. But Castile was brought to ruin by both classes; the former it lost, and the latter did not become incorporated with it; their home was elsewhere.

The decrease in the population was remarkable. It was asserted in England, in the year 1688, that the total number of men in all Spain amounted by an accurate census to 1,125,390, and no more †. To judge from other enumerations, in which the men from fifteen to sixty years of age were included, constituting somewhat above a fifth of the entire population, the above number would lead us to infer a gross population of 6,000,000. But there was a visible decrease under Philip III. Medina del Campo and its vicinity had previously 5000 inhabitants; they had 600 in the year 1607 ‡. Davila informs us that a census of the peasants in the bishopric of Salamanca was taken in 1600, and there were found to be 8384 of them, with 11,745 yokes of oxen; but that when they were numbered again in the year 1619, there were found no more than 4135 peasants, with 4822 yokes of oxen, so that a full half of this peasantry had perished §. It was almost every where alike. Individuals complained that a man might travel through fertile fields, and see them overrun with thorns and nettles, because there was no one to cultivate them. The council of Castile bewailed the matter; "the houses," it says, "are falling, and no one repairs them; the inhabitants flee away, the villages are deserted, the fields run wild, the churches empty." The cortes now dreaded the total ruin of the country. "If this goes on so, there will soon be no neighbours for the villages, no peasants for the fields, no pilots for the seas. There will be no more marriages. It cannot hold out another century ‖."

And what did the government do in this state of things? Philip IV. asked advice of every body. Many thought the Italian monti di pieta desirable, many were for new monetary arrangements, others suggested different expedients, and many a decree was issued. But did the court meanwhile restrict its own expenditure? Did it abandon its schemes? Even at this moment, in the beginning of the thirty years' war, the policy of Olivarez, and the wars Philip engaged in in Italy, Germany, and the Netherlands, made the Spanish monarchy more dreaded and more intrinsically weak than ever. "Upon this," says Cespedes, "the cortes bethought them not merely of human, but of grander and divine measures." And what were these? Mark the naïf simplicity of the catholic faith as held by the Spaniards. They nominated "the glorious and

---

* Consejo, quoted by Davila, and Davila himself on the year 1619.

† Remark in the same Consejo: also Davila as to the year 1601, p. 81.

‡ Davila, Felipe III. in detail, c. 85.

§ Remonstrances of the Cortes in Cespedes, Felipe IV. 583. These complaints are very old. The evil had already been denounced by the Cortes of 1552: "Por experiencia se vee que las haziendas estan todas en poder de yglesias, colegios, monasterios y hospitales." They made proposals for obviating this: but they were put off with the sorry answer, "No conviene que sobre esto se haga novedad." Petic. lv.

* Damian de Olivarez, Sancho di Moncada, Restauracion politica de España, ap. Capmany.

† Pepys, secretary of the admiralty, quoted by Anderson, History of Commerce, iv. 235. It appears from the Lettres du cardinal d'Ossat, n. lxx., what hopes Philip's enemies built on the scarcity of men in Spain.

‡ Capmany, Memorias, iii. c. iii. 357.

§ Davila from the registers, in detail, s. a. 1619.

‖ Cortes primeras de Felipe IV., Cespedes, p. 105.

illustrious virgin, St. Teresa de Jesus, patroness of their realms, for the sake of the special favours they hope to obtain from God through such intercession." This, however, was not unanimously approved of. Some feared " that perchance they ·might provoke their hitherto most glorious patron in heaven, St. Iago, under whose protection they had seen the world at their feet, and the land filled with knowledge and virtue, and that they might give him occasion to forget them *."

2. *Catalonia.*

Each of three main territories of the Aragonese crown had its own peculiar and distinctive advantage. Aragon proper had its constitution; Valencia had an agriculture that made its fields like a garden, surpassing those of all the rest of Europe ; Catalonia possessed such busy maritime activity, that a town like Barcelona, which had neither a harbour nor a very secure anchorage, could give maritime law to all nations. These advantages had all of them their origin in the wars carried on of yore against the Moors. In those days the request was often made to an Aragonese king, by his soldiers, " that he would permit them, in defiance of the enemy, to build a town under their very eyes ;" but, at the same time, to keep them in good cheer he had to confer on them privileges almost equivalent to entire freedom. The lands of Valencia were still cultivated in the beginning of the seventeenth century by 22,000 Moorish families. All the navigation of the Catalonians had its birth from the wars once waged by the counts of Ampurias against the Saracen sea-robbers, and they won warlike renown and wealth from the infidels. It is with some right therefore that this crown bears on its coat of arms the singular emblem of four severed Moors' heads. Their prosperity struck root in a soil fattened with blood.

We pass over the manner of its growth. In the times of which we are treating Aragon lost its immunities, Valencia its cultivators. With all the pains these kingdoms took to keep aloof from Castile, still, as members of the empire, they could not escape participating in the fortunes of the empire at large. Catalonia too lost her navigation at the same period.

Once there was a time when the fame of the Catalonian navy, to use the language of Don Pedro of Portugal, resounded in all lands, and was echoed in all histories † ; a time in which the Catalonian naval ordinances spoke of all contingencies that could befal a ship, but never of retreat, capitulation, or surrender ; in which five of their ships were always bound to give battle to seven of the enemy, and their generals to die at the foot of the royal oriflamme ‡. What a spectacle it was, when the fleet was ready for sea, the king and the people assembled on the strand, the three consecrated banners, the king's, the admiral's, and St. George's, were set up, the air rang with joyous acclamations, and all made sure beforehand of victory and spoil ? That time was gone by §.

But even in the beginning of the seventeenth century the trade of Barcelona was in tolerable vigour. It does not appear to have suffered greatly from the change effected in commerce generally, and in that with India in particular, by the discoveries of the Portuguese. We still find, year after year, Catalan caravels and baloneres proceeding from Alexandria to Barcelona ; we still find the city and the general deputation of the country busying themselves in the year 1552 to obtain the pope's absolution for all those whose business lay in the Egyptian countries *, a thing, as they expressed themselves, which concerned the interests of many citizens. Lastly, we find the Catalan merchants assembling in the mart in Cairo as late as the year 1525, and electing a council †. Till about this same time we trace the trade of the Barcelonese with Rhodes, with Ragusa, and with the coasts of Africa, which were re-opened by the conquests of the Castilians. We meet with Catalan consuls in Constantinople at least down to the latter part of the fifteenth century, and in 1499 their predatory vessels joined the Venetian fleet in the harbour of Modon, to make a combined resistance to the Ottomans. Catalonia boasts that even Charles V. said it was of more moment to him to be count of Barcelona, than to be Roman emperor ‡.

But, from this time forth, we see this life and activity dwindle away. The last fleet furnished by the remains of the Catalan naval power, was equipped by Charles V. in the year 1529 ; in the year 1535 we find the last consul in Tunis, and in 1539 the last in Alexandria. Very soon all thoughts of Constantinople, and the remote places on the Mediterranean, were given up. If the consul at Bruges was ever of any importance this ceased now. The old love for the sea could not be altogether suppressed, but it was kept within narrow limits, and had little sway. The general deputation was obliged to impose a tax towards the end of the century in order to equip four galleys against the corsairs.

Now if, as we have seen, the general revolution in commerce, though it had perhaps conduced to this result in a certain way, had yet not done so directly or decisively, the question is, by what other causes was this change brought about ?

Of all the causes alleged two only appear to me to have been actually influential in the matter. The first of these was the union of the country with Castile, the consequence of which was, that the whole Atlantic commerce, carried on by the peninsula in general, with Flanders and the north-east, devolved on the provinces which lay nearer, especially Biscay ; and this necessarily put an end to the peculiar system of sea plunder carried on by the Catalonians, now that they were bound up with the interests of a great monarchy. Capmany boasts § that his countrymen highly distinguished themselves in the battle of Lepanto ; that Pedro Roig carried home with him the Turkish admiral's flag for a trophy, as was well known to his native town San Felio de Gruxoles, where that trophy was depo-

---

* Transactions of the cortes, Cespedes, 290. 584.

† Extract from his letters, Capmany, Memorias, t. ii. Apendice de algunas notas, p. 19.

‡ Ordinaciones sobre lo feyt de la mar, per lo molt noble Bernat de Cabrera, Capmany, Mem. iii. c. i. p. 54.

§ Capmany, from the Ordinanzas Navales. Ibid. p. 57.

* Representacion hecha por la ciudad de Barcellona, Capmany, t. ii. Coll. Diplom. p. 344.

† Carta al Baxa de Egypto. Ibid. 346.

‡ Scattered notices in Capmany's Memorias, e. g. i. c. x. 167 ; i. c. ii. 67. 69, and elsewhere.

§ Memorias, i. c. i. 182. Pedro Roig y Jalpi in the Resumen historical de Gerona, in Capmany's work.

sited. The union however was very far from complete, and by no means secured the Catalans equal privileges with the Castilians. In many Castilian ports they would not allow the subjects of the Aragonese crown to be fully the king's vassals, on account of the great immunities they enjoyed *. They were excluded too from all American enterprises, though their natural activity might have been of the greatest service in this department.

Add to this the many unfavorable influences proceeding directly from Castile. The king, for instance, prohibited the exportation of iron, and yet the viceroy granted licenses for that purpose; but only for money, only to his friends and servants, whereby the advantages gained by individuals was an injury to the community. Again, the experiments upon the circulation, which distinguished the reign of Philip III., must have instantly produced their unhappy effects upon the market of Barcelona. The Genoese too, old rivals of the Catalans, were now in the interests of the monarchy, and were highly favoured. Taking all these things into account, we must own that the union of the crowns of Aragon and Castile, the foundation of the Spanish monarchy, was more prejudicial than advantageous to Catalonia.

But that which most especially decided the downfall of the Catalan trade was the supremacy of the Turkish marine in the Mediterranean. That supremacy was established by the advantages gained by Barbarossa and his Turks over the Spanish and Venetian fleets in the Ionian waters in 1538 ; by the league between Francis I. and Soliman, which carried the Turkish corsairs into the most remote bays of the Mediterranean, and, lastly, by the strong position taken up by the Barbary powers on the African coasts. Thenceforth not a single ship of Catalonia, engaged as it was in constant war with the Turks, could pursue its traffic in the eastern parts of the Mediterranean. Shipments strikingly decreased from the year 1537. In fact, the care of defending their own coasts was become a matter demanding the whole attention of the Catalans. The Turks showed themselves, in 1527, in the roads of Barcelona ; but, after 1538, they appeared more frequently, often to the number of twenty vessels, and in many instances one hundred. Castles were now built on the headlands, and on the mouths of the Ebro and the Llobregat, and the towns sent news to each other whenever they saw Turkish cruisers in the offing †. They had cause indeed for fear. Ciudadela, in Minorca, was captured and burned in the year 1558.

Thus thwarted by the great monarchy, and driven back on itself by the Turks, excluded from the west by the former, and from the east by the latter, Catalonia had to content itself with its Sicilian and Neapolitan trade. From time to time it made but fruitless attempts to revive the rest of its commerce.

The naval power of the Catalonians had been founded upon victories of Arabian Mahometans ; its decline was brought about by the triumphs of other Mahometans, the Ottoman Turks.

* This was complained of in Castile by the cortes of 1552, Petic. lxxx. " Los alcaldes de sacas proceden contra los que compran mercaderias de Aragoneses y Valencianos."
† Capmany, i. c. ii. 239; iii. 250; iv. 327 ; iii. c. ii. 226.

3. *Sicily, Milan, Naples.*

We have seen that the constitution of Sicily was distinguished for a dexterous parrying of all extraneous influence, and the duchy of Milan for a certain independence of its municipal administrations; that in Naples, on the other hand, the foreign government had taken firm footing, and if it maintained the rights of feudality, it did so only in as far as these operated from above downwards, not conversely. Now the question is, how far did the general circumstances of these countries correspond with their constitution.

Sicily.

In the year 1530 they counted in Sicily, among 936,267 inhabitants, 198,550 men from fifteen to fifty years of age, capable of bearing arms ; the property fixed and chattel was valued at 36,285,000 scudi*. Had they then sought to take part in general affairs, they would have been at least numerous and wealthy enough to obtain a certain weight.

But we do not find that they had any thoughts of the kind. They had contrived means to belong to the Spanish monarchy, and yet not to be partakers in its burthens and exertions. They made it their business to guard their rights against the encroachments of the government ; and they were sufficiently occupied with their insular disputes, with the discords that had long subsisted between the leading families, between the towns, and between the nobles and the communes. The general interest claimed but little of their regard. They were always in arms; but never in the field, never in war †.

It is only such endeavours as have some general interest for their object that can elevate the mind and fill it with high thoughts. Partial feuds indeed keep up an alert activity ; but as they compel men to keep in view rather the persons they wish to serve or to injure, than principles and a general laudable purpose and aim, they undoubtedly weaken the cogency of the moral impulse. We are told that the character of the Sicilians assumed a greater aptitude for subtlety, cunning, and tricks of all kinds, than for strength of mind and true wisdom.

Certain it is, however, that they kept their native land safe from the frequently arbitrary measures of the Spanish ministers, and in a prosperous condition. They had but little commerce with foreign countries. Lucca and Genoa indeed sent them silks, Catalonia and Florence cloth ; but silk was also wrought in Messina, and the coarse cloth, used by the more numerous class, was prepared in Sicily itself, and care was taken to restrict the

* Ragazzoni, Relatione di Sicilia : " L'anno 1530 d'ordine del vicerè fu fatta la descrittione dell' anime di detta isola di Sicilia et l'estimo generale di tutte le facoltà et beni dell' habitanti d'essa per assegnare ad ogn'uno la sua conveniente portione delle gravezze. Et fu trovato"—what is above stated.
† Ragazzoni: " Sono feroci et pronti d'ingegno, ma se bene sono rissosi tra loro et ogn'uno porti l'armi, non si però dilettano d'andar alla guerra, nè volentieri escono della sua patria, il che procede dalla fertilità del paese, dove stanno molto commodi et agiati." Scipio di Castro, Avvertimenti respecting Sicily.

privileges even of Catalonia, though so closely connected with the island. The importation of the country was amply counterpoised by the exportation of corn. The king never received more than moderate dues from the province, which was in every respect very tenacious of its own interests *. Thus, though the Sicilians did not enter on a new and improved career, still their constitution had this good effect, that they remained in the condition bequeathed them from former ages.

Milan.

Milan on the other hand displayed a new development of the national mind. The people of Lombardy have always preceded other races of men in working out municipal principles, and of all the men of Lombardy the Milanese have ever been the foremost in this respect. If the new achievements they now made in this way were not to be compared, for intrinsic value and vast results, with what they had previously done, still they are very deserving of our attention.

We will first take notice of the nobles, and next of the burghers.

The Milanese nobles were remarkable for their wealth. Not that there were absolutely many families possessed of extraordinary incomes; only some few were counted which had between 10,000 and 30,000 ducats yearly. About the year 1600 the incomes of the Medici of Marignano, and of the Sforza of Caravaggio, were estimated at 12,000 ducats, those of the Borromei at 15,000, those of the Trivulzj at 20,000, and those of the Serbelloni at 30,000. But, on the other hand, there was an enormous number of houses with incomes ranging from 2000 to 4000 ducats †. Now these nobles who kept aloof from all traffic, and who had no public employments to occupy their time, sought satisfaction in good cheer and gaiety. They had none of the ambitious craving for titles of the Neapolitans, but liked to be left to enjoy themselves quietly in their own way. They were to be seen daily in great troops in the streets, mounted on war chargers, or on the swift ginnetto, or on mules with velvet trappings. The carriages, adorned with gold and richly lined, were left to the use of the ladies. Nothing could be more splendid than the Milanese carnival. But on other occasions too, how rich and beautiful were the dresses worn, what brilliant arms were to be seen, what fine horses, what fre-

quent festivities ! The tone of society derived, as it well might, peculiar fascination and liveliness from the intercourse of the two sexes *.

All the arts that have reference to knightly exercises and social grace, were peculiarly cultivated in Milan. The art of fence was already perfected in all its modern movements, in its whole tactics. The dance was nowhere in higher vogue. Not only was a kind of glory won by individuals among the dancers, such as that Pompeo Diobono, who had also the reputation of being a perfectly handsome man, but upwards of a hundred cavaliers, and as many ladies, are recorded by name as perfect proficients in this art. The Milanese combined the two arts together to form the ingenious sword dance. A place where reigned such a spirit of pleasure was favourable ground for the theatre. The opera presented itself in its early stage in the intermezzos, in 1590, though at first it was thought very unnatural to represent Pluto as singing. How much the pious Borromeo accomplished here, it is hard to say ; but we are not inclined to think it was very much, when we look at the names then in use on the stage, and find among them Ersilias, Aurelias, Violantes, and so forth, borrowed from fable or from antiquity, but few names that remind us of saintly and Christian virtues †.

A character of such a cast gave Milan a certain influence in the world. We find Milanese at the courts of France, Spain, Lorraine, and Savoy, as masters in the various accomplishments of the cavalier. Milan is to be looked on as a centre for the corporeal training of the European nobility.

It possessed another source of influence in the inventions and useful arts, which issued from it over the whole world. These are to be ascribed to the burgher class ‡. The mechanical arts were plied with extraordinary and masterly skill in Milan. Whoever wished for handsome armour and weapons, or rare embroidery, never thought of searching further, if he could not find them in Milan. The senate was assiduous in its endeavours to attach manufactures closely to the city. There is extant a decree to the effect, that no one who wrought in wool, particularly no one who understood dyeing in scarlet, whether master, journeyman, or even apprentice, should leave the city without special permission, and that no one should attempt to seduce them away on pain of forfeiting all he possessed §. Trade flourished also in Como. Two thousand bales of wool were imported thither in the year 1580, two-thirds Spanish, one-third German, and the quantity of cloth made from it was such as to realize 250,000 scudi. Silk-works were

---

* Ragazzoni: "Vi si pesca il corallo a Trapani, et v'è bestiame assai. Vi si fanno alcuni panni grossi di lana et servono per vestito delli contadini. Gl'altri panni più fini vengono condotti in Sicilia da Catalogna di Spagna, et molta quantità di saje da Fiorenza et panni di seta, oltre di quelli che si fanno da Genova et da Lucca, et vi si traffica assai massime in Palermo per rispetto del negotio frumentario." The fair of Lentini served particularly for the home trade. Marii Aretii Siciliæ Chorographia, written in May 1537, p. 17.

† These details are from a relatione di tutti li stati signori et principi d'Italia, MS. With a slight deviation Leoni entirely agrees with it. "E rippena (la citta)" he says "di molta nobiltà, conservata tutta via da quei cavalieri con splendore et magnificenza. E ricchissima, ma di richezze più tosto communicate in molti che raccolte in pochi, perche non sono sopra tre o quattro quelle famiglie che giungono alli 25 o 30,000 scudi d'entrate et pochissime quelle da x mila. Nondimeno di due, di tre et quattro mila scudi di rendita ve ne scno infinite."

* A classical authority on this head is one of Bandello's novels, il secondo volume novella quarta, corroborated by the Travels of the Duc de Rohan, 229.

† Sketches, illustrated by engravings, chiefly from a work by Negri, a Milanese dancing-master, "Le grazie d'amore," in Verri, Storia di Milano, ii. 336.

‡ Leoni: "Le ricchezze delli cittadini non nobili nascono per li trafichi, di che quella città è copiosa. Ha infinita copia di artefici, sì che nominar si può seminario delle arti manuali. Et si può dire inventrice delle pompe et del uso del vestire, il che fa con tanta et richezza et bellezza et attillatura che tutte queste cose pare che l'altre città l'apprendano solamente da lei."

§ "Crida, che gli artefici di lana et tintoria con grana et cremosino non escano dallo stato, 6 Maggio 1554." Ordines Senatus Mediolan. p. 49.

set up there in 1554, by Pagano Marino, and prospered well ; and yet Como was not by a great deal the most flourishing of the Milanese towns. We find it petitioning in the year 1555, that it should be allowed the same privileges as to workmanship and commerce which were enjoyed by Milan and the other towns *.

A lively activity pervaded the country. The customs rose with the progress of manufactures, whilst the increasing quantity of cash diminished the rate of interest. Canals and roads were laid out ; alienated estates were bought back; the poor were provided for. The Comaschi built halls for their corn market, and appointed ediles. They advanced money for the printing of a work upon their native nobility ; proposals were made for having lectures on the institutions of the country delivered thrice a week. Como was more populous about the year 1600, than it has ever been †.

But the city of Milan was above all flourishing. To look at the wide circuit of its walls, and the multitude of its houses, says Leoni, one would not suppose there could be inhabitants enough for them ; but if one had an opportunity of once passing in review the enormous multitude of the people, he would fancy they could not all have dwellings. The city was thought to be, next after Naples, the most populous in Italy ‡.

Naples.

If there be no doubt that the maintenance of the customary state of things in Sicily, and the growth and progress of peculiar social and civil habits in Milan, were owing to the independence retained by the rural districts or the towns of those provinces, in Naples, on the other hand, this condition no longer subsisted. Here the whole sum and substance of the government lay in the absolute authority of the viceroy ; this pervaded the whole state from the highest to the lowest grade. To form a just conception of the state of things, it will be advisable to turn for a moment from general views, and look more closely into the individual character of some of these viceroys.

Our Relationi mention but two, with some fulness of detail, namely, Mondegar (1575 to 1579), and Ossuna (1616 to 1620). The former, who was already seventy years of age, held it his first duty to provide for his family. He gave one of his sons a company of horse, another a company of foot, a third rich abbeys. He had a wealthy heiress taken with armed force from a convent, and married into his house. He contrived also to procure for his wife a regular income of 7000 ducats. Moreover, so full was he of Spanish *sosiego,* that he seemed to be rather a king than a viceroy, and let the Neapolitan princes stand uncovered before him §. He kept the people in utter subjection.

Arbitrary acts, that would any where else have provoked rebellion, such as his invasion of the rights of the seggi in Naples, and his innovations with respect to the trade in provisions, here produced nothing beyond confusion and distress. New taxes were paid in obedience to his will and pleasure; and when new donatives were granted, those who voted could not even have the privilege of sending them by their own envoys to the king. Many were of opinion that the king might, if he pleased, have introduced even the inquisition *.

If Mondegar's age made him unbending, stern, and pertinacious in his arbitrary proceedings, Ossuna's vigorous youth prompted him to rude arrogance and extravagant schemes. Such a character was calculated to make friends and foes. His friends could not sufficiently extol him. "He has subjected the proceedings of the royal ministers to close scrutiny," they said ; " he has put an end to the mischievous patronage of the doctors ; he has visited the prisons in person, and heard the accused; his strictness has put a stop to the daily assassinations, and rooted out the robbers†." His enemies could not sufficiently censure him. "He has suborned false witnesses, to strike terror into those from whom he wished to extort money ; he has transformed donations into exactions, and has pardoned the greatest crimes for money ; all with the help of the Marchesana de Campilatar, his acknowledged mistress ; his lust has spared no convent, no church‡." We may be tempted to hold the praise and the blame as equally true ; we cannot acquit the duke of arrogance and despotism.

Nor were most of the other governors free from these faults. What a strange ambition possessed some of them to annul the acts of their predecessors. They did not scruple to leave unfinished fortresses begun by the latter, and to build others elsewhere. Some desired to become rich, others to have a train of dependents, others to win the favour of the court. But these are not the motives that should actuate the governors of kingdoms.

The viceroys set the precedent after which the whole business of the local administration was carried on. As they had the nomination to all places, nothing being left the colleges but the right of proposing three or four candidates for each, they did not employ this prerogative to select the worthiest out of those proposed, but allowed them to outbid each other. Hence, when any man had with great cost obtained the place of a counsellor or reggente, it followed of course that he strove, by all means, to indemnify himself for his expenditure, and took presents on his part also. The councillors had 600 ducats salary, and yet they amassed wealth.

---

* Novelli, Storia di Como, iii. c. 2, 109; 43. Petition of the Comaschi, 47, n. 6.

† Avvertimenti by Scipio di Castro and Rovelli.

‡ The number of inhabitants is illegible in Leoni. A correction has been made from 350,000 to 250,000. Respecting the condition of the city, see further Leander Alberti's Descriptio Italiæ, 681. He mentions a proverb of the day, " Qui Italiam reficere totam velit, eum destruere Mediolanum debere." [Whoever would reconstruct all Italy should begin by destroying Milan.]

§ Lippomano, Relatione di Napoli, mentions all this. He

adds, however, " E desideroso d'honore con tutto che viva più da privato marchese che da vicerè, conoscendo benissimo lui et la viceregina ogni suo avantaggio familiare. E ben vero che ha causa di sparmiare."

* Al Sr Landi: " E opinione di molti, che se adesso il re volesse mettervi l'inquisitione, tanto aborrita da costoro, che non haveria molto contrasto."

† Relatione dell' armata di mare uscita da Napoli per il golfo adriatico et del seguito di essa. Inform. ix. MS. "Con ingegnose et rigorose pragmatiche togliendo via le risse, costioni (questioni) et assassinamenti che giornalmente abondavono per tutto questo regno."

‡ Memorial y capitulos que dió a su Magestad el reyno de Napoles contra el duque de Ossuna. Copied in Daru's Histoire de Venise, viii. 178.

The same system extended to the subordinate places; the secretaries of the vicarie received money from the culprits they ought to have punished. The evil spread even to the lowest class of servants : to obtain audience of a councillor it was necessary to pay for it in coin to his porter. This wide-spread corruption was associated in all classes with pride, hardness of heart, and violence of temper *.

The functionaries regarded their rank as a portion delegated to them of the supreme authority, which they were empowered to use in the name of right and law, but in reality for their own advantage. Accordingly they were seen concluding treaties of peace, as it were, with those they were intended to punish or to control. The governors in the provinces are accused of having permitted gross crimes, and even murders, for lucre †. The capitani in the towns should have resisted the usurpations of the eletti, and these again the encroachments of the governors ; but how often did both come to an understanding and combine to ruin the towns. The inspectors of the fairs were bound to examine the weights and measures ; they took money from the dealers, and let them do just as they pleased. The protomedico sent out commissioners; but if these men only saw money, we are told, they gave themselves no concern as to whether the medicines sold were spurious or genuine. Promises were given to the towns that they should be relieved of the soldiers quartered upon them, if they would pay for the relief ; and this was in fact unlawful enough : but how shall we characterise the fact, that after the money had been received, and the soldiers withdrawn, another company was sent in their stead a fortnight afterwards ?

Public offices were regarded as estates, to be managed, not only with the greatest profit, but also with the utmost economy of expense. The commandants of the fortresses kept two-thirds fewer soldiers than they received pay for. The huomini d'armi, whose duties were exclusively those of cavalry, hired horses to undergo review, but kept none at any other time. The capitani, whose galleys should have been in readiness to repel any sudden attack, used to hire out their galley-slaves for service in the town ‡. The masters of the mint used to clip the silver to such an extent that people were obliged to take a gran for a half real. Attorneys and notaries contrived to make suits eternal. Justice was a trade ; ambition, avarice, jealousy, and the peculiar mania for revenge that actuated the people, occasioned monstrous and horrible things §.

In this general state of feeling, what might be expected of those whose rights were derived from the sword and were personal ? When the barons quitted the capital in debt and returned home, they enforced every right of theirs, even to barbarity. They sold offices at high prices to people who, as

Lippomano says, flayed their vassals alive. They converted their territories into close states, and obliged the dealers who drove their cattle from market to market to purchase safe conducts at an immoderate sum per head of cattle *. They permitted no inns on the roads but such as were leased from themselves at exorbitant rates, so that the landlords, like the proprietors, were forced to indemnify themselves by cruel extortions upon unfortunate travellers. And that no one might prosper, they bought up the silk and other produce of the country, and shut their subjects out from trade.

We are already aware that the clergy pursued the same course, that they shut the seminaries against those who had no means; that they managed the hospitals and lending houses, which should have benefited the poor, in a dishonest manner, and that they took illegal fees for every act and decree.

Does it not seem as though all these functionaries, nobles, and clergy were enemies who had conquered the land, and won the right perpetually to suck out its substance ?

They let each other feel their violence and harshness, but the main force of these fell on the unfortunate people, which was burthened besides with exorbitant taxation. With what keenness were the state debtors followed up ! How often, when a poor man had earned his real and half by his day's labour with his mattock, and thought to enjoy his earnings in the evening with his wife and children, did a soldier enter his door, whom he could barely satisfy with the whole of his scanty pittance. If he had no money, they sold all within his house. The poor widow, who had nothing but her bed, had it sold from under her. If nothing else could be laid hands on, they stripped the very roof from the house, and sold the materials †.

The victim of the law was now driven to desperation, and abandoned his wretched hut. Many left their villages and took to the mountains. Revolting against a form of society which contemptuously violated every principle for which society is constituted, they began to wage a war with it that filled the land with murder and rapine. Sometimes they united together, as for instance under that Marco Berardi, of Cosenza ‡, who combined the separate bands in a body 1500 strong, styled himself king Marco, routed the first Spaniards who were sent against him, and could only be vanquished by a sort of regular campaign. For the most part they acted singly. The name of a banished man or outlaw (bandito) became equivalent with that of assassin. Though more men of this kind were sent to the galleys in Naples than in all the rest of Italy and Spain put together, still the country was filled with them. The towns fell into decay; thriving places, like Giovenazzo, became

---

* Lettera al Cardinal Borgia : " E cosa grande il considerare le smisurate richezze che molti di essi sono stati soliti di accumulare in brevissimo tempo."

† Lettera : " I governatori accorduti con chi si sia, . . . si uccide poi l'inimico impune, facendosi apparire colpevole il morto."

‡ Al Signor Landi : " La ciurma vien noleggiata da capitani a mercanti nobili per scaricare navi, per altri servitii domestici.

§ A Landi : " Cose monstruosamente scandalose." All accounts agree in this.

* Lettera : " Prendere un passaporto sotto colore di assicurarsi da i furti con la nota del nome et cognome di quelli che gli hanno venduti o comprati, e ne esigono cosa esorbitante per ogni capo di bestiame."

† Tiepolo. A. Landi. Lippomano : " Fanno scoprire i tetti delle case et vendere coppi per pagarsi delle impositioni regie, cosa veramente crudele et che induce gli huomini disperatamente mettersi alla campagna a rubare, dove ne nasce che sia tutto il paese pieno di ladri e d'assassini."

‡ Parino, Teatro de' Vicerè, ii. 255. Thuanus, Hist. xxxvi. p. 719. Chiefly Adriani, Storia de suoi tempi, 709.

almost uninhabited * ; there was no travelling through Calabria except in caravans.

If the re-action against absolute authority in Sicily perhaps endangered public morality, but preserved the country in its old accustomed condition, and in Milan did not perhaps prevent all arbitrary conduct, but still rendered some municipal vigour possible ; in Naples, on the other hand, the same absolute authority, enhanced by the tyranny of those who wielded it, at once destroyed public morality and ruined the country.

That authority seemed to be exercised in the king's interest ; but how could the king's interest be promoted in such a manner ?

The king wished that the land should be profitable to the exchequer ; but this rapacious constitution consumed its own booty with the voracity of the spendthrift. The king desired to have the country secure from enemies: but there stood his fortresses unfinished, half garrisoned, fitter to entice the foe than to repel him ; his galleys lay at the mole, but without oars or rowers, soldiers or guns, whilst corsairs swarmed about all the coasts. Lastly, the king wished to have the land obedient and submissive ; but a part of his subjects reverted, as we have said, to the condition of nature ; the citizens of Naples showed a readiness to insurrection upon every slight dearth of bread; the Angevines among the nobility still retained the lilies in their coats of arms, and brooded over the losses they had suffered, and the insults they had endured †. All waited only a call to rise in rebellion.

Thus does despotism counteract its own purposes by the means it takes to gain them. A sorry consolation for mankind! The effect of despotism remains, namely, the destruction of virtue and prosperity.

4. The Netherlands.

So long as the Netherlands defrayed the greater part of the expenses of the Spanish empire, Castile was exempted from that burthen : the former, nevertheless, was in a thriving condition, while the latter prospered but ill. But from the time the Netherlands revolted, the whole burthen of the monarchy fell on Castile. The revolted provinces were convulsed and exhausted by the ravages of war, yet they speedily rose again in renovated vigour ; Castile on the contrary was ruined.

But these two countries, which had long been so closely connected together, stood in many other respects in stronger contrast with each other. We notice in the Spaniards, as in the Neapolitans, a decisive tendency to make themselves publicly prominent, to indulge in brilliant display. They long to be knights, to fill offices of state; they do not grudge purchasing a certain pomp of appearance in the streets, at the cost of penury and privation at home. Injuries prompt them to implacable hatred, kindness makes them devoted partisans. The men of the Netherlands on the other hand are fashioned entirely for the comforts of private life. In the first place, the house they

occupy must be well filled and furnished with neat and cleanly household apparatus of every kind. Then they are willing enough to fill some public office; but when this has once occurred, they are content and retire again to a private station. Their chief anxiety as to public affairs is, that they may not be troubled in their property by any violation of order or arbitrary acts ; they are less disposed to factions prompted by personal considerations *. The former are more warlike, the latter more pacific; the former bold assailants, the latter stouthearted defenders ; the former more intent on sudden gain, the latter on the acquisitions of patient industry.

How different were the popular pleasures on either side ;—here the horseman charging the bull with his lance, or driving him down the narrow way from the mountain cliffs to the river, where he perishes † ;—there the rhetorical guilds of the Flemish towns giving entertainments in which they visit each other, dressed in velvet and silk, in antique, richly adorned holiday carriages, to hold gorgeous spectacles, embodying in sensible imagery some wise saw or pregnant maxim. The delight of the Flemings was to see oxen roasted whole in the market-place, wine gushing from the pipes of the fountains, men climbing high poles, and women running races for prizes, and many hundred festive lanterns burning by night on the high tower of Antwerp ‡.

If the Spaniards discovered America, conquered it, and made booty of its silver, the real advantage which consisted in life and activity, industry and wealth, devolved upon the Netherlands, particularly on the city of Antwerp in the beginning of the sixteenth century.

Our Relationi remark that no country was more favourably situated for general commerce. It could be reached by sea in one day from England, in three from Scotland, in five from Denmark, in ten from Spain and Portugal : France and Germany were immediately contiguous to it. Antwerp gathered together the fruits of all these advantages. There were about a thousand foreign commercial houses in that city about the year 1566, a multitude of Spaniards who gained more there than they could do in their native land, and of Germans. It was said that more business was done in Antwerp in a month than in Venice in two years, though the latter city was still one of the first commercial marts. "I grew melancholy," says Marino Cavallo, "when I beheld Antwerp, for I saw Venice outdone §." The commerce of the city was promoted

* Description in the Relatione de costumi, richezze, etc. " Gli huomini et donne di corpo grande, di carnagione bianca, di fattezze delicate, di membri ben proportionati et composti. Sono grandissimi mercanti, laboriosi, diligenti, ingegnosi, moderati nell' una et nell' altra fortuna, temperati nello sdegno, nell' amore di donne et nel desiderio d'haver piacere, finalmente humani nel conversare." The author only finds fault with their credulity and obstinacy. Cf. Guicciardini, p. 57.

† It is to be remarked, however, that as early as 1555 the cortes expressed their disapprobation of the bull fights, Petic. 75.

‡ Meteren, Niederländische Historien, at the beginning.

§ Cavallo : " Anversa fa tante faccende di cambi reali et socchi, che loro chiamano finanzi (is this the origin of the word ?) et d'ogn'altra sorte di mercantie, che in vero mi sono attristato vedendole, pensando certissimo che superi questa città."

* Lippomano : " . . . . Perche le terre non dishabitino come ne sono alcune et tra l'altre Giovenazzo in Puglia."

† Relatione di tutti li stati d'Italia, MS. " Tutti odiano mortalmente gli Spagnoli e perche desiderano novità e perche hanno strapazzi e sono fatti mol o soggetti a huomini di robba lunga e li loro sudditi contra i signori favoriti."

by the lowness of the customs, though both a Brabantine and a Zealand rate was levied, and it was secured by the fortifications undertaken by the council. Cavallo calls the city the fountain head of trade.

This is not the place to go into the details of the subject. The instructive exposition given of it by Luigi Guicciardini, valuable for the light it sheds on the affairs of Europe generally in those days, has been incorporated in many other sufficiently familiar works[*]. A comparison between that author and our manuscripts suggests however one remark, which perhaps deserves consideration.

Though Cavallo had doubtless investigated the commerce of the Netherlands as accurately as possible, since he pressed upon the Venetians sundry counsels founded upon his observations[†]; though Guicciardini, who at first proposed to write only of Antwerp, manifests by the minuteness of his details, how well he was acquainted with the affairs of that city (his book was dedicated to the council of Antwerp), so that nothing can be objected to the testimony either of the one or the other, still their statements are very different from each other. This can only be explained from the circumstance, that the former author wrote in 1550, the latter in 1566. Precisely between these two years was the period of the highest prosperity ever enjoyed by the trade of Antwerp. Even though the facts put forward by our authors should prove now and then not to be quite accurate, still it is easy to conceive how important a collation of the two must be towards obtaining some general notions of the course and value of this trade.

Its progress thus estimated appears really wonderful. There was imported from Portugal in the year 1550, 300,000 ducats' worth of jewels, grocery, and sugar. The consumption of colonial produce increased to such a degree, that in 1566 the value of the sugar and grocery alone imported from Lisbon amounted to 1,600,000 ducats. There was brought from Italy in 1550 1,000,000, and sixteen years afterwards 3,000,000 ducats' worth of raw and manufactured silk, camlet, and cloth of gold. The importation from the Baltic countries generally, comprising corn, flax, and wood, amounted in 1550 to 250,000 ducats; and in 1566 the single item of corn was valued at upwards of a million and a half. Whereas the total value of the imports from France and Germany together was computed in 1550 at 800,000 ducats, that of French wine alone was reckoned at a million of écus in 1566, and that of Rhenish wine at a million and a half of ducats. Bruges received in 1550 350,000, in 1566 600,000 ducats' worth of Spanish wool. But the English trade had unquestionably taken the greatest leap of all. Cavallo valued the whole importation from England in his time, tin, wool, and cloth, at 300,000 ducats: Guicciardini, on the other hand, valued the wool at 250,000, and the cloth and stuffs at more than 5,000,000 of ducats, a startling fact if it be admitted, as commonly supposed, that the art

of cloth making was first carried into England by Flemish refugees. According to this, the Spanish trade with the Netherlands must have been almost doubled, the Portuguese, French, and German certainly trebled, whilst the English must have increased twenty-fold, a fact seemingly well nigh incredible. In truth, the Flemish traders in London had advanced within a space of forty years from their crockery and brush stalls to the most sumptuous warehouses stored with all the commodities of the world[*]. Whilst Cavallo sets down the silken stuffs, the spices, and all the other articles exported to England in 1550, at half a million, Guicciardini values the total traffic of both countries, in 1566, at twelve millions. This explains why Elizabeth was forced to keep on friendly terms with Philip before the revolt of the Netherlands, and with the provinces after that event.

But Antwerp was not alone in its prosperity. What Cavallo extols above all is the fact that industry throve throughout the whole land. Courtray, Tournay, and Lille, were chiefly engaged in the manufacture of cloth; camlet was wrought in Valenciennes; table cloths in Douay[†]; handsome carpets were manufactured in Brussels. Holland derived profit not only from its cattle, but also from its flax; Zealand yielded at least salt fish. The net proceeds from all these sources amounted yearly to a million of ducats. The consequence was that the whole land was filled with trade and plenty, that no one was so low or so incapable but that he was wealthy in proportion to his station[‡].

Now, whilst commerce promoted manufacturing industry, the improvement of the latter became associated with the fine arts. Nothing more excited Soriano's admiration than the Flemish carpets. Herein, he said, was exemplified what practised skill could accomplish: as the masters who work in mosaic can produce pictures of objects with little pieces of stone, so here the work put together with woollen and silken threads, is not only made to exhibit colour, but also light and shade, and to display figures in as perfect relief as the best painters could produce[§]. But the cultivation of the fine arts was not merely of this indirect kind; it was also direct, as every one knows.

But how transient is human fortune. The civil wars ensued, devastating the land and bringing sack and pillage on the towns, on Antwerp with the rest. When Guicciardini published a second edition of his work in 1580, he added the remark, that the present times were to those he described as night to day. Subsequently, after the conquest by the prince of Parma, Antwerp never could regain its old prosperity. It was reduced in the beginning of the seventeenth century from a population of certainly 150,000 inhabitants to somewhere about half that number[‖].

Were these the consequences of a war which the

---

[*] Giucciardini, Descriptio Belgii, 158—245. Anderson's History of Commerce, vol. iv. p. 61. Bor, too, Nederl. Oorlogen, has his "Beschryvinge der Stad van Antwerpen," as he says, "uit de Beschryvinge van Ludewijk Guicciardini Edelman van Florencen," p. 67.

[†] Cavallo: "Crederei che il medesimo potesse fare la Serenità Vostra con gran utile suo et de suoi sudditi."

[*] Wheeler quoted by Anderson, iv. 68.

[†] Cavallo. "Li mantili et tovaglie a Benoani;" in another copy, "Duoas," no doubt Douay.

[‡] Cavallo: "In ogni luogo corrono tanto i danari et tanto il spacciamento d'ogni cosa, che non vi è huomo, per basso et inerte che sia, che per il suo grado non sia ricco." Soriano: "Traffichi et industria porta tanto in quelli paesi le richezze dell' altre parti del mondo."

[§] Soriano: "Mostrando i rilevi delle figure con quella misura insieme che sanno fare i più eccelenti pittori."

[‖] Contarini gives the numbers 170,000 and 80,000.

country had undertaken with so much justice, and upon so many urgent motives?

The fact is so; all the results of that war were not fortunate. The division in religion, manners, and language, which is to this moment visible between two countries so nearly allied, was undoubtedly created by that cause. Commerce however, industry, trade, and active habits of life, were not put down by it; they found an asylum in Holland. Amsterdam took the place of Antwerp. If we ask how this occurred, let us remember that the prince of Parma conquered the soil indeed, but not the men. These fled before him, whether actuated by solicitude for their religion, or for the remnant of their wealth, or impelled by the fear of want *. It was chiefly the emigration of the active classes that transplanted commerce to Amsterdam, and gave its already rising trade so sudden and vigorous an impulse that it became the first in Europe.

Holland made the products of all the world tributary to its wealth. First of all it made itself the medium for the exchange of the necessaries of life between the eastern and western coasts of the neighbouring seas, of the wood and corn of the one, with the salt and wine of the other †. It sent out its ships to the herring fisheries of the northern waters, and conveyed the cargoes taken to the mouths of all the rivers flowing through southern lands from the Vistula to the Seine. The Rhine, the Maas, and the Scheldt, carried this article through their own territories ‡. They sailed to Cyprus for wool, to Naples for silk §; and the coasts of the ancient Phenicians paid tribute to the commercial enterprises of so far remote a Germanic race, whose abodes they themselves had hardly ever reached. Vast stocks of the various articles of trade were now collected by the Dutch. Contarini found 100,000 sacks of good wheat, and as much other corn in their granaries in 1610, and Raleigh asserts that they were always provided with 700,000 quarters of corn, so that they could even assist their neighbours in any pressing occasion of scarcity, of course not without considerable profit: one year of bad harvest was worth to them seven good years. Nor did they by any means confine themselves to dealing in raw produce, but even made it an important part of their business to apply their own skill to the wrought produce of

* Hugo Grotius, Historia, p. 85. Proof of this is given in John de Wit's Maxims of Holland.

† Sir Walter Raleigh's detailed essay on the English trade with Holland, Anderson, p. 361. Discorso intorno la guerra di Fiandra in Tesoro Politico, iii. p. 323, enumerates as articles of the eastern trade, "formento, cenere, mele, cera, tele, funi, pece, legno, ferro;" and as Spanish, "salo, lane, zuccari et le drogherie dell' Indie," before the Dutch navigation to India.

‡ Contarini remarks, "De danari cavati da questo pesce (aringa) si servono a lor bisogni et a mantener le guerre."

§ Contarini: "A Cipro et Soria fecero bene et sono andati molti per lane et cottoni sperando trarne grand utile."

other countries. They imported about 80,000 pieces of cloth every year from England, but in the undyed state; these they prepared for use, and so realized the larger profit in the sale.

Whilst they had thus so great a portion of European commerce in their hands, their most splendid profits, as well as the true renown of their shipping, were connected with the East Indies. Of all their hostilities against Spain, their expeditions to the Indies were what most alarmed the king and the nation, struck them the severest blow, and gave the most potent impulse to the energies of the Dutch themselves. Contarini regards with wonder the regularity with which they yearly dispatched thither from ten to fourteen ships: he states the capital of the company to have been 6,600,000 gulden. The grand and world-embracing spirit of exertion that animated them, led them ever onwards; their ships sailed even in search of unknown lands. Their efforts to discover a north-west passage, and the voyages of their Heemskerke, cast the maritime renown of other nations completely into the shade *.

Every harbour, bight, and bay of Holland were then seen swarming with ships, every canal in the interior covered with boats. It was a common significant saying, that there were as many living there on the water as on the land. There were reckoned 200 large ships, and 3000 of middle size, the chief station of which was at Amsterdam. Close by the town rose their thick dark forest of masts.

Amsterdam prospered uncommonly under these circumstances. It was twice considerably enlarged within thirty years. Six hundred new houses are said to have been built there in the year 1601 †. A scudo, says Contarini, was paid for as much ground as a foot could cover ‡. He reckons 50,000 inhabitants in the year 1610.

Manufactures flourished; the goods wrought by the Dutch were excellent. The rich continued moderate and frugal in their habits; many a man who sold the finest cloth, was content himself with coarse clothing; the poor had the means of subsistence; the idle were punished. It became a common thing to set off for India, and the seamen learned to sail with every wind. Every house was a school of navigation; there was none without sea charts. Were they men to give way before a foe, they who had so wholly mastered the sea? The Dutch ships had the reputation of rather burning than surrendering.

* Bentivoglio: "Relatione delle provincie unite di Fiandra, MS. in Berlin, but printed in 1601 by Ericius Puteanus, in the Relationi del Cardinal Bentivoglio, edit. 1667, p. 17.

† Isaac Pontanus in Laet, Belgium Confœderatum, p. 63.

‡ Contarini: "Il terreno per il concorso è prezzato assai e pagato di quanto si può coprire con un piede un scudo." What follows is from Contarini and Bentivoglio. See the somewhat later remarks of Sir William Temple, Remarques sur l'état des Provinces Unies, p. 217.

LIST

OF THE MORE IMPORTANT MANUSCRIPTS CONSULTED FOR THIS WORK.

Ottoman Empire.

1. Relatione di Constantinopoli del Cl^{mo} Signor Bernardo *Navagero*. MSS. Gothana, n. 218. 30 leaves. 1553.
2. Relatione del Cl^{mo} Marc Antonio *Barbaro* ritornato bailo a Constantinopoli da Sultan Selim imperatore de Turchi. MSS. Goth. n. 218. 66 leaves. 1573.
3. Relatione del Cl^{mo} M. A. *Barbaro* alla Ser^{ma} Signoria di Venetia delli negotii trattati da lui con Turchi. Informationi politiche, t. i. (MSS. Berol. Ital. n. 2.) 1573.
4. Discorso sopra il imperio del Turco (see p. 12) Inf. ix. 10 leaves. 1579.
5. Descrittione dell' imperio turchesco fatta dal capitan Pompeo *Floriani* [a Nostro Sign. Clemente VIII.] Inf. tom. xvii. 63 leaves. 1579.
6. Relatione o diario del viaggio fatto in Constantinopoli del Cl^{mo} Giacomo *Soranzo* an^{re} della Ser^{ma} Rep. di Venetia per il ritaglio di Mehemet figliuolo d'Amurath imperatore de Turchi l'anno 1551. Inf. i. 54 leaves. 1581.
7. Constantinopoli del 1584. Sommario della relatione di Constantinopoli dell' Illmo Signor Giovanni Francesco *Morosini*, hora cardinale. MSS. Goth. n. 218. 39 leaves. 1584.
8. Relatione di Constantinopoli e gran Turco, dove si ha intiera notitia del governo politico e de costumi e religione de Turchi. Inf. tom. xi. 68 leaves. 1590.
9. Relatione di Mons. Pietro *Cedolini* vescovo di Lesina del presente stato dell' imperio turchesco. Inf. i. 16 leaves. 1594.
10. Relatione dello stato nel quale si ritrova il governo dell' imperio turchesco quest' anno 1594. Inf. i. 33 leaves. 1594.
11. Relatione di Constantinopoli dell' Illmo Mr Christofano *Valieri* ritornato da quel bailaggio. Inf. xlvi. 118 leaves. 1617.
12. Relatione di Constantinopoli nell' anno 1637. Inf. xi. 53 leaves. 1637.

II. *The Spanish Empire.*

1. Relatione riferita nel consiglio de Pregadi per il Cl^{mo} *Gasparo Contarini*, ritornato ambasciatore da papa Clemente et dall' imperatore Carlo V. l'anno 1530. Inf. xxv. 16 leaves. 1530.
2. Relatione del Cl^{mo} *Nicolò Tiepolo* del convento di Nizza anno 1538. 58 leaves. 1538.
3. Relatione del Cl^{mo} Monsignore Marino *Cavallo* tornato ambasciatore dall' imperatore Carlo V. Informat. ix. 34 leaves. 1550.
4. Ordine della casa dell' imperatore. Inf. xvii.
5. Avvertimenti di Carlo V. al re Filippo suo figliuolo. Inf. xlvi. 126 leaves. Dubious. 1555.
6. Relatione del Cl^{mo} M. Gio. *Micheli* ritornato ambasc. alla regina d'Inghilterra (Mary, the wife

of Philip II.) l'anno 1557. MSS. Gothana, n. 217. 77 leaves. 1557.
7. Relatione di Spagna del cavallero Michele *Soriano* ambasciatore al re Filippo. MSS. Goth. n. 218. 75 leaves. 1559.
8. Lettera di Monsignor di *Terracina* nunzio di papa Pio IV. appresso il re catolica. Toledo, 22 Majo 1560. Inf. v. 23 leaves. 1560.
9. Sommario di tutte l'entrate e spese particolari di Sua Maestà catolica. MSS. Goth. 218. 7 leaves.
10. Relatione del clarissimo *M. Antonio Tiepolo* tornato ambasciatore del catolico re Filippo del 1567: a dì d'Ottobre. Informat. i. 67 leaves. Also MSS. Gothana, 219. 1567.
11. Sommario dell' ordine che si tiene alla corte di Spagna circa il governo delli stati del re catolico. Inf. ix. 7 leaves. 1570.
12. Relatione in forma di discorso de costumi, ricchezze, forze, qualità, sito e modo di governo delli paesi bassi. D'incerto autore. Inf. xi. 22 leaves. 1573.
13. Relatione del Cl^{mo} M. Girolamo *Lippomani* ritornato di Napoli ambasciatore al Serenissimo Signore Giovanni d'Austria l'anno 1575. Inf. tom. xxxv. 90 leaves. 1575.
14. Relatione del magnifico Signore Placido *Ragazzoni* ritornato agente per la Ser^{ma} Signoria nel regno di Sicilia. MSS. Goth. 219. 15 leaves. 1575.
15. Relatione compendiosa della negotiatione di Monsignor *Sega* vescovo della Ripa e di poi di Piacenza nella corte del re catolico. Inf. xxviii. 70 leaves. 1577.
16. Compendio degli stati et governi della Fiandra nel tempo del re Filippo, 1578. Inf. i. 20 leaves. 1579.
17. Nota di tutti li titolati di Spagna con le loro casate e rendite che tengono, dove hanno li loro stati et habitationi, di tutti gli arcivescovati e vescovati e entrate e così delli visconti, adelantadi, almiranti e priori, fatta nel 1581 alli 30 di Maggio. Inf. xv. 18 leaves. 1581.
18. Relatione delli negoti trattati in Spagna di Monsignor di *Piacenza* quando fu rimandato al re da Gregorio XIII. Inf. xxviii. 10 leaves. 1581.
19. Avvertimenti e ricordi al Signor Duca di Terranuova governator dello stato di Milano e capitano generale per S. M. Catolica in Italia. Inf. xi. 29 leaves. 1583.
20. Cause per le quali la Fiandra tumultuò, 1586. MSS. Italica Berolin. n. 49. 42 leaves. 1586.
21. Relatione di Milano e suo stato fatta nell' anno 1589 dal Signor Giov. Batt. *Leoni* al Ser^{mo} Duca di Ferrara. Inf. xi. 48 leaves. 1589.
22. Relatione del Cl^{mo} *Tomaso Contarini* ritornato ambasciatore di Spagna, 1593. Inform. xii. 37 leaves. 1593.
23. Al Rey nuestro Señor: signed Juan de *Velasco* Condestable. Milan, July 1, 1597. Spanish. Inf. xxix. 73 leaves. 1597.

24. Ragionamento del re Don Filippo negli ultimi giorni di sua vita al principe suo figliuolo. Inf. xlvi. 52 leaves. Dubious. 1598.
25. Relatione della vita del re di Spagna e delli privati. Inf. ix. 27 very closely written leaves. 1604.
26. Alla Santità di Nostro Signore Paolo V. Respecting Naples. Inf. xx. 34 leaves. 1607.
27. Relatione fatta dall' Illmo *Tomaso Contarini*. On the Netherlands. Inf. xi. 9 leaves. 1610.
28. Relatione delle cose di maggior consideratione in tutta la corte di Spagna fatto nell' anno di 1611. Informat. ix. 65 leaves. 1611.
29. Relatione dell' armata di mare uscita di Napoli per il golfo Adriatico e del seguito di essa. Also respecting Ossuna's administration. Inf. ix. 12 leaves. 1617.
30. Lettera scritta all' Illustrissimo e Reverend^{mo} Signore Cardinale Borgia, in Ragguaglio del modo col quale si deve governare nella sua carica di vicerè di Napoli, l'anno 1620. Inf. xx. 14 leaves. 1620.
31. Cagioni che condussero la Santità di N. S. Papa Gregorio XV. a levare la nuntiatura di Spagna a M. di Sangro. Inf. xxiv. 18 leaves. 1628.
32. Relatione di Spagna fatta dall' Ecc^{mo} Signor Leonardo *Moro* ambasciatore della Republica appresso la Maestà catolica. MS. in the author's possession. 53 leaves. 1629.

THE END.